Fourth Edition

BRIDGING THE GAP

COLLEGE READING

Brenda D. Smith
Georgia State University

 HarperCollinsCollegePublishers

To my Mother and Father

Sponsoring Editor: Mark Paluch
Developmental Editor: Susan Moss
Project Coordination: Hockett Editorial Service
Cover Design: Marsha Cohen, Parallelogram
Cover Photo: Skyway Bridge in St. Petersburg, Florida,
      by Eric Schweikardt/The Image Bank
Photo Researcher: Karen Koblik
Production/Manufacturing: Michael Weinstein/Paula Keller
Compositor: Graphic Sciences Corporation
Printer and Binder: R. R. Donnelley & Sons Company
Cover Printer: The Lehigh Press, Inc.

BRIDGING THE GAP: COLLEGE READING, Fourth Edition

Library of Congress Cataloging-in-Publication Data

Smith, Brenda D., 1944-
    Bridging the gap : college reading Brenda D. Smith. — 4th ed.
      p. cm.
    Includes bibliographical references and index.
    ISBN *0-673-46691-4* (student edition)
    ISBN *0-673-46692-2* (teacher edition)
    1. Reading (Higher education) 2. Study, Method of. I. Title.
LB2395.3.S64 1992
428.4′3—dc20
                                                92-22263
                                                CIP

93 94 95 9 8 7 6 5 4 3

CONTENTS

Chapter 4 Organizing Textbook Information 165

Selection 1 Pregnancy and Birth 185

"A baby weighing several pounds and composed of trillions of cells will be delivered about 266 days later."

Selection 2 Women in History 192

"Tens of thousands of women ran farms and businesses while the men were gone."

Selection 3 Creative Thinking and Critical Thinking 200

"Creative thinking leads to the birth of new ideas, while critical thinking tests ideas for flaws and defects."

Chapter 5 Rate Flexibility 213

Selection 1 A Chinese Reporter on Cape Cod 231

"No matter if you like it or not, you stay with your job."

Selection 2 The Right to Fail 235

"Who is to say, then, if there is any right path to the top, or even to say what the top consists of?"

Chapter 8   Critical Thinking   **320**

Chapter 9   Graphic Illustrations   **361**

Chapter 10   Test Taking   **389**

PREFACE

"Build knowledge networks, build knowledge networks, build knowledge networks," is the phrase I repeated to myself as I worked on the fourth edition of *Bridging the Gap*. My aim in this text is for students to recognize the importance of knowledge networks, for teachers to be assisted in explaining the process, and for this book to offer the opportunity for quality and meaningful practice.

Learning is like the creation of many webs poised to expand with the introduction of new material. Business courses, for example, stress the importance of networking with people to create opportunities for advancement. College students can realize these same benefits from networking new ideas with old knowledge for their own intellectual advancement.

The intent of the fourth edition is to draw heavily on the strengths of the learner by offering activities directed toward academic materials that personally *involve* the reader. Through intellectual and emotional interactions, and, hopefully, many stimulating class discussions, students can build knowledge networks that will prove to be "old friends" throughout the freshman course curriculum.

The cultural diversity in our classrooms is reflected in our new readings in this edition. I hope that the readings inspire thoughtful class discussions, growth, and a respect for cultural differences.

CONTENT AND ORGANIZATION

The fourth edition continues the tradition of previous editions by using actual college textbook material for teaching and practice. Designed for an upper-level course in college reading, each chapter introduces a new skill, provides short practice exercises to teach the skill, and then offers practice through longer selections that are arranged according to graduated readability levels. For vocabulary development, words are presented in context after most of the longer selections, as well as in short "Word Bridge" sections within selected chapters.

Presentation of skills in the text moves from the general to the specific. Initial chapters discuss concentration, study strategies, and organization, while later chapters teach rate flexibility, inference, point of view, critical thinking, and graphic illustrations. The reading and study skills discussions in the first portion of the book stress the need to construct the main idea of a passage and select significant supporting details. Exercises encourage "engaged thinking" before reading, while reading, and after reading. Four different methods of organizing textbook information for later study are explained.

The new critical thinking chapter is a culmination and application of main idea, inference, and point-of-view skills. The chapter on test-taking is designed to help students gain insights into text construction and the testing situation. The book concludes with an opportunity to apply all the skills to an actual chapter from a college textbook.

NEW FEATURES

Significant changes in the fourth edition include the following:

- Thirteen new reading selections from history, anthropology, political science, literature, business, and science.
- The addition of a variety of selections that reflect the cultural diversity of student readers.
- A new chapter on critical thinking that teaches students to identify issues and systematically assess supporting arguments and evidence.
- In the Textbook Application chapter, a new chapter-length selection entitled "Racial and Ethnic Minorities," which explores the history of ethnic groups in America. Taken from a freshman sociology textbook, this longer selection provides the opportunity to practice the transfer of skills while still including study questions and strategy suggestions. Both multiple-choice and essay questions are provided.
- Nineteen new "Connecting and Reflecting" articles after reading selections. This new feature is designed to stimulate thinking, reinforce learning, and encourage exploration and interaction.
- An expanded discussion in Chapter 1 of concentration and attention from the perspective of a cognitive psychologist.
- A revised main idea chapter based on current research, that includes patterns of organization.
- In selected chapters, manageable "Word Bridge" sections addressing vocabulary development.
- New practice readings on inference and point of view in Chapters 6 and 7, with more opportunities for written student responses.
- Increased opportunities for students to link knowledge and expand networks through reading selections and learning activities that overlap.

CONTINUING FEATURES

Other features of the book include the following:

- Actual textbook selections are used for practice exercises.
- Chapters contain selections having different levels of readability for greater individualization.
- Each selection has both explicit and inferential questions.
- Selections include essay questions for writing practice.
- Vocabulary is presented in context, and exercises on prefixes, suffixes, and roots are included.
- Although skills build and overlap, each chapter can be taught as a separate unit to fit individual class or student needs.
- Pages are perforated so that Students can tear out and hand in assignments.

The Instructor's Manual which accompanies this book, available from the publisher, contains the answers to all exercises as well as suggestions for additional practice. An interactive computer software program and a test packet are also available from the publisher. The test packet includes quizzes and reading selections for additional practice. The computer software provides the student with opportunities to apply specific strategies and receive immediate feedback from the program.

ACKNOWLEDGMENTS

I am indebted to my editorial friends at HarperCollins: Senior English Editor Jane Kinney, Sponsoring Editor Mark Paluch, and Developmental Editor Susan Moss. Jane is a long-time working partner and valued colleague who creates new ideas, seeks support, and delivers. Mark has carefully followed this book through production and energetically supported my work. Susan coordinated the review process and worked with me in making decisions on a chapter-by-chapter, page-by-page basis. This edition reflects Susan's attention to detail and enthusiasm for meeting the needs of teachers and students.

I was extremely privileged to have many learned professors of college reading review the manuscript for this edition. I have been educated by the reviewers' insightful comments and cannot thank them enough for their time and suggestions. Not only did they generate valuable advice, but their suggestions helped me solidify my own thoughts. Our profession is immeasurably strengthened by the following teachers and thinkers:

Bob Akin, Houston Community College System
Ellen H. Bell, Manatee Community College
Paul Beran, North Harris County College
Doralee E. Brooks, Community College of Allegheny County

Barbara Culhane, Nassau Community College
Karen Haas, Manatee Community College
Valerie Joy Huczko, Ocean County College
Margaret A. Hyde, Evergreen Valley College
Joyce Kammeraad, North Harris County College
Elizabeth Lindgren-Young, Skyline Community College
Joal M. Mayer, Southwestern College
Linda Moore, Skagit Valley College
Michael T. Moore, Georgia Southern University
Judith Olson-Fallon, Case Western Reserve University
Pamela R. Rupert, University of Akron
Karen Samson, Chicago State University
Douglas H. Schewe, Madison Area Technical College
Diane J. Starke, El Paso Community College
Sue P. Stultz, Brevard Community College
Dorothy K. Wamsley, Bethany College

Brenda D. Smith

CONCENTRATION

- What is it?
- How can you improve it?
- How does the brain "pay attention"?
- Can you do two things at once?
- What are common distractors?
- What are the cures?

WHAT IS CONCENTRATION?

Answer the following questions honestly:

1. Do you believe the power of concentration is an innate gift that some are born with and others lack?
2. Do you believe that the ability to concentrate is hereditary, like having blue eyes or brown hair?
3. If your father's side of the family is fidgety and can't concentrate, does that mean that you will be the same?

The answer to all three questions is an obvious *no*. Concentration is a skill that is developed through self-discipline and practice—not a mystical power, a hereditary gift, or a defective gene. It is a **habit** that requires time and effort to develop and careful planning for consistent success.

Concentration is no more than **paying attention**—that is, focusing your full attention on the task at hand. Someone once said that the mark of a genius is the ability to concentrate completely on one thing at a time. This is easy if the task is fun and exciting, but it becomes more difficult when you are required to read something that is not very interesting to you. At this point your mind begins to wander, and the words on the page remain just words for the eyes to see rather than becoming meaningful thoughts and ideas to engage your imagination.

When you are "trying hard to concentrate," what is your brain actually doing? To explain this mystery, cognitive psychologists hypothesize and conduct data-collecting experiments to test theories about our many mental processes. They then make inferences or educated guesses about how the brain operates.

WHAT IS COGNITIVE PSYCHOLOGY?

Cognitive psychology is the body of knowledge that describes how the mind works, or at least how experts think the mind works. Either fortunately or unfortunately, the activity of the brain in concentrating, reading, and remembering cannot be directly observed. These cognitive processes are invisible, just as thinking and problem solving are also invisible.

Since so little is actually known about thinking, the ideas of cognitive psychologists are frequently described as models or designs of something else we understand. For the last thirty years, for example, the computer has been a popular model for describing how the brain processes information. The human brain is more complex than a computer, but the analogy provides a comparison that can help us understand.

HOW DOES THE BRAIN SCREEN MESSAGES?

Cognitive psychologists use the word **attention** rather than concentration to describe a student's uninterrupted mental focus. Thinking and learning, they say, begin with attention. During every minute of the day the brain is bombarded with millions of sensory messages. How does the brain decide which messages to pay attention to and which to overlook? At this moment, are you thinking about the temperature of the room, outdoor noises, or what you are reading? Since all this information is available to you, how are you able to set priorities?

The brain relies on a dual command center to screen out one message and attend to another. According to a researcher at UCLA, receptor cells send millions of messages per minute to your brain.[1] Your reticular activating system (RAS), a network of cells at the top of the spinal cord that runs to the brain, tells the cortex in the brain not to bother with most of the sensory input. Your RAS knows that most sensory inputs do not need attention. For example, you are probably not aware at this moment of your back pressing against your chair or your clothes pulling on your body. Your RAS has decided not to clutter the brain with such irrelevant information unless there is an extreme problem, like your foot going to sleep because you are sitting on it.

The cortex can also make attention decisions. When you decide to concentrate your attention on a task, like reading your history assignment, your cortex

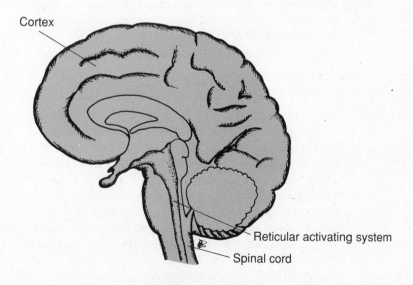

Cortex

Reticular activating system

Spinal cord

[1] H. W. Magoun, The Waking Brain, 2nd ed. (Springfield, Ill.: Charles C. Thomas, 1963).

tells your RAS not to bother it with trivial information. While you focus on learning, your RAS follows orders and "holds" the messages as if you were on an important long-distance call. The cortex and the RAS cooperate in helping you block out distractions and concentrate on learning.

IS DIVIDED ATTENTION EFFECTIVE?

Students often ask if it is possible to do two things at once, such as watching television and doing homework. Most psychologists agree that you can only attend to one thing at a time. An early researcher used a "switch model" to describe his belief, saying that attention operates like the on-off switch of a light fixture in that only one channel is "on" at a time.[2] The "cocktail party effect" illustrates this model. At a party with many available conversations within your listening range, you would probably attend to only one person at a time. If your name were spoken in a nearby group, however, your attention would be diverted. You would probably "switch" your attention to the nearby group to seek more information on such a fascinating topic while only pretending to listen to the original conversation. According to Broadbent's model, you would not be able to listen intently to both conversations at the same time.

Two later researchers conducted an experiment to test the effectiveness of divided attention.[3] They asked subjects to watch two televised sports events with one superimposed over the other. When subjects were instructed to attend to only one of the games, they did an excellent job of screening out the other and answering questions accurately. When asked to attend to both games simultaneously, subjects made eight times more mistakes than when focusing on only one game. This research seems to confirm the old adage, "You can't do two things at once and do them well."

CAN TASKS BECOME AUTOMATIC?

How can you walk and chew gum at the same time? Does every simple activity require your undivided attention? Many tasks—walking, tying shoelaces, and driving a car, for example—begin under controlled processing, which means that they are deliberate and require concentrated mental effort. After much practice, however, such tasks become automatic. Driving a car is an overlearned behavior that researchers would say becomes an automatic process after thousands of hours of experience. You can probably drive, change radio stations, and talk at the same time. Driving no longer requires your full cognitive

[2]D. E. Broadbent, *Perception and Communication* (London: Pergamon Press, 1958).

[3]U. Neisser and R. Becklen, "Selective Looking: Attending to Visually Significant Events," *Cognitive Psychology* 7 (1975): 480–494.

capacity unless conditions are hazardous. Similarly, a skilled athlete can dribble a basketball automatically while also attending to strategy and position. Attention is actually not divided because it can shift away from tasks that have become automatic.

Automatic Aspects of Reading

The idea of doing some things automatically is especially significant in reading. As a first-grade reader you had to concentrate on recognizing letters, words, and sentences, as well as trying to construct meaning. After years of practice and overlearning, much of the recognition aspect of reading became automatic. You no longer stop laboriously to decode each word or each letter. For example, can you look at the word *child* without processing the meaning? Because you automatically think the meaning, you can focus mental resources on understanding the *message* in which the word appears, rather than on understanding the word itself.

College textbooks tend to contain unfamiliar words that are not automatically processed. Attention to the message can be interrupted by the need to attend to an individual unit of thought. Such breaks are to be expected in college reading because of the newness of the material. You can become caught in the dilemma of trying to do two things at once; that is, trying to figure out word meaning as well as trying to understand the message. When this happens, your attention shifts to defining and then back to comprehending. After such a break, you can regain your concentration, and little harm is done if the breaks are infrequent. However, frequent lapses in this automatic aspect of reading can undermine your ability to concentrate on the message.

POOR CONCENTRATION: CAUSES AND CURES

The type of intense concentration that forces the RAS and cortex to close out the rest of the world is the state we would all like to achieve each time we sit down with a textbook. Too often, however, the opposite is true.

Students frequently ask, "How can I keep my mind on what I'm doing?" or "I finished the assignment, but I don't know a thing I read." The solution is not a simple mental trick to fool the brain; rather, it involves a series of practical short- and long-range planning strategies targeted at three offenders: external distractions, internal distractions, and lack of curiosity.

External Distractions

External distractions are the temptations of the physical world that divert your attention away from your work. They are the people in the room, the noise in the background, the time of day, or your place for studying. To control these external distractions, create an environment that says, "Now this is the place and the time for me to get my work done."

Place.   Start by establishing your own private study cubicle; it may be in the library, on the dining room table, or in your bedroom. Wherever it is, choose a straight chair and face the wall. Get rid of gadgets, magazines, and other temptations that trigger the mind to think of *play*. Stay away from the bed because it triggers *sleep*. Spread out your papers, books, and other symbols of studying and create an atmosphere in which the visual stimuli signal *work*.

Time.   To be successful, your study hour must be as rigid and fixed in your mind as your class hours. Leave nothing to chance because too often an unplanned activity never gets done. At the beginning of each new term, establish a routine study time for each day of the week and stick scrupulously to your schedule.

Schedule.   On the next page is a weekly activity chart. Analyze your responsibilities and in the squares on the chart write your fixed activities such as class hours, work time, meal time, and bedtime. Next, think about how much time you plan to spend studying and how much on recreation, and plug those into the chart. For studying, indicate the specific subject involved and the exact place.

Make a fresh chart at the beginning of each week since responsibilities and assignments vary. Learn to estimate the time usually needed for typical assignments. As the term progresses, include time for a regular review of lecture notes. Examinations require special planning. Many students do not realize how much time it takes to study for a major exam. Spread your study out over several days and avoid last-minute cramming sessions late at night. Plan additional time for special projects and term papers, so as not to get caught in a deadline crisis.

Successful people do not let their time slip away; they manage time, rather than letting time manage them. Plan realistically and then follow your schedule.

Ratio.   Even though it is not necessary to write this on the chart, remember that you need short breaks. Few students can study uninterrupted for two hours without becoming fatigued and losing concentration. Try the *50–10 ratio*— study hard for fifty minutes, take a ten-minute break, and then promptly go back to the books for another fifty minutes.

Habit.   Forming study habits is similar to developing the habit of brushing your teeth; the important word is *consistency.* Always study in the same place at the same times, and do not tolerate exceptions. After a number of repeated experiences, the places and times should become subconscious psychological signals for concentration.

Time	Sunday	Monday	Tuesday	Wednesday	Thursday	Friday	Saturday
8:00–9							
9:00–10							
10:00–11							
11:00–12							
12:00–1							
1:00–2							
2:00–3							
3:00–4							
4:00–5							
5:00–6							
6:00–7							
7:00–8							
8:00–9							
9:00–10							
10:00–11							
11:00–12							

Internal Distractions

Internal distractions are the concerns that come repeatedly into your mind as you try to keep your attention focused on the assignment. Rather than the noise or the conversations in a room, they are the nagging worries or doubts in your mind that disrupt your work.

Unfortunately, students, just like everyone else, have to run errands, pick up laundry, make telephone calls, and pay bills. The world does not stop just because George has to read four chapters for a test in "Western Civ." by Wednesday. Consequently, when George sits down to read, he worries about getting an inspection sticker for his car or about picking up tickets for Saturday's ball game rather than concentrating completely on the assignment.

Make a List. For the most part, the interferences that pop into the mind and break reading concentration are minor concerns rather than major problems. To gain control over these mental disruptions, make a list of what is bothering you. What is on your mind that is keeping you from concentrating on your studies? Jot down on a piece of paper each mental distraction and then analyze each to determine if immediate action is possible. If so, get up and take action. Make that phone call, write that letter, or finish that chore. Maybe it will take a few minutes or maybe half an hour, but the investment will have been worthwhile if the quality of your study time—your concentration power—has increased. Taking action is the first step in getting something off your mind.

For the big problems about which you can do nothing immediately, ask yourself, "Is it worth the amount of brain time I'm dedicating to it?" Take a few minutes to think and make notes on possible solutions. Jotting down necessary future action and forming a plan of attack will help relieve the worry and clear the mind for studying.

Right now, list five things that are on your mind that you need to remember to do. Alan Lakein, a specialist in time management, calls this a **to-do list.** In his book, *How to Get Control of Your Time and Your Life,*[4] Lakein claims that suc-

© 1993 HarperCollins College Publishers

To-Do List	**Sample**
1. _____	1. Get hair cut
2. _____	2. Do my book report
3. _____	3. Buy stamps
4. _____	4. Call power Co.
5. _____	5. Pay phone bill

[4]A. Lakein, *How to Get Control of Your Time and Your Life* (New York: Signet, 1974).

cessful business executives start each day with such a list. Rank the activities on your list in order of priority and then do the most important things first.

At the end of the day all the tasks may not be completed, but the leftovers can be transferred to tomorrow's list. Keep your to-do lists in a booklet, rather than on different scraps of paper, so that you can refer back to a previous day's activity as well as make notes for several days ahead. If you can't think of five things you need to do, think harder! In fact, most students will probably come up with more than five items.

Use a Pocket Calendar or Assignment Book. At the beginning of the quarter or semester record dates for tests, term papers, and special projects on a calendar that you can keep with your books. Use the planner to organize all course assignments. A look at the calendar will remind you of the need for both short- and long-term planning. Assigned tests, papers, and projects will be due whether you are ready or not. Your first job is to devise a plan for getting ready.

Increase your Self-Confidence. Saying "I'll never pass this course" or "I can't get in the mood to study" is the first step to failure. Concentration requires self-confidence. If you didn't think you could do it, you would not be in a college class reading this book. Getting a college degree is not a short-term goal. Your enrollment indicates that you have made a commitment to a long-term goal. Ask yourself the question, "Who do I want to be in five years?" In the following space, describe how you view yourself, both professionally and personally, five years from now.

Five years from now I hope to be _____

_____

Sometimes identifying the traits you admire in others can give you further insight into your own values and desires. Think about the traits you respect in others and your own definition of success. Answer the two questions that follow and consider how your responses mirror your own aspirations and goals.

Who is the person that you admire the most? _____

Why do you admire this person? _____

_____

_____

_____

Improve Your Self-Concept. Have faith in yourself and in your ability to be what you want to be. How many people do you know who have passed the particular course that is worrying you? Are they smarter than you? Probably not. Can you do as well as they did? Turn your negative feeling into a positive attitude. What are some of your positive traits? Are you a hard worker, an honest person, a loyal friend? Take a few minutes to pat yourself on the back. Think about your good points and, in the following spaces, list five positive traits that you believe you possess.

Positive Traits

1. _____

2. _____

3. _____

4. _____

5. _____

What have you already accomplished? Did you participate in athletics in high school, win any contests, or master any difficult skills? Recall your previous achievements, and in the following spaces, list three accomplishments that you view with pride.

Accomplishments

1. _____

2. _____

3. _____

Reduce Anxiety. Have you ever heard people say, "I work better under pressure"? This statement contains a degree of truth. A small amount of tension can help you to force yourself to direct full attention to an immediate task. For example, concentrated study for an exam is usually more intense two nights before, rather than two weeks before, the test.

On the other hand, too much anxiety can cause nervous tension and discomfort, which interfere with the ability to concentrate. Students operating under too much tension sometimes "freeze up" mentally and experience nervous physical reactions. The causes can range from fear of failure to lack of organization and preparation; the problem is not easily solved.

Anxiety is a behavior that is learned in response to situations that engender feelings of inadequacy. Because it is learned, it can also be unlearned. As an immediate, short-term response to tension, try muscle relaxation and visualization. For example, if you are reading a particularly difficult section in a chemistry book and becoming frustrated to the point that you can no longer concentrate, stop your reading and take several deep breaths. Use your imagination to visualize a peaceful setting in which you are calm and relaxed. Imagine yourself rocking back and forth in a hammock or lying on a beach listening to the surf. Use the image you created and the deep breathing to help relax your muscles and regain control. Take several deep breaths and allow your body to release the tension so that you can resume reading and concentrate on your work.

As a long-term solution, nothing works better than success. Just as failure fuels tension, success tends to weaken it. Each successful experience helps to desensitize feelings of inadequacy. Early success in a course can make a big psychological difference between final success and failure. Starting off with a passing grade on the first examination means that for the rest of the course the student is working to maintain a passing grade rather than fighting to overcome a failure. Maintaining a good grade creates far less tension and pressure than trying to overcome a bad one. The counseling center of most colleges offers special help for stress management and test anxiety.

Network with Other Students.

You are not in this alone; you have lots of potential buddies who can offer mutual support. Collect the names and phone numbers of a few classmates who are willing to help you if you do not understand the homework, miss a day of class, or need help on an assignment. Be prepared to help your classmates in return for their support.

Classmate _____ Phone _____

Classmate _____ Phone _____

Classmate _____ Phone _____

Form a Study Group.

Research experiments involving college students have shown that study groups can be very effective. Students learn to collaborate and form academic bonds that increase their chances of academic success. Studying with others is not cheating; it is a wise use of available resources. In many colleges such groups have become so popular that counselors assist students in finding study partners. If asked, many professors will assist networking efforts by distributing copies of the class roll on which willing participants have provided phone numbers. A developmental studies student testified upon receiving a scholarship as a dean's list junior, "I call my study buddy when I have a problem. One time I called about an English paper because I couldn't think of my thesis. She asked what it was about. I told her and she said, 'That's your thesis.' I just couldn't see it as clearly as she did."

Collaborate.

When participating in group learning activities, set expectations for group study so that each member contributes, and try to keep the studying on target. As a group activity, ask several classmates to join you in discussing the resources that are available for students on your campus. Brainstorm with the group for the answers, or information leading to the answers, to the following questions.

Where are the academic advisors located?

What kind of help is offered in the learning lab?

Does the college offer a study skills workshop?
Where can you use a word processor?
Where is your professor's office and what is the phone number?
Can you get individual help in the writing lab?
What services can the dean's office offer to students?
How late is the library open on the weekend?
What kind of help does the counseling center offer?

Curiosity

Do you start an assignment with a desire to learn and an interest in the subject? If so, you are lucky and you will probably have no trouble concentrating. If you are not quite so enthusiastic, you will want to look to yourself and the material for stimulation and motivation.

Spark an Interest.   Have you ever wondered why it is that the same student who barely plods through Book A can pick up Book B, a text of equal difficulty, and become completely engrossed in the subject matter, read for hours, and later remember most of what was read? This has probably happened to you. How can the success with Book B be applied to Book A? The student obviously finds Book B very interesting and therefore enjoyable and easy to read. How then can you generate an interest in material that has not previously seemed exciting?

Potentially dull material, like seemingly dull people, needs some background work. Ask some questions, get some ideas, and do some thinking before starting to read. If the material was assigned, it must have merit, and finding it will make your job easier. Make a conscious effort to stimulate your curiosity before reading, even if in a contrived manner. Make yourself want to learn something. First look over the assigned reading for words or phrases that attract your attention, glance at the pictures, check the number of pages, and then ask yourself the following question: What do *I* want to learn about this?

With practice, this method of thinking before reading can create a spark of enthusiasm that will make the actual reading more purposeful and make concentration more direct and intense.

Set a Time Goal.   An additional trick to spark your interest is to set a time goal. Study time is not infinite and short-term goals create a self-imposed pressure to pay attention, speed up, and get the job done. After looking over the material, project the amount of time you will need to finish it. Estimate a reasonable completion time and then push yourself to meet the goal. The purpose of a time goal is not to "speed read" the assignment, but rather to be realistic about the amount of time to spend on a task and to learn how to estimate future study time.

Learning Styles

Did you know that many experts believe that your ability to concentrate on learning may be affected by the manner in which the information is presented to you? For example, could you be a right-brain thinker in a left-brain classroom? Are you an intuitive type working with concrete details? Do you have a learning style preference?

Many psychologists believe that individuals develop a preference for a particular style or manner of learning at an early age and that these preferences affect concentration and learning. For example, some people learn easily by reading, but others benefit more readily from a demonstration or a diagram. Similarly, engineers like to work with details while politicians prefer broad generalizations. Learning style theorists focus on strengths, not weaknesses; there is no right or wrong way. These researchers believe that instruction is best when it matches the learner's particular preference.

Learning Style Preferences.
One popular measure of individual learning style preferences is the Myers-Briggs Type Indicator (MBTI). Based on psychologist Carl Jung's theory of personality types, it measures individual learning style preferences in four categories. Although the MBTI is not accepted by all educators, the following brief description of its four categories gives an idea of the kinds of issues that its proponents consider significant:

1. Extroverted—Introverted
Extroverts prefer to talk with others and learn through experience, while introverts prefer to think alone about ideas.
2. Sensing—Intuitive
Sensing types prefer working with concrete details and tend to be patient, practical, and realistic. Intuitive types like abstractions and are creative, impatient, and theory oriented.
3. Thinking—Feeling
Thinking types tend to base decisions on objective criteria and logical principles. Feeling types are subjective and consider the impact of the decision on other people.
4. Judging—Perceiving
Judging types are time-oriented and structured, whereas perceivers are spontaneous and flexible.

Right- vs. Left-Brain Dominance.
Another popular learning style theory is concerned with right- or left-brain dominance. Proponents of this theory believe that left-brain dominant people are analytical and logical and excel in verbal skills. Right-brain people, on the other hand, are intuitive, creative, and emotional, and tend to think in symbols. Albert Einstein, for example, said

that he rarely thought in words, but that his concepts appeared in symbols and images.

Learning style theorists offer another way of looking at attention and learning. If you are "turned off" by an assignment, maybe it is the manner in which the material is presented and not the topic itself. Perhaps a presentation more in tune with your learning preferences would capture your attention and engender enthusiasm. A compatible approach may "turn on" your imagination.

SUMMARY

Concentration means focusing your full attention on the job at hand. It is a skill that is developed through self-discipline and practice. Research by cognitive psychologists indicates that the brain seems to attend selectively to certain inputs and to block out others. The ability to do several tasks at once depends on the amount of cognitive resources required for each. Experienced readers automatically process word meaning and thus are able to use cognitive resources to comprehend ideas.

Common causes of poor concentration are external and internal. External distractions are physical temptations that divert your attention. Make an effort to remove these distractions, and establish a private study place, a daily time, and a weekly schedule for effective learning. Internal distractions are more difficult to control. They are the mental wanderings that vie for your attention. Making a daily to-do list gets some of the distractions out of your head. To keep yourself working hard, estimate a reasonable completion time for an assignment and then push yourself to meet your goal.

Concentration requires self-confidence, self-discipline, and persistence. Have faith in yourself, develop your abilities, and expect to succeed. Network with other students. Research shows that study groups can be very effective in helping students form academic bonds and increasing their chances of success.

Many psychologists suggest that individuals develop a preference for a particular style or manner of learning at an early age. These preferences may affect concentration and learning.

Selection **1**

PSYCHOLOGY

Skill Development: Concentration

Preview

Directions: Before reading the first selection, take a few moments to analyze your potential for concentration, preview the selection, and answer the following questions.

1. *Look at your physical environment. Where are you and what time is it?*

_____

Is this your usual study time and place or are you deviating today for some special reason?

_____

What, if any, are your external distractions?

_____

_____

_____

_____

2. *Is anything popping into your mind that you need to remember to do? Do you feel confident that you understand the assignment and can do well? What, if any, are your internal distractions?*

_____

_____

_____

_____

3. *Now the big question is "Do you have any interest in what you are about to read?" The title of the selection is "Critical-Period Hypothesis," and it is taken from a book on human behavior. Do you know what* imprinting *means? Glance over the selection and see what words attract your attention. You may notice words and phrases like* critical-period hypothesis, Lorenz, goslings, baby chicks, the maternal instinct in rats, overcoming the critical period, baby geese, *and others. What do you think you would like to know about the topic? What about it is of interest to you?*

_____

_____

_____

_____

4. *Set approximate time goals for yourself. How long do you think it will take you to read this selection? _____ minutes. Look at the comprehension and vocabulary questions that follow the selection. How long do you think it will take you to answer the questions? _____ minutes*

Learning Strategy

Even though most of this excerpt describes animal behavior, the textbook is concerned with human behavior; therefore, be alert to links between the two. Be able to define and give examples of the two major terms in this selection.

Word Knowledge

Review the ten vocabulary items that follow the selection. Look up unfamiliar words in the dictionary.

As you begin to read, record your starting time. _____

CRITICAL-PERIOD HYPOTHESIS

From James V. McConnell, *Understanding Human Behavior*

There is some evidence that the best time for a child to learn a given skill is at the time the child's body is just mature enough to allow mastery of the behavior in question. This belief is often called the

© 1993 HarperCollins College Publishers

critical-period hypothesis—that is, the belief that an organism must
have certain experiences at a *particular time* in its developmental
sequence if it is to reach its mature state.

There are many studies from animal literature supporting the
critical-period hypothesis. For instance, German scientist Konrad
Lorenz discovered many years ago that birds, such as ducks and
geese, will follow the first moving object they see after they are
hatched. Usually the first thing they see is that mother, of course, who
has been sitting on the eggs when they are hatched. However, Lorenz
showed that if he took goose eggs away from the mother and hatched
them in an incubator, the fresh-hatched *goslings* would follow him
around instead.

After the goslings had waddled along behind Lorenz for a few
hours, they acted as if they thought he was their mother and that they
were humans, not geese. When Lorenz returned the goslings to their
real mother, they ignored her. Whenever Lorenz appeared, however,
they became very excited and flocked to him for protection and
affection. It was as if the visual image of the first object they saw
moving had become so strongly *imprinted* on their consciousness
that, forever after, that object was "mother."

During the past 20 years or so, scientists have spent a great deal of
time studying *imprinting* as it now is called. The effect occurs in
many but not in all types of birds, and it also seems to occur in
mammals such as sheep and seals. Whether it occurs in humans is a
matter for debate. Imprinting is very strong in ducks and geese,
however, and they have most often been the subjects for study.

The urge to imprint typically reaches its strongest peak 16 to 24
hours after the baby goose is hatched. During this period, the baby
bird has an innate tendency to follow anything that moves, and will
chase after its mother (if she is around), or a human, a bouncing
football or a brightly painted tin can that the experimenter dangles in
front of the gosling. The more the baby bird struggles to follow after
this moving object, the more strongly the young animal becomes
imprinted to the object. Once the goose has been imprinted, this very
special form of learning cannot easily be reversed. For example, the
geese that first followed Lorenz could not readily be trained to follow
their mother instead; indeed, when these geese were grown and
sexually mature, they showed no romantic interest in other geese.
Instead, they attempted to court and mate with humans.

If a goose is hatched in a dark incubator and is not allowed to see
the world until two or three days later, imprinting often does not
occur. At first it was thought that the "critical period" had passed and
hence the bird could never become imprinted to anything. Now we
know differently. The innate urge to follow moving objects does

appear to reach a peak in geese 24 hours after they are hatched, but it
does not decline thereafter. Rather, a second innate urge—that of
50 fearing and avoiding new objects—begins to develop, and within 48
hours after hatching typically overwhelms the prior tendency the bird
had to follow after anything that moves. To use a human term, the
goose's *attitude* toward strong things is controlled by its genetic
blueprint—at first it is attracted to, then it becomes afraid of, new
55 objects in its environment. As we will see in a moment, these
conflicting "attitudes" may explain much of the data on "critical
periods" in both animals and humans.

(*Question:* How might these two apparently conflicting behavioral
tendencies help a baby goose survive in its usual or natural
60 environment?)

In other experiments, baby chickens have been hatched and raised
in the dark for the first several days of their lives. Chicks have an
innate tendency to peck at small objects soon after they are
hatched—an instinctive behavior pattern that helps them get food as
65 soon as they are born. In the dark, of course, they cannot see grain
lying on the ground and hence do not peck (they must be hand-fed
in the dark during this period of time). Once brought into the light,
these chicks do begin to peck, but they do so clumsily and
ineffectively, as if their "critical period" for learning the pecking skill
70 had passed. Birds such as robins and blue jays learn to fly at about
the time their wings are mature enough to sustain flight (their parents
often push them from the nest as a means of encouraging them to
take off on their own). If these young birds are restrained and not
allowed to fly until much later, their flight patterns are often clumsy
75 and they do not usually gain the necessary skills to become good fliers.

The "Maternal Instinct" in Rats

Suppose we take a baby female rat from its mother at the moment of
its birth and raise the rat pup "by bottle" until it is sexually mature.
Since it has never seen other rats during its entire life (its eyes do not
open until several days after birth), any sexual or maternal behavior
80 that it shows will presumably be due to the natural unfolding of its
genetic blueprint—and not due to learning or imitation. Now,
suppose we inseminate this hand-raised female rat artificially—to
make certain that she continues to have no contact with other rats.
Will she build a nest for her babies before they are born, following
85 the usual pattern of female rats, and will she clean and take care of
them during and after the birth itself?

The answer to that question is yes—*if.* If, when the young female
rat was growing up, there were objects such as sticks and sawdust and

90 string and small blocks of wood in her cage, and which she played
with. Then, when inseminated, the pregnant rat will use these "toys"
to build a nest. If the rat grows up in a bare cage, she won't build a
nest *even though we give her the materials to do so once she is
impregnated.* If this same rat if forced to wear a stiff rubber collar
around her neck when she is growing up—so that she cannot clean
95 her sex organs, as rats normally do—she will not usually lick her
newborn babies clean *even though we take off the rubber collar a
day or so before she gives birth.* The genetic blueprint always operates
best within a particular environmental setting. If an organism's early
environment is abnormal or particularly unusual, later "innate"
100 behavior patterns may be disrupted.

Overcoming the "Critical Period"

All of these examples may appear to support the "critical-period"
hypothesis—that there is one time in an organism's life when it is
best suited to learn a particular skill. These studies might also seem
to violate the general rule that an organism can "catch up" if its
105 development has been delayed. However, the truth is more
complicated (as always) than it might seem from the experiments we
have *cited* so far.

Baby geese will normally not imprint if we restrict their visual
experiences for the first 48 hours of their lives—their fear of strange
110 objects is by then too great. However, if we give the geese
tranquilizing drugs to help overcome their fear, they can be imprinted
a week or more after hatching. Once imprinting has taken place, it
may seem to be irreversible. But we can occasionally get a bird
imprinted on a human to accept a goose as its mother, if we coax it
115 enough and give it massive rewards for approaching or following its
natural mother. Chicks raised in darkness become clumsy eaters—but
what do you think would happen if we gave them special training in
how to peck, rather than simply leaving the matter to chance? Birds
restrained in the nest too long apparently learn other ways of getting
120 along and soon come to fear heights; what do you think would
happen if we gave these birds tranquilizers and rewarded each tiny
approximation to flapping their wings properly?

There is not much scientific evidence that human infants have the
same types of "critical periods" that birds and rats do. By being born
125 without strong innate behavior patterns (such as imprinting), we
seem to be better able to adjust and survive in the wide variety of
social environments human babies are born into. Like many other
organisms, however, children do appear to have an inborn tendency to
imitate the behavior of other organisms around them. A young rat will
130 learn to press a lever in a Skinner box much faster if it is first allowed
to watch an adult rat get food by pressing the lever. This learning is

even quicker if the adult rat happens to be the young animal's mother.
Different species of birds have characteristic songs or calls. A
European thrush, for example, has a song pattern fairly similar to a
135   thrush in the United States, but both sound quite different from blue
jays. There are *local dialects* among songbirds, however, and these are
learned through imitation. If a baby thrush is isolated from its parents
and exposed to blue jay calls when it is very young, the thrush will
sound a little like a blue jay but a lot like other thrushes when it
140   grows up. And parrots, of course, pick up very human-sounding
speech patterns if they are raised with humans rather than with other
parrots.

Record reading time. _____

Comprehension Questions

After reading the selection, answer the following questions with *a, b, c,*
or *d.*

1. The best statement of the main idea of this selection is
   a. studies show that goslings can be imprinted on humans.
   b. a particular few days of an animal's life can be a crucial time for
      developing long-lasting "natural" behavior.
   c. imprinting seems to occur in mammals but is very strong in ducks
      and geese.
   d. the "crucial period" of imprinting is important but can be overcome
      with drugs.

2. The critical-period hypothesis is the belief that
   a. there is a "prime time" to develop certain skills.
   b. most learning occurs during the first few days of life.
   c. fear can inhibit early learning.
   d. the "maternal instinct" is not innate but is learned.

3. In Lorenz's studies, after the goslings imprinted on him, they would do
   all of the following except
   a. follow him around.
   b. flock to him for protection.
   c. return to their real mother for affection.
   d. become excited when Lorenz appeared.

4. The author points out that in Lorenz's studies the early imprinting of
   geese with humans
   a. was easily reversed with training.
   b. caused the geese to be poor mothers.
   c. produced later sexually abnormal behavior in the geese.
   d. made it difficult for the goslings to learn to feed themselves.

————————— 5. The author suggests that after 24 hours the innate urge to imprint in geese is
  a. decreased significantly.
  b. increased.
  c. overwhelmed by the avoidance urge.
  d. none of the above.

————————— 6. In its natural environment the purpose of the avoidance urge that develops within 48 hours of hatching might primarily be to help a small gosling
  a. learn only the behavior of its species.
  b. follow only one mother.
  c. escape its genetic blueprint.
  d. stay away from predators.

————————— 7. The author suggests that there is a critical period for developing all of the following except
  a. desire to eat.
  b. pecking.
  c. flying.
  d. cleaning young.

————————— 8. The studies with rats suggest that nest building and cleaning behavior are
  a. totally innate behaviors.
  b. totally learned behaviors.
  c. a combination of innate and learned behaviors.
  d. neither innate nor learned behaviors.

————————— 9. Abnormal imprinting during the critical period can later be overcome by using all of the following except
  a. tranquilizing drugs.
  b. natural tendencies.
  c. special training.
  d. massive reward.

————————— 10. Because humans do not seem to have strong innate behavior patterns, the author suggests that humans
  a. are better able to adapt to changing environments.
  b. have more difficulty learning early motor skills.
  c. find adjustment to change more difficult than animals.
  d. need more mothering than animals.

Answer the following with *T* (true) or *F* (false).

————————— 11. The author states that whether imprinting occurs in humans is a matter of debate.

————————— 12. The author implies that a goose can be imprinted on a painted tin can.

————————— 13. In the author's opinion, studies show that organisms can catch up adequately without special training when skill development has been delayed past the critical period.

_____ 14. If an abandoned bird egg is hatched and raised solely by a human, the author suggests that the bird will be abnormal.

_____ 15. The author suggests that the urge to imitate is innate in both humans and animals.

Vocabulary

According to the way the italicized word was used in the selection, select *a, b, c,* or *d* for the word or phrase that gives the best definition.

____ 1. "The critical-period *hypothesis*" (04)
    a. association
    b. tentative assumption
    c. law
    d. dilemma

____ 2. "in an *incubator*" (14)
    a. cage
    b. electric enlarger
    c. nest
    d. artificial hatching apparatus

____ 3. "its *genetic* blueprint" (53)
    a. sexual
    b. emotional
    c. hereditary
    d. learned

____ 4. "an *instinctive* behavior pattern" (64)
    a. desirable
    b. innate
    c. early
    d. newly acquired

____ 5. "to *sustain* flight" (71)
    a. support
    b. imitate
    c. begin
    d. imagine

____ 6. "birds are *restrained*" (73)
    a. pressured
    b. pushed
    c. held back
    d. attacked

____ 7. "suppose we *inseminate*" (82)
    a. imprison
    b. artificially impregnate
    c. injure
    d. frighten

____ 8. "may be *disrupted*" (100)
    a. thrown into disorder
    b. repeated
    c. lost
    d. destroyed

____ 9. "seem to be *irreversible*" (113)
    a. temporary
    b. changeable
    c. frequent
    d. permanent

____ 10. "*coax* it enough" (114)
    a. encourage fondly
    b. punish
    c. feed
    d. drill

Record total time for reading and responding. _____

Written Response

Use information from the text to respond to the following:
Does a critical period exist during which an organism must have certain experiences in order to reach its normal mature state?

Response Strategy: Define the critical-period hypothesis and describe three to five examples from the text that support the hypothesis. (Use your own paper for this response.)

Connecting and Reflecting

Many selections in this text are followed by a brief passage that relates to the longer selection. The passages may be an academic or emotional appeal, and they may agree or disagree with previously stated ideas. The passages were chosen to stimulate thinking, reinforce learning, and encourage you to explore new ideas and interact with them. Answers will reflect your insight, enlightenment, and personal connection with the material.

According to researchers, many animals have a critical period, or a particular time in their genetic blueprint, at which certain experiences should occur in order for them to achieve a normal mature state. Current research has not confirmed that these same critical periods exist for humans although future research may do so. If you had a newborn today, not knowing what scientists will discover tomorrow, would you be concerned about the effects of early experiences on the child's later maturation? What experiences would you engineer and repeat for your newborn during the first month of life in hopes that this early experience would positively influence later development?

Read the following passage for more information, and use your own paper to respond. List six experiences that you would offer a newborn, and explain why you think each one should be introduced early.

What Newborn Infants Can and Can't Do

Are there "critical periods" in human development? As it turns out, we cannot answer this question satisfactorily without knowing what things newborn infants can and can't do. A century ago, many scientists believed that a neonate had few if any innate abilities.

In recent years, however, the pendulum of scientific opinion has begun to swing back toward a "naturist" position. For instance, we now know that almost from birth, an infant can not only see and

5

hear with great precision, but also can sort out stimuli, remember,
and predict future inputs. Neonates apparently can recognize their
own names by two weeks of age, and they can distinguish among
colors by the time they are three months old. They seem to
develop depth perception by the fourth month of life. There is
even some evidence that fetuses can acquire simple associations
while still in the womb (Mussen 1983).

In a recent experiment, DeCasper and Melanie Spence asked
pregnant women to "talk" to their fetuses daily. During the last six
weeks of their pregnancy, the women read aloud from *The Cat in
the Hat* (a children's book) twice a day. Then, shortly after the
infants were born, DeCasper and Spence tested them. The infants
preferred hearing their mothers read aloud from *The Cat in the
Hat* than from another children's book. In a second study,
DeCasper and Spence had pregnant women repeat a phrase aloud,
several times a day, during the last weeks of their pregnancy. After
birth, the infants preferred the spoken phrase to other similar
phrases (DeCasper & Spence 1986). DeCasper concludes that
"Prenatal auditory experience is sufficient to influence postnatal
auditory preferences" (cited in Kolata 1984).

Princeton researchers J.L. and Carol G. Gould believe that the
genes *sensitize* newly born organisms to certain aspects of their
environments. But both the environment, and the training
techniques actually used, determine what infants learn. Simple
animals—such as bees and birds—inherit rather rigid "learning
programs," the Goulds say. These programs specify rather precisely
what the animals can (and can't) learn from their environments,
and when in the developmental sequence this learning should take
place (Gould & Gould 1981).

The restrictions on human learning are much more subtle. You
were born with the ability (and the desire) to learn almost
anything. However, you do best when your environment "shapes"
you following the laws of learning.

From James V. McConnell, Understanding Human Behavior

Skill Development: Concentration

When you have finished each part of the assignment, evaluate your reading and study time.

How long did you take to read the selection? _____ minutes

How long did you take to answer the questions? _____ minutes

Did you work steadily or were you interrupted? _____

Did setting a time goal help you keep your mind on your work? _____

If you had been given the concentration pop quiz while reading this selection, would your score have been high _____, medium _____, or low _____?

Now that you have completed this selection, how much time would you plan for the next selection? _____ minutes

Selection

2

PSYCHOLOGY

Skill Development: Concentration

Directions: Before reading the second selection, take a few moments to analyze your potential for concentration, preview the selection, and answer the following questions.

1. Where are you? _____ What time is it? _____

Is this study time and place written on your weekly time schedule? What, if any, are your external distractions?

_____

_____

_____

_____

2. *Is anything special on your mind at the moment? Are you ready to "attack" the material? What, if any, are your internal distractions?*

_____

_____

_____

3. *Do you have any interest in reading the next selection? It is called "Memory Retrieval" and comes from a psychology textbook. Do you have a good memory? Do you use "tricks" to help you remember things? Looking over the pages, you might notice words and phrases like* recall, recognition, retrieval, methods of loci, *and* imagery. *Do these phrases give you ideas you may want to explore? What ideas are of interest to you?*

_____

_____

_____

_____

4. *Set approximate time goals for yourself.*
   How long do you think you will take to read this section?
   _____ *minutes*

As you begin to read, record your starting time. _____

© 1993 HarperCollins College Publishers

MEMORY RETRIEVAL

From Richard R. Bootzin et al., *Psychology Today: An Introduction*

Memory would be very limited if we lacked a system for the long-term storage of information. Anything we perceived would

*From *Psychology Today: An Introduction*, Fifth Edition by Bootzin et al., pages 212-220. Copyright © 1975, 1979, 1983 by McGraw-Hill, Inc. Reprinted by permission of Mc-Graw-Hill, Inc.

simply fade away moments after we shifted our attention from it.
Nothing we ever looked at, heard, felt, smelled, or tasted would
ever seem familiar to us. Life would be a steady stream of new
experiences. In short, we would be incapable of learning.

Schemas

As they build upon simple relations among concepts, people create
increasingly complex networks of knowledge. We store large
clusters of interrelated concepts regarding people and objects
(human anatomy, for instance, or automobile engines), as well as
events and procedures (what the Fourth of July is like or how to fix
a leaky faucet). These large clusters of interrelated concepts, which
provide us with general concepts of people, objects, events, and
procedures, are called **schemas.**

Once formed, schemas help you record new experiences.
Suppose you hear that your friend John got a part-time job at the
Super Store, a new supermarket. You add such facts to memory
partly by creating new relationships between existing concepts and
schemas. For instance, you can take your schema "has a job" and
record in memory that this relationship holds between two familiar
concepts, John and the Super Store. Here you are storing new
knowledge by arranging the old in new ways. Notice the efficiency
of these approaches to storing new information. You do not
approach each new experience as if it were entirely novel,
unrelated to anything you know. Instead, you form associations
between new experiences and old information, thus saving yourself
cognitive effort.

Another advantage of relating new information to existing
schemas is that it puts the new information into a meaningful
context, which makes it easier to learn and retain. Studies have
demonstrated this effect (Bransford 1979; Ross and Bower 1981).
For instance, when people are instructed to learn seemingly
unrelated words ("ropes, lights, canvas, bell"), they learn them
slowly. But when a schema that provides a meaningful framework is
suggested to them ("boxing ring"), learning occurs much faster.
Schemas also have a powerful effect on the ability to understand
and remember simple sentences. Consider these:

The notes were sour because the seams split.
The voyage was delayed because the bottle did not break.
The haystack saved him because the cloth ripped.

If these sentences are puzzling to you, it is because you are having
trouble relating them to your schemas. Without appropriate
schemas, you are likely to forget the words quickly, even if you do
manage to memorize them for a while. But when given the right

45 schemas—bagpipe, ship christening, parachutist—your confusion changes to insight. Now the sentences are easy to understand and recall (Bransford and Johnson 1973).

Retrieval Cues

A *retrieval cue* is a piece of information that helps us to retrieve information from long-term memory. It can be a word, a sight, an
50 odor, a texture that reminds us of the information we are seeking—or that summons unbidden an event from the past. For example, the odor of evergreens may suddenly evoke the memory of Christmases past. Retrieval cues are taken seriously by the legal system and often used in court to remind a witness of some event.
55 In one court decision, the range of possible retrieval cues was described as "the creaking of a hinge, the whistling of a tune, the smell of seaweed, the sight of an old photograph, the taste of nutmeg, the touch of a piece of canvas" (*Fanelli* v. *U.S. Gypsum Co.,* 1944). Many aspects of memory—including recognition and
60 recall, state-dependent memory, and the elusiveness of information that remains stubbornly on the tip of the tongue—can be understood by applying the concept of retrieval cues.

Recognition and Recall.   Retrieval takes two basic forms: recognition and recall. *Recognition* requires us to realize whether something that is before us has been seen or heard in the past. The
65 process seems to occur automatically and is usually accurate. A familiar act of recognition occurs in answering multiple-choice questions. Three possible answers are in view; the task is to recognize the correct item. *Recall* requires us to retrieve specific
70 pieces of information in the information's absence. The process often demands an active search of long-term memory. To answer the question, "What is your mother's family name?" the item must be recalled from memory.

Recognition is easier than recall because the most effective
75 possible retrieval cue is present—the original information. There is no need to search long-term memory for it. Recognition for visual memories is often extraordinarily good. In one experiment (Haber and Standing 1969), people looked at 2,560 photographs of various scenes, studying each for ten seconds. When shown a group of
80 photographs on a subsequent day, the subjects were able to recognize between 85 and 95 percent of the pictures they had seen before.

In contrast, recall is often difficult because retrieval cues may be sparse or absent. The most common recall failure is the inability to
85 retrieve any information at all, as when people grope for a word they want or fail to remember a name they thought they knew.

False recall is rare. When it does occur, it can usually be explained in terms of strong familiar associations. For example, most grandchildren are used to having a grandparent call them by a
90 parent's name.

Relearning.   Sometimes information can be neither recalled nor recognized with certainty, as when a student seems to have forgotten everything learned in last year's German class. Yet if that student were to begin studying German again, she would be able to
95 relearn the language in less time than the original learning required. Although the information is no longer accessible, it apparently leaves a trace in long-term memory that facilitates new storage and retrieval, when cued by relearning.

State-Dependent Memory.   Many people have experienced an
100 inability to recall on the following morning events that accompanied heavy drinking the night before. Such losses of memory may be due in part to the absence of retrieval cues, for several experiments (e.g., Weingartner et al. 1976; Bartlett and Santrock 1979) have shown that a person's internal state—whether
105 sober or drunk, happy or sad—can serve as a retrieval cue. In *state-dependent memory,* information learned while in one physiological state is difficult to retrieve when a person is in a different state, but when the original condition is restored, the information can again be retrieved.

110 *"Tip-of-the-Tongue" Phenomenon.*   Sometimes we produce our own retrieval cues internally, although they're not always successful, as the *"tip-of-the-tongue" phenomenon* indicates. When we have a word or a number on the tip of the tongue, we are certain that we know the word but simply cannot pull it out of
115 storage. The condition has been described as "a state of mild torment, something like the brink of a sneeze" and when the word is finally retrieved, there is a feeling of considerable relief (Brown and McNeill 1966).

Aiding Retrieval

It is possible for anyone to improve her or his memory. *Mnemonic,*
120 or memory-assisting, systems have been known for thousands of years and were practiced in ancient Greece. Mnemonic systems organize information so that it can be remembered, using imagery, association, and meaning to accomplish their purpose, and they all make use of information already stored in semantic memory.
125 However, the boost to ordinary memory they provide will not take the work out of learning. At first these devices may take more time

than traditional rote memorization, but people who learn to use mnemonic systems gain two advantages. First, routine things are memorized more efficiently, freeing their minds for tasks that
130 involve understanding and reason. Second, facts required for tasks involving reasoning and understanding are remembered better (Higbee 1977).

Method of Loci.   One mnemonic system is called the *method of loci,* and it involves the use of a series of loci, or places, that are
135 firmly implanted in memory. Items to be remembered are placed along a familiar route.

Anyone can use this method. Suppose, for example, that you must learn the names of the presidents of the United States in chronological order. Simply visualize a familiar place—say, the
140 house in which you grew up—and imagine each president in a particular location. George Washington greeting you at the front door, John Adams and Thomas Jefferson talking in the entrance hall, James Madison playing backgammon with John Quincy Adams on the stairway, and so on until you find Ronald Reagan chopping
145 wood in the back yard. Thus, by taking a mental journey through the house along the same route, you will be able to visualize and recall the presidents. The same loci could be used to recall information about each of Shakespeare's plays or the chemical reactions involved in photosynthesis.
150 Another mnemonic system based on loci is called the peg-word system, which uses twenty simple words as loci. Once memorized, these words act as pegs upon which any arbitrary series of information can be hung. Each of the twenty words stands for one of the numbers from one to twenty. For example:

155 One is a bun.
Two is a shoe.
Three is a tree.
Four is a door.
Five is a hive.
160 Six is sticks.
Seven is heaven.
Eight is a gate.
Nine is a line.
Ten is a hen.

165 Each item to be remembered is visualized as interacting with one of these words. Suppose the memory task involves a shopping list, consisting of tomato soup, potatoes, spaghetti, and pickles. Imagine tomato soup being poured over a large bun, a potato resting in a shoe, strands of spaghetti hanging over a tree limb, and pickles

170 sticking like knives into a door. Once at the market, it's fairly easy to run through the familiar peg words and recall the image that has been hung on each. The list of presidents could be learned the same way with, for example, George Washington gnawing on a bun, John Adams complaining of a hole in his shoe, and so forth.

175 *Imagery.* The method of loci is based on imagery and uses the principle that it is easier to remember something if the object can be pictured in some way. Imagery is most helpful when the items to be remembered are concrete rather than abstract. For example, compare the word combinations "gorilla-piccolo" and
180 "omniscience-euphony." The first pair of words, both concrete nouns, immediately suggests specific images, but the second pair, both abstract nouns, either suggests no images at all or suggests images that are not uniquely tied to the words to be remembered. Abstract nouns can be remembered through images, but there is
185 always the risk that "choir," chosen as the image for "euphony," will bring "harmony" instead of "euphony" to mind on later recall.
　　Memory for visual images improves further if the images are woven into some sort of scene. Studies (e.g., Bower 1973) have shown that when a pair of words, such as "pig-ice," must be
190 remembered, people who imagine the words interacting in some way, such as a pig skating on ice, will remember the words better than someone who creates unconnected images for both words. The images need not be bizarre—ordinary scenes work just as well. But it is helpful to imagine a scene with a strong emotional impact.
195 In one study (Sadalla and Loftness 1972), people were shown lists of noun pairs and told to form images about the words that would later help them to recall the second noun in the pair when they were given the first. Some of the people were instructed to form neutral images, vivid but without emotional content; others to form
200 positive images, full of pleasant feelings; the rest to form negative images, which were "horrifying" and "uncomfortable to think about." On later memory tests it was clear that associating any strong emotion with an image was more effective than none; both positive and negative images helped people recall missing words
205 far better than did neutral images.
　　Why imagery is such a powerful tool of memory is not completely understood. It may be because imagery is processed in the nonlinguistic systems of the brain. In this view, words plus images are more likely to be remembered than words alone for the
210 same reason that it is better to have two reminder notes—one at home and one in a pocket—than to have only one. The two kinds of "notes"—verbal and visual—make it twice as likely that the message will be remembered.

215 Research with people who are totally blind from birth indicates that imagery can be used to improve memory even among those who have never had visual experiences. In one experiment (Jonides, Kahn, and Rozin 1975), both sighted and congenitally blind adults showed improved memory when they were given word pairs such as "locomotive-dishtowel" and told to imagine a
220 relationship between the words of each pair—for example, the locomotive wrapped in the dishtowel. The fact that imagery instructions improved the memory of blind subjects as well as sighted ones indicates that imagery effects do not rely on vision. The reason for imagery's effectiveness with the blind is unclear;
225 attempts to relate its success to other sensory channels, such as hearing or touch, have been successful.

The Key Word System.   The key word system has been successfully used to learn foreign languages, and it relies on linking English words (key words) with foreign words that have
230 similar sounds. The imagery used is much like that suggested to the blind. For example, if the word to be learned is *pato* (pronounced "pot-o"), the Spanish word for duck, an effective image is a duck with a *pot* (key word) on its head. To learn the French word for skin, *peau* (pronounced "poe"), imagine Edgar
235 Allan Poe with a beautiful complexion. Students who use this method have learned almost twice as many words in the same study time as students who use rote memorization. In addition, since some key words are better than others, the system works best if an instruction booklet suggests the key word but students create their
240 own images (Bower 1978).

Rhymes and Acronyms.   Unlike the mnemonic systems we have been discussing, rhymes and acronyms are specific. They can be used only once, so that although they are effective, they require a good deal of effort to create. Most, therefore, are handed down and
245 apply to common information that many people must learn. There are many mnemonic rhymes: "*I* before *E* except after *C*"; "Thirty days hath September, April, June, and November . . ."; and so on. The rhyme system is based on the fact that people have no difficulty remembering the individual items (the letters or the
250 months); the problem is remembering something about them (letter order, number of days). Acronyms are created by taking the first letter of each word in a series that must be remembered and making a word for them. For example, ROY G. BIV represents the order of the colors in the spectrum: red, orange, yellow, green,
255 blue, indigo, violet.

Record reading time. _____

Comprehension Questions

After reading the selection, answer the following questions with *a, b, c,* or *d.*

_____ 1. The best statement of the main idea of this selection is
   a. memory is dependent on retrieval clues and can be enhanced by their manipulation.
   b. the ability to recall information is more significant than recognition.
   c. mnemonic devices can enhance short-term memory.
   d. retrieval clues for memory are state-dependent.

_____ 2. A retrieval cue can be all of the following except
   a. a bit of information that helps recall thoughts from long-term memory.
   b. a word that reminds us of the information we are seeking.
   c. an odor or a sight that evokes the past.
   d. the word that seems to be on the tip of your tongue but cannot be pulled from storage.

_____ 3. Recall is a more difficult memory form for the retriever than recognition because
   a. the most effective retrieval clue is present.
   b. the original information is presented.
   c. the retrieval clue must come from the retriever.
   d. the information in the long-term memory is sparse.

_____ 4. The author attributes the tip-of-the-tongue phenomenon to
   a. state-dependent memory.
   b. an inability to produce successful internal retrieval clues.
   c. the lack of information in long-term memory.
   d. the absence of the information from storage.

_____ 5. The author suggests that mnemonic systems
   a. take the work out of learning.
   b. use imagery alone.
   c. use information already stored in semantic memory.
   d. are faster initially than rote memorization.

_____ 6. The method of loci is a better memory system than the key word method for learning
   a. foreign languages.
   b. items in a series.
   c. definitions of vocabulary words.
   d. brand names for grocery items.

_____ 7. A schema is
   a. a network or cluster of knowledge.
   b. a new idea.
   c. an unrelated concept.
   d. an experience that is not yet connected.

_____ 8. The author believes that the types of scenes and images that are most helpful to memory are
   a. bizarre.
   b. neutral.
   c. strongly emotional.
   d. positive rather than negative.

_____ 9. The initial link or retrieval clue in the key word system of memory is
   a. place.
   b. a similar sounding word.
   c. numbers in a series.
   d. an acronym.

_____ 10. According to the author, the disadvantage of rhymes and acronyms as memory systems is
   a. they apply to common information.
   b. they have a more generalized use than other systems.
   c. they are specific to one bit of information.
   d. they apply only to letters rather than concepts.

Answer the following questions with *T* (true) or *F* (false).

_____ 11. According to the author's explanation, answering a multiple-choice test would be considered an easier task than answering an essay exam.

_____ 12. Relearning a forgotten foreign language takes less time than the original learning required.

_____ 13. Mnemonic memory systems were first used by scientists in the United States.

_____ 14. Abstract nouns are easier to remember through imagery than concrete nouns.

_____ 15. Blind people are not able to use imagery effectively as a memory system.

Vocabulary

According to the way the italicized word was used in the selection, select *a, b, c,* or *d* for the word or phase that gives the best definition.

____ 1. "the *elusiveness* of information" (60)
   a. inaccuracy
   b. hopelessness
   c. frustration
   d. evasiveness

____ 2. "cues may be *sparse*" (83)
   a. few
   b. frequent
   c. forgotten
   d. misleading

—— 3. "people *grope* for a word"
(85)
    a. think aloud
    b. search uncertainly
    c. stutter
    d. wish

—— 4. "the *brink* of a sneeze"
(116)
    a. end
    b. beginning
    c. verge
    d. threat

—— 5. "stored in *semantic* memory"
(124)
    a. relating to language
    b. relating to nerves
    c. long-term
    d. ordinary

—— 6. "traditional *rote*
memorization" (127)
    a. regular
    b. familiar
    c. reliable
    d. by mechanical repetition

—— 7. "any *arbitrary* series of
information" (152)
    a. random
    b. structured
    c. compatible
    d. organized

—— 8. "Washington *gnawing* on a
bun" (173)
    a. agonizing
    b. crying
    c. chewing
    d. banging

—— 9. "in the *nonlinguistic* systems
of the brain" (207)
    a. unmeaningful
    b. without nerves
    c. stationary
    d. not associated with
       language

—— 10. "*congenitally* blind adults"
(217)
    a. existing from birth
    b. completely
    c. recently
    d. severely

Record total time for reading and responding. ——————

Written Response

Use information from the text to respond to the following:
Can a person improve memory by improving retrieval cues?
Response Strategy: Define retrieval cues and discuss three to four systems for forming retrieval cues and thus improving memory. (Use your own paper for this response.)

Connecting and Reflecting

In order to associate events in history, certain dates form crucial reference points and must be committed to memory. In United States history, the following dates are reference points. How can you use schemata and mnemonics to remember these dates? Form a collaborative study group for this activity and assign several dates to each group member. Seek additional knowledge about each date from group members and other sources in order to form clusters of meaningful ideas. **Working as a group, develop schemata and mnemonics for remembering the dates.**

1492 Columbus discovers America
1620 *Mayflower* lands English Pilgrims in Plymouth, Mass.
1776 Declaration of Independence
1865 Civil War ends
1929 Stock market crash and start of Great Depression
1945 World War II ends
1973 Vietnam War ends

Read the following passage to expand your knowledge on schemata and memory. Develop and share group strategies for remembering the dates with the class.

Schemata and Expert Memorizers

Sometimes experts in a particular area seem to have remarkable memories for information in their own specialty. For example, the famous conductor Toscanini is reported to have had an extraordinary memory for music. Just before the start of a concert, an agitated musician appeared before him. The musician reported that the key for the lowest note on his bassoon was broken—how would he play the concert? Toscanini shaded his eyes, thought for a moment, and then said, "It's all right—the note does not occur in tonight's concert." Not only did Toscanini know every note for every instrument in that concert, but it has been estimated that he knew by heart every note for every instrument in about 250 symphonic works, the words and music for 100 operas, plus a volume of chamber music, piano music, cello and violin pieces, and songs (Marek 1982). How could Toscanini memorize so much information? One view holds that experts can memorize information in their field because they already have well-developed schemata or frameworks to place the information in (Alba & Hasher 1983; Horton & Mills 1984).

A study by Chiesi, Spilich, and Voss (1979) demonstrated the role of schemata in memory. This experiment showed that people who knew a lot about baseball could remember more about a fictitious baseball game than those who knew less about the sport. Baseball knowledge was first assessed by a test used to divide subjects into high- and low-knowledge groups. Both groups were given an account of one half of an inning in a fictitious baseball game and were then asked to recall the information. Presumably

© 1993 HarperCollins College Publishers

because they could more easily map the new information onto their existing knowledge structure or schema, the high-knowledge subjects remembered significantly more.

30   Schemata may also be helpful to students. For example, you may have noticed that when you are first studying a subject it is difficult to learn and remember the new terms and concepts. Yet the more you study the subject, the easier it becomes to learn additional information. Perhaps you have developed schemata for the material

35   that help you to organize and remember the new information.

From Andrew B. Crider et al., *Psychology*

Skill Development: Concentration

When you have finished each part of the assignment, evaluate your reading and study time.

How long did you take to read the selection? _____ minutes

How long did you take to answer the questions? _____ minutes

Did you work steadily or were you interrupted? _____

Did setting a time goal help you keep your mind on your work? _____

If you had been given the concentration pop quiz while reading this selection, would your score have been high _____, medium _____, or low _____?

How much time do you think you will need to complete the next selection? _____ minutes

© 1993 HarperCollins College Publishers

WORD BRIDGE
Remembering New Words

While reading, you come across the following words:

autocrat   monotonous   prenatal

What do they mean? Should you stop reading immediately, look up each word in the dictionary, and jot down the definitions for future drill? That's ambitious, but unrealistic.

Your purpose for reading is to get information and ideas from the text, not to make word lists. Stopping to look up a particular word in the dictionary may improve your vocabulary, but it interrupts your train of thought and detracts from your comprehension of the material. Good readers use several strategies to get an approximate meaning of a word before going to the dictionary. They begin by using context and structural clues and then seek further clarification in the glossary or dictionary if necessary.

How to Remember New Words

Have you ever made lists of unknown words that you wanted to remember? Did you dutifully write down the word, a colon, and a definition, and promise to review the list at night before going to bed? Did it work? Probably not! Memorization can be an effective cramming strategy, but it does not seem to produce long-term results. Recording only the word and definition does not establish the associations necessary for long-term memory.

The best way to expand your vocabulary is to place yourself in an environment where challenging words are used. As children, this is the way we learn new words. Although changing households may not be an option, books afford a similarly rich verbal environment for those who are willing and eager to learn. Books both introduce and reinforce new words. The more you read, the more you will notice new words. With a little effort, these "new" words will gradually become "old." Once you start noticing words, you will probably be surprised at how often they recur. The following suggestions can help you make new words into old friends.

Associate Words in Phrases.   Never record a word in isolation. Think of the word and record it in a phrase that suggests its meaning. The phrase may be part of the sentence in which you first encountered the word, or it may be a vivid creation of your own imagination. Such a phrase provides a setting for the word and enriches the links to your long-term memory.

For example, the word *caravel* means a *small sailing ship.* Record the word in a phrase that creates a memorable setting, like "a caravan of gliding caravels shimmering on the sea."

Associate Words in Families.   Words, like people, have families that share the same names. In the case of words, the names are called **prefixes, roots,** and **suffixes.** A basic knowledge of word parts can help you unlock the meaning to thousands of associated family members.

The prefix *ambi* means *both,* as in the word *ambivert,* which means being both introverted and extroverted. Although this word is seldom used, it can be easily remembered because of its association with the other two more common words. A useful transfer occurs, however, when the knowledge of *ambi* is applied to new family members like *ambidextrous, ambiguous,* and *ambivalence.*

Associate Words in Images.   Expand the phrase chosen for learning the word into a vivid mental image. Create a situation or an episode for the word. Further enrich your memory link by drawing a picture of your mental image. Such a picture may ultimately prove to be a more useful memory tool than writing the word in a sentence.

The "caravan of gliding caravels on the shimmering sea" is an engaging illustration. Another example is the word *candid,* which means *frank and truthful.* A suggestive phrase for learning the word might be "his candid reply hurt her feelings."

Seek Reinforcement.   Look and listen for your new words. As suggested previously, you will probably discover that they are used more frequently than you ever thought. Notice them, welcome them, and congratulate yourself on your newfound wisdom.

Create Concept Cards.   The following blocks represent the front and back of index cards for recording information on new words. Each word is already presented in a phrase on the front of the card, along with a notation of where the word was encountered. On the back of each card, write an appropriate definition, use the word in a sentence, and draw an image illustrating the word. Review the cards to reinforce the words.

Front

Back

Example "birds are *restrained*" from "Imprinting"	 held back, not allowed to move The sheriff restrained the prisoner with handcuffs.
"the brink of a *sneeze*" from "Memory Retrieval"	
"a form of *quackery*" from "Acupuncture"	
"controlled by its genetic *blueprint*" from "Imprinting"	

READING AND STUDY STRATEGIES

- Why use a study system?
- What is a study system?
- What are the three stages of reading?
- How do you preview?
- Why should you activate your schemata?
- How do good readers think?
- What is metacognition?
- Why recall or self-test what you have read?

WHY USE A STUDY SYSTEM?

When a professor ends a class by saying, "Read the assigned pages for your next class meeting," both the students and the professor know the real message is, "Read *and study* the assigned pages for our next class meeting." Reading a textbook means "reading to learn," which means studying and thus includes a number of steps required to master material.

Textbook reading therefore demands an organized approach. To be successful, the techniques for reading novels and textbooks must differ. Reading a murder mystery may provide an escape into intrigue and adventure, whereas the purpose of textbook reading is to learn and remember a body of information. Each chapter, and even each page, of a textbook may contain a heavy load for the reader.

Students need to be aware of the activities involved in the learning process. According to experts on learning theory, students should first analyze the reading task to determine appropriate prereading strategies. As reading progresses, these strategies should be monitored and may need to be altered. To enhance understanding and recall while reading, students should engage in predicting, summarizing, self-testing, and establishing relationships to prior knowledge.[1] Obviously, all of these activities involve more than simply opening a book and moving from one word to another.

WHAT IS A STUDY SYSTEM?

In 1946, after years of working with college students at the Ohio State University, Francis P. Robinson developed a textbook-study system called SQ3R. The system was designed to help students efficiently read and learn from textbooks and effectively recall relevant information for subsequent exams. The letters in Robinson's acronym, SQ3R, stand for the following five steps: survey, question, read, recite, and review.

Numerous variations have been developed since SQ3R was introduced. One researcher, Norman Stahl, analyzed 65 textbook study systems and concluded that there are more similarities than differences among the systems.[2] The commonalities in the systems include a previewing stage, a reading stage, and a final self-testing stage. In the *previewing* stage students ask questions, activate past knowledge, and establish a purpose for reading. During the *reading* stage, students answer questions and continually integrate old and new knowledge. The *self-testing* stage of reading involves review to improve recall, evalu-

© 1993 HarperCollins College Publishers

---

[1] A. L. Brown, J. C. Campione, and J. E. Day, "Learning to Learn: On Training Students to Learn from Text," *Educational Researcher* 10 (1981): 14–21.

[2] N. A. Stahl, *Historical Analysis of Textbook Study-Systems* (Ph.D. diss., University of Pittsburgh, 1983).

ation to accept or reject ideas, and integration to blend new information with existing knowledge networks. Strategies used in these stages are depicted in the chart below and are discussed in this chapter.

STAGE 1: PREVIEWING

What is Previewing?

Previewing is a method of assessing your knowledge and needs before starting to read. When you preview, you decide what the material is about, what you already know about the topic, what needs to be done, and how to go about doing it. You formulate a reading strategy and then read to meet those goals.

Textbook Study Strategies

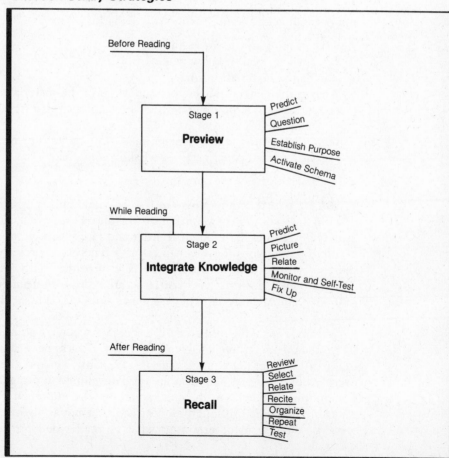

Even though previewing may take a few extra minutes in the beginning, the increased involvement that results makes it worth the time.

How to Preview

What to Ask.   To preview, look over the material, think, and ask questions. The process is similar to the concentration technique of sparking an interest before reading, except that in previewing, the questions are more directly related to purpose. The focus is, "What do I already know, what do I need to know, and how do I go about finding it out?"

More specifically, ask the following questions before beginning to read:

1. What is the topic of the material?
   What does the title suggest? What do the subheadings, italics, and summaries suggest?
2. What do I already know?
   What do I already know about this topic or a related topic?
   Is this new topic a small part of a larger idea or issue that I have thought about before?
3. What is my purpose for reading?
   What will I need to know when I finish?
4. How is the material organized?
   What is the general outline or framework of the material? Is the author listing reasons, explaining a process, or comparing a trend?
5. What will be my plan of attack?
   What parts of the textbook seem most important? Do I need to read everything with equal care? Can I skim some parts? Can I skip some sections completely?

What to Read.   A narrative tells a story and moves from one event to another in the resolution of a conflict. Novels and short stories are narratives. They usually develop in chronological order and rarely have such signposts as subheadings, italic type, or even chapter titles. Therefore, previewing a novel or a short story is difficult because of the lack of reader signposts.

Textbooks, however, are written in an expository manner in order to inform, explain, and discuss. They use many signposts to assist the reader in previewing the material so as to anticipate what is to come.

A public speaking rule says, "Tell them what you are going to tell them, tell them, and then tell them what you told them." This same organizational pattern frequently applies to textbook material. Typically, a chapter begins with a brief overview of the topic. The ideas are then developed in paragraphs or sections. Concluding statements at the end summarize the important points the author wants remembered. Although this pattern does not apply in every case, it can serve as a guide in determining what to read when previewing textbook material.

Previewing can be a hit-or-miss activity since there may or may not be an introductory or concluding statement. Because of differences in writing styles, no one set of rules will work for all material. The following points should be considered in previewing.

Title.   Titles are designed to attract attention and reflect the contents of the material. The title of an article, a chapter, or a book is the first and most obvious clue to its content. Think about the title and turn it into a question. If the article is entitled "Acupuncture," a major concern in your reading would probably be to find out "What is acupuncture?" Use the "five W technique" that newspaper stories often use in the first paragraph: Ask *who, what, when, where,* and *why* of the title.

Introductory Material.   To get an overview of an entire book, refer to the table of contents and preface. Sophisticated students use the table of contents as a study guide, turning the chapter headings into possible exam items. When you are seeking specific information in a book for research, the table of contents can help you to locate relevant material quickly. For novels, read the book jackets or paperback covers for a preview.

The first paragraphs in textbook chapters and articles frequently introduce the topic to be covered and give the reader a sense of perspective. For both articles and chapters, italicized inserts are sometimes used to overview and highlight the contents.

Subheadings.   Subheadings are titles for sections within chapters. The subheadings, usually appearing in **boldface print** or *italics,* outline the main points of the author's message and thus give the reader an overview of the organization and the content. Turn these subheadings into questions that need to be answered as you read.

Italics, Boldface Print, and Numbers.   Italics and boldface print are used to highlight words that merit special attention and emphasis. These are usually new words or key words that students should be prepared to define and remember. For example, a discussion of sterilization in a biology text might emphasize the words *vasectomy* and *tubal ligation* in italics or boldface print. Numbers usually signal a list of important details. In another book on the same subject, the two forms of sterilization might be emphasized with enumeration, by indicating (1) vasectomy and (2) tubal ligation.

Concluding Summary.   Many textbooks include summaries at the end of the chapters to highlight the important points within the material. The summary can serve not only as a review to follow reading, but also as an introduction for overviewing the chapter.

Exercise 1: Previewing this Textbook for the Big Picture

To get an overview of this text, look over the table of contents to get an idea of the scope and sequence of the book. Think about how the different chapter topics fit into the goals of college reading. Glance through the chapters to get a sense of the organization, and then use your previewing to answer the following questions.

1. Who is the author? Is the author a teacher?
2. The book is divided into how many major sections?
3. What seems to be the purpose of the reading selections?
4. List seven different college disciplines that are represented in the longer reading selections.
5. What seems to be the purpose of the "Connecting and Reflecting" segments?
6. Which chapter do you think you need the most?
7. Which chapter do you think you will like the most?
8. Why does the last chapter have only one reading selection?
9. Does the text have any study aids such as an index, a glossary, or summaries?
10. Which reading selection do you think will be most interesting?

Exercise 2: Previewing this Chapter

To get an overview of this chapter, look first at the table of contents and then read the list of questions at the beginning of the chapter. Read the chapter summary and scan to understand the subheadings and italicized words. Use your previewing to answer the following questions.

1. What is a study system?
2. Why are questions listed at the beginning of this chapter?
3. Why is reading considered in three stages rather than one stage?
4. What is a schema?
5. What is metacognition?
6. What is the purpose of a recall diagram?
7. Why does this chapter have a summary?
8. Which reading selection do you think will be most interesting?
9. What is a context clue?
10. What are the five thinking strategies used by good readers?

Preview to Activate Schemata

Despite what you may sometimes think, you are not an empty bucket into which the professor is pouring information. You are a learner who already knows a lot, and you are actively selecting, eliminating, and connecting information.

What do you bring to the printed page? The reader has a responsibility to think and interact before, during, and after reading. Your previewing of material helps you predict the topic. Then, as a further part of the prereading stage, you need to activate your schema for what you perceive the topic to be.

A **schema** is the skeleton of knowledge in your brain on a particular subject. As you learn more about the subject, you flesh out the skeleton with new information, and the skeleton grows. A schema is like a computer chip in your brain that holds all you know on a subject. Each time you learn something new, you pull out the computer chip on that subject, add the new information, and return the chip to storage.

Before reading, your previewing should lead you to activate the relevant computer chip. Actually, you will probably activate several **schemata,** which will stimulate interest and get you ready to interact with the text. Then the reading will expand your knowledge and add to your chips before you return them to storage.

The depth of the schema or the amount of information on the chip varies according to previous experience. A scientist would most likely have a more detailed computer chip for DNA than would a freshman biology student. If the student can define the concept or recall an instance in which DNA appeared, however, the beginning of a rather sketchy schema exists.

All college students have a schema for Shakespeare. Suppose your previewing of a ten-page essay led you to predict that the discussion focused on the strength of the main characters in five of Shakespeare's plays. Next you would ask, "What existing knowledge do I have on the subject?" or "What is on my computer chip labeled 'Shakespeare'?" Most students would immediately think of *Macbeth* and *Hamlet,* both the characters and the plays. Others who have studied Shakespeare more might recall *King Lear,* the comedies, and a model of the Globe Theater. The richness of your background determines the amount you can activate. In general, the more you are able to activate, the more meaningful the reading will be.

STAGE 2: INTEGRATING KNOWLEDGE WHILE READING

Importance of Relating Prior Knowledge

Is it easier to understand a passage if you already know something about the topic? You already know that the answer is *yes.* Read the following paragraphs for a demonstration.

Passage A: Life Expectancy

The **life span** is the age that a person actually attains, whereas **life expectancy** is the statistical probability of living to a particular age. When the Bible spoke of some people living threescore and ten years 2000 years ago, most humans were fortunate to reach their early 30s. Life expectancies had increased to the late 30s by the Middle Ages. Life expectancy for all Americans born in 1900 averaged about 47 years; it is now about 75 years. On the average, females live longer than males and the difference between the sexes is increasing. Life expectancy for all male American infants today is about 71 years, but it is almost 79 years for females. Lower life expectancies are found among various American subcultures and in most populations in developing nations.

John Cunningham, *Human Biology*

Passage B: Echinoderms (i kĭ′ nə dərms′)

Echinoderms have protective skeletal elements embedded in their body walls. They also have an unusual feature called a water vascular system, which is used as a kind of hydraulic pump to extend the soft, pouchlike *tube feet,* with their terminal suckers. They are sluggish creatures with poorly developed nervous systems. However, they are tenacious foragers. Some species feed on shellfish, such as oysters. They wrap around their prey and pull relentlessly until the shells open just a bit. Then they evert their stomachs, squeezing them between the shells, and digest the flesh of the oysters on the spot.

Robert Wallace, *Biology: The World of Life*

Even if you are a biology major, the first passage is probably easier to read than the second. Everyone is interested in life expectancy, particularly their own. Thus, most people have greater prior knowledge of life expectancy issues than of echinoderms. This prior knowledge makes reading more interesting, easier to visualize, and therefore easier to understand. Linking the old with the new provides a schema on which to hang the new ideas.

Before and while reading, good readers ask, "What do I already know about this topic?" and "How does this new information relate to my previous knowledge?" Although textbook topics may at times seem totally unfamiliar, seldom are all of the ideas completely new. Usually there is a link, an old bit of knowledge that you can associate with the new ideas. For example, although you may not be familiar with the echinoderms described in Passage B, you probably know what an oyster looks like and can visualize the tenacity needed to open its shell.

On the other hand, your choice of Passage A or B might have been different if you had known before reading the second paragraph that starfish are echinoderms. You might have found the description of mealtime downright exciting. Reread the passage with this knowledge and visualize the gruesome drama.

Later in this chapter you will read another passage on echinoderms. Be ready to pull out your already developed "echinoderm knowledge network."

Expanding Knowledge

Most experts agree that the single best predictor of your reading comprehension is what you already know. In other words, **the rich get richer.** The good news about this conclusion is that once you have struggled and learned about a subject, the next time you encounter the subject, learning about it will be easier. Forming new schemata is much more difficult than adding to existing ones. Does this help to explain why some experts say that the freshman year is the hardest? Frequently, students who barely make C's in introductory courses end up making A's and B's during their junior and senior years. Although the later courses are more advanced than the introductory ones, the students profit from the initial struggle of building schemata. Their intellectual energies during the junior and senior years can go into assimilating and arranging new information into previously established frameworks rather than striving to build schemata. Be comforted to know that during that initial struggle with new subjects, you are building schemata that you will later reuse. Tell yourself, "The smart get smarter, and I'm getting smart!"

Integrating Ideas: How Do Good Readers Think?

Understanding and remembering complex material requires as much thinking as reading. Both consciously and subconsciously, the good reader is predicting, visualizing, and drawing comparisons in order to assimilate new knowledge. The following list, devised by a reading researcher, represents the kind of thinking strategies good readers employ.[3]

1. *Make predictions.* (Develop hypotheses.)
   "From the title, I predict that this section will give another example of a critical time for rats to learn a behavior."
   "In this next part, I think we'll find out why the ancient Greeks used mnemonic devices."
   "I think this is a description of an acupuncture treatment."
2. *Describe the picture you're forming in your head from the information.* (Develop images during reading.)
   "I have a picture of this scene in my mind. My pet is lying on the table with acupuncture needles sticking out of its fur."
3. *Share an analogy.* (Link prior knowledge with new information in text.) We call this the *"like-a" step.*
   "This is like my remembering, 'In 1492 Columbus sailed the ocean blue.'"

[3]B. Davey, "Think Aloud—Modeling for Cognitive Processes of Reading Comprehension," *Journal of Reading* 27 (October 1983): 44–47.

4. *Verbalize a confusing point.* (Monitor your ongoing comprehension.)
   "This just doesn't make sense."
   "This just doesn't make sense. How can redwoods and cypress trees both be part of the same family?"
   "This is different from what I had expected."
5. *Demonstrate fix-up strategies.* (Correct your lagging comprehension.)
   "I'd better reread."
   "Maybe I'll read ahead to see if it gets clearer."
   "I'd better change my picture of the story."
   "This is a new word to me—I'd better check context to figure it out."

The first three thinking strategies used by good readers are perhaps the easiest to understand and the quickest to develop. Young readers quickly learn to predict actions and outcomes as the excitement of an adventure escalates. Vivid descriptions and engaging illustrations nurture the imagination to create exciting mental images. Questions, discussions, and feelings of self-worth encourage the inclusion of past experience.

Up until this point, reading is like going to the movies, whether the reading is about Mafia gangsters or cholesterol's slow accumulation in the blood vessels. The moviegoer, as well as the reader, can be totally absorbed and integrated into the topic. When the ideas get more complicated, however, the last two thinking strategies become essential elements in the pursuit of meaning. College textbooks are tough and require constant use of monitoring strategies and frequent use of correction strategies.

These last two strategies involve a higher level of thinking than just picturing an oyster. They reflect a deeper understanding of the process of getting meaning and suggest a reader who both knows and controls. This ability to know and control is called *metacognition*.

Metacognition

The term **metacognition** is a coined word. **Cognition** refers to knowledge or skill that you possess. The Greek prefix *meta-* suggests an abstract level of understanding as if viewed from the outside. Thus, metacognition not only means having the knowledge but also refers to your own awareness and understanding of the processes involved and your ability to regulate and direct the processes. In reading, if you know how to read, you are operating on the cognitive level. To operate on a metacognitive level, you must know the processes involved in reading and be able to regulate them. If you are reading a chemistry assignment and are failing to understand, you must first of all recognize that you are not comprehending. Then you must identify what and why you don't understand. Remember, you can do this because you understand the skills involved in the reading process. Next, you select another tactic. You attempt a fix-up strategy. If it doesn't work, you try another and remain confident that you will succeed. The point is that you understand how to get meaning, you know when you

Metacognition

Cognition
1. Predict
2. Picture
3. Relate

4. Monitor
5. Fix up

don't have it, and you know what to do about getting it. One researcher calls this "knowing about knowing."[4]

Comparing reading to a similar activity, do you know when you are really studying? Do you know the difference between really studying and simply going through the motions of studying? Sometimes you can study intensely for an hour and accomplish a phenomenal amount. Other times you can put in twice the time with books and notes but learn practically nothing. Do you know the difference and do you know what to do about it? Some students do not.

Many poor readers do not know that they don't know. They seem unaware that gaps of knowledge exist. They continue to read and do not notice comprehension failures. Not only do they fail to monitor and recognize, but they probably do not know enough about the reading process to be able to attempt a fix-up strategy to correct faulty comprehension.

Poor readers see their failure to comprehend as a lack of ability and feel that nothing can be done about it. Successful readers see failure only as a need to reanalyze the task. They know they will eventually correct their problems and succeed.

Develop a Metacognitive Sense for Reading

Research studies indicate that students can learn to develop a metacognitive sense for reading. With instruction and practice, students can improve their total reading performance. Awareness and improvement activities center around the following areas:

1. *Knowing about reading.* Good readers are aware of the many strategies they use to comprehend. These include knowledge about words, main ideas and supporting details, and implied ideas. They also understand the organization of the text and where meaning can be found. In other words, they understand the underlying elements of process and presentation.

[4]A. L. Brown, "The Development of Memory: Knowing, Knowing about Knowing, and Knowing How to Know," in H. W. Reese, ed., *Advances in Child Development and Behavior,* vol. 10 (New York, N.Y.: Academic Press, 1975), 104–146.

2. *Knowing how to monitor.* Monitoring is the ongoing process of predicting, clarifying, questioning, and self-testing. The advocates of SQ3R focus on predicting and questioning in the preview stage, while metacognitive proponents stress the occurrence of these activities throughout the reading. Monitoring is an ongoing process of questioning and predicting with subsequent corroborations or discards. Clarification and self-testing both reinforce learning and pinpoint gaps in comprehension.

3. *Knowing how to correct failures.* Knowledge of the reading process offers choices for correction. Perhaps rereading to reprocess a complex idea systematically will solve the comprehension failure. Maybe the writing style is confusing, and the idea must be unraveled on a sentence level. Then again, perhaps the idea is slowly unfolding, and reading ahead will bring enlightenment. In some cases, correction may lie beyond the text. You may need to consult the dictionary for additional word knowledge or peruse other sources to fill in background knowledge you lack.

Examples. Apply both your congnitive and metacognitive knowledge to the reading of the following sentences. Interact with the material, monitor, and predict the ending phrase before reading the options. Some of the thoughts of the reader are highlighted in handwriting.

Picture → *How horrible!*

1. Leeches used to be a favorite means of treating bruises (especially black eyes) and were also used for bloodletting. Pharmacies in some countries still stock them

   Didn't work   *not here*

   Key word?   *(At the drugstore?*

   a. for historical value.

   b. but they are never used.

   c. to entertain customers.

   d. for medicinal purposes. ← *The word still suggests some use*

   Picture   pollutes and kills

2. What is euphemistically called an "oil spill" can very well become an oil disaster for marine life. This is particularly true when refined or semirefined products are being transported. As the tankers get bigger, so do the accidents, yet we continue to

   Wants to make more money →

   Key word   *P. 1040*

   a. fight for clean water.

   b. search for more oil.

   c. use profits for clean up.

   d. build larger vessels. ← *shows a parallel idea*

   Robert Wallace, *Biology: The World of Life*

The following passage illustrates the use of these thinking strategies with longer textbook material. The thoughts of the reader are highlighted in handwriting. Keep in mind that each reader reacts differently to material, depending on background and individual differences. This example merely represents one reader's attempt to integrate knowledge.

Viruses *Makes you sick?*

too small to imagine

Viruses are remarkable small organisms, about 1/20,000 the size of

how big? *difficult to kill* bacteria, that reproduce entirely inside cells. Viruses are unique

strange?

among living things—if, in fact, they are alive. Outside of a living cell

they are completely inert. In some cases they look like crystals, and

good image

as lifeless as ordinary table salt. As soon as a virus enters a living cell,

however, it begins to take over the metabolic machinery of that cell. It

reorganizes the cell's processes so that the cell begins to engage in

is it cancer?

producing more viruses instead of continuing its normal activities.

forces cell to kill itself

Finally, when the cell ruptures, new viruses are released to take over

will they later?

yet other cells. To date, no viruses have been implicated in human

cancer, but some viruses have definitely been shown to cause cancer

in other animals. *p. 161*

How can they be killed without killing host?

Robert Wallace, *Biology: The World of Life*

The example may be confusing to read because many of the thoughts that are highlighted normally occur on the subconscious rather than the conscious level. Stopping to consciously analyze these reactions seems artificial and interrupting. It is important, however, to be aware that you are incorporating these thinking strategies into your reading. The following exercises are designed to make you more aware of this interaction.

Exercise 3: Integrating Knowledge While Reading

For each of the following passages, demonstrate with written notes the way you use the five thinking strategies as you read. The passages are double-spaced so that you can insert your thoughts and reactions between the lines. Make a conscious effort to experience all of the following strategies as you read:

1. Predict (Develop hypotheses.)

2. Picture (Develop images during reading.)
3. Relate (Link prior knowledge with new ideas.)
4. Clarify points (Monitor your ongoing comprehension.)
5. Use fix-up strategies (Correct your lagging comprehension.)

Sea Stars

Let's take a look at one class of echinoderms—the sea stars. Sea stars (starfish) are well known for their voracious appetite when it comes to gourmet foods, such as oysters and clams. Obviously, they are the sworn enemy of oystermen. But these same oystermen may have inadvertently helped the spread of the sea stars. At one time, when they caught a starfish, they chopped it apart and vengefully kicked the pieces overboard. But they were unfamiliar with the regenerative powers of the starfish. The central disk merely grows new arms, and a single arm can form a new animal.

Stars are slow-moving predators, so their prey, obviously, are even slower-moving or immobile. Their ability to open an oyster shell is a testimony to their persistence. When a sea star finds an oyster or clam, the prey clamps its shell together tightly, a tactic that discourages most would-be predators, but not the starfish. It bends its body over the oyster and attaches its tube feet to the shell, and then begins to pull. Tiring is no problem since it uses tube feet in relays. Finally, the oyster can no longer hold itself shut, and it opens gradually—only a tiny bit, but it is enough. The star then protrudes its stomach out through its mouth. The soft stomach slips into the slightly opened shell, surrounds the oyster, and digests it in its own shell.

Robert Wallace, *Biology: The World of Life*

At first glance, you probably recognized *echinoderm* as an old friend and activated your newly acquired schema from a previous page. The description of the starfish lends itself to a vivid visualization. Were some of your predictions corroborated as you read the passage? Did you find yourself monitoring to reconcile new facts with old ideas? Did you need to use any fix-up strategies? Has your computer chip been expanded?

STAGE 3: RECALLING FOR SELF-TESTING

What is Recalling?

Recalling is telling yourself what you have learned, what you wish to remember, and relating it to what you already know. It is taking those few extra minutes to digest what you have read and having a short conversation with yourself or a friend about the new material. Rather than being formal, long, and involved, the recalling process is a brief overviewing that helps you "pull together" what you have learned, as well as fill in any gaps. Before saying, "Hallelujah, I've finished!" good readers invest a few more minutes in remembering and arranging. Researchers have proven that recalling pays off. In experiments students who actively recalled what they had read scored higher on tests than students who did not recall or who merely reread the material. Recall is part of the monitoring in metacognition. It is the final self-testing good readers require of themselves.

Recall also involves arranging new information into old schemata and creating new schemata. Not only are you recalling what you just read, but you are also recalling old knowledge and seeking to make connections. While "sorting through" ideas, you are accepting and rejecting information, making decisions about storage, rearranging old networks, and creating new ones. Good readers make an effort to make connections.

Why Recall?

Engaging in recall immediately after reading forces the reader to select the most important points and to relate new with existing information.

1. *Select the most important points.*
   The poor student wants to remember everything—facts have equal importance and thus no priorities are set. In short, no decisions have been made, and the student has failed to sift through the reading and pull out the important issues.
   Good readers look for order and importance. They recognize issues and identify significant support information.
2. *Relate the information.*
   Facts are difficult to learn in isolation. For example, many first-year college students have difficulty with history courses because they have

no framework or schemata into which to fit new information. Events appear to be isolated happenings rather than results of previous occurrences or parts of ongoing trends. Juniors and seniors, on the other hand, who have worked hard to establish knowledge networks, can more readily relate historical happenings into existing frameworks.

How to Recall

To recall, simply take a few minutes after that last "*Hallelujah!* period" to recap what you have learned. This can be done in your head or on paper. To visualize the main points graphically, make a recall diagram. On a straight line across the top, briefly state the topic, or what the selection seems to be mainly about. Indented underneath the topic, state the supporting details that seem to be most significant. Next, take a few seconds to make a connection. What do you already know that seems to relate to this information? Each reader's answer will be unique because you are connecting the material to your own knowledge networks. Draw a dotted line, your thought line, and recall a related idea, issue, or concern. The following is an example of a recall diagram.

What is the material mainly about?

significant supporting examples
(or) significant related facts
(or) significant clarifying phrases

Related idea   What idea connects to this?

Example: Autopsies
Today, many dead people receive some form of **autopsy** or postmortem examination. At least two main reasons for this are (1) the desire of the family to know the exact cause of death, and (2) the fact that increased medical knowledge results. Because of the important moral and legal restrictions on human experimentation, much of our knowledge of pathology comes from autopsies. This fact prompts many people to donate their bodies to medical schools and/or donate certain organs for possible transplantation.

John Cunningham, *Human Biology*

(topic) *Why autopsies are done*

(significant details)

To know exact cause of death
To increase medical knowledge
— thus donations

(related idea) *Will this relieve the need for much animal research?*

Exercise 4: Recall Diagrams

After reading the following passages, stop to recall what the passage contained. Use the recall diagrams to record what the passage seems to be mainly about, list significant supporting details, and identify a related idea, issue, or concern to which you feel the information is connected.

Passage A: Postwar Boom

A number of factors were responsible for the post–Civil War industrial boom. The United States possessed bountiful raw materials, and the government was willing to turn them over to industry for little or no money. Coupled with the abundance of natural resources was a home market steadily expanding through immigration and a high birth rate. Both capital and labor were plentiful. The increase in trade and manufacturing in the Northeast in the years before the war produced an accumulation of savings, while additional millions of dollars came from European investors. Unbroken waves of European immigration provided American industry with workers as well as with customers. From 1860 to 1900 about 14 million immigrants came to the United States, most of whom settled in cities and became industrial workers.

Carl N. Degler et al., *The Democratic Experience**

(topic) _____

(significant details)

(related idea) _____

*From Carl N. Degler et al., *The Democratic Experience*, 4th edition. Copyright © 1977, Scott, Foresman and Company, HarperCollinsCollege Publishers.

Passage B: Kangaroos

Kangaroos and Australia are synonymous for most people, and the abundance of the large kangaroos has gone up since the British colonized Australia. The increase in kangaroo populations has occurred in spite of intensive shooting programs, since kangaroos are considered pests by ranchers and are harvested for meat and hides. The reason seems to be that ranchers have improved the habitat for the large kangaroos in three ways. First, in making water available for their sheep and cattle, the ranchers have also made it available for the kangaroos, removing the impact of water shortage for kangaroos in arid environments. Second, ranchers have cleared timber and produced grasslands for livestock. Kangaroos feed on grass, and so their food supply has been increased as well as the water supply. Third, ranchers have removed a major predator, the dingo. The dingo is a doglike predator, the largest carnivore in Australia. Because dingoes eat sheep, ranchers have built some 9660 kilometers of fence in southern and eastern Australia to prevent dingoes from moving into sheep country. Intensive poisoning and shooting of dingoes in sheep country, coupled with the dingo fence that prevents recolonization, has produced a classic experiment in predator control. There is a spectacular increase in the abundance of red kangaroos when dingoes are eliminated. Densities of kangaroos are 166 times higher in New South Wales than in South Australia. Dingoes are able to hold kangaroo numbers low in South Australia because the dingoes are not solely dependent on the kangaroos as food supply. They have alternate prey such as rabbits and rodents to sustain them. Dingoes eat sheep and, by getting rid of one problem, the ranchers have helped to accentuate the kangaroo problem.

Charles Krebs, *The Message of Ecology*

(topic) _____

(significant details)

(related idea) _____

SUMMARY

Reading is an active rather than a passive process and requires that thinking occur before, during, and after the act. All study systems include a previewing stage to ask questions and establish a purpose for reading, a reading stage to answer questions and integrate knowledge, and a final stage of self-testing and review to improve recall.

Previewing is a method of assessing your needs before starting to read by deciding what the material is about, what needs to be done, and how to go about doing it. Activate your schemata before reading; the more you are able to activate, the more meaningful the reading will become.

The second stage of reading involves thinking while reading. The thinking strategies are to predict, to picture, to relate, to monitor, and to fix up. Good readers operate on a metacognitive level, which means they control and direct these thinking strategies as they read.

Recalling what you have read immediately after reading is the last stage. It forces the reader to select the most important points, relate the supporting details, and connect new information into existing networks of knowledge.

Selection **1**

PSYCHOLOGY

Skill Development

Stage 1: Preview

> *Preview the next selection to predict purpose, organization, and a learning plan.*

Preview
Overlearning seems to mean

_____

After reading this selection, I will need to know

_____

Activate Schema
> *Can you recite the Pledge of Allegiance to the flag? Why?*
> *Does "free" learning for an exam occur between study sessions?*
> *If a fellow student declares, "I've read this three times. I've really studied," are you impressed?*

Learning Strategy
> *Be able to define the terms and relate them to college study.*

Word Knowledge
> *Review the ten vocabulary items that follow the selection. Seek an understanding of unfamiliar words.*

Stage 2: Integrate Knowledge While Reading

> *Since each reader interacts with material in a unique manner, it is artificial to require certain thinking strategies to be used in certain places. In order to heighten awareness, however, several questions have been inserted within this selection. Briefly respond in the margin to the inserted questions. In addition, make a note in the margin of at least one other instance when you used each of the following strategies:*

> **1. Predict 2. Picture 3. Relate 4. Monitor 5. Fix up**

OVERLEARNING

From Jerome Kagan and Ernest Havemann, *Psychology: An Introduction*

Adults are often surprised by how well they remember something they learned as children but have never practiced in the meantime. A man who has not had a chance to go swimming for years can still swim as well as ever when he gets back in the water. He can get on a

5 bicycle after several decades and still ride away. He can play catch and swing a baseball bat as well as his son. A mother who has not thought about the words for years can teach her daughter the poem that begins "Twinkle, twinkle, little star" or recite the story of Cinderella or Goldilocks and the three bears.

(Describe your mental pictures.)

10 One explanation is the *law of overlearning,* which can be stated as follows: Once we have learned something, additional learning trials increase the length of time we will remember it. A laboratory demonstration of this law is shown in the figure.

How Overlearning Aids Remembering

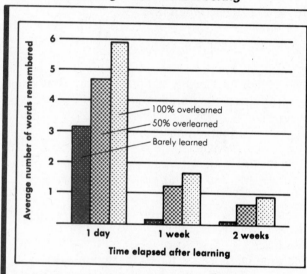

These are the results of an experiment in which subjects learned a list of twelve single-syllable nouns. Sometimes they stopped studying the list as soon as they were able to recall it without error—in the words used in the chart, as soon as they had "barely learned" the words. At other times they were asked to continue studying the list for half again as many trials as bare learning required (50 percent overlearned) or to continue studying for the same number of extra trials as the original learning had required (100 percent overlearned). Whether measured after a day or at later intervals, the subjects who had overlearned by 50 percent remembered considerably more than those who had barely learned, and the subjects who had overlearned by 100 percent remembered most of all. (20)

15 In childhood we usually continue to practice such skills as swimming, bicycle riding, and playing baseball long after we have learned them. We continue to listen to and remind ourselves of jingles such as "Twinkle, twinkle, little star" and childhood tales such as Cinderella and Goldilocks. We not only learn but overlearn.

20 Earlier in the chapter, it was mentioned that the multiplication tables are an exception to the general rule that we tend to forget rather quickly the things that we learn in school by rote. An explanation was promised later—and now, of course, you have it, for the multiplication tables are another of the things we overlearn in 25 childhood.

The law of overlearning explains why cramming for an examination, though it may result in a passing grade, is not a satisfactory way to learn a college course. By cramming, a student may learn the subject well enough to get by on the examination, but he is likely soon to
30 forget almost everything he learned. A little overlearning, on the other hand, is usually a good investment toward the future.

Distribution of Practice

Another argument against cramming is that it represents an attempt to learn through what is called *massed practice*—that is, a single long learning session. Studies of a wide range of situations involving both
35 human and animal learning have indicated that massed practice is generally less efficient than *distributed practice*—that is, a series of shorter learning periods. The same total amount of time spent in learning is often strikingly more efficient when invested in short, separated periods than all at once.
40 Three possible explanations have been suggested for the superiority of distributed practice:

1. Distributed practice reduces the fatigue that often accompanies massed practice in motor learning and the boredom that often occurs in massed practice in verbal learning.
45 **2.** In the intervals between distributed practice sessions the learner may continue to mull over the material he has learned, even without knowing that he is doing so. This process is called *covert rehearsal* and results in what is called *consolidation* of what has been learned.
50 **3.** In many kinds of learning it seems likely that we learn not only what we want to learn but a number of useless and irrelevant habits that may actually interfere. A student learning to type, for example, might at the same time learn to grit his teeth, squint, and blink his eyes—habits that do not help his skill but hurt it. During the
55 intervals between distributed practice sessions these extraneous habits may be forgotten more quickly than the basic subject matter of the learning. The process is called *differential forgetting*.

(Have you improved a skill by forgetting a bad habit?)

It must be added, however, that distributed practice does not always
60 give such spectacular results. It seems less helpful in learning by logical rule than in learning by rote, possibly because rule learning involves less boredom. In learning situations that require a lot of "cranking up" time—getting out several books and notebooks, finding some reference works on the library shelves, and finding a
65 comfortable and well-lighted place to work—short practice periods may be less efficient than long ones. Moreover, distributed practice

does not appear to have much effect if any on how well the learning
is remembered; even when it results in substantial savings of the time
required for learning, it does not seem to improve retention. But
70 the general idea of distributed practice is a useful tool in the

(How does this make sense?)

management of learning. Probably all learning tasks can be best
accomplished through some pattern of distributed practice—in some
cases many short periods separated by long intervals, in some cases
75 fewer and longer periods separated by shorter intervals, and in some
cases perhaps a combination. The trick is to find the pattern that best
suits the particular situation.

Recitation

We come now to the last of the questions posed at the beginning of
the chapter: Is it better just to keep reading when you study or to
80 read a while and then attempt to recite? . . .

(What is the answer?)

Experimenters have found that it makes no difference whether the
subjects are children or adults or whether the material being learned
is nonsense syllables, spelling, mathematics, or a foreign vocabulary.
85 In every case it is more efficient to read and recite than to read alone.
Let us say that you have eight hours to devote to learning this
chapter and that reading through the chapter takes you two hours. The
least efficient way to spend your study time would be to read through
the chapter four times. You would do much better to spend more
90 time in trying to recite what you have learned than in reading—for . . .
devoting as much as 80 percent of study time to recitation may be
more efficient by far than mere reading.
Recitation seems to assist learning in a number of ways. It certainly
helps make the stimulus more distinctive; it casts a telling searchlight
95 on what you have grasped quickly and what you have not, on what
you understand and what you still find obscure. It provides a form of
feedback that sharpens your attention. It helps you find
meaningfulness and logical principles in the material. Of all study
techniques, recitation is the one of most clearly proved value.
100 Recitation is the heart of a widely recommended study method
called the SQ3R system,* which holds that the most efficient way to
study a chapter is to approach it through five steps:

  1. *Survey.* That is, study the outline at the beginning of the
chapter (if there is one) and then glance through the chapter to get a

*SQ3R system from F. P. Robinson, *Effective Study* (New York: Harper, 1961).

105 general idea of how much attention is devoted to each point in the outline and to the subheadings.

2. *Question.* Look through the chapter again in a more inquisitive fashion, asking yourself questions that the headings and subheadings suggest; let the topics you find there whet your curiosity.

110 **3.** *Reading.* Now read the chapter straight through, without taking notes.

4. *Recitation.* You have made a survey of the chapter, asked some questions about it, and read it. Now see how much of the chapter you can recite, either silently to yourself or out loud to a cooperative friend.

115 **5.** *Reviewing.* Go through the chapter again, making another survey of its topics and noting how much of it you were able to recite and what points you left out. The reviewing process will show you where you must devote further study.

(How do these five steps relate to the three stages described in this 120 chapter?)

Skill Development: Study-Reading

Stage 2. Review your answers to the inserted questions and your marginal notes to see if you are using all five thinking strategies as you read. Which did you use the most?

_____

Stage 3. Stop to self-test and relate. Recall important points in the selection. Use the recall diagram to record what the passage seems to be mainly about, list significant supporting details, and identify a related idea, issue, or concern to which you feel the information is connected.

(topic) _____

(significant details)

(related ideas) _____

Comprehension Questions

After reading the selection, answer the following questions with *a, b, c,* or *d*.

_____   1. The best statement of the main idea of this selection is
   a. recitation explains why cramming for an exam is an ineffectual method of study.
   b. overlearning, distributed practice, and recitation improve the efficiency of the learning process.
   c. effective learning means remembering the material at least two weeks later.
   d. forgetting is caused by a failure to apply the principles of learning in an efficient manner.

_____   2. The author uses all of the following as examples of the success of overlearning except
   a. bicycling.
   b. nursery jingles.
   c. multiplication tables.
   d. examination cramming.

_____   3. The difference between distributed practice and mass practice is
   a. the number of hours spent studying.
   b. the complexity of the material studied.
   c. the time intervals between study periods.
   d. the recitation after study units.

_____   4. The process of covert rehearsal between distributed practice sessions is
   a. a conscious recitation.
   b. an unconscious review.
   c. an organized consolidation.
   d. a selective forgetting.

_____   5. The author implies that the differential forgetting process that occurs between distributed practice sessions would probably be the most important in
   a. learning to play tennis.
   b. memorizing a poem.
   c. studying for a history examination.
   d. learning multiplication tables.

_____   6. Distributed practice sessions have been shown to do all of the following except
   a. cut down on fatigue.
   b. improve retention.
   c. give an opportunity for covert rehearsal.
   d. relieve boredom.

_____ 7. The author suggests that the most effective method of spending four hours studying a chapter for an exam would be to
   a. read it once and then recite as many times as possible.
   b. read it once, recite, and then read it again.
   c. read it twice and then recite.
   d. read it three times.

_____ 8. The author suggests that the key success factor in the SQ3R study method is
   a. recitation.
   b. a combination of distributed practice and recitation.
   c. the final review that follows the recitation.
   d. looking over the material and asking questions before beginning the reading.

_____ 9. The author suggests that the most efficient study technique for a college student to use in remembering material is
   a. rereading.
   b. distribution of practice.
   c. covert rehearsal.
   d. recitation.

_____ 10. The author would consider an adult's forgetting how to tie a shoe an example of a failure in
   a. overlearning.
   b. distribution of practice.
   c. recitation.
   d. SQ3R.

Answer the following with _T_ (true) or _F_ (false).

_____ 11. The author implies that short distributed practice periods would be the most efficient method for writing a research paper.

_____ 12. The author suggests that recitation is similar to a self-imposed examination.

_____ 13. Remembering the words to a popular hit song usually would combine the laws of overlearning, distributed practice, and recitation.

_____ 14. Consolidation is the result of covert rehearsal.

_____ 15. The author considers the initial reading to be the most important key to remembering.

© 1993 HarperCollins College Publishers

Vocabulary

According to the way the italicized word was used in the selection, select _a,_ _b, c,_ or _d_ for the word or phrase that gives the best definition.

_____ 1. "learn in school by *rote*"
(22)
a. rules
b. short time sessions
c. logic
d. repetition without
meaning

_____ 2. "to *mull* over" (46)
a. ponder
b. work
c. progress
d. refine

_____ 3. "*covert* rehearsal" (47)
a. planned
b. hidden
c. required
d. repetitious

_____ 4. "*consolidation* of what has
been learned" (48)
a. strengthening
b. reorganization
c. magnification
d. repetition

_____ 5. "*Irrelevant* habits" (51)
a. annoying
b. conditioned
c. detrimental
d. unrelated

_____ 6. "these *extraneous* habits"
(55)
a. extraordinary
b. nonessential
c. dangerous
d. disliked

_____ 7. "still find *obscure*" (96)
a. unnecessary
b. ridiculous
c. vague
d. uninteresting

_____ 8. "a form of *feedback*" (96)
a. rekindling
b. internal review
c. instructions
d. demonstrating

_____ 9. "a more *inquisitive* fashion"
(107)
a. vindictive
b. intellectual
c. curious
d. studious

_____ 10. "*whet* your curiosity" (109)
a. kill
b. fancy
c. find
d. excite

Written Response

Use information from the text to answer the following question:

Why is a series of study periods better than one long cramming session when studying for an exam?

Response Strategy: Define both methods and point out the advantages of short, separated periods of study. (Use your own paper for this response.)

Connecting and Reflecting

In this chapter and throughout the text you will be reading about scientific experiments conducted by researchers. Many of the research studies involve learning, and the results of those studies affect the way in which students are taught. Much remains unknown about learning, and accepted ideas are often proven incorrect. Scientists, however, try to be accurate and to base their conclusions on ideas that are tested in an experimental manner.

What are some of your own ideas about learning, memory, and studying? How would you design an experimental study using your classmates as subjects to prove or disprove your hunches about improving learning? Join together in collaborative groups to design a research study. In order to conduct your experiment, first select a hypothesis or notion that the group would like to test. Use the following sentence stem to guide, but not to restrict, your selection:
Hypothesis: Student learning improves when . . .

In order to prove or disprove your hypothesis, design a treatment to evaluate whether the idea works. To test the treatment, use at least two groups of students. Your experimental subjects—the treatment group—will be those students with whom you do something special. This special treatment can be done once or many times over a period of several weeks. Your control subjects will be a similar group of students who do not receive any special treatment. You may want to use only your classmates or you might want to compare your classmates with other college students. After you have completed your treatment you will need to administer a test to verify your results and compare the performance of each group.

Think creatively and state a hypothesis, explain your treatment, describe your subjects, and discuss your testing, methods, and materials. Read the following passages to stimulate your thinking about the endless possibilities of research. (Please do not, however, attempt this kind of research with your classmates or professor!) Working together in a collaborative group, describe each of the following parts of your experiment.
Hypothesis:
Treatment:
Subjects (experimentals and controls):
Testing, methods, and materials:

Memory Transfer by Cannibalism and Injection
All of these experiments led me to believe that memory formation somehow involved the creation of new molecules, and that RNA played some part in the process. But how to prove it?

© 1993 HarperCollins College Publishers

About 1960, it occurred to me that if two worms learned the same task, the chemical changes that took place inside their bodies might also be identical. If this were so, it might not matter how the chemicals got inside the worms. Provided the right molecules were present, the worm should "remember" whatever its chemical engrams told it to remember. Our attempts to test this odd notion took us not to the heart of the matter, but to the worm's digestive system.

In 1960 Reeva Jacobson, Barbara Humphries, and I classically conditioned a bunch of "victim" planarians, then chopped them in bits and fed the "trained" pieces to untrained cannibalistic flatworms (our experimental group). We fed untrained victims to another group of cannibals (our control group). After we had given both groups of cannibals a couple of days to "consolidate" their meals, we trained both groups. To our delight, the planarians that had eaten educated victims learned much faster than did the worms that had consumed their untrained brethren. We seemed to have "transferred an engram" from one animal to another (McConnell, Jacobson, & Humphries 1961).

A year or so later, my colleagues and I extracted RNA from trained worms and injected it into untrained animals. These animals showed a "transfer effect," but worms injected with RNA from untrained planarians did not (Zelman et al. 1963).

In 1964 scientists working in the US, Denmark, and Czechoslovakia reported similar success using rats rather than worms. And by 1984 several hundred successful memory-transfer experiments had been reported in the scientific literature. However, we are still far from proving conclusively that memories are coded in RNA, or that engrams can be transferred from one animal to another.

James V. McConnell, *Understanding Human Behavior*

Selection **2**

HISTORY

Skill Development

Stage 1: Preview

Before reading the next selection, preview to (1) establish a purpose, (2) size up how the material is organized, and (3) plan an attack. Read any introductory material, the first paragraph, the subheadings, the boldface and italicized print, the first sentence of some paragraphs, and the last paragraph. Think about the selection as a whole and then complete the following sentences. Use the questions that are provided to activate your schema on the subject.

Preview
Was cowboy life glamourous?

_____

After reading this selection, I will need to know

_____

Activate Schema
> *Did Roy Rogers and Dale Evans ever get dirty?*
> *Did cowboys get drunk and shoot in saloons?*
> *How did cowboys avoid getting lost on the range?*

Learning Strategy
> *What economic and industrial factors caused first the demand for and then the demise of the cowboy?*

Word Knowledge
> *Review the ten vocabulary items that follow the selection. Seek an understanding of unfamiliar words.*

Stage 2: Integrate Knowledge While Reading

> *Since each reader interacts with material in a unique manner, it is artificial to require certain thinking strategies to be used in certain places. In order to heighten awareness, however, several questions have been inserted within this selection. Briefly respond in the margin to the inserted questions. In addition, make a note in the margin of at least one other instance when you used each of the following strategies:*

1. Predict 2. Picture 3. Relate 4. Monitor 5. Fix up

COWBOYS AND THE CATTLE INDUSTRY

From Joseph Conlin, *The American Past*

The First Buckaroos

Acre for acre, cattlemen won more of the West than any other group of pioneers. They were motivated to bring the vastness of the Great Plains into the American economy by the appetite of the burgeoning cities for cheap meat, and they were encouraged in their venture by
5 the disinterest in the rolling, arid grasslands of anyone save the Indians. Their story thrills Americans (and other peoples) to this day partly because it was romanticized, partly because the cattle kingdom was established so quickly and just as quickly destroyed.

   The cowboy first rode into American legend just before the Civil
10 War. In the late 1850s, enterprising Texans began to round up herds of the half-wild longhorns that ranged freely between the Nueces River and the Rio Grande. They drove them north over a trail that had been blazed by Shawnee Indians to Sedalia, Missouri, a railroad town with connections to Chicago. Although the bosses were English-
15 speaking, many of the actual workers were Mexican. They called themselves *vaqueros*.

Vaquero, "cowboy," entered the English language as buckaroo. Indeed, while Anglo-Americans soon comprised the majority of this mobile work force, and former black slaves were a substantial
20 minority of it, much of what became part of American folklore and parlance about the buckaroos was of Mexican derivation. The cowboy's colorful costume was an adaptation of functional Mexican work dress. The bandana was a washcloth that, when tied over the cowboy's mouth, served as a dust screen, no small matter when a
25 thousand cattle were kicking up alkali grit. The broad-brimmed hat was not selected for its picturesque qualities but because it was a shield against sun and rain. Manufactured from first-quality beaver felt, the *sombrero* also served as a drinking pot and washbasin.

The pointed, high-heeled boots, awkward and even painful when
30 walking, were designed for riding in the stirrups, where a *vaquero* spent his workday. The "western" saddle was of Spanish design, quite unlike the English tack that Americans in the East used. Chaps, leather leg coverings, got their name from chaparral, the ubiquitous woody brush against which they were designed to protect the cowboy.

35 (Describe your mental picture.)

Meat for Millions
The Civil War and Missouri laws against importing Texas cattle (because of hoof-and-mouth disease) stifled the cattle-driving business before it was fairly begun. However, in 1866, when the transcontinental railroad reached Abilene, Kansas, a wheeler-dealer
40 from Illinois, Joseph G. McCoy, saw the possibilities of underselling steers raised back East with Texas Longhorns. McCoy built a series of holding pens on the outskirts of the tiny Kansas town, arranged to ship cattle he did not then have with the Kansas Pacific Railroad, and dispatched agents to southern Texas to induce Texans to round up
45 and drive cattle north to Abilene on a trading route called the Chisholm Trail.

(How can this make sense?)

In 1867, McCoy shipped 35,000 "tall, bony, coarse-headed, flat-sided, thin-flanked" cattle to Chicago. In 1868, 75,000 of the beasts,
50 next to worthless in Texas, passed through Abilene with Chicago packers crying for more. In 1871, 600,000 "critters" left the pens of several Kansas railroad towns to end up on American dinner tables.

The profits were immense. A steer that cost about $5 to raise on public lands could be driven to Kansas at the cost of one cent a mile
55 ($5 to $8) and sold for $25 or, occasionally, as much as $50. Investors from as far as England went west to establish ranches that were as comfortable as big-city gentlemen's clubs. The typical cattleman at

the famous Cheyenne Club never touched a gun, and he sat on a
horse only for the photographer. Instead, he sank into plush easy
60 chairs, ignited a Havana cigar, and discussed account books, very
often in a proper English accent, with his fellow businessmen.

The railhead continued to move westward, and with it went the
destination of the cowboys, who were soon arriving from the North as
well as the South. The migration of the raihead was alright with most
65 of the citizens of towns like Abilene. They concluded after a few
seasons that the money to be made as a cattle trading center was not
worth the damage done to their own ranches and farms by hundreds
of thousands of cattle. The wild atmosphere given their towns by the
rambunctious cowboys, many of them bent on a blow-out after
70 months on the trail, was even less conducive to respectable civic life.
As a cow town grew, its "better element" demanded churches and
schools in place of saloons, casinos, and whorehouses. The stage was
set for the "taming" of a town, which is the theme of so many popular
legends.
75 Never, though, did the cowboys lack for someplace to take their
herds. There were always newer, smaller towns to the west to
welcome them. In Kansas alone, Ellsworth, Newton, Wichita, Dodge
City, and Hays had their "wide-open" period.

Disaster

The cattle kingdom lasted only a generation, ending suddenly as a
80 result of greed in collaboration with two natural disasters.

(What will be covered in this next part?)

The profits to be made in cattle were so great that exploiters
ignored the fact that grassland has its limits as the support of huge
herds. Vast as the plains were, they were overstocked by the mid-
85 1880s. Unlike the bison, which had migrated vast distances each
season, allowing the Plains to rest, the cattle stayed put. Clear-running
springs were trampled into unpotable mudholes. Weeds never before
noticed replaced the grasses that had invited overgrazing. Hills and
buttes were scarred by cattle trails. Some species of migratory birds
90 that once passed through twice a year simply disappeared; the
beefsteaks on hoof had beaten them to their food.

Then, on January 1, 1886, a great blizzard buried the eastern and
southern plains. Within three days, three feet of snow drifting into 20-
and 30-foot banks suffocated the range. Between 50 and 85 percent of
95 the livestock froze to death or died of hunger. About 300 cowboys
could not reach shelter and were killed; the casualties among the
Indians never were counted. When spring arrived, half the American
plains reeked of death.

The summer of 1886 brought ruin to many cattlemen who had
survived the snows. Grasses that had weathered summer droughts for
millennia were unable to do so in their overgrazed condition; they
withered and died, starving cattle already weakened by winter. Then,
the next winter, the states that had escaped the worst of the blizzard
of 1886 got 16 inches of snow in 16 hours and weeks more of
intermittent fall.

(Summarize the disasters.)

The End of a Brief Era
The cattle industry recovered, but only when more prudent and
methodical businessmen took over the holdings of the speculators of
the glory days. Cattle barons like Richard King of southern Texas
foreswore risking all on the open range. Through clever manipulation
of land laws, King built a ranch that was as large as the state of Rhode
Island. If not quite so grandiose in their success, others imitated
King's example in Texas, Wyoming, Montana, and eastern Colorado.
Even more important in ending the days of the long drive and the
cowboy as a romantic knight-errant was the expansion of the railroad
network. When new east-west lines snaked into Texas and the states
on the Canadian border, and the Union Pacific and Kansas Pacific sent
feeder lines north and south into cow country, the cowboy became a
ranch hand, a not-so-freewheeling employee of large commercial
operations.

The Cowboy's Life
Even in the days of the long drive, the world of the cowboy bore
scant resemblance to the legends that came to permeate American
popular culture. Despite the white complexion of the cowboys in
popular literature and in Western films of the twentieth century, a
large proportion of cowboys were Mexican or black. In some cases,
these workers and the whites acted and mixed as equals. Just as often,
however, they split along racial lines when they reached the end of
the trail, frequenting segregated restaurants, barber shops, hotels,
saloons, and brothels.
Black, white, or Hispanic, they were indeed little more than boys.
Photographs that the buckaroos had taken in cow towns like Abilene
and Dodge City (as well as arrest records, mostly for drunk and
disorderly conduct), show a group of very young men, few apparently
much older than 25. The life was too arduous for anyone but
youths—days in the saddle, nights sleeping on bare ground in all
weather. Moreover, the cowboy who married could not afford to be
absent from his own ranch or farm for as long as the cattle drives
required.

(Is this the way cowboys were depicted in the old movies?)

140   The real buckaroos were not constantly engaged in shooting scrapes such as made novels and movies so exciting. Their skills lay in horsemanship and with a rope, not with the Colt revolver that they carried to signal co-workers far away. Indeed, toting guns was forbidden in railhead towns. With a drunken binge on every cowboy's
145 itinerary, the sheriff or marshal in charge of keeping the peace did not tolerate shooting irons on every hip. Those who did not leave their revolvers in camp outside town checked them at the police station.

Skill Development: Study-Reading

Stage 2.   Review your answers to the inserted questions and your marginal notes to see if you are using all five thinking strategies as you read. Which did you use the most?

_____

Stage 3.   Stop to self-test and relate. Recall important points in the selection. Use the recall diagram to record what the passage seems to be mainly about, list significant supporting details, and identify a related idea, issue, or concern to which you feel the information is connected.

(topic) _____

(significant
details)

(related ideas) _____

Comprehension Questions

    After reading the selection, answer the following questions with *a, b, c,* or *d.*

_____ 1. The best statement of the main idea of this selection is
   a. the western cowboy traditions are derived from Mexican folklore.
   b. the brief era of the cattle drives brought high profits to owners and a romanticization of the western cowboy.
   c. natural disasters prevented the destruction of the West by greedy cattlemen.
   d. the cowboys of the western movies are more fiction than fact.

_____ 2. According to the author, the first cattle herded to a railhead were
   a. raised by rancher Joseph G. McCoy.
   b. owned by Mexican workers.
   c. shipped east from Abilene during the Civil War.
   d. taken from herds of free-ranging longhorns.

_____ 3. The majority of the western cowboys were
   a. Mexican.
   b. Indian.
   c. Black.
   d. Anglo-American.

_____ 4. The author uses the example of the bandana to show all of the following except
   a. the lack of protection offered by the cowboy outfit.
   b. the usefulness of the parts of the cowboy outfit.
   c. the Mexican derivation of the cowboy outfit.
   d. the blend of color and function in the cowboy outfit.

_____ 5. The major reasons that Kansas towns overtook those in Missouri as cattle trading centers are all of the following except
   a. the transcontinental railroad's extension to Kansas.
   b. the Cheyenne Club.
   c. the Civil War.
   d. laws regarding hoof-and-mouth disease.

_____ 6. The author mentions Joseph G. McCoy because
   a. he established the organization for shipping vast numbers of cattle east from Abilene.
   b. he bought ranches in Texas to supply the packers in Chicago.
   c. he owned the Kansas Pacific Railroad.
   d. he assembled the largest cattle-producing ranch in the West.

_____ 7. The author suggests that cowboys brought all of the following to a popular railhead town except
   a. money.
   b. damage to nearby farms.
   c. saloons and whorehouses.
   d. respectability.

_____ 8. All of the following contributed to the demise of the glory days of the cattle industry except
   a. overgrazed grasslands.
   b. a reduced demand for beef.

———— c. the blizzard of 1886.
　　　 d. the drought of 1886.

———— 9. According to the author, western cowboys were most likely to be
　　　 a. young.
　　　 b. bandits.
　　　 c. married.
　　　 d. trigger-happy gunslingers.

———— 10. The major reason long cattle drives eventually became unnecessary was
　　　 a. clever manipulation of land laws.
　　　 b. the expansion of the railroad network.
　　　 c. the consolidation of ranch holdings.
　　　 d. the trend toward large-scale ranches in many western states.

Answer the following with *T* (true) or *F* (false).

———— 11. The Shawnee Indians were the first cowboys to drive herds to Missouri.
———— 12. The chaparral is a thicket that cowboys wished to avoid.
———— 13. The author suggests that Joseph McCoy built holding pens for cows that he did not yet have.
———— 14. Cattlemen made profits on cattle that was raised on public lands.
———— 15. The author suggests that the buffalo overgrazed the plains in previous years.

Vocabulary

—— 1. "appetite of the *burgeoning* cities" (3)
　　 a. newborn
　　 b. fast-growing
　　 c. hungry
　　 d. highly productive

—— 2. "encouraged in their *venture*" (4)
　　 a. greed
　　 b. motivation
　　 c. soul
　　 d. risky undertaking

—— 3. "*ubiquitous* woody brush" (33)
　　 a. present everywhere
　　 b. dangerous
　　 c. thorn bearing
　　 d. poisonous

—— 4. "*rambunctious* cowboys" (69)
　　 a. tired
　　 b. friendly
　　 c. unruly
　　 d. drunken

—— 5. "less *conducive* to respectable civic life" (70)
　　 a. appealing
　　 b. contributing
　　 c. limiting
　　 d. meaningful

—— 6. "not quite so *grandiose*" (112)
　　 a. impressive
　　 b. reckless
　　 c. clever
　　 d. timid

____ 7. "bore *scant* resemblance" (121)
 a. absolutely no
 b. little
 c. immediate
 d. historical

____ 8. "to *permeate* American popular culture" (122)
 a. enliven
 b. refresh
 c. convert
 d. penetrate

____ 9. "life was too *arduous*" (134)
 a. difficult
 b. boring
 c. threatened
 d. unhealthy

____ 10. "on every cowboy's *itinerary* (144)
 a. tombstone
 b. conscience
 c. route of a journey
 d. criminal record

Written Response

Use information from the text to answer the following question:
What conditions contributed to the sudden rise and fall of the western cowboy?
Response Strategy: Divide the question into parts. First explain reasons for the rise of the cattle industry, and then describe factors contributing to its fall.

Connecting and Reflecting

Many movies of the past have presented a blend of fact with a heavy dose of fiction in a romantization of the Old West. Pretend that you have been hired to direct a multimillion dollar western film project. The script involves the men and women of a small western town and the adventure of a cattle drive. As the director, you are given great freedom of interpretation. Knowing the truth about the many myths of the West, how would you portray the people, the life, and the conditions of the Old West? What myths would you keep, and which ones would you reject? In a meeting with the crew which is scheduled for tomorrow, you will announce your interpretive guidelines. After explaining to them that you understand the myths of the West, you plan to list four myths or fictions that you will retain in the film and four that you will reject. In anticipation of their questions, you will have notes to explain your reasons for each choice. Read the following passage for more information about the West, and then **prepare your list and notes on the four myths you will retain and the four you will reject.**

The Wild West in American Culture

The legend of the cowboy as a romantic, dashing, and quick-drawing knight of the wide-open spaces was not a creation of a later era. On the contrary, all the familiar themes of the Wild West were well formed when the cold, hard reality was still alive on the plains. Rather more oddly, the myths of the Wild West were embraced not only by easterners in their idle reveries, but by the cowboys themselves.

Play-Acting. The most important creator of the legendary Wild West was a none-too-savory character named E. Z. C. Judson. A former Know-Nothing who was dishonorably discharged from the Union Army, Judson took the pen name Ned Buntline, and between 1865 and 1886, churned out more than 400 romantic, blood, guts, and chivalric novels about western heroes. Some of his characters he invented; others were highly fictionalized real people.

American Heroes. In the pulps and later in films, Americans discovered that the bank and train robbers Jesse and Frank James, and several cohorts from the Clanton family, were really modern-day Robin Hoods who gave the money they took to the poor. When Jesse was murdered, his mother made a tourist attraction of his grave, charging admission and explaining that her son had been a Christian with an inclination to read the Bible in his spare time.

Belle Starr, the moniker of one Myra Belle Shirley, was immortalized as "the bandit queen," as pure in heart as Jesse James was socially conscious. Billy the Kid (William Bonney), a Brooklyn-born homicidal maniac, was romanticized as a tragic hero who had been forced into a life of crime by a callous society. James Butler "Wild Bill" Hickok, a gambler and clothes-horse who killed perhaps six people before he was shot down in Deadwood Gulch, South Dakota, in 1876, was attributed with dozens of killings, all in the cause of making the West safe for women, children, and psalmbooks. Calamity Jane (Martha Cannary), later said to have been Wild Bill's paramour, wrote her own romantic autobiography in order to support a drinking problem.

Joseph Conlin, *The American Past*

Selection

3

SOCIOLOGY

© 1993 HarperCollins College Publishers

Skill Development

Stage 1: Preview

> Preview the next selection to predict purpose, organization, and a learning plan.

Preview

> Unity in diversity is a paradox. What does it seem to mean?

_____

> After reading this selection, I will need to know

_____

Activate Schema

> Is it wrong for primitive tribal people to wear no clothes?
> Does social status exist in primitive cultures?
> Could you eat insects if doing so meant survival?

Learning Strategy

How do the examples explain the different principles and the overall idea of cultural unity?

Word Knowledge

Review the ten vocabulary items that follow the selection. Seek an understanding of unfamiliar words.

Stage 2: Integrate Knowledge While Reading

Since each reader interacts with material in a unique manner, it is artificial to require certain thinking strategies to be used in certain places. In order to heighten awareness, however, several questions have been inserted within this selection. Briefly respond in the margin to the inserted questions. In addition, make a note in the margin of at least one other instance when you used each of the following strategies:

1. Predict 2. Picture 3. Relate 4. Monitor 5. Fix up

UNITY IN DIVERSITY

From Donald Light, Jr., and Suzanne Keller, *Sociology**

(Does this title make sense or are these words opposites?)

What is more basic, more "natural" than love between a man and woman? Eskimo men offer their wives to guests and friends as a gesture of hospitality; both husband and wife feel extremely offended if the guest declines (Ruesch 1951, pp. 87–88). The Banaro of New
5   Guinea believe it would be disastrous for a woman to conceive her first child by her husband and not by one of her father's close friends, as is their custom.

> The real father is a close friend of the bride's father. . . . Nevertheless the first born child inherits the name and possessions of the husband. An American
> 10   would deem such a custom immoral, but the Banaro tribesmen would be equally shocked to discover that the first born child of an American couple is the offspring of the husband. (Haring 1949, p. 33)

The Yanomamö of Northern Brazil, whom anthropologist Napoleon A. Chagnon (1968) named "the fierce people," encourage what we
15   would consider extreme disrespect. Small boys are applauded for striking their mothers and fathers in the face. Yanomamö parents would laugh at our efforts to curb aggression in children, much as they laughed at Chagnon's naïveté when he first came to live with them.

(What would your parents do if you slapped either of them in the face?)

*From *Sociology,* 4th Edition by Donald Light and Suzanne Keller, pages 74-77.
Copyright © 1986 by McGraw-Hill, Inc. Reproduced by permission of McGraw-Hill, Inc.

20 The variations among cultures are startling, yet all peoples have customs and beliefs about marriage, the bearing and raising of children, sex, and hospitality—to name just a few of the universals anthropologists have discovered in their cross-cultural explorations. But the *details* of cultures do indeed vary: in this country, not so many years ago, when a girl was serious about a boy and he about 25 her, she wore his fraternity pin over her heart; in the Fiji Islands, girls put hibiscus flowers behind their ears when they are in love. The specific gestures are different but the impulse to symbolize feelings, to dress courtship in ceremonies, is the same. How do we explain this unity in diversity?

Cultural Universals

30 *Cultural universals* are all of the behavior patterns and institutions that have been found in all known cultures. Anthropologist George Peter Murdock identified over sixty cultural universals, including a system of social status, marriage, body adornments, dancing, myths and legends, cooking, incest taboos, inheritance rules, puberty 35 customs, and religious rituals (Murdock 1945, p. 124).

The universals of culture may derive from the fact that all societies must perform the same essential functions if they are to survive—including organization, motivation, communication, protection, the socialization of new members, and the replacement of those who die. 40 In meeting these prerequisites for group life, people inevitably design similar—though not identical—patterns for living. As Clyde Kluckhohn wrote, "All cultures constitute somewhat distinct answers to essentially the same questions posed by human biology and by the generalities of the human situation" (1962, p. 317).

45 The way in which a people articulate cultural universals depends in large part on their physical and social environment—that is, on the climate in which they live, the materials they have at hand, and the peoples with whom they establish contact. For example, the wheel has long been considered one of the humankind's greatest inventions, 50 and anthropologists were baffled for a long time by the fact that the great civilizations of South America never discovered it. Then researchers uncovered a number of toys with wheels. Apparently the Aztecs and their neighbors did know about wheels; they simply didn't find them useful in their mountainous environment.

(Describe your mental picture.)

55 **Adaptation, Relativity, and Ethnocentrism**
Taken out of context, almost any custom will seem bizarre, perhaps cruel, or just plain ridiculous. To understand why the Yanomamö encourage aggressive behavior in their sons, for example, you have to

try to see things through their eyes. The Yanomamö live in a state of
chronic warfare; they spend much of their time planning for and
defending against raids with neighboring tribes. If Yanomamö parents
did *not* encourage aggression in a boy, he would be ill equipped for
life in their society. Socializing boys to be aggressive is *adaptive* for
the Yanomamö because it enhances their capacity for survival. "In
general, culture is . . . adaptive because it often provides people with
a means of adjusting to the physiological needs of their own bodies,
to their physical-geographical environment and to their social
environments as well" (Ember and Ember 1973, p. 30).

In many tropical societies, there are strong taboos against a mother
having sexual intercourse with a man until her child is at least two
years old. As a Hausa woman explains,

> A mother should not go to her husband while she has a child such is sucking
> . . . if she only sleeps with her husband and does not become pregnant, it will
> not hurt her child, it will not spoil her milk. But if another child enters in, her
> milk will make the first one ill. (Smith, in Whiting 1969, p. 518)

Undoubtedly, people would smirk at a woman who nursed a
two-year-old child in our society and abstained from having sex with
her husband. Why do Hausa women behave in a way that seems so
overprotective and overindulgent to us? In tropical climates protein is
scarce. If a mother were to nurse more than one child at a time, or if
she were to wean a child before it reached the age of two, the
youngster would be prone to *kwashiorkor,* an often fatal disease
resulting from protein deficiency. Thus, long postpartum sex taboos
are adaptive. In a tropical environment a postpartum sex taboo and a
long period of breast-feeding solve a serious problem (Whiting, in
Goodenough 1969, pp. 511–24).

No custom is good or bad, right or wrong in itself; each one must
be examined in light of the culture as a whole and evaluated in terms
of how it works in the context of the entire culture. Anthropologists
and sociologists call this *cultural relativity.* Although this way of
thinking about culture may seem self-evident today, it is a lesson that
anthropologists and the missionaries who often preceded them to
remote areas learned the hard way, by observing the effects their best
intentions had on peoples whose way of life was quite different from
their own. In an article on the pitfalls of trying to "uplift" peoples
whose ways seem backward and inefficient, Don Adams quotes an old
Oriental story:

> Once upon a time there was a great flood, and involved in this flood were two
> creatures, a monkey and a fish. The monkey, being agile and experienced, was
> lucky enough to scramble up a tree and escape the raging waters. As he
> looked down from his safe perch, he saw the poor fish struggling against the
> swift current. With the very best intentions, he reached down and lifted the
> fish from the water. The result was inevitable. (1960, p. 22)

(What is the difference between adaptation and relativity?)

Ethnocentrism is the tendency to see one's own way of life,
105 including behaviors, beliefs, values, and norms as the only right way
of living. Robin Fox points out that "any human group is ever ready to
consign another recognizably different human group to the other side
of the boundary. It is not enough to possess culture to be fully
human, you have to possess *our* culture" (1970, p. 31).

110 **Values and Norms**
The Tangu, who live in a remote part of New Guinea, play a game
called *taketak,* which in many ways resembles bowling. The game is
played with a top that has been fashioned from a dried fruit and with
two groups of coconut stakes that are driven into the ground (more or
115 less like bowling pins). The players divide into two teams. Members
of the first team take turns throwing the top into the batch of stakes;
every stake the top hits is removed. Then the second team steps to
the line and tosses the top into their batch of stakes. The object of the
game, surprisingly, is not to knock over as many stakes as possible.
120 Rather, the game continues until both teams have removed the *same*
number of stakes. Winning is completely irrelevant (Burridge 1957,
pp. 88–89).

(What will be covered in this next part?)

In a sense games are practice for "real life"; they reflect the values
of the culture in which they are played. *Values* are the criteria people
125 use in assessing their daily lives, arranging their priorities, measuring
their pleasures and pains, choosing between alternative courses of
action. The Tangu value equivalence: the idea of one individual or
group winning and another losing bothers them, for they believe
winning generates ill-will. In fact, when Europeans brought soccer to
130 the Tangu, they altered the rules so that the object of the game was
for two teams to score the same number of goals. Sometimes their
soccer games went on for days! American games, in contrast, are
highly competitive; there are *always* winners and losers. Many rule
books include provisions for overtime and "sudden death" to prevent
135 ties, which leave Americans dissatisfied. World Series, Superbowls,
championships in basketball and hockey, Olympic Gold Medals are
front page news in this country. In the words of the late football
coach Vince Lombardi, "Winning isn't everything, it's the only thing."
Norms, the rules that guide behavior in everyday situations, are
140 derived from values, but norms and values can conflict, as we
indicated in Chapter 3. You may recall a news item that appeared in
American newspapers in December 1972, describing the discovery of

survivors of a plane crash 12,000 feet in the Andes. The crash had
occurred on October 13; sixteen of the passengers (a rugby team and
their supporters) managed to survive for sixty-nine days in near-zero
temperatures. The story made headlines because, to stay alive, the
survivors had eaten parts of their dead companions. Officials,
speaking for the group, stressed how valiantly the survivors had tried
to save the lives of the injured people and how they had held
religious services regularly. The survivors' explanations are quite
interesting, for they reveal how important it is to people to justify
their actions, to resolve conflicts in norms and values (here, the
positive value of survival vs. the taboo against cannibalism). Some of
the survivors compared their action to a heart transplant, using parts
of a dead person's body to save another person's life. Others equated
their act with the sacrament of communion. In the words of one
religious survivor, "If we would have died, it would have been suicide,
which is condemned by the Roman Catholic faith" (Read 1974).

Skill Development: Study-Reading

Stage 2.   Review your answers to the inserted questions and marginal notes
to see if you are using all five thinking strategies as you read. Which did you use
the most?

_____

(topic) _____

(significant _____
details)

_____

_____

_____

_____

(related idea) _____

Stage 3. Stop to self-test and relate. Recall important points in the selection. Use the recall diagram to record what the passage seems to be mainly about, list significant supporting details, and name a related idea, issue, or concern to which you feel the information is connected.

Comprehension Questions

After reading the selection, answer the following questions with *a, b, c,* or *d.*

_____ 1. The best statement of the main idea of this selection is
   a. the variety of practices and customs in society show few threads of cultural unity.
   b. the unusual variations in societies gain acceptability because of the cultural universals in all known societies.
   c. a variety of cultural universals provides adaptive choices for specific societies.
   d. cultural universals are found in all known societies even though the details of the cultures may vary widely.

_____ 2. The author believes that the primary cultural universal addressed in the Eskimo custom of offering wives to guests is
   a. bearing and raising of children.
   b. social status.
   c. hospitality.
   d. incest taboos.

_____ 3. The custom of striking practiced by the Yanomamö serves the adaptive function of
   a. developing fierce warriors.
   b. binding parent and child closer together.
   c. developing physical respect for parents.
   d. encouraging early independence from parental care.

_____ 4. *Cultural universals* might be defined as
   a. each culture in the universe.
   b. similar basic living patterns.
   c. the ability for cultures to live together in harmony.
   d. the differences among cultures.

_____ 5. The author implies that universals of culture exist because of
   a. a social desire to be more alike.
   b. the differences in cultural behavior patterns.
   c. the competition among societies.
   d. the needs of survival in group life.

_____ 6. The author suggests that the wheel was not a part of the ancient Aztec civilization because the Aztecs

a. did not need wheels.

b. were not intelligent enough to invent wheels.

c. were baffled by inventions.

d. did not have the materials for development.

_____ 7. The underlying reason for the postpartum sexual taboo of the Hausa is

a. sexual.

b. nutritional.

c. moral.

d. religious.

_____ 8. The term *cultural relativity* explains why a custom can be considered

a. right or wrong regardless of culture.

b. right or wrong according to the number of people practicing it.

c. right in one culture and wrong in another.

d. wrong if in conflict with cultural universals.

_____ 9. The author relates Don Adams' oriental story to show that missionaries working in other cultures

a. should be sent back home.

b. can do more harm than good.

c. purposefully harm the culture to seek selfish ends.

d. usually do not have a genuine concern for the people.

_____ 10. The tendency of ethnocentrism would lead an American to view the Eskimo practice of wife sharing as

a. right.

b. wrong.

c. right for Eskimos but wrong for Americans.

d. a custom about which an outsider should have no opinion.

Answer the following questions with *T* (true) or *F* (false).

_____ 11. An American's acceptance of the Banaro tribal custom of fathering the firstborn is an example of an understanding by cultural relativity.

_____ 12. The author feels that the need to symbolize feelings in courtship is a cultural universal.

_____ 13. The author feels that culture is not affected by climate.

_____ 14. The author states that all societies must have a form of organization if they are to survive.

_____ 15. The author implies that the rugby team which crashed in the Andes could have survived without eating human flesh.

Vocabulary

According to the way the italicized word was used in the selection, select *a*, *b*, *c*, or *d* for the word or phrase that gives the best definition.

_____ 1. "efforts to *curb* aggression"
(17)
    a. stabilize
    b. release
    c. promote
    d. restrain

_____ 2. "at Chagnon's *naïveté*" (18)
    a. lack of knowledge
    b. gentle manner
    c. jolly nature
    d. clumsiness

_____ 3. "body *adornments*" (33)
    a. ailments
    b. treatments
    c. scars
    d. decorations

_____ 4. "*articulate* cultural
universals" (45)
    a. remember
    b. design
    c. express clearly
    d. substitute

_____ 5. "will seem *bizarre*" (55)
    a. phony
    b. unjust
    c. grotesque
    d. unnecessary

_____ 6. "*smirk* at a woman" (76)
    a. refuse to tolerate
    b. smile conceitedly
    c. lash out
    d. acknowledge approvingly

_____ 7. "*abstained* from having sex"
(77)
    a. matured
    b. regained
    c. refrained
    d. reluctantly returned

_____ 8. "long *postpartum* sex
taboos" (83)
    a. after childbirth
    b. awaited
    c. subcultural
    d. complicated

_____ 9. "being *agile* and
experienced" (99)
    a. eager
    b. nimble
    c. young
    d. knowledgeable

_____ 10. "ready to *consign*" (106)
    a. assign
    b. remove
    c. reorganize
    d. overlook

Written Response

Use the information in this selection to answer the following question.

What issues should an American health worker consider while planning a hygiene program for a village in a remote mountain region of northern Afghanistan?

Response Strategy: Define the cultural concepts listed in the text and relate them to the plans, methods, and possibilities for improving hygiene. (Use your own paper for this response.)

Connecting and Reflecting

As a student and an employee, you may have seen or experienced the pain of ethnocentric attitudes. Next year your favorite first cousin will be entering college, as well as starting a new part-time job. You would like to **sensitize your cousin to some of the ethnocentrism that exists in college and on the job.** You feel that you could do this best by giving examples. Prepare your notes for a talk with your cousin, including three examples of situations in which you or someone else was hurt by the ethnocentrism of others. What would be your advice to your cousin in coping with and ultimately preventing similar occurrences? Read the following passage to get an idea of what someone else has written on this topic and then **describe the three examples and the advice you will relate to your cousin.**

Ethnocentrism in the Classroom

In New Mexico, students also complain about ethnocentrism in the classroom.

"There are certain pieces of literature that are very offensive," says Madrid. "You study long enough and all of a sudden you say, 'Hey, maybe that's not right,' even the way the Pulitzer Prize-winning authors depict things in Southwest Studies. You're from the area and you're proud of your people and you're sitting here reading something by Willa Cather about fat, greasy Mexicans who, all they want to do is have kids. And you know, it may be written so it sounds kind of nice, but you're sitting there saying, 'God, this is offensive.' That's what your professors want you to read. They don't want you to read something by Raulfo Acuna, talking about occupied America. And you don't study people like Rejes Tijerina, or the disputes over the treaty of Guadalupe Hidalgo land grants. You've got to teach yourself that stuff."

Ruth Conniff, *The Progressive,* December 1988

WORD BRIDGE

Context Clues

Context clues are the most common method of unlocking the meaning of unknown words. The context of a word refers to the sentence or paragraph in which it appears. Readers use several types of context clues. In some cases, words are defined directly in the sentences in which they appear; in other instances, the sentence offers clues or hints that enable the reader to arrive indirectly at the meaning of the word. The following are examples of how each type of clue can be used to figure out word meaning in textbooks.

1. Definition

Complex scientific material has a heavy load of specialized vocabulary. Fortunately, new words are often directly defined as they are introduced in the text. Do you know the meaning of *erythrocytes* and *oxyhemoglobin*? Read the following textbook sentence in which these two words appear, and then select the correct definition for each word.

When oxygen diffuses into the blood in external respiration, most of it enters the red blood cells, or erythrocytes, and unites with the hemoglobin in these cells, forming a compound called oxyhemoglobin.

Willis H. Johnson et al., *Essentials of Biology*

_____ *Erythrocytes* means
a. diffused oxygen.
b. red blood cells.
c. respiration process.

_____ *Oxyhemoglobin* means
a. hemoglobin without oxygen.
b. dominant oxygen cells.
c. combination of oxygen and hemoglobin.

The answers are *b* and *c*. Notice that the first word is defined as a synonym in an appositive phrase, and the second is defined in the sentence.

2. Elaborating Details

In political science you will come across the term *gerrymander*. Keep reading and see if you can figure out the meaning from the hints in the following sentence.

Since Governor Elbridge Gerry's newly engineered electoral district "had the shape of the salamander," it quickly came to be labeled a "gerrymander," and since its widely convoluted shape seemed to typify the widespread practice of forming districts with distorted boundaries, the usage of the term spread.

Theodore J. Lowi, *American Government: Incomplete Conquest*

_____ ***Gerrymander* means**
a. dividing voting districts unevenly to give unfair advantage.
b. member of the salamander family.
c. voting in a new electoral district.

_____ ***Convoluted* means**
a. twisted.
b. inflated.
c. reduced.

The answers are *a.* Both of these words can be figured out from details within the sentence.

3. Examples

In psychology you will frequently encounter a complicated word describing something you have often thought about but not named. Read the following sentence to find out what *psychokinesis* means.

Another psychic phenomenon is *psychokinesis,* the ability to affect physical events without physical intervention. You can test your powers of psychokinesis by trying to influence the fall of dice from a mechanical shaker. Are you able to have the dice come up a certain number with a greater frequency than would occur by chance?

Douglas W. Matheson, *Introductory Psychology: The Modern View*

_____ ***Psychokinesis* means**
a. extrasensory perception.
b. an influence on happenings without physical tampering.
c. physical intervention affecting physical change.

The answer is *b.* Here the word is first directly defined in a complicated manner and then the definition is clarified by a simple example.

4. Comparison

Economics uses many complex concepts that are difficult to understand. The use of a familiar term in a comparison can help the reader relate to the new idea. Can you explain *monopolistic competition*? The following comparison will help.

Monopolistic competition is similar to monopoly because each individual firm claims to produce a distinctly unique product: the *only* socially accepted toothpaste or haircream, the *only* truly tasteful soft drink, the *only* fully nutritious breakfast cereal. Monopolistic competition is similar to competition because there are many firms in the industry.

Marilu McCarty, Dollars and Sense[*]

_____ **_Monopolistic competition_ means that industries are competing to sell**
a. vastly different products.
b. only slightly differentiated products.
c. overpriced products.

The answer is *b*. In this case, both the comparison and the example aid the reader in understanding the concept.

5. Contrast

Can you explain what transsexuals are and how they differ from homosexuals? The following sentences will give you some clues.

Transsexuals are people (usually males) who feel that they were born into the wrong body. They are not homosexuals in the usual sense. Most homosexuals are satisfied with their anatomy and think of themselves as appropriately male or female; they simply prefer members of their own sex. Transsexuals, in contrast, think of themselves as members of the opposite sex (often from early childhood) and may be so desperately unhappy with their physical appearance that they request hormonal and surgical treatment to change their genitals and secondary sex characteristics.

Rita Atkinson et al., Introduction to Psychology

_____ **_A transsexual_ is a person who thinks of himself as**
a. a homosexual.
b. a heterosexual.
c. a member of the opposite sex.
d. a person without sex drive.

The answer is *c*. By comparing *homosexual* and *transsexual,* the reader is better able to understand the latter and distinguish between the two.

Limitations of Context Clues

While the clues in the sentence in which an unknown word appears are certainly helpful in deriving the meaning of a word, these clues will not always give a complete and accurate definition. To understand totally the meaning of a word, it is frequently necessary to take some time after your reading is completed to look the word up in a glossary or a dictionary. Context clues operate just as the name suggests; they are hints and not necessarily complete definitions.

*From *Dollars and Sense.* Third Edition, by Marilu Hurt McCarty, pp 67-68. Copyright © 1982 by Scott, Foresman and Company, HarperCollinsCollege Publishers.

Part B:

Instructions. The purpose of Part B is to demonstrate how context clues assist the reader in clarifying or unlocking the meaning of unknown words. Each of the italicized words on the preceding list appears in a sentence from a college textbook. Using the context clues in the sentences, again place *a, b, c,* or *d* in the numbered space for the definition that you feel best fits each italicized word. Check your answers, record your total number correct, and compare your scores on Part A and Part B. Did reading the word in context help? Were you uncertain of any word as it appeared on the list, but then were able to figure out the meaning after reading it in a sentence?

1. _____   6. _____   11. _____   16. _____

2. _____   7. _____   12. _____   17. _____

3. _____   8. _____   13. _____   18. _____

4. _____   9. _____   14. _____   19. _____

5. _____   10. _____   15. _____   20. _____

Total number correct = _____

Words in Context

1. Henry, to the end of his life, thought of himself as a pious and orthodox Catholic who had restored the independent authority of the Church of England *usurped* centuries before by the Bishop of Rome.

   Shepard B. Clough et al., *A History of the Western World*

2, 3. But his own income was *derived* largely from other sources. He regained much of the royal domain and its revenues that had previously passed out of the crown's hand and added to it by confiscating the estates of his *adversaries*.

   ibid.

4. When members of a minority group wish to give up what is distinctive about them and become just like the majority, they take an *assimilationist* position. An example is the Urban League.

   Reece McGee et al., *Sociology: An Introduction*

5. George Simmel was one of the first sociologists to suggest that the number of members in a group radically transforms its properties. He began with an analysis of what happens when a *dyad,* a two member group, becomes a triad, a three member group.

   ibid.

6. Rogers believes that everyone has a tendency toward *self-actualization,* the realization of one's potentials, and stresses that the human need for acceptance and approval is essential if self-actualization is to occur.

ibid.

7, 8, 9. However, the United States has lived in rather close *proximity* to its own Constitution and can by virtue of that fact at least claim, with some *plausibility,* that as a country we have managed to maintain conquest over an immensely *heterogeneous* society without falling prey to tyranny.

Theodore J. Lowi, *American Government: Incomplete Conquest*

10. The gut is essentially an elaborate *gastrovascular* cavity.

Willis H. Johnson et al., *Essentials of Biology*

11. Locomotion ranges from the generally nonmotile tapeworms to freely moving flatworms such as *planarians,* that glide on a slime they secrete by ciliary action of their epidermal cells and generalized muscular contractions of the body.

ibid.

12. The body can produce some natural *anticoagulants* such as heparin or dicumarol, which are formed in the liver. Also, some animals that depend on blood for nutrition—such as fleas and leeches—secrete substances to inhibit clotting.

ibid.

13. If France's sharp regional differences in development and prosperity are to be *ameliorated,* the Southeast and the West must be encouraged to grow more rapidly.

Jesse H. Wheeler, Jr., et al., *Regional Geography of the World*

14. Under a decree of September 1952, the government *expropriated* several hundred thousand acres from large landholders and redistributed this land among the peasants.

ibid.

15. One of the fundamental features of Hinduism has been the division of its *adherents* into the most elaborate caste system ever known.

ibid.

16. While we are sleeping, for example, we are hardly aware of what is happening around us, but we are aware to some degree. Any loud noise or other abrupt *stimulus* will almost certainly awaken us.

Gardner Lindzey et al., *Psychology*

17. However, anyone who has passed through several time zones while flying east or west knows how difficult it can be to change from one sleep schedule to another. This "jet lag" can be so *debilitating* that many corporations will not allow their executives to enter negotiations for at least two days after such a trip.

ibid.

18. *Autocratic* leadership can be extremely effective if the people wielding it have enough power to enforce their decisions and if their followers know that they have it. It is especially useful in military situations where speed of decision is critical. Among its disadvantages are the lack of objectivity and the disregard for opinions of subordinates.

David J. Rachman and Michael Mescon, *Business Today*

19. Many social critics decry profits as an *incentive* but have proposed no practical alternative in a free society. The only other incentive that has worked is the one used most often in communist countries: severe punishment for nonproductive persons.

ibid.

20. Disseminated Magmatic Deposits are the simplest of the magmatic deposits. The valuable mineral is *disseminated* or scattered throughout the igneous body. In the diamond deposits of South Africa, for example, the diamonds are disseminated in unusual rock, somewhat similar to peridotite.

Robert J. Foster, *Physical Geology*

Exercise 6: Context Clues

The following sentences appeared in this chapter. Use your memory of the passage and the context of the sentence to determine the meaning, or an approximate guess at the meaning, of each of the following italicized words.

1. Then they *evert* their stomachs, squeezing them between the shells, and digest the flesh of the oyster on the spot.

Robert Wallace, *Biology: The World of Life*

Evert means _____

2. But they were unfamiliar with the *regenerative* powers of the starfish. The central disk merely grows new arms, and a single arm can form a new animal.

ibid.

Regenerative means _____

3. To our delight, the *planarians* that had eaten educated victims learned much faster than did the worms that had consumed their untrained brethren.

ibid.

Planarians are _____

4. In the *pulps* and later in films, Americans discovered that the bank and train robbers Jesse and Frank James, and several *cohorts* from the Clanton family, were really modern-day Robin Hoods who gave the money they took to the poor.

Joseph Conlin, *The American Past*

Pulps are _____

Cohorts are _____

5. Belle Starr, the *moniker* of one Myra Belle Shirley, was immortalized as "the bandit queen," as pure in heart as Jesse James was socially conscious.

ibid.

Moniker means _____

6. Calamity Jane (Martha Cannary), later said to have been Wild Bill's *paramour,* wrote her own romantic autobiography in order to support a drinking problem.

ibid.

A *paramour* is _____

CHAPTER · 3

MAIN IDEA

- What is a topic?
- What is a main idea?
- What are significant details?

WHAT IS THE POINT?

Many experts agree that the most important skill in reading is understanding the **main idea,** or the particular point the author is trying to convey about the subject in a passage. They say that comprehending the main idea is crucial to the comprehension of text. In fact, if all reading comprehension techniques were reduced to one basic question, that question might be, "What is the main idea the author is trying to get across?"

In order to answer the question, the reader must first determine the **topic** being discussed, that is the general subject under which the key ideas in a passage may be grouped. Then, after considering the contributing details, he or she must decide what point or statement the author is trying to make about the topic. For example, if a friend commented favorably on a recent article, your first question would be, "What was it about?" and then you would ask, "What was the point?" The first answer is the topic and the second is a statement of the main idea. *The point being made about the topic is the main idea.*

IMPORTANCE OF PRIOR KNOWLEDGE IN MAIN IDEA

Although identifying the main idea is proclaimed as the most important reading skill, until the last few years little research has been done on the processes readers use to construct main ideas. One researcher asked graduate students and university professors to "think aloud" as they read passages on both familiar and unfamiliar topics.[1] These expert readers spoke their thoughts to the researcher before, during, and after they had finished reading. From these investigations, Afflerbach concluded that expert readers use different strategies for familiar and unfamiliar materials.

This research showed that *already knowing something about the topic is the key to easy reading.* When the readers were already familiar with the material, constructing the main idea was effortless and, in many cases, automatic. These readers quickly assimilated the unfolding text into already well-developed knowledge networks. They seemed to organize text into chunks for comprehension and later retrieval. These "informed" readers did not have to struggle with an information overload.

By contrast, expert readers with little prior knowledge of the subject were absorbed in trying to make meaning out of unfamiliar words and confusing sentences. Because they were struggling to recognize ideas, few mental resources remained for constructing a main idea. These "uninformed" experts were reluctant to guess at a main idea and to predict a topic. Instead, they preferred to read

[1]P. Afflerbach, "How Are Main Idea Statements Constructed? Watch the Experts!," *Journal of Reading* 30 (1987): 512–518; and "The Influence of Prior Knowledge on Expert Readers' Main Idea Construction Strategies," *Reading Research Quarterly* 25 (1990): 31–46.

all of the information before trying to make sense out of it. Constructing the main idea was a difficult and deliberate task for these expert readers.

MAIN IDEA STRATEGIES

The following strategies for getting the main idea were reported by Afflerbach's expert readers. Can you see the differences in the thinking processes of the informed and uninformed experts?

Expert Readers Who Knew about the Subject

Strategy 1: The informed expert readers skimmed the passage before reading and took a guess at the main idea. Then they read for corroboration.

Strategy 2: The informed experts automatically paused while reading to summarize or reduce information. They frequently stopped at natural breaks in the material to let ideas fall into place.

Expert Readers with No Prior Knowledge of the Subject

Strategy 1: Expert readers who knew very little about the subject were unwilling to take a guess at the main idea. Instead, they read the material, decided on a topic, and then looked back to pull together a main idea statement.

Strategy 2: The uninformed experts read the material and then reviewed to find key terms and concepts. They tried to bring the key terms and concepts together into a main idea statement.

Strategy 3: The uninformed experts read the material and then proposed a main idea statement. They double-checked the passage to clarify or revise the main idea statement.

Since introductory college textbooks address many topics that are new and unfamiliar, freshmen readers will frequently need to use the last three strategies listed above to comprehend the main ideas of their college texts. Until prior knowledge is built for the different college courses, main idea construction for course textbooks is likely to be a conscious effort rather than an automatic phenomenon.

WHAT IS A TOPIC?

The topic of a passage is like a title. It is a word or phrase that labels the subject but does not reveal the specific contents of the passage. The topic is a general, rather than specific, term and forms an umbrella under which the specific ideas or details in the passage can be grouped. For example, what general term would pull together and unify the following items?

Items: carrots
lettuce
onions
potatoes

} Topic? _____

Exercise 1: Identifying Topics

Each of the following lists includes four specific ideas that could relate to a single topic. At the end of each list, write a general topic that could form an umbrella under which the specific ideas can be grouped.

1. shirt	2. psychology	3. democracy	4. Bermuda	5. coffee
pants	history	autocracy	Cuba	tea
jacket	sociology	oligarchy	Haiti	cola
sweater	political science	monarchy	Tahiti	chocolate
_____	_____	_____	_____	_____

How Do Topics and Main Ideas Differ?

Topics are general categories, like titles, but they are not main ideas. In the previous list, caffeine is a general term or topic that unifies the items, coffee, tea, cola, and chocolate. If those items were used as details in a paragraph, the main idea could not be expressed by simply saying "caffeine." The word *caffeine* would answer the question, "What was the passage about?" but not the second question, "What is the author's main idea?"

A writer could actually devise several very different paragraphs about caffeine using the same four details as support. If you were assigned to write a paragraph about caffeine, using the four items as details, what would be the main idea or thesis of your paragraph?

Topic: Caffeine

Main idea or thesis: _____

Read the following examples of different main ideas that could be developed in a paragraph about caffeine.

1. Consumption of caffeine is not good for your health. (Details would enumerate health hazards associated with each item.)
2. Americans annually consume astonishing amounts of caffeine. (Details would describe amounts of each consumed annually.)
3. Caffeine can wake up an otherwise sluggish mind. (Details would explain the popular use of each item as a stimulant.)

4. Reduce caffeine consumption with the decaffeinated version of popular caffeinated beverages. (Details would promote the decaffeinated version of each item.)

MAIN IDEA STATEMENTS

Remember: the main idea of a passage is a statement of what the author says about the topic. Similar to the topic, the main idea is general rather than specific and forms a summary statement for the specific ideas in the paragraph. Reading specialists use several different terms in referring to the author's main idea. In this book, all of the following terms are synonymous with *main idea*.

main point
central focus
gist
controlling idea
central thought
thesis

In all cases, the reader's statement of main idea of a passage must be in a complete sentence. Constructing anything less, such as expanding a phrase or narrowing a subject, remains only a designation of topic.

Exercise 2: Differentiating Topic, Main Idea, and Details

Below are examples of a topic, main idea, and supporting detail.

Topic   **Early Cognitive Development**

Main idea   Cognitive psychologists sometimes study young children to observe the
Detail   very beginnings of cognitive activity. For example, when children first begin to utter words and sentences, they overgeneralize what they know and make language more consistent than it actually is.

Christopher Peterson, *Introduction to Psychology*

The topic pulls our attention to a general area, and the main idea provides the focus. The detail offers elaboration and support.

The following exercise is designed to check your ability to differentiate statements of main idea from topics and specific supporting details. Compare the items within each group and indicate whether each one is a statement of main idea (*MI*), a topic (*T*), or a specific supporting detail (*D*).

Group 1

_____ a. In 1981 Henry Cisneros of San Antonio became the first Mexican-American mayor of a large city.
_____ b. Mexican-American political gains
_____ c. Since 1960 Mexican-Americans have made impressive political gains.

James Martin et al., *America and Its People*

Group 2

_____ a. For poor farm families, life on the plains meant a sod house or a dugout carved out of the hillside for protection from the winds.
_____ b. One door and usually no more than a single window provided light and air.
_____ c. Sod houses on the plains

James W. Davidson et al., *Nation of Nations*

Group 3

_____ a. As individuals, Americans tend to value the knowledge and skills transmitted by the schools, not for their own sake but because they hope to translate those skills into good jobs and money.
_____ b. Social mobility through education
_____ c. As one study indicates, many students are attracted to college because of job and career considerations.

Alex Thio, *Sociology*

Group 4

_____ a. For example, human babies require about twice as many calories per unit of body weight than adults.
_____ b. Although children need less total food than adults, their metabolic needs exceed those of adults in proportion to their body weight.
_____ c. Metabolic needs of children

John Cunningham, *Human Biology*

Group 5

_____ a. The question of a bill of rights
_____ b. First, Hamilton wrote in *Federalist* 84 that a Bill of Rights might be necessary to restrict a king, but not a government established by the people; such a government, he said, possesses only the powers given to it by the people.
_____ c. A serious objection raised against the Constitution by those who opposed its ratification was that it contained no Bill of Rights.

Fred Harris et al., *Understanding American Government*

Questioning for the Main Idea

To determine the main idea of a paragraph, an article, or a book, ask the three basic questions listed in the box below. The order of the questions may vary depending on your prior knowledge of the material. If the material is familiar, main idea construction may be automatic and thus a selection of significant details would follow. If the material is unfamiliar, as frequently occurs in textbook reading, identifying the details through key terms and concepts would come first and from them you would form a main idea statement.

Finding the Main Idea

1. Establish the topic. Ask, "Who or what is this about?" The response is a general word or phrase that names the subject. The topic should be broad enough to include all the material, yet restrictive enough to reflect the details. For example, identifying the topic of an article as "politics," "federal politics," or "corruption in federal politics" might all be correct, but the last may be the most descriptive of the actual contents.

2. Ask the question, "What are the major details?" The response should include key terms and concepts within the passage. List the details that seem to be significant to determine if they point in any one particular direction. If so, this direction could be the topic or focus that leads to the main idea. Details such as kickbacks to senators, overspending on congressional junkets, and lying to the voters could support the idea of "corruption in federal politics."

3. Sharpen the impact of the topic. Ask, "What is the main idea the author is trying to convey about the topic?" This statement of the main idea should be:

A. A complete sentence
B. Broad enough to include the significant details
C. Slanted enough to reflect the author's treatment of the topic

In the example about corruption in federal politics, the author's main idea might be that voters need to ask for an investigation of seemingly corrupt practices by federal politicians.

Read the following example, and answer the questions for determining the main idea.

New high-speed machines also brought danger to the workplace. If a worker succumbed to boredom, fatigue, or simple miscalculation, disaster could strike. Each year of the late nineteenth century some

35,000 wage earners were killed by industrial accidents. In Pittsburgh iron and steel mills alone, in one year 195 men died from hot metal explosions, asphyxiation, and falls, some into pits of molten metal. Men and women working in textile mills were poisoned by the thick dust and fibers in the air; similar toxic atmospheres injured those working in anything from twine-making plants to embroidery factories. Railways, with their heavy equipment and unaccustomed speed, were especially dangerous. In Philadelphia over half the railroad workers who died between 1886 and 1890 were killed by accidents. For injury or death, workers and their families could expect no payment from employers, since the idea of worker's compensation was unknown.

James W. Davidson et al., *Nation of Nations*

1. Who or what is this about? *Injuries from machines*

2. What are the major details? *35,000 killed, 195 died from explosions, etc., poisoned by dust. Half of rail workers killed.*

3. What is the main idea the author is trying to convey about the topic? *New high-speed machines brought danger to the workplace.*

STATED AND UNSTATED MAIN IDEAS

Like paragraphs, pictures also suggest main ideas. Artists compose and select to communicate a message. Look at the picture on the following page, and state the topic of the picture, the details that seem important, and the main idea that the artist is trying to convey.

What is the general topic of the picture? _____

_____

What details seem important? _____

_____

What is the main idea the artist is trying to convey about the topic? _____

_____

The topic is smoking or the pollution from smoking. The details compare the smoker's head to a cigarette and to a factory smokestack. The main idea is that smoking pollutes both you and the environment. In this case the main idea is stated directly in the slogan printed on the picture.

Now look at the picture on the following page, which does not include a slogan or directly stated appeal. Again, state the topic of the picture, the important details, and the main idea the artist is trying to get across.

What is the general topic of the picture? _____

_____

What details seem important? _____

_____

What is the main idea the artist is trying to convey about the topic? _____

_____

The topic is child labor. The details are the two young children, the huge machinery of a textile mill, and the small hands and bare feet that are doing the work. The main idea is that children were ill used as child laborers in textile mills. The main idea of the picture is strongly communicated in the frail body, torn clothes, and bare feet of the first child. Although the point is unstated, do you sense the injustice to the children and the despair and danger they most likely face?

As in the pictures, an author's main point can either be directly stated in the material or it can be unstated. When the main idea is stated in a sentence, the statement is called a **topic sentence or thesis statement.** Such a general statement is helpful to the reader because it provides an overview of the material. It does not, however, always express the author's opinion of the subject. For that reason, while helpful in overviewing, the topic sentence may not always form a complete statement of the author's main point.

Frequency of Stated Main Idea

Research shows that students find passages easier to comprehend when the main idea is directly stated within the passage. How often do stated main ideas appear in college textbooks? Should the reader expect to find that most paragraphs have stated main ideas?

For psychology texts, the answer seems to be about half and half. In a recent study,[2] stated main ideas appeared in *only 58 percent* of the sampled paragraphs in introductory psychology textbooks. In one of the books, the main idea was directly stated in 81 percent of the sampled paragraphs, and the researchers noted that the text was particularly easy to read.

Given these findings, we should recognize the importance of being skilled in locating and, especially in constructing, main ideas. In pulling ideas together to construct a main idea, you will be looking at the big picture and not be bound to the text in search of any single suggestive sentence.

Location of Stated Main Ideas

Should college readers wish for all passages in all textbooks to begin with stated main ideas? Indeed, research indicates that when the main idea is stated at the beginning of the passage, the text tends to be most easily comprehended. In their research, however, Smith and Chase found only 33 percent of the stated main ideas to be positioned as the first sentence of the paragraph.

Main idea statements can be positioned at the beginning, in the middle, or at the end of a paragraph. Both the beginning and concluding sentences of a passage can be combined for a main idea statement. The following examples and diagrams demonstrate the different possible positions for stated main ideas within paragraphs.

1. An introductory statement of the main idea at the beginning of the paragraph

main idea
1. detail
2. detail
3. detail
4. detail

Under hypnosis, people may recall things that they are unable to remember spontaneously. Some police departments employ hypnotists to probe for information that crime victims do not realize they have. In 1976, twenty-six young children were kidnaped from a school bus near Chowchilla, California. The driver of the bus caught a quick glimpse of the license plate of the van in which he and the children were driven away. However, he remembered only the first two digits. Under hypnosis, he recalled the other numbers and the van was traced to its owners.

David Dempsey and Philip Zimbardo, *Psychology and You*[*]

[2]B. Smith and N. Chase, "The Frequency and Placement of Main Idea Topic Sentences in College Psychology Textbooks," *Journal of College Reading and Learning* 24 (1991): 46–54.
[*]From *Psychology & You* by David Dempsey and Philip G. Zimbardo. Copyright © 1978 by Scott, Foresman and Company, HarperCollinsCollege Publishers.

2. A concluding statement of the main idea at the end of the paragraph

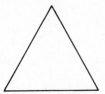

1. detail
2. detail
3. detail
4. detail
main idea

Research is not a once-and-for-all-times job. Even sophisticated companies often waste the value of their research. One of the most common errors is not providing a basis for comparisons. A company may research its market, find a need for a new advertising campaign, conduct the campaign, and then neglect to research the results. Another may simply feel the need for a new campaign, conduct it, and research the results. Neither is getting the full benefit of the research. When you fail to research either the results or your position *prior* to the campaign, you cannot know the effects of the campaign. *For good evaluation you must have both before and after data.*

Edward Fox and Edward Wheatley, *Modern Marketing**

3. Beginning with details to arouse interest and then a statement of main idea in the middle of the paragraph

1. detail
2. detail
main idea
3. detail
4. detail

What happens when foreign materials do enter the body by breaking through the skin or epithelial linings of the digestive, circulatory, or respiratory systems and after the clotting process is complete? The next line of defense comes into action. Phagocytic cells (wandering and stationary) may engulf the foreign material and destroy it. But there is another and very complicated aspect of the process. *This is the production of specific antibody molecules. Antibodies may circulate in the blood as mentioned or they may be bound to cells;* less is known about these cell-bound antibodies. Antibodies inactivate or destroy the activity of antigens by combining with them. The reaction is a manifestation of the immune response, and the discipline primarily devoted to its study is immunology. Generally immunity is considered to be peculiar to the vertebrates, but recent evidence suggests that a form of immunity occurs in invertebrate animals also.

Willis H. Johnson et al., *Essentials of Biology*

*From *Modern Marketing* by Edward J. Fox and Edward W. Wheatley. Copyright © 1978 by Scott, Foresman and Company, HarperCollinsCollege Publishers.

4. Both the introductory and concluding sentences state the main idea.

main idea
1. detail
2. detail
3. detail
4. detail
main idea

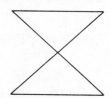

A speech of tribute is designed to create in those who hear it a sense of appreciation for the traits or accomplishments of the person or group to whom tribute is paid. If you cause your audience to realize the essential worth or importance of the person or group, you will have succeeded. But you may go further than this. You may, by honoring a person, arouse deeper devotion to the cause he or she represents. Did this person give distinguished service to community or country? Then strive to enhance the audience's sense of patriotism and service. Was this individual a friend to young people? Then try to arouse the conviction that working to provide opportunities for the young deserves the audience's support. Create a desire in your listeners to emulate the person or persons honored. *Make them want to develop the same virtues, to demonstrate a like devotion.*

Douglas Ehninger et al., *Principles of Speech Communication**

Unfortunately, readers cannot always rely on a stated main idea being provided. For example, fiction writers rarely, if ever, use stated main ideas. The following is an example of a paragraph with an unstated main idea.

5. Details combine to make a point but the main idea is not directly stated.

1. detail
2. detail
3. detail
4. detail

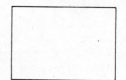

This creature's career could produce but one result, and it speedily followed. Boy after boy managed to get on the river. The minister's son became an engineer. The doctor's sons became "mud clerks;" the wholesale liquor dealer's son became a bar-keeper on a boat; four sons of the chief merchant, and two sons of the county judge, became pilots. Pilot was the grandest position of all. The pilot, even in those days of trivial wages, had a princely salary—from a hundred and fifty to two hundred and fifty dollars a month, and no board to pay. Two months of his wages would pay a preacher's salary for a year. Now some of us were left disconsolate. We could not get on the river—at least our parents would not let us.

Mark Twain, *Life on the Mississippi*

*From *Principles of Speech Communication,* 9th Brief Edition, by Douglas Ehninger, Bruce E. Gronbeck, and Alan H. Monroe. Copyright © 1984, Scott, Foresman and Company, HarperCollinsCollege Publishers.

Main idea: Young boys in the area have a strong desire to leave home and get a job on the prestigious Mississippi River.

WHAT DO DETAILS DO?

Look at the details in the following picture to decide what message the photographer is trying to communicate. Determine the topic of the picture, propose a main idea using your prior knowledge, and then list some of the significant details that support this point.

What is the topic? _____

What are the significant supporting details? _____

_____

What is the point the artist is trying to convey about the topic? _____

_____

The topic of the picture is the sad plight of the refugees, and the main idea is that the refugees must bury their dead children in a shallow grave with no coffin. The young are dying and there are no resources even for a proper burial. The significant details are the grave, the pick and shovel, the small bundle wrapped in white cloth, the sad faces, the tents, the barren mountain landscape, and the headdress which suggests the Kurds. In this case, the details develop the main idea and make the picture into a strong and moving statement about the despair of these displaced refugees who are living in tents.

Details support, develop, and explain a main idea. Specific details can include reasons, incidents, facts, examples, steps, and definitions.

The task of a reader is to recognize the major details and to pull them together into a main idea. Being able to pick out major details implies that the reader has some degree of prior knowledge on the subject and has probably already begun to form some notion of the main idea.

Textbooks are packed full of details, but fortunately all details are not of equal importance. Major details tend to support, explain, and describe main ideas, whereas minor details tend to support, explain, and describe the major details. Ask the following questions to determine which details are major in importance and which are not:

1. Which details logically develop the main idea?
2. Which details help you understand the main idea?
3. Which details validate the main idea?

Noticing key words that form transitional links from one idea to another can sometimes help the reader distinguish between major and minor details. The following terms are frequently used to signal significance:

Key words for major details: one, first, another, furthermore, also, finally

Key words for minor details: for example, to be specific, that is, this means

Example of Stated Main Idea

Managers can regain control over their time in several ways. One is by meeting whenever possible in someone else's office, so that they can leave as soon as their business is finished. Another is to start meetings on time without waiting for late-comers. The idea is to let late-comers adjust their schedules rather than everyone else adjusting theirs. A third is to set aside a block of time to work on an important project without interruption. This may require ignoring the telephone, being protected by an aggressive secretary, or hiding out. Whatever it takes is worth it.

Reitz and Jewell, *Managing*

1. Who or what is this about?
   (The passage is about managers controlling their time.)
2. What are the major details?
   (The details are: meet in another office, start meetings on time, and block out time to work.)
3. What is the main idea the author is trying to convey about the topic?
   (The main idea, stated in the first sentence, is that managers can do things to control their time.)

Exercise 3: Stated Main Ideas

Read the following passages and use the three-question system to determine the author's main idea. For each passage in this exercise, the answer to the third question will be stated somewhere within the paragraph.

Passage A
Courting behavior in birds is also believed to be instinctive. In one experiment Daniel Lehrman of Rutgers University found that when a male blond ring dove was isolated from females, it soon began to bow and coo to a stuffed model of a female—a model that it had previously ignored. When the model was replaced by a rolled-up cloth, he began to court the cloth; and when this was removed the sex-crazed dove directed his attention to a corner of the cage, where it could at least focus its gaze. It seems that the threshold for release of the behavior pattern became increasingly lower as time went by without the sight of a live female dove. It is almost as though some specific "energy" for performing courting behavior were building up within the male ring dove.

Robert Wallace, *Biology: The World of Life*

1. Who or what is this about? _____

_____

2. What are the major details?

_____

_____

3. What is the main idea the author is trying to convey about the topic? Underline the main idea.

Passage B
The nations whose lands were crossed by white wagon trains reacted in a number of ways to the westward tide. The Sioux, who had long

been trading with whites, were among the tribes who regularly visited overlanders to trade for blankets, clothes, cows, rifles, and knives. The Sioux were sharp negotiators, who "in every case get the best of the bargain," remarked one overlander, while another, Catherine Haun, asserted that the Indian was "a financier of no mean ability and invariably comes out Al in a bargain." As white migrants flooded the overland routes, they took a heavy toll on the Plains Indians' way of life: the emigrant parties scared off game and reduced buffalo herds, overgrazed the grass, and depleted the supply of wood. Having petitioned unsuccessfully in 1846 for government compensation, the Sioux decided to demand payment from the wagon trains crossing their lands. Whether parties paid or not depended on the relative strength of the two groups, but whites complained bitterly of what seemed to them naked robbery.

James W. Davidson et al., *Nation of Nations*

1. Who or what is this about? _____

_____

2. What are the major details?

_____

_____

3. What is the main idea the author is trying to convey about the topic? Underline the main idea.

Passage C

Consider, for example, how a physician's office influences patterns of social interaction. This setting is carefully crafted by the physician and the medical staff to convey appropriate information to their audience of patients. Physicians enjoy a position of considerable prestige and power in American society. Usually this fact is suggested immediately upon entering the office, as the physician is nowhere to be seen. Instead, within what Goffman describes as the "front region" of the setting, the patient encounters a receptionist. This person functions as a gatekeeper, deciding if and when the patient can meet the physician. The physician's private office—the "back region" of the setting—contains various props, such as medical books and at least one framed degree that serve as a reminder that the physician, not the patient, has the specialized knowledge necessary to guide their social interaction. Just as important, the physician usually receives the patient while sitting behind a large desk—a symbol of power—while the patient is provided with only a chair. Slightly changing the seating arrangement could considerably lessen the hierarchy in this setting.

© 1993 HarperCollins College Publishers

The physician could sit down next to the patient on a couch, putting both people on more equal terms.

John Macionis, *Sociology**

1. Who or what is this about? _____

_____

2. What are the major details?

_____

_____

3. What is the main idea the author is trying to convey about the topic? Underline the main idea.

Example of an Unstated Main Idea

Michael Harner (1977) proposes an ecological interpretation of Aztec sacrifice and cannibalism. He holds that human sacrifice was a response to certain diet deficiencies in the population. In the Aztec environment, wild game was getting scarce, and the population was growing. Although the maize-beans combination of food that was the basis of the diet was usually adequate, these crops were subject to seasonal failure. Famine was frequent in the absence of edible domesticated animals. To meet essential protein requirements, cannibalism was the only solution. Although only the upper classes were allowed to consume human flesh, a commoner who distinguished himself in a war could also have the privilege of giving a cannibalistic feast. Thus, although it was the upper strata who benefited most from ritual cannibalism, members of the commoner class could also benefit. Furthermore, as Harner explains, the social mobility and cannibalistic privileges available to the commoners through warfare provided a strong motivation for the "aggressive war machine" that was such a prominent feature of the Aztec state.

Serena Nanda, *Cultural Anthropology*

1. Who or what is this about?
   (This passage is about Aztec sacrifice and cannibalism.)
2. What are the major details?
   (The major details are: diet deficiencies occurred, animals were not available, and upper class members and heros could eat human flesh.)
3. What is the main idea the author is trying to convey about the topic?
   (The author's main idea is that Aztec sacrifice and cannibalism met protein needs of the diet and motivated warriors to achieve.)

*John J. Macionis, SOCIOLOGY, © 1987, pp. 128-129, 176, 323-325, 328-329, 332-334, 341-343. Reprinted by permission of Prentice-Hall, Inc., Englewood Cliffs, N.J.

Exercise 4: Unstated Main Ideas

Read the following passages and use the three-question system to determine the author's main idea. Pull the ideas together to state the main ideas in your own words.

Passage A

Leonardo da Vinci was the illegitimate son of Piero, a notary from the town of Vinci, and a peasant girl named Caterina. The third wife of Leonardo's father later bore a son named Bartolommeo, who idolized Leonardo although he was forty-five years younger. After the death of the legendary Leonardo, Bartolommeo attempted an amazing experiment. He studied every detail of his father's relationship with Caterina. Then Bartolommeo, himself a notary by family tradition, returned to Vinci and found another peasant wench who seemed similar to Caterina, according to all Bartolommeo knew. He married her and she bore him a son whom they called Piero. Strangely, the child actually looked like Leonardo and was brought up with encouragement to follow in the great man's footsteps. Surprisingly, the boy became an accomplished artist and was becoming a talented sculptor when he died, thus ending the experiment.

Robert Wallace, *Biology: The World of Life*

1. Who or what is this about? _____

_____

2. What are the major details?

_____

_____

3. What is the main idea the author is trying to convey about the topic? ___

_____

_____

Passage B

At the age of thirty-five, Eleanor Roosevelt, one of the most widely admired American women, wrote in her diary: "I do not think I have ever felt so strangely as in the past year . . . all my self-confidence is gone and I am on the edge, though I never was better physically I feel sure" (cited in Sheehy 1976:260). What explains Eleanor Roosevelt's self-doubt? Perhaps she was troubled by the attention her husband was paying to another, younger woman; perhaps as she looked into the future, she could not see what challenges or accomplishments might bring a sense of satisfaction to her life. As she experienced what we might today describe as a "midlife crisis," there was much that she could not foresee. Although her husband, Franklin Delano Roosevelt, was shortly to suffer the crippling debilities of poliomyelitis, his rising political career would lead ultimately to thirteen consecutive years as his country's president. And Eleanor Roosevelt would become perhaps the most active and influential of all First Ladies.

John J. Macionis, *Sociology*˙

1. Who or what is this about? _____

_____

2. What are the major details?

_____

_____

3. What is the main idea the author is trying to convey about the topic? ____

_____

_____

Passage C

The Aswan High Dam, built in Egypt with Russian support, was supposed to provide hydroelectric power and to increase Egypt's food supply by controlling the unpredictable Nile River. The project meant that great art treasures were flooded as submerged land was drained for cultivation. However, only one tenth of an acre of land was made available for each person added to Egypt's population during the period of construction. One result of the dam was that the Nile no longer flooded the delta farmlands annually. These annual floods served to restore the farmland fertility with deposited silt. This no longer the case, the quality of the farmland decreased. The dam also cut off the nutrients that had been washed to the Mediterranean Sea as a result of the annual floodings. Because of this, or the change in the salinity of the sea that the dam produced, the sardine catch dropped from 18,000 tons per year to 500 tons per year. The stable lake created by the dam allowed aquatic snails to flourish. The snails serve as an intermediate host to a blood fluke that bores into humans causing the dreaded disease, schistosomiasis. The construction of the dam had important political implications at the time. These tombs had to be moved to be saved from the dam's waters. The political scene has changed now. So has the environmental one.

Robert Wallace, *Biology: The World of Life*

˙John J. Macionis, SOCIOLOGY, © 1987, pp. 128-129, 176, 323-325, 328-329, 332-334, 341-343. Reprinted by permission of Prentice-Hall, Inc., Englewood Cliffs, N.J.

1. Who or what is this about? _____

_____

2. What are the major details?

_____

_____

3. What is the main idea the author is trying to convey about the topic? ____

_____

_____

PATTERNS OF ORGANIZATION

The main idea and the pattern of organization chosen by a writer to deliver this idea are closely interwoven. Identifying one will often help identify the other, because the message can dictate the structure. A **pattern of organization** is a vehicle or structure for a message. Before beginning to write, an author must ask, "If this is what I want to say, what is the best way to organize my message?"

From a number of possible patterns, an author chooses the organizational structure that seems most appropriate. For example, if he or she wanted to convey the message or main idea that freshmen receive more support at junior colleges than at large universities, the author would probably organize the message through a pattern of comparison and contrast. On the other hand, if the writer wanted to explain that a college degree can lead to expanded opportunities, upward mobility within companies, later salary increases, and ultimately greater job satisfaction, the idea might best be communicated through a pattern of cause and effect, although words like *expanded* and *greater* also suggest a comparison.

Suppose you were writing an orientation article describing support services available at your own college. You could summarize the resources in a list pattern, or you could discuss them in the order in which a freshman is likely to need them. Within your article, you might use a separate paragraph to describe or define a relatively unknown service on campus, with examples of how it has helped others. Thus, one long article might have an overall list pattern of organization yet contain individual paragraphs which follow other patterns. The organizational pattern is a choice you make for structuring your message.

The importance of identifying organizational patterns is that they signal how facts will be presented. They are blueprints for you to use while reading. The number of details in a textbook can be overwhelming. Identifying the author's pattern can help you to master the complexities of the material by allowing you to predict the format of upcoming information.

Although key words can signal a particular pattern, the most important clue to the pattern is the main idea itself. In a single selection several patterns can be employed. Your aim as a reader is to anticipate the overall pattern and place the supporting details into its broad perspective.

The following are examples of the patterns of organization that are found most frequently in textbooks.

Simple Listing

Items are randomly listed in a series of supporting facts or details. These supporting elements are of equal value, and the order in which they are presented is of no importance. Changing the order of the items does not change the meaning of the paragraph.

Signal words often used as transitional words to link ideas in a paragraph with a pattern of simple listing: *in addition, also, another, several, for example, a number of.*

Signal Sentence: Insecticides are harmful in a number of ways.

Definition

Frequently in a textbook, an entire paragraph is devoted to defining a complex term or idea. The concept is defined initially and then expanded with examples and restatements.

Signal Sentence: Hallucinations are vivid images in the absence of stimuli. *For example, . . .*

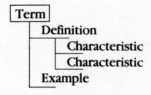

Description

Description is like listing; the characteristics that make up a description are no more than a definition or a simple list of details.

Signal Sentence: The hermit crab is a creature with many interesting characteristics.

© 1993 HarperCollins College Publishers

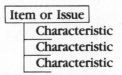

Time Order or Sequence

Items are listed in the order in which they occurred or in a specifically planned order in which they must develop. In this case, the order is important, and changing it would change the meaning.

Signal words often used for time order or sequence: *first, second, third, after, before, when, until, at last, next, later.*

Signal Sentence: The events leading up to the treaty strengthened the hand of the allies.

Comparison-Contrast

Items are presented according to similarities and differences among them.

Signal words often used for comparison-contrast: *different, similar, on the other hand, but, however, bigger than, in the same way, parallels.*

Signal Sentence: The United States and England are both alike and different.

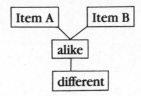

Cause and Effect

In this pattern, one element is shown as producing another element. One is the *cause* or the "happening" that stimulated the particular result or *effect.*

Signal words often used for cause and effect: *for this reason, consequently, on that account, hence, because, made.*

Signal Sentence: Stress can cause disease.

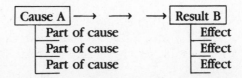

Exercise 5: Patterns of Organization and Main Idea

Read the following passages and use the three-question system to determine the author's main idea. In addition, indicate the dominant pattern of organization used by the author. Select from the following list:

Simple listing
Definition
Description
Time order
Comparison-contrast
Cause and effect

Passage A
Let us follow the story of how rabbits were introduced into Australia. European rabbits reached Australia with the first European settlers in 1788 and repeated introductions followed. By the early 1800s rabbits were being kept in every large settlement and had been liberated many times. All the early rabbit introductions either died out or remained localized. No one knows why.

On Christmas Day, 1859, the brig HMS *Lightning* arrived at Melbourne with about a dozen wild European rabbits bound for an estate in western Victoria. Within three years rabbits had started to spread, after a bush fire destroyed the fences enclosing one colony. From a slow spread at first the colonization picked up speed during the 1870s, and by 1900 the European rabbit had spread 1000 miles to the north and west, changing the entire economy of nature in southeastern Australia.

Charles Krebs, *The Message of Ecology*

1. Who or what is this about? _____

_____

2. What are the major details? _____

_____

_____

3. What is the overall pattern of organization? _____

_____

4. What is the main idea the author is trying to convey about the topic? ____

_____

Passage B

The disadvantage faced by children who attempt morning schoolwork on an empty stomach appears to be at least partly due to hypoglycemia. The average child up to the age of ten or so needs to eat every four to six hours to maintain a blood glucose concentration high enough to support the activity of the brain and nervous system. A child's brain is as big as an adult's, and the brain is the body's chief glucose consumer. A child's liver is considerably smaller, and the liver is the organ responsible for storing glucose (as glycogen) and for releasing it into the blood as needed. The liver can't store more than about four hours' worth of glycogen; hence the need to eat fairly often. Teachers aware of the late-morning slump in their classrooms wisely request that a midmorning snack be provided; it improves classroom performance all the way to lunch time. But for the child who hasn't had breakfast, the morning may be lost altogether.

Eva May Nunnelley Hamilton et al., *Nutrition*

1. Who or what is this about? _____

_____

2. What are the major details? _____

_____

3. What is the overall pattern of organization? _____

_____

4. What is the main idea the author is trying to convey about the topic? ____

_____

Passage C

An orange grown in Florida usually has a thin and tightly fitting skin, and it is also heavy with juice. Californians say that if you want to eat a Florida orange you have to get into a bathtub first. California oranges are light in weight and have thick skins that break easily and come off in hunks. The flesh inside is marvelously sweet, and the segments almost separate themselves. In Florida, it is said that you can run over a California orange with a ten-ton truck and not even wet the pavement. The differences from which these hyperboles arise will prevail in the two states even if the type of orange is the same. In arid climates, like California's, oranges develop a thick albedo, which is the white part of the skin. Florida is one of the two or three most rained-upon states in the United States. California uses the Colorado River and similarly impressive sources to irrigate its oranges, but of course irrigation can only do so much. The annual difference in rainfall between the Florida and California orange-growing areas is one million one hundred and forty thousand gallons per acre. For years, California was the leading orange state, but Florida surpassed California in 1942, and grows three times as many oranges now. California oranges, for their part, can safely be called three times as beautiful.

John McPhee, *Oranges*

1. Who or what is this about? _____

_____

2. What are the major details? _____

_____

3. What is the overall pattern of organization? _____

_____

4. What is the main idea the author is trying to convey about the topic? ____

_____

Passage D

The left hemisphere is sometimes known as the **major hemisphere** because it controls language, an important human skill. The right hemisphere, which controls spatial skills, has been treated as somewhat of a second-class citizen and has often been referred to as the **minor hemisphere** (Nebes 1974). However, psychologists have recently begun to recognize the talents of the right or minor hemisphere. The left or language hemisphere may give us the ability to solve a brainteaser or tell a wonderful story, but without the right hemisphere, we can't so much as copy a simple shape. Only the excellent spatial talents of the right hemisphere enable us to draw complex figures. In fact, one view stresses the idea that the reason many people are poor artists is that they are dominated by their left or verbal hemisphere (Edwards 1979). Without the right hemisphere, we may have difficulty recognizing complex figures like a face. When the left hemisphere is damaged, people may lose their ability to speak and write, but they are still able to compose music.

Andrew B. Crider et al., *Psychology*

1. Who or what is this about? _____

_____

2. What are the major details? _____

_____

© 1993 HarperCollins College Publishers

3. What is the overall pattern of organization? _____

_____

4. What is the main idea the author is trying to convey about the topic? ___

_____

GETTING THE MAIN IDEA OF LONGER SELECTIONS

Understanding the main idea of longer selections requires a little more thinking than finding the main idea of a single paragraph. Since longer selections such as articles or chapters involve more material, the challenge of tying the ideas together can be confusing and complicated. Each paragraph of a longer selection usually represents a new aspect of a supporting detail. In addition, several major ideas may contribute to developing the overall main idea. The reader, therefore, must fit the many pieces together under one central theme.

For longer selections, the reader needs to add an extra step between the two questions, "What is the topic?" and "What is the main idea the author is trying to convey?" The step involves organizing the material into manageable subunits and then relating those to the whole. Two additional questions to ask are, "Under what subsections can these ideas be grouped?" and "How do these subsections contribute to the whole?"

Use the following suggestions to determine the main idea of longer selections. The techniques are similar to those used in previewing and skimming, two skills that also focus on the overall central theme.

1. Think about the significance of the title. What does the title suggest about the topic?
2. Read the first one or two paragraphs for a statement of the topic or thesis. What does the selection seem to be about?
3. Read the subheadings and, if necessary, glance at the first sentences of some of the paragraphs. From these clues what does the article seem to be about?
4. Look for clues that indicate how the material is organized.
   a. Is the purpose to define a term, to prove an opinion, to explain a concept, to describe a situation, or to persuade the reader towards a particular point of view?
   b. Is the material organized into a list of examples, a time order or sequence, a comparison or contrast, or a cause and effect relationship?
5. As you read, organize the paragraphs into subsections. Give each subsection a title. These become your significant supporting details.
6. Determine how the overall organization and subsections relate to the whole, and answer the question, "What is the main idea the author is trying to convey in this selection?"

SUMMARY WRITING: A MAIN IDEA SKILL

What Is a Summary?

A summary is a brief, concise statement in your own words of the main idea and the significant supporting details. The first sentence should state the main idea or thesis, and subsequent sentences should incorporate the significant details. Minor details and material irrelevant to the learner's purpose should be omitted. The summary should be in paragraph form and should always be shorter than the material being summarized.

Why Summarize?

Summaries can be used for textbook study and are particularly useful in anticipating the organization of answers for essay exam questions. For writing research papers, summarizing is an essential skill. Using your own words to put the essence of an article into concise sentences requires a thorough understanding of the material. As one researcher noted, "Since so much summarizing is necessary for writing papers, students should have the skill before starting work on research papers. How much plagiarism is the result of inadequate summarizing skills?"[3]

Writing a research paper may mean that you will have to read as much as thirty articles and four books over a period of one or two months. After each reading you want to take enough notes so you can write your paper without returning to the library for another look at the original reference. Since you will be using so many different references, the notetaking should be done carefully. The complete sentences of a summary are more explicit than underscored text or the highlighted topic-phrase format of an outline. Your summary should demonstrate a synthesis of the information.

How to Summarize

1. Keep in mind the purpose of your summary. Your projected needs will determine which details are important and how many should be included.
2. Decide on the main idea the author is trying to convey. Make this main idea the first sentence in your summary.
3. Decide on the major ideas and details that support the author's point. Include in your summary the major ideas and as many of the significant supporting details as your purpose demands.
4. Do not include irrelevant or repeated information in your summary.

[3]K. Taylor, "Can College Students Summarize?," *Journal of Reading* 26 (March 1983): 540–544.

Example of Summarizing

Read the following summary of an excerpt on the circulatory system that appears in the next chapter. Notice that a statement of the main idea is followed by major details. For additional illustrations of summary writing, read the summary at the end of the introductory portion of each chapter of this book.

There are two types of circulatory systems, the open and closed, by which blood reaches all the cells of an animal. In the open system, found mostly in insects and other arthropods, blood moves through the body and bathes the cells directly. The blood moves slower than in the closed system, and oxygen is supplied from outside air through tubes. In the closed system, blood flows through a system of vessels, oxygen is carried by the blood so it must move quickly, and the heart serves as a pumping mechanism. All vertebrates, as well as earthworms, have closed systems.

Exercise 6: Summarizing

On a sheet of notebook paper, write a summary of the following passage. Your purpose is to note the main idea and major supporting details as a later reference for a research paper on gun control. Be brief, but include the essential elements.

Murder

Homicide occurs most frequently during weekend evenings, particularly on Saturday night. This holds true largely for lower-class murderers but not for middle- and upper-class offenders, who kill on any day of the week. One apparent reason is that higher-class murders are more likely than lower-class homicides to be premeditated— hence less likely to result from alcohol-induced eruptions during weekend sprees.

Whatever their class, murderers most often use handguns to kill. Perhaps seeing a gun while embroiled in a heated argument may incite a person into murderous action. As Shakespeare said, "How oft the sight of means to do ill deeds, makes ill deeds done." Of course, firearms by themselves cannot cause homicide, nor can their absence reduce the motivation to kill. It is true that "Guns don't kill, people do." Still, were guns less available, many heated arguments would have resulted in aggravated assaults rather than murders, thereby reducing the number of fatalities. One study suggests that attacks with knives are five times *less* likely to result in death than are attacks with guns (Wright et al. 1983). In fact, the use of less dangerous weapons such as knives in attempted murders has been estimated to cause 80 percent fewer deaths (Newton and Zimring 1969). Given the enormous number of guns in private hands (about 120 million), it is not surprising that far more deaths result from gun attacks in this country than in Canada, England, and Japan (Rodino 1986).

Ironically, murder is the most personal crime, largely committed against acquaintances, friends, and relatives. According to the latest national statistics, in cases where the relationship of the victim to the killer is known, 56 percent involve acquaintances, friends, and spouses while only 23 percent involve strangers (Malcolm 1989). Many of us may find it incredible that the people we know or even love are more likely to kill us than are total strangers. "This should really not be very surprising," Donald Mulvihill and Melvin Tumin (1969) have explained. "Everyone is within easy striking distance from intimates for a large part of the time. Although friends, lovers, spouses, and the like are a main source of pleasure in one's life, they are equally a main source of frustration and hurt. Few others can anger one so much." The act of murder requires a great deal of emotion. It is a crime of passion carried out under the overwhelming pressure of a volcanic emotion. It may be more difficult for us to kill a stranger for whom we don't have any sympathetic or antagonistic feelings. Only psychotic or professional killers can do away with people in a cold-blooded, unemotional manner. But such impersonal killings are rare.

© 1993 HarperCollins College Publishers

Alex Thio, *Sociology*

SUMMARY

Getting the main idea the author is trying to convey is the single most important reading comprehension skill. To do this the reader must first determine the topic, a general term that forms an umbrella for the specific ideas presented. The main idea is the point the author is trying to convey about the topic. In some passages the main idea is stated in a sentence, and in others it is unstated. Details support, develop, and explain the main idea; some are major and some are minor. Organizational patterns for presenting details and developing ideas can vary, and anticipating the pattern can help the reader. Summaries condense material and include the main ideas and major details.

Selection

PSYCHOLOGY

Skill Development: Stage 1

Preview

The author's main purpose is to describe the infant-mother love relationship.

agree ☐   *disagree* ☐

After reading this selection, I will need to know the meaning of contact comfort.

agree ☐   *disagree* ☐

Activate Schema
Do parents who were abused as children later abuse their own children?

Learning Strategy
Be able to explain the needs of the infant monkey and the effect that deprivation of those needs can have on the whole pattern of psychological development. Relate these findings to human behavior.

Word Knowledge
Review the ten vocabulary items that follow the selection. Seek an understanding of unfamiliar words.

Stage 2: Integrate Knowledge While Reading

Use thinking strategies as you read:

1. Predict 2. Picture 3. Relate 4. Monitor 5. Fix up

MONKEY LOVE

From James V. McConnell, *Understanding Human Behavior*

The scientist who has conducted the best long-term laboratory experiments on love is surely Harry Harlow, a psychologist at the University of Wisconsin. Professor Harlow did not set out to study love—it happened by accident. Like many other psychologists, he was
5   at first primarily interested in how organisms learn. Rather than working with rats, Harlow chose to work with monkeys.

Since he needed a place to house and raise the monkeys, he built the Primate Laboratory at Wisconsin. Then he began to study the effects of brain lesions on monkey learning. But he soon found that
10 young animals reacted somewhat differently to brain damage than did older monkeys, so he and his wife Margaret devised a breeding program and tried various ways of raising monkeys in the laboratory. They rapidly discovered that monkey infants raised by their mothers often caught diseases from their parents, so the Harlows began taking
15 the infants away from their mothers at birth and tried raising them by hand. The baby monkeys had been given cheesecloth diapers to serve as baby blankets. Almost from the start, it became obvious to the Harlows that their little animals developed such strong attachments to the blankets that, in the Harlows' own terms, it was often hard to tell

20 where the diaper ended and the baby began. Not only this, but if the Harlows removed the "security" blanket in order to clean it, the infant monkey often became greatly disturbed—just as if its own mother had deserted it.

The Surrogate Mother.   What the baby monkeys obviously needed
25 was an artificial or *surrogate* mother—something they could cling to as tightly as they typically clung to their own mother's chest. The Harlows sketched out many different designs, but none really appealed to them. Then, in 1957, while enjoying a champagne flight high over the city of Detroit, Harry Harlow glanced out of the
30 airplane window and "saw" an image of an artificial monkey mother. It was a hollow wire cylinder, wrapped with a terry-cloth bath towel, with a silly wooden head at the top. The tiny monkey could cling to this "model mother" as closely as to its real mother's body hair. This surrogate mother could be provided with a functional breast simply
35 by placing a milk bottle so that the nipple stuck through the cloth at an appropriate place on the surrogate's anatomy. The cloth mother could be heated or cooled; it could be rocked mechanically or made to stand still; and, most important, it could be removed at will.
      While still sipping his champagne, Harlow mentally outlined much
40 of the research that kept him, his wife, and their associates occupied for many years to come. And without realizing it, Harlow had shifted from studying monkey learning to monkey love.

Infant-Mother Love

The chimpanzee or monkey infant is much more developed at birth than the human infant, and apes develop or mature much faster than
45 we do. Almost from the moment it is born, the monkey infant can move around and hold tightly to its mother. During the first few days of its life the infant will approach and cling to almost any large, warm, and soft object in its environment, particularly if that object also gives it milk. After a week or so, however, the monkey infant
50 begins to avoid newcomers and focuses its attentions on "mother"—real or surrogate.
      During the first two weeks of its life warmth is perhaps the most important psychological thing that a monkey mother has to give to its baby. The Harlows discovered this fact by offering infant monkeys a
55 choice of two types of mother-substitutes—one wrapped in terry cloth and one that was made of bare wire. If the two artificial mothers were both the same temperature, the little monkeys always preferred the cloth mother. However, if the wire model was heated, while the cloth model was cool, for the first two weeks after birth the baby primates
60 picked the warm wire mother-substitutes as their favorites. Thereafter

they switched and spent most of their time on the more comfortable cloth mother.

Why is cloth preferable to bare wire? Something that the Harlows called *contact comfort* seems to be the answer, and a most powerful influence it is. Infant monkeys (and chimps too) spend much of their time rubbing against their mothers' skins, putting themselves in as close contact with the parent as they can. Whenever the young animal is frightened, disturbed, or annoyed, it typically rushes to its mother and rubs itself against her body. Wire doesn't "rub" as well as does soft cloth. Prolonged "contact comfort" with a surrogate cloth mother appears to instill confidence in baby monkeys and is much more rewarding to them than is either warmth or milk. Infant monkeys also prefer a "rocking" surrogate to one that is stationary.

According to the Harlows, the basic quality of an infant's love for its mother is *trust*. If the infant is put into an unfamiliar playroom without its mother, the infant ignores the toys no matter how interesting they might be. It screeches in terror and curls up into a furry little ball. If its cloth mother is now introduced into the playroom, the infant rushes to the surrogate and clings to it for dear life. After a few minutes of contact comfort, it apparently begins to feel more secure. It then climbs down from the mother-substitute and begins tentatively to explore the toys, but often rushes back for a deep embrace as if to reassure itself that its mother is still there and that all is well. Bit by bit its fears of the novel environment are "desensitized" and it spends more and more time playing with the toys and less and less time clinging to its "mother."

Good Mothers and Bad.   The Harlows found that, once a baby monkey has come to accept its mother (real or surrogate), the mother can do almost no wrong. In one of their studies, the Harlows tried to create "monster mothers" whose behavior would be so abnormal that the infants would desert the mothers. Their purpose was to determine whether maternal rejection might cause abnormal behavior patterns in the infant monkeys similar to those responses found in human babies whose mothers ignore or punish their children severely. The problem was—how can you get a terry-cloth mother to reject or punish its baby? Their solutions were ingenious—but most of them failed in their main purpose. Four types of "monster mothers" were tried, but none of them was apparently "evil" enough to impart fear or loathing to the infant monkeys. One such "monster" occasionally blasted its babies with compressed air; a second shook so violently that the baby often fell off; a third contained a catapult that frequently flung the infant away from it. The most evil-appearing of all had a set of metal spikes buried beneath the terry cloth; from time to time the spikes

would poke through the cloth making it impossible for the infant to
cling to the surrogate.

The baby monkeys brought up on the "monster mothers" did show
a brief period of emotional disturbance when the "wicked"
temperament of the surrogates first showed up. The infants would cry
for a time when displaced from their mothers, but as soon as the
surrogates returned to normal, the infant would return to the
surrogate and continue clinging, as if all were forgiven. As the
Harlows tell the story, the only prolonged distress created by the
experiment seemed to be that felt by the experimenters!

There was, however, one type of surrogate that uniformly "turned
off" the infant monkeys. S. J. Suomi, working with the Harlows, built a
terry-cloth mother with ice water in its veins. Newborn monkeys
would attach themselves to this "cool momma" for a brief period of
time, but then retreated to a corner of the cage and rejected her forever.

From their many brilliant studies, the Harlows conclude that the
love of an infant for its mother is *primarily a response to certain
stimuli the mother offers.* Warmth is the most important stimulus for
the first two weeks of the monkey's life, then contact comfort
becomes paramount. Contact comfort is determined by the softness
and "rub-ability" of the surface of the mother's body—terry cloth is
better than are satin and silk, but all such materials are more effective
in creative love and trust than bare metal is. Food and mild "shaking"
or "rocking" are important too, but less so than warmth and contact
comfort. These needs—and the rather primitive responses the infant
makes in order to obtain their satisfaction—are programmed into the
monkey's genetic blueprint. The growing infant's requirement for
social and intellectual stimulation becomes critical only later in a
monkey's life. And yet, if the baby primate is deprived of contact with
other young of its own species, its whole pattern of development can
be profoundly disturbed.

Mother-Infant Love

The Harlows were eventually able to find ways of getting female
isolates pregnant, usually by confining them in a small cage for long
periods of time with a patient and highly experienced normal male.
At times, however, the Harlows were forced to help matters along by
strapping the female to a piece of apparatus. When these isolated
females gave birth to their first monkey baby, they turned out to be
the "monster mothers" the Harlows had tried to create with
mechanical surrogates. Having had no contact with other animals as
they grew up, they simply did not know what to do with the furry
little strangers that suddenly appeared on the scene. These
motherless mothers at first totally ignored their children, although if

© 1993 HarperCollins College Publishers

the infant persisted, the mothers occasionally gave in and provided the baby with some of the contact and comfort it demanded.

Surprisingly enough, once these mothers learned how to handle a baby, they did reasonably well. Then, when they were again
150 impregnated and gave birth to a second infant, they took care of this next baby fairly adequately.

Maternal affection was totally lacking in a few of the motherless monkeys, however. To them the newborn monkey was little more than an object to be abused the way a human child might abuse a doll or a
155 toy train. These motherless mothers stepped on their babies, crushed the infant's face into the floor of the cage, and once or twice chewed off their baby's feet and fingers before they could be stopped. The most terrible mother of all popped her infant's head into her mouth and crunched it like a potato chip.

160 We tend to think of most mothers—no matter what their species—as having some kind of almost-divine "maternal instinct" that makes them love their children and take care of them no matter what the cost or circumstance. While it is true that most females have built into their genetic blueprint the tendency to be interested in (and to
165 care for) their offspring, this inborn tendency is always expressed in a given environment. The "maternal instinct" is strongly influenced by the mother's past experiences. Humans seem to have weaker instincts of all kinds than do other animals—since our behavior patterns are more affected by learning than by our genes, we have greater
170 flexibility in what we do and become. But we pay a sometimes severe price for this freedom from genetic control.

Normal monkey and chimpanzee mothers seldom appear to inflict real physical harm on their children; human mothers and fathers often do. Serapio R. Zalba, writing in a journal called *Trans-action,*
175 estimated in 1971 that in the United States alone, perhaps 250,000 children suffer physical abuse by their parents each year. Of these "battered babies," almost 40,000 may be very badly injured. The number of young boys and girls killed by their parents annually is not known, but Zalba suggests that the figure may run into the thousands.
180 Parents have locked their children in tiny cages, raised them in dark closets, burned them, boiled them, slashed them with knives, shot them, and broken almost every bone in their bodies. How can we reconcile these facts with the much-discussed maternal and paternal "instincts"?

185 The research by the Harlows on the "motherless mothers" perhaps gives us a clue. Mother monkeys who were themselves socially deprived or isolated when young seemed singularly lacking in affection for their infants. Zalba states that most of the abusive human parents that were studied turned out to have been abused and
190 neglected *themselves* as children. Like the isolated monkeys who

seemed unable to control their aggressive impulses when put in
contact with normal animals, the abusive parents seem to be greatly
deficient in what psychologists call "impulse control." Most of these
parents also were described as being socially isolated, as having
195 troubles adjusting to marriage, often deeply in debt, and as being
unable to build up warm and loving relationships with other
people—including their own children. Since they did not learn how
to love from their own parents, these mothers and fathers simply did
not acquire the social skills necessary for bringing up their own
200 infants in a healthy fashion.

Stage 3: Recall

Stop to self-test and relate to issues.

Skill Development: Summarizing

Using this selection as a source, summarize on index cards the information
that you might want to include in a research paper entitled "Animal Rights: Do
Scientists Go Too Far?"

Skill Development: Main Idea

Directions: Write the answers to the following questions.

1. In the first section, which includes the first four paragraphs, what is the
   point the author is trying to convey about Harlow's experiments? _____

   _____

2. In the second section, entitled "Infant-Mother Love," what is the point
   the author is trying to convey about that love? _____

   _____

3. In the beginning of the section entitled "Good Mothers and Bad," what is
   the point the author is trying to convey about these mothers? _____

   _____

4. In the beginning of the section entitled "Mother-Infant Love," what is the
   point the author is trying to convey about that love? _____

   _____

5. What is the author's overall pattern of organization for this selection? ___

_____

Comprehension Questions

1. Who or what is the topic? _____

   What is the main idea the author is trying to convey about the topic?

   _____

After reading the selection, answer the following questions with *a, b, c,* or *d.*

_____ 2. When Harry Harlow originally started his experiments with monkeys, his purpose was to study
   a. love.
   b. breeding.
   c. learning.
   d. disease.

_____ 3. The reason that the author mentions Harry Harlow's revelations on the airplane is to show
   a. that he had extrasensory perception.
   b. that he liked to travel.
   c. that he was always thinking of his work.
   d. in what an unexpected way brilliant work often starts.

_____ 4. In his experiments Harlow used all of the following in designing his surrogate mothers except
   a. a terry-cloth bath towel.
   b. real body hair.
   c. a rocking movement.
   d. temperature controls.

_____ 5. Harlow manipulated his experiments to show the early significance of warmth by
   a. heating wire.
   b. changing from satin to terry cloth.
   c. equalizing temperature.
   d. creating "monster mothers."

_____ 6. Harlow feels that for contact comfort the cloth mother was preferable to the wire mother for all of the following reasons except
   a. the cloth mother instilled confidence.
   b. the wire mother doesn't "rub" as well.
   c. the wire mother was stationary.
   d. with the cloth mother, the infant feels a greater sense of security when upset.

7. Harlow's studies show that when abused by its mother, the infant will
   a. leave the mother.
   b. seek a new mother.
   c. return to the mother.
   d. fight with the mother.

8. For an infant to love its mother, Harlow's studies show that in the first two weeks the most important element is
   a. milk.
   b. warmth.
   c. contact comfort.
   d. love expressed by the mother.

9. In Harlow's studies with motherless monkeys, he showed that the techniques of mothering are
   a. instinctive.
   b. learned.
   c. inborn.
   d. natural.

10. The Harlows feel that child abuse is caused by all of the following problems except
   a. parents who were abused as children.
   b. socially isolated parents.
   c. parents who cannot control their impulses.
   d. parents who are instinctively evil.

Answer the following with *T* (true) or *F* (false).

11. The author feels that love in infant monkeys has a great deal of similarity to love in human children.
12. The author implies that isolated monkeys have difficulty engaging in normal peer relationships.
13. After learning how to handle the first baby, many motherless mothers became better parents with the second infant.
14. Zalba's studies support many of the findings of the Harlow studies.
15. Harlow had initially planned to perform drug experiments on the monkeys.

Vocabulary

According to the way the italicized word was used in the selection, indicate *a, b, c,* or *d* for the word or phrase that gives the best definition.

1. "the *surrogate* mother" (25)
   a. mean
   b. thoughtless
   c. loving
   d. substitute

2. "a *functional* breast" (34)
   a. mechanical
   b. operational
   c. wholesome
   d. imitation

___ 3. "on the surrogate's *anatomy*"
(36)
a. body
b. head
c. offspring
d. personality

___ 4. "begins *tentatively* to
explore" (82)
a. rapidly
b. hesitantly
c. aggressively
d. readily

___ 5. "fears of the *novel*
environment" (84)
a. hostile
b. literary
c. dangerous
d. new

___ 6. "fears . . . are *desensitized*"
(84)
a. made less sensitive
b. made more sensitive
c. electrified
d. communicated

___ 7. "solutions were *ingenious*"
(96)
a. incorrect
b. noble
c. clever
d. honest

___ 8. "*deprived of* contact" (132)
a. encouraged
b. denied
c. assured
d. ordered into

___ 9. "if the infant *persisted*"
(146)
a. stopped
b. continued
c. fought
d. relaxed

___ 10. "to be greatly *deficient*"
(192)
a. lacking
b. supplied
c. overwhelmed
d. secretive

Written Response

Use information from the text to support the following statement:
**How does a trusting relationship with a mother give an infant the
confidence to explore the environment and the ability to love?**
Response Strategy: Describe the elements necessary in the development of
the trusting relationship needed for confidence and for love. Use Harlow's experiments to support your statements. (Use your own paper for this response.)

Connecting and Reflecting

In the following passage, Margaret Mead is quoted as saying that "fathers are a biological necessity but a social accident." Do you believe
this statement is fair or unfair to fathers? To explore this issue, organize

into collaborative groups and discuss the modern father's role in parenting. Does a child need a father in the home? Does a father contribute something to a child's development that a mother cannot add? After a discussion, each group should list five areas in which a father makes a significant impact on the development of a child and note why the father is important to the child in each. Read the following passage for additional ideas about fathers.

The Father's Role in Infant Development

The noted anthropologist Margaret Mead once said that "fathers are a biological necessity but a social accident." However, data gathered by developmental psychologists tend not to support Dr. Mead's viewpoint (Robinson & Barret 1986).

As Michael Lamb notes, fathers contribute significantly to an infant's emotional growth, although the father's contributions are often quite different from the mother's. While the father is just as capable of taking care of an infant as is the mother, one of the father's chief roles (at least in our society) seems to be that of *playmate* to the child (Lamb 1981).

Lamb reports several studies suggesting that men are just as likely to nurture and stimulate their children as are the mothers. In fact, there is some evidence that fathers are more likely to hold their infants and to look at them than are the mothers. Furthermore, fathers are just as likely to interpret correctly the cues the infants give as are mothers. However, in most real-life settings, men are less likely to feed infants and change their diapers than are women. This difference in parental behaviors seems due to cultural roles, however, and not to innate differences in male-female "instincts" (Pleck, Lamb, & Levine 1985–1986).

T. Berry Brazelton and his colleagues at Harvard found that fathers talked to their infants less than did the mothers. However, the men were much more likely to touch or hug the child than were the women. The fathers primarily engaged in rough-and-tumble play with their children, while the mothers were more likely to play conventional games, such as peek-a-boo. Brazelton notes that "When several weeks old, an infant displays an entirely different attitude—more wide-eyed, playful, and bright-faced—toward its father than toward its mother." One explanation for this, Brazelton says, is that the fathers apparently *expect* more playful responses from their children. And the children then respond to the father's expectations (Brazelton 1986).

James V. McConnell, Understanding Human Behavior

Selection

2

GOVERNMENT

Shays' Rebellion. Massachusetts citizens rallied against high taxes during Shays' Rebellion in 1786. The uprising served to influence the framers of the Constitution.

© 1993 HarperCollins College Publishers

Stage 1: Preview

Preview the next selection to predict purpose, organization, and a learning plan.

Preview

Shays' Rebellion seems to refer to

_____

After reading this selection, I will need to know

_____

Activate Schema

Was the U.S. Constitution written on July 4, 1777?
Who wrote the Constitution?
Who signed the Constitution?

Learning Strategy
   Find out how Shays' Rebellion influenced the U.S. Constitution.

Word Knowledge
   *Review the ten vocabulary items that follow the selection. Seek an
   understanding of unfamiliar words.*

Stage 2: Integrate Knowledge While Reading
   *Since each reader interacts with material in a unique manner, it would
   be artificial to require certain thinking strategies to be used in certain
   places. As you read the following selection, make a note in the margin of
   at least one instance when you used each of the following strategies.*

   1. Predict 2. Picture 3. Relate 4. Monitor 5. Fix up

SHAYS' REBELLION AND THE CONSTITUTION

Fred Harris et al., *Understanding American Government*

What kind of system do we have? And how is it supposed to work?
These are the questions which we will consider. But, in order to
understand the system, we must first understand what was happening
when it was designed and what people were thinking. We need to
5 know more about the historical background which helped produce
the U.S. Constitution (a background in which Shays' Rebellion figures
prominently). How does the United States happen to have the
Constitution it has?
   The Declaration of Independence stated a set of political
10 principles. It did not attempt to establish a government to carry them
out. That practical task was taken up, at the state level, in written state
constitutions. At the national level, the form and workings of a central
government were first embodied in the Articles of Confederation and,
finally, in the U.S. Constitution.
15 Written constitutions all too often read the way marble feels—solid
and heavy, but cold and lifeless. They are the work of lawyers, who
choose their words and phrases cautiously to ensure precision of
meaning. This is certainly true of the United States Constitution.
Unlike the Declaration of Independence, which Thomas Jefferson
20 imbued with his passionate warmth, the Constitution is coldly
legalistic. It was the product of Jefferson's more cautious friend,
James Madison, and a committee dominated by men of legal training.
The contemporary reader, however, should not be led astray by the
style of the document. For like Jefferson and the Declaration of
25 Independence, the framers of the Constitution were feeling men, as

subject to fear, desire, love, and hate as any other individuals. When
they arrived in Philadelphia in the spring of 1787, they were charged
with a sense of mission. They wanted to save America from the
divisive forces which seemed to be tearing it apart.

30   For many of the Constitutional delegates, **Shays' Rebellion** was a
symbol of the nation's real and potential problems. Strains of greed,
suffering, anarchy, and violence ran through the Massachusetts
uprising. Certainly several of the delegates could not get the rebellion
out of their minds as they traveled slowly to Philadelphia. Thoughts of

35   the cold winter along the Connecticut River and Americans lying in
the snow disturbed their thoughts. As Revolutionary War hero Baron
von Steuben said, "When a whole people complains . . . something
must be wrong."

Complaints from Farmers

What was to become known as Shays' Rebellion began with honest,

40   heartfelt complaints. According to western farmers, Massachusetts had
become a rich man's state. Life throughout America was difficult
during the early 1780s, but the postwar depression and the terrible
monetary troubles seemed worse in western Massachusetts. Part of the
trouble was the state legislature, which met in Boston and was

45   dominated by representatives of eastern mercantile interests. "Thieves,
knaves, and robbers," complained one westerner, ran the Bay State.

There were solid grounds for their complaints. Farmers,
hardpressed to pay their taxes, demanded the acceptance of paper
money, but the eastern merchants and creditors defeated all soft

50   money plans. In fact, the Easterners pushed through a bill of their
own which called for the redemption of state wartime securities,
which they had purchased using inflated paper money, with hard
money. The act doubled the state debt and created a need for more
and heavier taxes.

55   Westerners shouldered the new taxes. A land tax placed duties on
land regardless of its value. An acre of rocky soil in the Berkshire
foothills was taxed at the same rate as an acre of prime Boston real
estate. In addition, a head tax demanded equal sums from the
wealthiest Boston shipping merchant and the poorest western farmer.

60   Every male over the age of sixteen had to pay the head tax. And to
add injury to insult, the tax had to be paid in hard money.

Even if they had wanted to pay—and they certainly did not—many
western farmers simply could not. Hard money during hard times,
they grumbled, was as difficult to come by as an honest lawyer. In

65   unprecedented numbers farmers fell into debt. Virginia, Connecticut,
and Delaware solved similar problems with "stay laws," which
suspended the payment of outstanding personal debts until economic

conditions improved. Other states turned to paper money, risking inflation but allowing farmers to save their farms. But the
70 Massachusetts legislature was not interested in imaginative plans to help Westerners. It wanted its taxes paid in hard money, and for those who couldn't pay, there were lawyers ready to foreclose and prisons for debtors.

These were no idle threats. Creditors and tax collectors forced
75 many men from central and western Massachusetts into debtor prison. In 1785–86 there were over four thousand suits for debt, twice as many as in the preceding two years. During the same period, the number of people imprisoned for debt increased more than one thousand percent. In fact, during 1786, debtors outnumbered all other
80 criminals in Worcester County prisons 3 to 1. By the middle 1780s, farmers were wondering just why and for whom they had fought a revolution.

They protested in a most legal and circumspect manner. They sent petitions to the legislature demanding redress. They called for
85 reduction of court and lawyers' fees, issuance of paper money, redistribution of the tax load, reduction of salaries for state officials, and other changes. They were as patient as poor men with their backs to the wall could be. But their petitions went unanswered and their patience unrewarded. And then their moods turned uglier, and talk of
90 violence became louder.

Mob Reaction
Local courts provided a logical target. As an historian of Shays' Rebellion noted, "A court that did not sit could not process foreclosures, pass judgments on debts, or confiscate property for defaulted taxes." In August, 1786, a mob of angry men "armed with
95 guns, swords, and other deadly weapons, and with drums beating and fifes playing" closed the county courthouse in Northhampton. During September and October similar mobs closed courts in Middlesex, Bristol, and Worcester counties. As winter drew nearer, sprigs of hemlock, the symbol of the rebel cause, adorned thousands of hats in
100 western Massachusetts.

Along the eastern seaboard of the Bay State, news of the mob successes caused fear and anger. Governor James Bowdoin condemned the "riot, anarchy, and confusion" and prepared to confront force with force. Using a public subscription of 5,000, he
105 raised an army drawn largely from the militia of the eastern counties. In command of the army he placed Major General Benjamin Lincoln, a Revolutionary veteran noted as much for his humanity as his military leadership.

Daniel Shays

In the western part of the state, new leaders were also emerging. The most famous was Daniel Shays. Although the rebellion would eventually be linked with his name, he did not start the conflict. In fact, he was a moderate, considerate man, slow to anger and reluctant to take up arms. Like many of his followers, he was hit hard by the postwar depression and the rising taxes. Similarly, like many of his followers, he had served his country during the Revolution, facing the Red Coats at Bunker Hill, Ticonderoga, Saratoga, and Stony Point. Promoted to captain, he proved a brave and efficient officer. Toward the end of the war, the Marquis de Lafayette presented a handsome sword to Shays for his service. But debt had forced him to sell the sword, and poverty had convinced him to join the rebel cause.

Winter came early and hard. Blizzards swept the land and temperatures fell to as low as thirty degrees below zero. Snowdrifts as high as the tallest rebels formed along the Connecticut River. But the weather did not stop the revolutionary activities. In January, 1787, the rebellion became more focused. The Hampshire County Court was scheduled to meet in Springfield in late January. Springfield was also the site of a federal arsenal, and without arms and gunpowder the rebellion was doomed. And so to Springfield Shays and his army moved. Waiting there was General William Shepard, commander of the arsenal's garrison.

Shays and several other rebel leaders planned a coordinated attack, which they scheduled for January 25. On the appointed day, Shays launched a frontal assault on the arsenal. Due to bad communication, however, he received no support from the other leaders. Shepard was prepared for the attack. He fired two warning cannon shots. Shays' force of 1,200 men kept coming. Shepard ordered the third volley to be fired into the rebels. Three rebels fell dead, a fourth was mortally wounded. The rest turned and ran. The battle was over.

As the battle was ending, General Lincoln arrived in Springfield. He quickly moved north after the fleeing rebels. On the night of February 2, he marched his men the thirty miles between Holiday and Petersham in a blinding snowstorm. He was able to catch Shays' forces unguarded and destroy the rebel army. By the end of February, what the legislature had condemned as a "horrid and unnatural Rebellion and war . . . traitorously raised and levied against the Commonwealth" was over.

Had the rebellion accomplished anything? Yes. Although Shays' Rebellion caused little destruction of property or loss of life, its impact was widely felt. In the spring elections Massachusetts citizens voted into office a government sympathetic to the farmers' plight. It pardoned the rebels and enacted a more equitable tax system. Perhaps more important, Shays' Rebellion gave a sense of urgency to

the Spring Constitutional Convention in Philadelphia. When he saw
the document that emerged from Philadelphia, Thomas Jefferson
155 remarked, "our convention has been too much impressed by the
insurrection of Massachusetts." Was Jefferson correct? What parts of
the Constitution might have been written with the Rebellion in mind?
Does the Constitution provide safeguards against future rebellions?

The Constitutional Convention of 1787

The Convention which was called to order in the Philadelphia State
160 House—now called Independence Hall—in the spring of 1787 did
not confine its work to proposing revisions in the Articles of
Confederation, which would have required approval by all thirteen of
the state legislatures. Instead, the delegates chose a vastly more
sweeping undertaking: they decided to write a new constitution. They
165 agreed to submit it to popularly elected state conventions for
ratification, not to the state legislatures, as had been done with the
Articles. Thus, the delegates had to be mindful of what the voters
would accept. In addition, the delegates decided that the new
constitution would go into effect only when nine of the thirteen states
170 had approved it.

The Delegates and Their Motives

The Convention was able to agree on writing a wholly new
Constitution partly because a number of those who could have been
counted on to oppose it—men such as Richard Henry Lee, who had
made the motion for independence in the Second Continental
175 Congress, and Patrick Henry, whose oratory had helped win
Americans to the Revolutionary cause—were not present. Henry had
refused to be a delegate because, he said, "I smelt a rat"—meaning
he suspected that there would be an attempt to make the national
government stronger than he thought advisable. (Both Henry and Lee
180 were among those who later opposed the ratification of the
Constitution, but by then it was too late.)

Seven of those who did attend the Constitutional Convention had
been signers of the Declaration of Independence. Thomas Jefferson
was not at the Convention because he had gone to France as U.S.
185 Ambassador to that country. Washington and Benjamin Franklin were
among the best known of the Revolutionary leaders present.
Washington, 55 years old, was unanimously chosen to chair the
proceedings. Franklin, at 81 the oldest delegate, was a philosopher
and statesman of world renown. Because of his age, Franklin's
190 speeches had to be read to the Convention by James Wilson. His
discourses were listened to attentively, as was his counsel, although
on most issues Franklin was willing to accord more power to the
people than were most of the delegates. A number of the delegates

195 were fairly young. Hamilton was thirty. A majority of the delegates
were college graduates.

The man we now think of as the "father of his country," George
Washington, might not have taken part in the writing of our
Constitution if not for Shays' Rebellion. Washington had been elected
by the Virginia legislature as a delegate to the constitutional
200 convention in Philadelphia but had not planned to go. He felt that in
leading the Revolutionary War army he had done enough. But
Washington had long felt that the nation's government needed to be
strengthened, particularly to maintain order, and the news of Shays'
Rebellion confirmed him in this view. He decided to go to the
205 Philadelphia convention after all, and help write a new constitution
for America.

A **constitution** is the fundamental and supreme law of a society.
Governments are based upon rules or guidelines that determine how
they are organized and what powers they have. These rules matter
210 because they define the relationship among the people in a society;
they determine what each person is entitled to expect from the
others—and from the government. And no rules matter more than
those embodied in a nation's constitution. Ours is a written
constitution, all in one document (unlike the constitution of Great
215 Britain, which is a partly written, partly unwritten body of various
declarations, statutes, practices, and precedents).

But just because a constitution is written does not necessarily mean
that it will be followed and enforced. Some countries have
constitutions that have not proven to be reliable guarantees against
220 illegal takeovers and rule of force. If a nation's constitution is to be
effective in restraining government and protecting citizens' rights, it
must enjoy general respect and support from the citizens of the
country. Ours does. It is the oldest living written constitution in the
world, 200 years old in 1987.

Stage 3: Recall

Stop to self-test and relate to issues.

Skill Development

Write the answers to the following questions on your own paper.

1. What is the author's overall pattern for organizing this selection?
2. In the section titled, "Daniel Shays," what is the overall pattern of
organization?
3. What is the main idea of the section titled, "Daniel Shays"?

4. What is the main idea of the section titled, "The Delegates and Their Motives"?
5. What is the pattern of organization for the next to the last paragraph, beginning "A constitution is . . ."?

Comprehension Questions

1. Who or what is the topic of this selection? _____

   What is the main idea the author is trying to convey about the topic?

   _____

After reading the selection, answer the following questions with *a, b, c,* or *d.*

_____ 2. The author of the Declaration of Independence was
  a. Thomas Jefferson.
  b. James Madison.
  c. George Washington.
  d. Benjamin Franklin.

_____ 3. The "western farmers" in this selection were from
  a. Boston.
  b. west of the Mississippi.
  c. the western part of Massachusetts.
  d. Virginia and Delaware.

_____ 4. The western farmers objected to all of the following acts of the legislature except
  a. the head tax.
  b. the land tax.
  c. taxes paid in hard money.
  d. "stay laws."

_____ 5. The author suggests that the first targets of the rebels were the county courthouses because
  a. legislators would listen to the courts.
  b. court and lawyers' fees were too high.
  c. closed courts could not process foreclosures.
  d. increased taxes supported court officials.

_____ 6. The "Bay State" refers to
  a. Virginia.
  b. Massachusetts.
  c. Connecticut.
  d. Delaware.

_____ 7. The purpose of Shays' attack on Springfield was
  a. to defeat General Lincoln.
  b. to gain a stronghold on the Connecticut River.
  c. to get arms and gunpowder for the rebels.
  d. to move the state militia out of the eastern counties.

_____ 8. The main purpose of a constitution is to declare
   a. freedom.
   b. equal voting rights.
   c. the powers of the government.
   d. the rate of taxation by the states.

_____ 9. Ratification of the U.S. Constitution required approval by
   a. all thirteen state legislatures.
   b. nine state legislatures.
   c. thirteen elected state conventions.
   d. nine elected state conventions.

_____ 10. The author suggests that Shays' Rebellion dramatized the need for
   a. stronger states' rights.
   b. increased power for the national government.
   c. the Declaration of Independence.
   d. taxation for the rich and poor.

Answer the following with *T* (true) or *F* (false).

_____ 11. States other than Massachusetts devised inventive plans to help the farmers save their property.

_____ 12. The western farmers did not engage in any formal protest with the legislature prior to Shays' Rebellion.

_____ 13. Sprigs of holly were used in Massachusetts to symbolize the rebel cause.

_____ 14. Prior to the Constitution the national government had no national military to maintain order.

_____ 15. Patrick Henry was against the ratification of the Constitution.

Vocabulary

According to the way the italicized word was used in the selection, indicate *a, b, c,* or *d* for the word or phrase that gives the best definition.

____ 1. "*ensure* precision of meaning" (17)
   a. hope for
   b. demand
   c. guarantee
   d. read with

____ 2. "*imbued* with his passionate warmth" (20)
   a. wrote
   b. filled
   c. united
   d. overburdened

____ 3. "*divisive* forces" (29)
   a. divided by disagreement
   b. unequal
   c. sly
   d. unsympathetic

____ 4. "*redemption* of state wartime securities" (51)
   a. cancellation
   b. increased interest rate
   c. pay off
   d. default

___ 5. "no *idle* threats" (74)
a. insignificant
b. evil
c. helpful
d. legal

___ 6. "*petitions* went unanswered" (88)
a. messengers
b. letters
c. farmers
d. appeals

___ 7. "*insurrection* of Massachusetts" (156)
a. debate
b. argument
c. revolt
d. politics

___ 8. "conventions for *ratification*" (165)
a. approval
b. election
c. clarification
d. signatures

___ 9. "*accord* more power" (192)
a. deny
b. lessen
c. intervene
d. grant

___ 10. "*embodied* in a nation's constitution" (213)
a. voted
b. incorporated
c. sold
d. imagined

Written Response

Use information from the text to answer the following:

Describe how Shays' Rebellion changed the governmental system of the United States.

Response Strategy: Describe the cause and effect relationship between the rebellion and the issues addressed in the U.S. Constitution.

Connecting and Reflecting

The U.S. Constitution has been amended only twenty-six times in its more than 200 years of life. Suppose a twenty-seventh amendment were now before Congress and ready for a vote. Pretend that you are adamant about this amendment, which states that the President of the United States does not have to be born in the United States. Write a letter to your senator in support of or in opposition to this amendment. Explain at least three reasons why you support or oppose it.

Read the following passage for an explanation of how amendments are ratified and a list of the constitutional amendments passed in the twentieth century.

Amending the Constitution

An amendment to the Constitution (or a completely new constitution) may be *proposed* either by a two-thirds vote in both the House and Senate or by a new constitutional convention called by Congress on the application of two-thirds of the state legislatures. All of the amendments adopted to date were proposed by a two-thirds vote of Congress. No new constitutional convention has ever been held. From time to time, a number of one-issue movements, such as the antiabortion group called Americans for a Constitutional Convention, have unsuccessfully advocated a new constitutional convention to deal with their favorite cause.

Once an amendment (or a new constitution) has been proposed, it may be *ratified* in one of two ways decided upon by Congress: by approval of three-fourths of the state legislatures; or by approval of three-fourths of the ratification conventions called for that purpose in each of the states. The state convention method has been used only once (in the ratification of the Twenty-first Amendment in 1933 for the repeal of Prohibition).

Sixteenth Amendment: Giving Congress the power to levy an income tax (1913).

Seventeenth Amendment: Providing for the direct popular election of U.S. Senators (1913).

Eighteenth Amendment: Prohibiting the manufacture, sale, and transportation of intoxicating liquors (1919).

Nineteenth Amendment: Guaranteeing the right of women to vote (1920).

Twentieth Amendment: Changing the beginning of the President's term to January 20 (instead of March 4) and that of the Congress to January 3 (1933).

Twenty-First Amendment: Repealing the Eighteenth Amendment on prohibition (1933).

Twenty-Second Amendment: Limiting the President to two terms (1951).

Twenty-Third Amendment: Giving residents of the District of Columbia the right to vote in presidential elections (1961).

Twenty-Fourth Amendment: Prohibiting the poll tax in federal elections (1964).

Twenty-Fifth Amendment: Providing for filling a vacancy in the office of Vice-President, establishing procedure for determining when the President is unable to discharge the duties of the office, and listing the line of succession (1967).

Twenty-Sixth Amendment: Guaranteeing the right to vote to those eighteen years of age or older (1971).

Fred Harris et al., *Understanding American Government*

Selection **3**

ANTHROPOLOGY

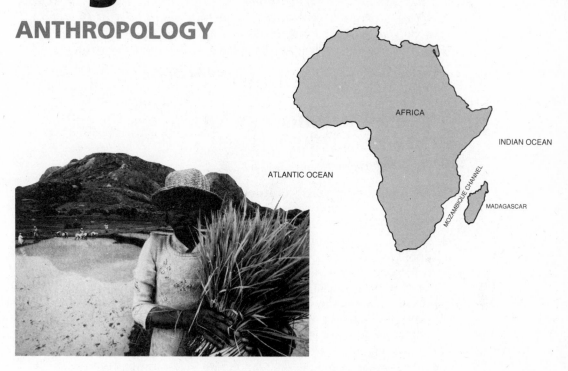

Stage 1: Preview

Preview the next selection to predict purpose, organization, and a learning plan.

Preview

The Betsileo live in _____

After reading this selection, I will need to know

_____

Activate Schema

How do isolated cultural groups without refrigeration share protein?

Learning Strategy

Be able to describe the Betsileo economy, family, and ceremonies.

Word Knowledge

Review the ten vocabulary items that follow the selection. Seek an understanding of unfamiliar words.

Stage 2: Integrate Knowledge While Reading

Since each reader interacts with material in a unique manner, it would be artificial to require certain thinking strategies to be used in certain places. As you read the following selection, make a note in the margin of at least one instance when you used each of the following strategies.

1. Predict 2. Picture 3. Relate 4. Monitor 5. Fix up

AN ETHNOGRAPHIC VIEW OF BETSILEO CULTURE

From Conrad, *Anthropology*

How Ethnographers Study Cultures
Ethnographers don't study animals in laboratory cages. The experiments that psychologists do with pigeons, chickens, guinea pigs, and rats are very different from ethnographic procedure. Anthropologists don't systematically control subjects' rewards and
5 punishments or their exposure to certain stimuli. Our subjects are not speechless animals but human beings. It is not part of ethnographic procedure to manipulate them, control their environments, or experimentally induce certain behaviors.

One of ethnography's characteristic procedures is *participant*
10 *observation,* which means that we take part in community life as we study it. As human beings living among others, we cannot be totally impartial and detached observers. We must also take part in many of the events and processes we are observing and trying to comprehend. During the fourteen months I lived in Madagascar, for example, I
15 simultaneously observed and participated in many occasions in Betsileo life. I helped out at harvest time, joining other people who climbed atop—in order to stamp down on and compact— accumulating stacks of rice stalks. One September, for a reburial ceremony, I bought a silk shroud for a village ancestor. I entered the
20 village tomb and watched people lovingly rewrap the bones and decaying flesh of their ancestors. I accompanied Betsileo peasants to town and to market. I observed their dealings with outsiders and sometimes offered help when problems arose.

Agricultural Methods

Food   For the Betsileo of Madagascar, there is no way of saying "to
25 eat" without saying "to eat rice," their favorite and staple food. So strong is their preference for rice that they garnish it with beans, potatoes, and other starches. Eels cooked in their own grease are a

delicacy for the Betsileos' honored visitors, a category in which I
feared being included because of my cultural aversion to eel meat
30 (although I did tolerate grasshoppers cooked in peanut oil; they
tasted like peanuts). In northeastern Brazil I grew to like chicken
cooked in its own blood, a favorite there.

The Rice Fields   The Betsileo of central Madagascar (Kottak 1980)
sow rice in nursery beds. When the seedlings get big enough, they
35 are transplanted into flooded rice fields. Before transplanting, the
Betsileo till and flood their fields. Cattle are brought to trample the
prepared fields just before transplanting. Young men yell at and beat
the cattle, striving to drive them into a frenzy so that they will trample
the fields properly. Trampling breaks up clumps of earth and mixes
40 irrigation water with soil to form a smooth mud into which women
transplant seedlings. Like many other agriculturalists, the Betsileo
collect manure from their animals, using it to fertilize their plots, thus
increasing the yield.

Irrigation   While horticulturalists must await the rainy season,
45 agriculturalists can schedule their planting in advance, because they
control water. The Betsileo irrigate their fields with canals from rivers,
streams, springs, and ponds. Irrigation makes it possible to cultivate a
plot year after year. Irrigation enriches the soil because the irrigated
field is a unique ecosystem with several species of plants and animals,
50 many of them minute organisms, whose wastes fertilize the land.
    An irrigated field is a capital investment that increases in value. It
takes time for a field to start yielding; it reaches full productivity only
after several years of cultivation. The Betsileo, like other irrigators,
have farmed the same fields for generations. In some agricultural
55 areas, including the Middle East, however, salts carried in the
irrigation water can make fields unusable after fifty or sixty years.

Terracing   Terracing is another agricultural technique that the
Betsileo have mastered. Central Madagascar has small valleys
separated by steep hillsides. Because the population is dense, people
60 need to farm the hills. However, if they simply planted on the steep
hillsides, fertile soil and crops would be washed away during the
rainy season. To prevent this, the Betsileo, like the rice-farming Ifugao
of the Philippines, cut into the hillside and build stage after stage of
terraced fields rising above the valley floor. Springs located above the
65 terraces supply their irrigation water. The labor necessary to build and
maintain a system of terraces is great. Terrace walls crumble each year
and must be partially rebuilt. The canals that bring water down
through the terraces also demand attention.

The Family

Marriage   The household is the main productive unit. The more
wives, the more workers. Increased productivity means more wealth.
This wealth in turn attracts additional wives. Wealth and wives bring
greater prestige to the household and head. In many societies, the
first wife requests a second wife to help with household chores. The
second wife's status is lower than that of the first; they are senior and
junior wives. The senior wife sometimes chooses the junior one from
among her close kinswomen.

Among the Betsileo of Madagascar, the different wives always lived
in different villages. A man's first and senior wife, called "Big Wife,"
lived in the village where he cultivated his best rice field and spent
most of his time. However, the Betsileo inherit from several different
ancestors and cultivate different areas. High-status men with several
rice fields had households near each field. They spent most of their
time with the senior wife but visited the others occasionally
throughout the year.

Children   Among the world's cultures, infanticide may be overt or
covert. When there is another small child or many children in the
family, if a baby is not killed at birth, it is often neglected until it
dies. This is covert infanticide.

If the baby survives, the mother may change her strategy and begin
to invest more in its care, particularly if it shows culturally valued
characteristics (Scheper-Hughes 1987). Most cultures that practice
overt infanticide justify it by excluding newborn babies from their
definition of human life.

The ancestors of the Betsileo of Madagascar, whom I studied in
1966–1967, practiced occasional infanticide. Their culture did not
define it as murder, because in the Betsileo view it takes several years
for a child to become fully human. Parental and social investment
gradually increases as the child survives and matures.

Even today, although infanticide has ended, the Betsileo do not
define a baby as fully human. When a baby is born, an astrologer
calculates its lifetime horoscope. Formerly, when the horoscope was
unlucky or seemed to threaten the parents or the group, the infant
could be subjected to a death ordeal. It was placed at the entrance to
the cattle corral, where it was likely to be trampled by livestock
returning in the evening. If it survived, it was assumed to have
positive qualities that offset its apparent negative destiny.

Although infanticide has ended, the process by which a Betsileo
child grows into a human being (the acquisition of personhood) is
still gradual. During the first two years of its life, people call the baby
such derogatory names as "little dog," "slave," and "pile of feces." By

devaluing the child in this way, the Betsileo think they are increasing
its chances for survival. They are trying to divert ancestral spirits who
might want to seize the child for the spirit world. The American
anthropologist, whom a different culture has trained to say, "Oh, how
115   cute," must repress the urge to compliment a baby and produce an
insult instead. If a Betsileo baby dies during its first two years, it is
buried in the rice fields. Until adolescence, it can be buried in the
children's tomb. Only in adolescence does it acquire full personhood
and the right to a place in the ancestral tomb, which has tremendous
120   cultural significance in Betsileo culture.

Ceremonies

Ancestral Tombs   The Betsileo live in dispersed hamlets and
villages. Hamlets begin as small settlements with two or three
households. Over time many grow into villages. All the settlements
have ancestral tombs, which are very important in Betsileo culture. It
125   costs much more to build a tomb than to build a house. It's right to
spend more on the tomb, say the Betsileo, because one spends
eternity in it. A house is only a temporary home.
       Betsileo may be buried in the same tomb as any one of their eight
great-grandparents. When a woman has children, she also earns burial
130   rights in her husband's tomb. Most men belong to their father's
descent group, live in his village, and will be buried in his tomb.
Nevertheless, Betsileo attend ceremonies at all their ancestral tombs,
in all of which they have burial rights.
       After the annual rice harvest in April and May comes the ceremonial
135   season, when agricultural work is least taxing. Ceremonies honor the
ancestors as the Betsileo open the tombs. Sometimes they simply
rewrap corpses and bones in new shrouds. Sometimes, in more
elaborate ceremonies, they take the bodies and bones outside, dance
with them, wrap them in new cloth, and return them to the tomb.
140   Whenever a tomb is built, bodies and bones are moved in from an
older family tomb.
       During their ceremonies, the Betsileo kill cattle. They offer a small
part of the beef to the ancestors; living people eat the rest. After
offering meat to the ancestors, people remove it from the altar and
145   eat it as well. The custom of cattle sacrifice developed at a time when
there were no markets and the Betsileo lived in small hamlets. At that
time, ceremonial distribution was the Betsileo's only source of beef.
It was not feasible to slaughter and eat an entire animal in a small
hamlet, because there were too few people to consume it. Nor could
150   the Betsileo buy meat in markets. They got beef by attending
ceremonials in villages where they had kinship, descent, and marriage
links.

Funerals   Betsileo also kill cattle for funerals. Again, some beef is dedicated to the ancestors but eaten by the living. People attend the
155 funerals of neighbors, kin, in-laws, and fictive kin. Because funerals occur throughout the year, the Betsileo eat beef and thus obtain animal protein regularly. However, although people can die at any time, Betsileo deaths cluster in certain seasons—especially November to February, the rainy season. This is a period of food shortages, when
160 much of the rice harvested the previous April has been eaten. Many funerals, occasions on which beef and rice are distributed, occur at precisely the time of year (the preharvest season of food scarcity) when people are hungriest. In Betsileo cultural adaptation, funerals distribute food beyond the local group and to the poorest people,
165 helping them survive the lean season.

     Today, settlements are larger and the Betsileo have markets. Ceremonies persist, but there are fewer big postharvest feasts than there once were. Naturally, any discussion of the adaptive functions of Betsileo religion raises the question whether the Betsileo created the
170 ceremonies because they recognized their potential adaptive usefulness. The answer is no, but the question is instructive.

     The Betsileo maintain these rituals because they honor, commemorate, or appease ancestors, relatives, fictive kin, in-laws, and neighbors. The tomb ceremonies serve many of the social and
175 psychological functions of religion. However, although Betsileo receive invitations to several ceremonies each year, they don't attend them all. What determines the individual's decision to attend? If a distant relative or acquaintance dies when people are eating well, they may decide not to go or to send someone junior in their place.
180 However, if an equally distant relative dies during the season of scarcity, many Betsileo, especially poorer people, opt for a day or two of feasting. Some of my Betsileo friends, usually those with small rice fields, became funeral hoppers during the lean season. They used a series of personal connections to attend every available funeral and
185 ceremony. Betsileo ceremonies do not simply maintain social solidarity. They also play a role in cultural adaptation by regulating access to strategic resources, including the nutrients that people need to resist disease and infection and to survive (Kottak 1980).

Stage 3: Recall

Stop to self-test and relate to issues.

Skill Development: Summarizing

Using this selection as a source, summarize on index cards the information that you might want to include in a research paper entitled "Polygamy: Reasons and Reality."

Main Idea

Write the answers to the following questions on your own paper.

1. What is the main idea the author is trying to convey in the first two paragraphs?
2. What is the overall pattern of organization in the first two paragraphs?
3. What is the main idea the author is trying to convey in the section entitled "Children"?
4. What is the overall pattern of organization in the section entitled "Food"?
5. What is the main idea the author is trying to convey in the last paragraph?
6. What is the overall pattern of organization in the last paragraph?

Comprehension Questions

1. Who or what is the topic of this selection? _____

   What is the main idea the author trying to convey about the topic?

   _____

After reading the selection, answer the following questions with *a, b, c,* or *d.*

_____ 2. Ethnographers
   a. study chickens and rats in laboratories.
   b. manipulate rewards and punishments for their subjects.
   c. participate in the community under observation.
   d. induce certain community behaviors for observation.

_____ 3. The agricultural technique of terracing is used to
   a. prevent soil erosion.
   b. distinguish farm ownership.
   c. bring organisms to the soil.
   d. restrict animals to the fields.

_____ 4. All of the following are true about the irrigated fields of the Betsileo except
   a. planting can be scheduled in advance.
   b. irrigation enriches the fields with minute organisms.
   c. it takes a few years to reach maximum yield.
   d. salts in the irrigation waters have made some fields immediately unusable.

_____ 5. The author implies that among the Betsileo the first wife usually views a second wife in the family as
  a. a threat to authority.
  b. a household helper.
  c. a drain on limited wealth.
  d. a loss of prestige.

_____ 6. The Betsileo devalue children during the first two years of life because they believe such an attitude will
  a. enhance chances of survival.
  b. improve predicted horoscopes.
  c. replace covert infanticide.
  d. prevent murder.

_____ 7. The author states that a greater number of Betsileo deaths occur during
  a. the annual rice harvest.
  b. the rainy season.
  c. rice planting.
  d. June, July, and August.

_____ 8. The author implies that the Betsileo who are most likely to attend the most funerals
  a. are poor.
  b. have many close relatives.
  c. have strong family ties.
  d. sacrifice in order to attend.

_____ 9. The ancestral tombs of the Betsileo
  a. contain the bodies of young children.
  b. are opened for ceremonies honoring the dead.
  c. are built for burial of only one generation of family members.
  d. are used to store grain during the rainy season.

_____ 10. The author implies that the Betsileo created the burial rituals
  a. in order to save food.
  b. to resist disease and infection.
  c. to honor the dead.
  d. to keep meat from spoiling.

Answer the following with *T* (true) or *F* (false).

_____ 11. The Betsileo use cattle to create mud in the rice fields.
_____ 12. The staple food of the Betsileo is rice.
_____ 13. The Betsileo still engage in infanticide.
_____ 14. After a Betsileo ceremony, uneaten meat is sealed in the tomb as a sacrifice for the ancestors.
_____ 15. The author feels that larger villages and available markets have reduced the adaptive need for Betsileo ceremonial feasts.

Vocabulary

According to the way the italicized word was used in the selection, select *a, b, c,* or *d* for the word or phrase that gives the best definition.

—— 1. "*detached* observers" (12)
    a. unnoticed
    b. unfeeling
    c. unknown
    d. unscientific

—— 2. "cultural *aversion* to eel" (29)
    a. allergy
    b. custom
    c. habit
    d. dislike

—— 3. "infanticide may be *overt*" (85)
    a. open
    b. accidental
    c. sneaky
    d. hostile

—— 4. "*covert* infanticide" (88)
    a. illegal
    b. concealed
    c. within the family
    d. inhumane

—— 5. "pile of *feces*" (110)
    a. dirt
    b. excrement
    c. garbage
    d. filth

—— 6. "*dispersed* hamlets" (121)
    a. diseased
    b. small
    c. scattered
    d. primitive

—— 7. "least *taxing*" (135)
    a. tiring
    b. commercial
    c. rewarding
    d. important

—— 8. "*feasible* to slaughter" (148)
    a. lucky
    b. possible
    c. traditional
    d. adaptive

—— 9. "*opt* for a day" (181)
    a. wish
    b. hint
    c. travel
    d. choose

—— 10. "social *solidarity*" (185)
    a. entrance
    b. unity
    c. resources
    d. strategy

Written Response

Use information from the text to answer the following question:
Explain the culturally adaptive functions of the Betsileo ceremonies.

Response Strategy: Describe the ceremonies and explain how they help the people survive so that the culture continues.

Connecting and Reflecting

Anthropologists describe infanticide in primitive cultures, but they do not make judgments. **How do you think an anthropologist, writing a hundred years from now, would describe abortion in our own culture?** (1) From the perspective of a future anthropologist, write a paragraph describing the function of abortion in modern culture. (2) Next, state your own opinion on abortion. (3) Finally, explain three reasons for your position.

Read the following passage about the Yanomamo of Brazil for another example of an anthropologist's description of infanticide.

The Yanomamo

Feuding and warfare appear to be constant in many tribal societies. Among the Yanomamo intertribal hostility and warfare are almost a way of life. Yanomamo villages organize and conduct war parties against one another not for land, but to steal each other's women. In a Yanomamo raid, as many men as possible are killed, and as many women as possible are captured. According to their ethnographer, Chagnon (1983), the constant warfare and militant ideology of the Yanomamo are a way of preserving village autonomy. Because the Yanomamo have not been able to control conflict within villages, fights often break out among individuals. This leads to the division of villages into independent and hostile camps. In order to be able to survive as an independent unit in an environment of constant warfare, members of a village adopt a hostile and aggressive stance toward other villagers. Yanomamo aggressiveness is encouraged from childhood and reinforced by a cultural pattern that demands a display of ferocity on the part of males. This ferocity is demonstrated not only in the fights between men but also in the way husbands treat their wives.

Warfare among the Yanomamo, as well as among other horticultural groups, has been explained as a way of controlling population. Divale and Harris (1976) argue that war regulates population indirectly by leading to female infanticide, not by causing deaths in battle. In societies where warfare is constant, there is a cultural preference for fierce and aggressive males who can become warriors. Because male children are preferred over females, female infants are frequently killed. Among the Yanomamo, the shortage of women that results from female infanticide appears as a strong *conscious* motivation for warfare, thus providing a continuing "reason" for the Yanomamo to keep fighting among themselves. In the absence of effective contraception and abortion, the most effective and widespread means of regulating population growth is reducing the number of fertile females.

Serena Nanda, *Cultural Anthropology*

WORD BRIDGE

Structure

What is the longest word in the English language and what does it mean? Maxwell Nurnberg and Morris Rosenblum in *How to Build a Better Vocabulary* (Prentice-Hall, Inc. 1949) say that at one time the longest word in Webster's *New International Dictionary* was

pneumonoultramicroscopicsilicovolcanokoniosis

Look at the word again and notice the smaller and more familiar word parts. Do you know enough of the smaller parts to figure out the meaning of the word? Nurnberg and Rosenblum unlock the meaning as follows:

pneumono: pertaining to the lungs, as in *pneu*monia
ultra: beyond, as in *ultra*violet rays
micro: small, as in *micro*scope
scopic: from the root of Greek verb *skopein,* to view or look at
silico: from the element *silicon,* found in quartz, flint, and sand
volcano: the meaning of this is obvious
koni: the principal root, from a Greek word for dust
osis: a suffix indicating illness, as trichin*osis*

Now, putting the parts together again, we deduce that *pneumonoultra-microscopicsilicovolcanokoniosis* is a disease of the lungs caused by extremely small particles of volcanic ash and dust.

This dramatic example demonstrates how an extremely long and technical word can become more manageable by breaking it into smaller parts. The same is true with many of the smaller words that we use every day. A knowledge of word parts will help you unlock the meaning of literally thousands of words. One vocabulary expert identified a list of thirty prefixes, roots, and suffixes and claims that knowing these thirty word parts will help unlock the meaning to 14,000 words.

Words, like people, have families and, in some cases, an abundance of close relations. Clusters, or what might be called *word families,* are comprised of words with the same base or root. For example, *bio* is a root meaning *life.* If you know that *biology* means *the study of life,* it becomes easy to figure out the definition of a word like *biochemistry.* Word parts form new words as follows:

prefix + root   root + suffix   prefix + root + suffix

Prefixes and suffixes are added to root words to change the meaning. A prefix is added to the beginning of a word and a suffix is added to the end. For example, the prefix *il* means *not*. When added to the word *legal*, the resulting word, *illegal*, becomes the opposite of the original. Suffixes can change the meaning or change the way the word can be used in a sentence. The suffix *cide* means to *kill*. When added to *frater* which means *brother*, the resulting word, *fratricide*, means to *kill one's brother*. Adding *ity* or *ize* to *frater* changes both the meaning and the way the word can be used grammatically in a sentence.

To demonstrate how prefixes, roots, and suffixes overlap and make families, start with the root *gamy*, meaning *marriage*, and ask some questions.

1. What is the state of having only one wife called? _____
   (*mono* means *one*)
2. What is a man who has two wives called? _____
   (*bi* means *two* and *ist* means *one who*)
3. What is a man who has many wives called? _____
   (*poly* means *many*)
4. What is a woman who has many husbands called? _____
   (*andry* means *man*)
5. What is a hater of marriage called? _____
   (*miso* means *hater of*)

In several of the *gamy* examples, the letters change slightly to accommodate language sounds. Such variations of a letter or two are typical when working with word parts. Letters are often dropped or added to maintain the rhythm of the language, but the meaning of the word part remains the same regardless of the change in spelling. For example, the prefix *con* means *with* or *together* as in *conduct*. This same prefix is used with variations in many other words:

  cooperate   collection   correlate   communicate   connect

Thus, *con, co, col, cor,* and *com* are all forms of the prefix that means *with* or *together*.

Exercise 7: Word Families

Create your own word families from the word parts that are supplied. For each of the following definitions, supply a prefix, root, or suffix to make the appropriate word.

Prefix: *bi* means *two*

1. able to speak two languages: bi _____

2. having two feet, like humans: bi _____

3. representing two political parties: bi _____

4. occurs at two-year intervals: bi _____

5. having two lenses on one glass: bi _____

6. cut into two parts: bi _____

7. mathematics expression with two terms: bi _____

8. instrument with two eyes: bi _____

9. tooth with two points: bi _____

10. coming twice a year: bi _____

Root: *vert* means *to turn*

1. to change one's beliefs: _____ vert

2. to go back to old ways again: _____ vert

3. a car with a removable top: _____ vert _____

4. to change the direction of a stream: _____ vert

5. activities intended to undermine or destroy: _____ vers _____

6. an outgoing, gregarious person: _____ vert

7. a quiet, introspective, shy person: _____ vert

8. conditions that are turned against you; misfortune:

   _____ vers _____

9. one who deviates from normal behavior, especially sexual: _____ vert

10. one who is sometimes introspective and sometimes gregarious:

    _____ vert

Suffix: *ism* means *doctrine, condition,* or *characteristic.*

1. addiction to alcoholic drink: _____ ism

2. a brave and courageous manner of acting: _____ ism

3. doctrine of the fascists of Germany: _____ ism

4. doctrine concerned only with fact and reality: _____ ism

5. system using terror to intimidate: _____ ism

6. using someone's words as your own: _____ ism

7. driving out an evil spirit: _____ ism

8. purification to join the church: _____ ism

9. informal style of speech using slang: _____ ism

10. characteristic of one region of the country: _____ ism

Exercise 8: Prefixes, Roots, and Suffixes

Using the prefix, root, or suffix provided, write the words that best fit the following definitions.

1. *con* means *with*

   infectious or catching: con _____

2. *contra* means *against*

   to speak against another's statement: contra _____

3. *post* means *after*

   to delay or set back: post _____

4. *psych* means *mind*

   a physician who studies the mind: psych _____

5. *pel* means *drive* or *push*

   to push out of school: _____ pell

6. *therma* means *heat*

   device for regulating furnace heat: therm _____

7. *ven* means *come*

   a meeting for people to come together: _____ ven _____

8. *rupt* means *break* or *burst*

   a volcanic explosion: _____ rupt _____

9. *meter* means *measure*

   instrument to measure pressure: _____ meter

10. *naut* means *voyager*

    voyager in the sea: _____ naut

CHAPTER 4

ORGANIZING TEXTBOOK INFORMATION

- What is a knowledge network?
- What is annotating?
- What is notetaking?
- What is outlining?
- What is mapping?

THE DEMANDS OF COLLEGE STUDY

Your first assignment in most college courses will be to read Chapter 1 of the appointed textbook, at which time you will immediately discover that a textbook chapter contains an amazing amount of information. Your instructor will continue to make similar assignments designating the remaining chapters in rapid succession. Your problem is to select the information that needs to be remembered and organize it to facilitate future study. In many cases, future study could be for a midterm or a final exam that might be several weeks or months away.

In a recent study, three researchers looked at the demands on students in several introductory college history courses.[1] They observed classes for a ten-week period and analyzed the actual reading demands, finding that students were asked to read an average of 825 pages in each class over the ten-week period. The average length of weekly assignments was over 80 pages, but the amount varied both with the professor and the topic. In one class, students had to read 287 pages in only ten days.

College professors expected students to be able to see relationships between parts and wholes, to place people and events into a historical context, and to retain facts. Professors spent 85 percent of the class time lecturing and 6 percent of the time testing. Interaction was surprisingly limited. Student-student exchanges occurred 4 percent of the time in the only class that broke into groups, and student-instructor exchanges occurred a meager 2 1/2 percent of the average class time. However, students were expected to organize textbook material efficiently and effectively to prepare for that crucial 6 percent of test-taking time.

BUILDING KNOWLEDGE NETWORKS

The old notion of studying and learning is that studying is an information-gathering activity. Knowledge is the "product" and the student acquires "it" by transferring information from the text to memory. With this view, good learners locate important information, review it, and then transfer the information into long-term memory. The problem with this model is that review does not always guarantee recall, and rehearsal is not always enough to ensure that information is encoded into long-term memory.

More recent theories of studying and learning reflect the thinking of cognitive psychologists and focus on schemata, prior knowledge, and the learner's own goals. To understand and remember, the learner hooks new information to already existing schemata, or networks of knowledge. As the reader's personal knowledge expands, new networks are created. The learner, not the professor,

[1]N. Chase, J. Carson, and S. Gibson, "Literacy Demands of Undergraduate Curriculum," *Reading Research and Instruction* (in press).

decides how much effort should be expended and adjusts studying according to the answers to questions such as "How much do I need to know?," Will the test be multiple-choice or essay?," and "Do I want to remember this forever?" The learner makes judgments and selects the material to be remembered and integrated into knowledge networks.

In the following article three biology professors describe their plan for getting students actively involved in their own learning. Read the article and compare their course to your own past experience with biology.

Biology: A Big-Picture, Active Approach for Long-Term Learning

Biology 100, The Living World, is a nonmajors, one-semester introductory biology course taught at Arizona State University. For many students, BIO 100 is their first and last opportunity to learn science during college. During the past few years BIO 100 has undergone major changes in its goals and teaching methodology, which have been accompanied by an increase in enrollment from approximately 350 students per semester to our current level of over 900 per semester.

A substantial portion of students who enroll in BIO 100 have poorly developed scientific reasoning skills. They also vary widely in their understanding of important biological concepts and frequently hold misconceptions derived from poor instruction or from misleading personal experience. Further, they are largely unaware of the important implications that many biological phenomena have for their own lives and for their society and their world in general.

We have incorporated a number of significant innovations into the course. These include
• exploring biological phenomena in the labs before the introduction of related terminology;
• asking students to generate their own answers to biological questions and to design their own lab procedures to answer these questions rather than the standard practice of telling students what they will find and how to find it;
• initiating the course with the big picture, i.e., the biosphere and ecology, prior to introducing lower levels of organization; we do this primarily because going from whole to parts is more consistent with the scientific inquiry process, which we wish to emulate;
• basing both lab investigations and lectures on specific biological questions and on student conceptions (and in some cases, misconceptions);
• incorporating a historical perspective into lectures as a means of focusing attention on scientific reasoning;

• discussing implications and applications of the biological principles. For example, lung cancer is emphasized over memorization of pulmonary physiology; and Agent Orange and dioxin as contaminants of synthetic plant hormones are discussed at the end of the lecture material on plant hormones.

Anton Lawson et al., *Journal of College Science Teaching*

How was your own past experience in biology similar to or different from this course? _____

_____

How does this course help students build knowledge networks?

_____

All of your college professors may not be as dedicated to helping you participate and connect with your own learning as the biologists who created the new Biology 100 at Arizona State University. Regardless of your professor's approach, however, you are ultimately in charge of your own learning. Borrow from the success of the Arizona State biologists and try to connect with the material on a personal and global level. However you organize material—by annotating, notetaking, outlining, or mapping—seek to make meaning by making connections.

METHODS OF ORGANIZING TEXTBOOK INFORMATION

This chapter will discuss four methods of organizing textbook information for future study: annotating, notetaking, outlining, and mapping. In a recent review of more than five hundred research studies on organizing textbook information, two college developmental reading professors concluded that "no one study strategy is appropriate for all students in all study situations."[2] They encourage students to develop a repertoire of skills. They feel that students need to know, for example, that underlining takes less time than notetaking, but notetaking produces better test results. In addition, outlining and mapping require even more time than notetaking but tend further to improve test scores.

Your selection of a study strategy for organizing textbook material will vary according to the announced testing demands, the nature of the material, the amount of time you have to devote to the study effort, and your preference for a particular strategy. Being familiar with all four strategies affords a repertoire of choices.

[2]D. Caverly and V. Orlando, *Textbook Strategies in Teaching Reading and Study Strategies at the College Level* (Newark, N.J.: International Reading Association, 1991), 86–165.

ANNOTATING

Which of the following would seem to indicate the most effective use of the textbook as a learning tool?

1. A text without a single mark—not even the owner's name has spoiled the sacred pages
2. A text ablaze with color—almost every line is adorned with a red, blue, yellow, and/or green magic marker
3. A text with a scattered variety of markings—underlines, numbers, and stars are interspersed with circles, arrows, and short, written notes

Naturally number three is the best, but unfortunately the first two are not just silly examples; they are commonplace in every classroom. The student's rationale for the first is probably for resale of the book at the end of the course. The reason for the second is procrastination in decision making, which is a result of reading without thinking. In other words, the student underlines everything and relies on coming back later to figure out what is *really* important and worth remembering. Both of these extremes are inefficient and ineffective methods of using a college textbook.

Why Annotate?

The textbook is a learning tool and should be used as such; it should not be preserved as a treasure. A college professor requires a particular text because it contains information vital to your understanding of the course. The text places a vast body of knowledge in your hands, much more material than the professor could possibly give in class. It is your job to wade through this information, to make some sense out of it, and to select the important points that need to be remembered.

Annotating is a method of highlighting main ideas, significant supporting details, and key terms. The word **annotate** means to add marks. By using a system of symbols and notation and not just magic markers, you mark the text after the first reading so that a complete rereading will not be necessary. The markings indicate pertinent points to review for an exam.

Marking in the textbook itself is frequently faster than summarizing, outlining, or notetaking. In addition, since your material and personal reactions are all in one place, you can view them at a glance for later study rather than referring to separate notebooks. Your textbook has become a workbook.

Students who annotate, however, will probably want to make a list of key terms and ideas on their own paper in order to have a reduced form of the information for review and self-testing.

When to Annotate

Annotating ideas as they are first read is a mistake. The annotations should be done after a unit of thought has been presented and the information can be viewed as a whole. This may mean marking after a single paragraph or after three pages; marking varies with the material. When you are first reading, every sentence seems of major importance as each new idea unfolds, and the tendency is to annotate too much. Overmarking serves no useful purpose and wastes both reading and review time. If you wait until a complete thought has been developed, the significant points will emerge from a background of lesser details. You will then have all the facts, and you can decide what you want to remember. At the end of the course your textbook should have that worn, but well-organized look.

How to Annotate

Develop a System of Notations.   Highlighting material is not underlining; it is circling and starring and numbering and generally making an effort to put the material into perspective visually. Notations vary with the individual, and each student develops a number of original techniques. **Anything that makes sense to you is a correct notation.** Here is an example of a marking system:

Main idea

Supporting material

Major trend or possible essay exam question

Important smaller point to know for multiple-choice item

Word that you must be able to define

Section of material to reread for review

Numbering of important details under a major issue

Didn't understand and must seek advice

Notes in the margin

Questions in the margin

Indicating relationships

Related issue or idea

Examples of Annotating.   The following passage is taken from a biology textbook. Notice how the notations have been used to highlight main ideas and significant supporting details. This same passage will be used throughout this chapter to demonstrate each of the five methods of organizing textbook material.

Circulatory Systems

When we examine the systems by which blood reaches all the cells of an animal, we find two general types, known as open and closed circulatory systems.

Def. I

Open Circulatory Systems

The essential feature of the **open circulatory system** is that the blood moves through a body cavity—such as the abdominal cavity—and bathes the cells directly. The open circulatory system is particularly characteristic of insects and other arthropods, although it is also found in some other organisms.

In most insects the blood does not take a major part in oxygen transport. Oxygen enters the animal's body through a separate network of branching tubes that open to the atmosphere on the outside of the animal. (This type of respiratory system will be discussed in more detail in the next chapter.) Blood in an open circulatory system moves somewhat more slowly than in the average closed system. The slower system is adequate for insects because it does not have to supply the cells with oxygen.

Def. II

Closed Circulatory Systems

In a **closed circulatory system,** the blood flows through a well-defined system of vessels with many branches. In the majority of closed systems the blood is responsible for oxygen transport. To supply all the body cells with sufficient oxygen, the blood must move quickly through the blood vessels. A closed circulatory system must therefore have an efficient pumping mechanism, or heart, to set the blood in motion and keep it moving briskly through the body.

All vertebrates possess closed circulatory systems. Simple closed systems are also found in some invertebrates, including the annelid worms. A good example of such a simple closed circulatory system can be seen in the earthworm.

R → regeneration?

Victor A. Greulach and Vincent J. Chiapetta, eds., *Biology*

Exercise 1: Annotating

Using a variety of notations, annotate the following passage as if you were preparing for a quiz on the material. Remember, do not underscore as you read, but wait until you finish a paragraph or a section and then mark the important points.

Purposes of the Peer Group

If you were to ask most teenagers why they have joined a particular clique, club, or gang, they would probably tell you it is because they like the people in the group, or they like the kind of things the group is doing. Actually, there are many other purposes fulfilled by membership in a peer group. Rogers (1977) has summarized a number of these:

The "radar" function. One peer group function is to help the members find out how well they are doing in life. Adolescents can try out some behaviors by "bouncing" them off their peers who act as a radar screen. They then receive a message back as to how well others feel they are performing, and can alter their behavior accordingly.

Replacement for father. Although many, perhaps most, teenagers try to repudiate their father's authority during adolescence, the need for a father figure remains. The group leader often replaces one's father during the transition toward independence.

Support for independence. Closely related is the need for support from others while struggling against parental authority. Most adolescents need to learn to assert themselves, which often gives them strong guilt feelings and fear that their parents will reject them. Mutual support can be relied on among those who have similar concerns.

Ego building. Adolescence is a time of confusion as to who one is. At this low ebb of self-confidence, the peer group often serves the purpose of making one feel at least minimally good about oneself.

Psychic attachment. All human beings experience a deep need for psychological closeness and intimacy with others. In the past, this need was met largely by one's family. Today one's peers, especially in adolescence, have largely taken over this role.

Values orientation. We like to think we select our values by carefully considering how we feel about things and coming to our own conclusions as to what we shall believe. In fact, if we were forced to make up our minds about most things without any outside information, we would find it very difficult indeed. The peer group serves as a setting for the discussion of values, so that one has a better chance of seeing a wide range of options and making better choices.

Status setting. All societies have their hierarchy of status, in fact, several of them. Each of us needs to know something about how others regard us in the hierarchy of life. The peer group allows adolescents to learn more about how dominant and subordinate they are, thus giving them a better image of how they appear to others.

Negative identity. Often, youth join groups not so much because they believe in the goals of the group, but because they want to demonstrate their antagonism toward someone else. For example, a person whose parents overcontrol him may join an unruly gang even though he dislikes the occasional violence the group engages in. Nevertheless, he may view membership in the group as proof that he is more independent than his parents believe he is.

The avoidance of adult requirements. When the requirements of the peer group conflict with the requirements of adult society, the latter may be shunted aside. For example, teachers may insist that their students spend a considerable amount of time on homework; being a member of the basketball team may make it difficult to schedule both homework and practice sessions. Therefore, belonging to the basketball team may serve the purpose of excusing the teenager, at least to himself, from doing the homework that he didn't want to do anyway.

John Dacey, *Adolescents Today*[*]

Review your annotations. Have you sufficiently highlighted the main idea and the significant supporting details?

NOTETAKING

What Is Notetaking?

Many students prefer to jot down on their own paper brief sentence summaries of important textbook information. Margin space to the left of the summaries can be used to identify topics. Thus, topics of importance and explanations are side-by-side on notepaper for later study. In order to reduce notes for review, key terms can be further highlighted with a yellow marker to trigger thoughts for self-testing.

Why Take Textbook Notes?

Students who prefer this method say that working with a pencil and paper while reading keeps them involved with the material and thus improves con-

[*]From *Adolescents Today*, Second Edition, by John S. Dacey, pp. 218-219. Copyright © 1982 by Scott, Foresman and Company, HarperCollinsCollege Publishers.

centration. Notetaking takes longer than annotating, but sometimes a student who has already annotated the text may feel the need, based on later testing demands, time, and the complexity of the material, to organize the information further into notes.

Although the following notetaking system recommends sentence summaries, writing short phrases can sometimes be more efficient and still adequately communicate the message for later study.

How to Take Notes

One of the most popular systems of notetaking is called the Cornell Method. The steps are as follows:

1. Draw a line down your paper two and one-half inches from the left side to create a two-and-one-half-inch margin for noting key words and a six-inch area on the right for sentence summaries.
2. After you have finished reading a section, tell yourself what you have read and jot down sentence summaries in the six-inch area on the right side of your paper. Use your own words and make sure you have included the main ideas and significant supporting details. Be brief, but use complete sentences.
3. Review your summary sentences and underline key words. Write these key words in the column on the left side of your paper. These words can be used to stimulate your memory of the material for later study.

The Cornell Method can be used for taking notes on classroom lectures. The following explanation, developed by Norman Stahl and James King, both explains the procedure and gives a visual display of the results.

Example of Notetaking

The example on page 176 applies the Cornell Method of notetaking to the biology passage on the circulatory system which you have already read.

Exercise 2: Notetaking

In college courses, you will usually take notes on lengthy chapters or entire books. For practice with notetaking here, use the passage, "Purposes of the Peer Group," which you have already annotated. Prepare a two-columned sheet and take notes using the Cornell Method.

Taking Class Notes: The Cornell Method[3]

← 2½ INCHES → REDUCE IDEAS TO CONCISE JOTTINGS AND SUMMARIES AS CUES FOR RECITING.	← 6 INCHES → RECORD THE LECTURE AS FULLY AND AS MEANINGFULLY AS POSSIBLE.
Cornell Method	This sheet demonstrates the Cornell Method of taking classroom notes. It is recommended by experts from the Learning Center at Cornell University.
Line drawn down paper	You should draw a line down your notepage about 2½ inches from the left side. On the right side of the line simply record your classroom notes as you usually do. Be sure that you write legibly.
After the lecture	<u>After the lecture</u> you should read the notes, fill in materials that you missed, make your writing legible, and underline any important materials. Ask another classmate for help if you missed something during lecture.
Use the recall column for key phrases	The <u>recall column</u> on the left will help you when you study for your tests. Jot down any important words or <u>key phrases</u> in the recall column. This activity forces you to rethink and summarize your notes. The key words should stick in your mind.
Five Rs	The <u>Five Rs</u> will help you take better notes based on the Cornell Method.
Record	1. <u>Record</u> any information given during the lecture which you believe will be important.
Reduce	2. When you <u>reduce</u> your information you are summarizing and listing key words/phrases in the recall column.
Recite	3. Cover the notes you took for your class. Test yourself on the words in the recall section. This is what we mean by <u>recite</u>.
Reflect	4. You should <u>reflect</u> on the information you received during the lecture. Determine how your ideas fit in with the information.
Review	5. If you <u>review</u> your notes you will remember a great deal more when you take your midterm.
Binder & paper	Remember it is a good idea to keep your notes in a <u>standard-sized binder</u>. Also you should use only full-sized binder <u>paper</u>. You will be able to add mimeographed materials easily to your binder.
Hints	Abbreviations and symbols should be used when possible. Abbrev. & sym. give you time when used auto.

[3]From N. A. Stahl and J. King, "A Language Experience Model for Teaching College Reading, Study and Survival" (Paper delivered at the twenty-fifth College Reading Association Annual Conference, Louisville, Ky., 30 October 1981).

Circulatory System

Two types Open and Closed	There are two types, the open and the closed, by which blood reaches all the cells of an animal.
Open	In the open system, found mostly in insects and other arthropods, blood moves through the body and bathes the cells directly.
Bathes cells	The blood moves slower than in the closed system, and oxygen is supplied from outside air through tubes.
Oxygen from outside	In the closed system, blood flows through a system of vessels, oxygen is carried by the blood so it must move quickly, and the heart serves as a pumping mechanism. All vertabrates, as well as earthworms, have closed systems.
Blood vessels Blood carries oxygen Heart pumps	

OUTLINING

What Is an Outline?

An outline organizes and highlights major points and subordinates items of lesser importance. In a glance the indentations, Roman numerals, numbers, and letters quickly show how one idea relates to another and how all aspects relate to the whole. The layout of the outline is simply a graphic display of main ideas and significant supporting details.

The following example is the picture-perfect version of the basic outline form. In practice your "working outline" would probably not be as detailed or as regular as this.

Use the tools of the outline format, **especially the indentations and numbers** to devise your own system for organizing information.

Title

I. First main idea
  A. Supporting idea
    1. Detail
    2. Detail
    3. Detail
      a. Minor detail
      b. Minor detail
  B. Supporting idea
    1. Detail
    2. Detail
  C. Supporting idea

II. Second main idea
  A. Supporting idea
  B. Supporting idea

Why Outline?

Students who outline usually drop the preciseness of picture-perfect outlines, but make good use of the numbers, letters, indentations, and mixture of topics and phrases from the system to take notes and show levels of importance. A quick look to the far left of an outline indicates the topic with subordinate ideas indented underneath. The letters, numbers, and indentations form a visual display of the significance of the parts that make up the whole. Good outliners use plenty of paper so the levels of importance are evident at a glance.

Another use of the outline is to organize notes from class lectures. During class most professors try to add to the material in the textbook and put it into perspective for students. Since the notes taken in class represent a large percentage of the material you need to know in order to pass the course, they are extremely important. While listening to a class lecture, you must almost instantly receive, synthesize, and select material and, at the same time, record something on paper for future reference. The difficulty of the task demands order and decision making. Do not be so eager to copy down every detail that you miss the big picture. One of the most efficient methods of taking lecture notes is to use a modified outline form, a version with the addition of stars, circles, and underlines to emphasize further the levels of importance.

How to Outline

Professors say that they can walk around the classroom and look at the notes students have taken from the text or from a lecture and tell how well each has understood the lesson. The errors most frequently observed fall into the following categories:

1. Poor organization
2. Failure to show importance
3. Writing too much
4. Writing too little

To avoid these pitfalls the most important thing to remember in outlining is *"What is my purpose?"* You don't need to include everything and you don't need a picture-perfect version for study notes. Include only what you feel you will need to remember later, and use the numbering system and the indentations to show how one thing relates to another. Several other important guidelines to remember are as follows:

1. Get a general overview before you start.
   (How many main topics do there seem to be?)
2. Use phrases rather than sentences.
   (Can you state it in a few short words?)
3. Put it in your own words.
   (If you cannot paraphrase it, do you really understand it?)
4. Be selective.
   (Are you highlighting or completely rewriting?)

After outlining, indicate key terms with a yellow marker so that they will be highly visible for later review and self-testing.

Example of Outlining

The following is an outline of the biology passage on the circulatory system. Notice how the numbers and letters, as well as the distance from the left side of the paper, show levels of importance.

I. Open circulatory system
   A. Blood moves through body and bathes cells directly
   B. Examples — insects and other arthropods
   C. Oxygen supplied from outside air through tubes
   D. Slower blood movement since not supplying cells with oxygen

II. Closed circulatory system
   A. Blood flows through system of vessels
   B. Oxygen carried by blood so it must move quickly
   C. Heart serves as pumping mechanism
   D. Example — all vertebrates
   E. Example — earthworms

Exercise 3: Outlining

Outline the key ideas in the following selection as if you were planning to use your notes to study for a quiz. You may want to annotate before you outline.

Reacting to Stress with Defense Mechanisms

Stress may occasionally promote positive outcomes. Motivated to overcome stress and the situations that produce it, we may learn new and adaptive responses. It is also clear, however, that stress involves a very unpleasant emotional component. **Anxiety** is a general feeling of tension or apprehension that often accompanies a perceived threat to one's well-being. It is this unpleasant emotional component that often prompts us to learn new responses to rid ourselves of stress.

There are a number of techniques, essentially self-deceptive, that we may employ to keep from feeling the unpleasantness associated with stress. These techniques, or tricks we play on ourselves, are not adaptive in the sense of helping us to get rid of anxiety by getting rid of the source of stress. Rather, they are mechanisms that we can and do use to defend ourselves against the *feelings* of stress. They are called **defense mechanisms.** Freud believed defense mechanisms to be the work of the unconscious mind. He claimed that they are ploys that our unconscious mind uses to protect us (our *self* or *ego*) from stress and anxiety. Many psychologists take issue with Freud's interpretation of defense mechanisms and consider defense mechanisms in more general terms than did Freud, but few will deny that defense mechanisms exist. It *is* true that they are generally ineffective if consciously or purposively employed. The list of defense mechanisms is a long one. Here, we'll review some of the more common defense mechanisms, providing an example of each, to give you an idea of how they might serve as a reaction to stress.

Repression. The notion of **repression** came up earlier in our discussion of memory. In a way, it is the most basic of all the defense mechanisms. It is sometimes referred to as *motivated forgetting,* which gives us a good idea of what is involved. Repression is a matter of conveniently forgetting about some stressful, anxiety-producing event, conflict, or frustration. Paul had a teacher in high school he did not get along with at all. After spending an entire semester trying his best to do whatever was asked, Paul failed the course. The following summer, while walking with his girlfriend, Paul encountered this teacher. When he tried to introduce his girlfriend, Paul could not remember his teacher's name. He had repressed it. As a long-term reaction to stress, repressing the names of people we don't like or that we associate with unpleasant, stressful experiences is certainly not a very adaptive reaction. But at least it can protect us from dwelling on such unpleasantness.

Denial. **Denial** is a very basic mechanism of defense against stress. In denial, a person simply refuses to acknowledge the realities of a stressful situation. When a physician first tells a patient that he or she has a terminal illness, a common reaction is denial; the patient refuses to believe that there is anything seriously wrong.

Other less stressful events than serious illness sometimes evoke denial. Many smokers are intelligent individuals who are well aware of the data and the statistics that can readily convince them that they are slowly (or rapidly) killing themselves by continuing to smoke. But they deny the evidence. Somehow they are able to convince themselves that they aren't going to die from smoking; that's something that happens to other people, and besides, they *could* stop whenever they wanted.

Rationalization. **Rationalization** amounts to making excuses for our behaviors when facing the real reasons for our behaviors would be stressful. The real reason Kevin failed his psychology midterm is that he didn't study for it and has missed a number of classes. Kevin hates to admit, even to himself, that he could have been so stupid as to flunk that exam because of his own actions. As a result, he rationalizes: "It wasn't really *my* fault. I had a lousy instructor. We used a rotten text. The tests were grossly unfair. I've been fighting the darn flu all semester. And Marjorie had that big party the night before the exam." Now Susan, on the other hand, really did want to go to Marjorie's party, but she decided that she wouldn't go unless somebody asked her. As it happens, no one did. In short order, Susan rationalized that she "didn't want to go to that dumb party anyway"; she needed to "stay home and study."

Compensation. We might best think of **compensation** in the context of personal frustration. This defense mechanism is a matter of overemphasizing some positive trait or ability to counterbalance a shortcoming in some other trait or ability. If some particular goal-directed behavior becomes blocked, a person may compensate by putting extra effort and attention into some other aspect of behavior. For example, Karen, a seventh grader, wants to be popular. She's a reasonably bright and pleasant teenager, but isn't—in the judgment of her classmates—very pretty. Karen *may* compensate for her lack of good looks by studying very hard to be a good student, or by memorizing jokes and funny stories, or by becoming a good musician. Compensation is not just an attempt to be a well-rounded individual. It is a matter of expending *extra* energy and resources in one direction to offset shortcomings in other directions.

Fantasy. **Fantasy** is one of the more common defense mechanisms used by college students. It is often quite useful. Particularly after a hard day when stress levels are high, isn't it pleasant to sit in a comfortable chair, kick off your shoes, lie back, close your eyes, and daydream, perhaps about graduation day, picturing yourself walking across the stage to pick up your diploma—with honors.

When things are not going well for us, we may retreat into a world of fantasy where everything always goes well. Remember that to engage from time to time in fantasizing is a normal and acceptable response to stress. You should not get worried if you fantasize occasionally. On the other hand, you should realize that there are some potential dangers here. You need to be able to keep separate those activities that are real and those that occur in your fantasies. And you should realize that fantasy in itself will not solve whatever problem is causing you stress. Fantasizing about academic successes may help you feel better for awhile, but it is not likely to make you a better student.

Projection. **Projection** is a matter of seeing in others those very traits and motives that cause us stress when we see them in ourselves.

Under pressure to do well on an exam, Mark may want to cheat, but his conscience won't let him. Because of projection, he may think he sees cheating going on all around him.

Projection is a mechanism that is often used in conjunction with hostility and aggression. When people begin to feel uncomfortable about their own levels of hostility, they often project their aggressiveness onto others, coming to believe that others are "out to do me harm," and "I'm only defending myself."

Regression. To employ **regression** is to return to earlier, even childish, levels of behavior that were once productive or reinforced. Curiously enough, we often find regression in children. Imagine a four year old who until very recently was an only child. Now Mommy has returned from the hospital with a new baby sister. The four year old is no longer "the center of the universe," as her new little sister now gets parental attention. The four year old reverts to earlier behaviors and starts wetting the bed, screaming for a bottle of her own, and crawling on all fours in an attempt to get attention. She is regressing.

Many defense mechanisms can be seen on the golf course, including regression. After Doug knocks three golf balls into the lake, he throws a temper tantrum, stamps his feet, and tosses his three-iron in the lake. His childish regressive behavior won't help his score, but it may act as a release from the tension of his stress at the moment.

Displacement. The defense mechanism of **displacement** is usually discussed in the context of aggression. Your goal-directed behavior becomes blocked or thwarted. You are frustrated, under stress, and somewhat aggressive. You cannot vent your aggression directly at the source of the frustration, so you displace it to a safer outlet. Dorothy expects to get promoted at work, but someone else gets the new job she wanted. Her goal-directed behavior has been frustrated. She's upset and angry at her boss, but feels (perhaps correctly) that blowing her top at her boss will do more harm than good. She's still frustrated, so she displaces her hostility toward her husband, children, and/or the family cat.

Displacement doesn't have to involve hostility and aggression. A young couple discovers that having children is not going to be as easy as they thought. They want children badly, but there's an infertility problem that is causing considerable stress. Their motivation for love, sharing, and caring may be displaced toward a pet, nephews and nieces, or some neighborhood children—at least until their own goals can be realized with children of their own.

The list of defense mechanisms provided above is not an exhaustive one. These are among the most common, and this list gives you an idea of what defense mechanisms are like.

Josh Gerow, *Psychology: An Introduction*

MAPPING

What is Mapping?

Mapping is a visual system of condensing material to show relationships and importance. A map is a diagram of the major points, with their significant subpoints, that support a topic. The purpose of mapping as an organizing strategy is to improve memory by grouping material in a highly visual way.

Why Map?

Proponents of popular learning style theories would say that mapping offers a visual organization that appeals to learners with a preference for spatial representation, as opposed to the linear mode offered by outlining and notetaking. A map provides a quick reference to overviewing an article or a chapter and can be used to reduce notes for later study.

How to Map

Use the following steps for mapping.

1. Draw a circle or a box in the middle of a page and in it write the subject or topic of the material.
2. Determine the main ideas that support the subject and write them on lines radiating from the central circle or box.
3. Determine the significant details and write them on lines attached to each main idea. The number of details you include will depend on the material and your purpose.

Maps are not restricted to any one pattern, but can be formed in a variety of creative shapes, as the following diagrams illustrate:

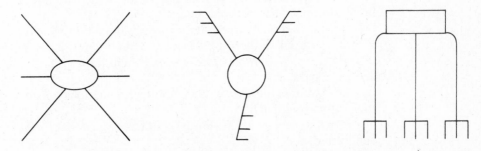

Example of Mapping

The following map highlights the biology passage on the circulatory system. Notice how the visual display emphasizes the groups of ideas supporting the topic.

Exercise 4: Mapping

Refer to Exercise 3 and design a map for the passage entitled, "Reacting to Stress," which you previously outlined. Use your outline to help you in making the map. Experiment with several different shapes for your map patterns on notebook or unlined paper.

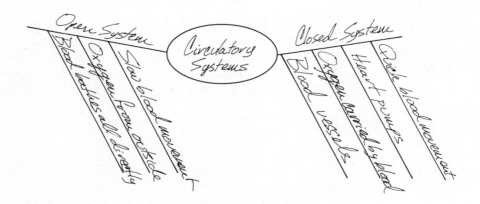

SUMMARY

Textbook reading is study reading. It is reading to learn and involves establishing knowledge networks. Students must select the textbook information to remember and organize it to facilitate future study. The following systems can be used to organize textbook information:

Annotating is a method of using symbols and notations to highlight main ideas, significant supporting details, and key terms.

The *Cornell Method of notetaking* includes writing summary sentences and marginal notes.

The layout of the *outline* is a graphic presentation of main ideas and significant supporting details.

Mapping is a visual system of condensing material to show relationships and importance.

Selection

1

BIOLOGY

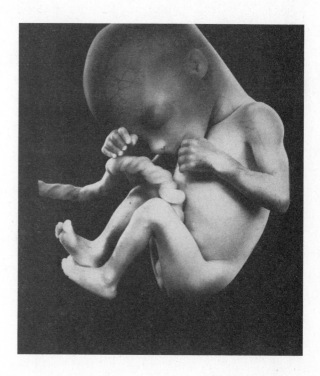

Stage 1

Preview

This selection is divided into how many sections? _____

After reading this selection, I will need to know

_____

Activate Schema

What hour of which day were you born? _____

How much did you weigh? _____

Learning Strategy

Be able to describe fetal growth in each trimester.

Stage 2: Integrate Knowledge While Reading

1. Predict 2. Picture 3. Relate 4. Monitor 5. Fix up

Skill Development: Outlining

Outline the key ideas in each section as if you were planning to use your notes to study for a quiz.

PREGNANCY AND BIRTH

From Robert Wallace, *Biology: The World of Life*

Descriptions in bus-station novels notwithstanding, fertilization occurs with the mother-to-be totally unaware of the event. If there are sperm cells thrashing around in the genital tract at any time within forty-eight hours before ovulation to about twelve hours after, the odds are
5 very good that pregnancy will occur. As soon as the egg is touched by the head of a sperm, it undergoes violent pulsating movements which unite the twenty-three chromosomes of the sperm with its own genetic complement. From this single cell, about 1/175 of an inch in diameter, a baby weighing several pounds and composed of trillions
10 of cells will be delivered about 266 days later.

For convenience, we will divide the 266 days, or nine months, into three periods of three months each. We can consider these *trimesters* separately, since each is characterized by different sorts of events.

The First Trimester

In the first trimester the embryo begins the delicate structural
15 differentiations that will lead to its final form. It is therefore particularly susceptible during this period to any number of factors that might influence its development. In fact the embryo often fails to survive this stage.

The first cell divisions result in cells that all look about alike and
20 have roughly the same potentials. In other words, at this stage the cells are, theoretically anyway, interchangeable. Seventy-two hours after fertilization the embryo will consist of sixteen such cells. (So, how many divisions will have taken place?) Each cell will divide before it reaches the size of the cell that has produced it; hence the
25 cells will become progressively smaller with each division. By the end of the first month the embryo will have reached a length of only ⅛ inch, but it will consist of millions of cells.

In the second month the features of the embryo become more recognizable. Bone begins to form throughout the body, primarily in
30 the jaw and shoulder areas. The head and brain are developing at a much faster rate than the rest of the body, so that at this point the ears appear and open, lidless eyes stare blankly into the amniotic fluid. The circulatory system is developing and blood is pumped

*From *Biology: The World of Life,* 3rd Edition, by Robert A. Wallace. Copyright © 1981 by Scott, Foresman and Company, HarperCollinsCollege Publishers.

through the umbilical cord out to the chorion, where it receives
life-sustaining nutrients and deposits the poisons it has removed from
the developing embryo. The nitrogenous wastes and carbon dioxide
filter into the mother's bloodstream, where they will be circulated to
her own kidneys and lungs for removal. At about day 46 the
primordial reproductive organs begin to form, either as testes or
ovaries, and it is now, for the first time, that the sex of the embryo
becomes apparent. Near the end of the second month fingers and
toes begin to appear on the flattened paddles which have formed
from the limb buds. By this time the embryo is about two inches long
and is more or less human in appearance; it is now called a *fetus*.
Growth and differentiation continue during the third month, but now
the fetus begins to move. It breathes the amniotic fluid in and out of
bulblike lungs and swallowing motions become distinct. At this point
individual differences can be distinguished in the behavior of fetuses.
The clearest differences are in their facial expressions. Some frown a
lot; others smile or grimace. It would be interesting to correlate this
early behavior with the personality traits that develop after birth.

The Second Trimester

In the second trimester the fetus grows rapidly, and by the end of the
sixth month it may be about a foot long, although it will weigh only
about a pound and a half. Whereas the predominant growth of the
fetus during the first trimester was in the head and brain areas, during
the second trimester the body grows at a much faster relative rate
than the brain and begins to catch up in size with the head.

The fetus is by this time behaving more vigorously. It is able to
move freely within its sea of amniotic fluid and the delighted mother
can feel it kicking and thrashing about. Interestingly, the fetus must
sleep now, so there are periods when it is inactive. It is capable of
reacting to more types of stimuli as time passes. For example, by the
fifth month the eyes are sensitive to light, although there is still no
sensitivity to sound. Other organs seem to be complete, but remain
nonfunctional. For example, the lungs are developed, but they cannot
exchange oxygen. The digestive organs are present, but they cannot
digest food. Even the skin is not prepared to cope with the
temperature changes in the outside world. In fact, at the end of the
fifth month the skin is covered by a protective cheesy paste consisting
of wax and sweatlike secretions mixed with loosened skin cells
(*vernix caseosa*). The fetus is still incapable in nearly all instances of
surviving alone.

By the sixth month the fetus is kicking and turning so constantly
that the mother often must time her own sleep periods to coincide
with her baby's. The distracting effect has been described as similar
to being continually tapped on the shoulder, but not exactly. The
fetus moves with such vigor that its movements are not only felt from

the inside, but can be seen clearly from the outside. To add to the mother's distraction, the fetus may even have periods of hiccups. By this stage it is so large and demanding that it places a tremendous drain on the mother's reserves.

At the end of the second trimester the fetus has the unmistakable appearance of a human baby (or a very old person, since its skin is loose and wrinkled at this stage). In the event of a premature birth around the end of this trimester, the fetus may be able to survive.

The Third Trimester

During the third trimester the fetus grows until it is no longer floating free in its amniotic pool. It now fills the abdominal area of the mother. The fetus is crowded so tightly into the greatly enlarged uterus that its movement is restricted. In these last three months the mother's abdomen becomes greatly distended and heavy, and her posture and gait may be noticeably altered in response to the shift in her center of gravity. The mass of tissue and amniotic fluid that accompanies the fetus ordinarily weighs almost twice as much as the fetus itself. Toward the end of this period, milk begins to form in the mother's mammary glands, which in the previous trimester have undergone a sudden surge of growth.

At this time, the mother is at a great disadvantage in several ways in terms of her physical well-being. About 85 percent of the calcium she eats goes to the fetal skeleton, and about the same percentage of her iron intake goes to the fetal blood cells. Of the protein she eats, much of the nitrogen goes to the brain and other nerve tissues of the fetus.

Some interesting questions arise here. If a woman is unable to afford expensive protein-rich foods during the third trimester, what is the probability of a lowered I.Q. in her offspring? On the average the poorer people in this country show lower I.Q. scores. Are they poor because their I.Q.'s are low, or are I.Q.'s low because they are poor? Is there a self-perpetuating nature about either of these alternatives?

In the third trimester, the fetus is large. It requires increasingly greater amounts of food, and each day it produces more poisonous wastes for the mother's body to carry away. Her heart must work harder to provide food and oxygen for two bodies. She must breathe, now, for two individuals. Her blood pressure and heart rate rise. The fetus and the tissues maintaining it form a large mass that crowds the internal organs of the mother. In fact, the crowding of the fetus against the mother's diaphragm may make breathing difficult for her in these months. Several weeks before delivery, however, the fetus will change its position, dropping lower in the pelvis (called "*lightening*") and thus relieve the pressure against the mother's lungs.

There are important changes occurring in the fetus in these last three months, and some of these are not very well understood. The effects of these changes, however, are reflected in the survival rate of babies delivered by Caesarian section (an incision through the
125 mother's side). In the seventh month, only 10 percent survive; in the eighth month, 70 percent; and in the ninth, 95 percent survive.

Interestingly, there is another change in the relationship of the fetus and mother at this time. Whereas measles and certain other infectious diseases would have affected the embryo during the first
130 trimester of pregnancy, at this stage the mother's antibodies confer an immunity to the fetus, a protection that may last through the first few weeks of infancy.

At some point about 255 to 265 days from the time of conception the life-sustaining placenta begins to break down. Certain parts shrink,
135 the tissue structure begins changing, and the capillaries begin to disintegrate. The result is a less hospitable environment for the fetus, and premature births at this time are not unusual. At about this time the fetus slows its growth, and drops into position with its head toward the bottom of the uterus. Meanwhile, the internal organs
140 undergo the final changes that will enable the newborn to survive in an entirely different kind of world. Its home has been warm, rather constant in its qualities, protected, and confining. It is not likely to encounter anything quite so secure again.

Birth

The signal that there will soon be a new member of the earth's most
145 dominant species is the onset of *labor,* a series of uterine contractions that usually begin at about half-hour intervals and gradually increase in frequency. Meanwhile, the sphincter muscle around the cervix dilates, and as the periodic contractions become stronger, the baby's head pushes through the extended cervical canal to the opening of
150 the vagina. The infant is finally about to emerge into its new environment, one that, in time, may give it the chance to propel its own genes into the gene pool of the species.

Once the baby's head emerges, the pattern of uterine contractions changes. The contractions become milder and more frequent. After
155 the head gradually emerges through the vaginal opening, the smaller shoulders and the body appear. Then with a rush the baby slips into a new world. As soon as the baby has emerged, the umbilicus by which it is attached to the placenta is tied off and cut. The placenta is expelled by further contractions as the *afterbirth.* The mother
160 recovers surprisingly rapidly. In other species, which deliver their young unaided, the mother immediately chews through the umbilicus and eats the afterbirth so that it will not advertise to predators the

presence of a helpless newborn. Fortunately, the behavior never became popular in our own species.

165   The cutting of the umbilicus stops the only source of oxygen the infant has known. There is a resulting rapid buildup of carbon dioxide in the blood, which affects a breathing center in the brain. An impulse is fired to the diaphragm, and the baby gasps its first breath. Its exhaling cry signals that it is breathing on its own.

170   In American hospitals the newborn is then given the first series of the many tests it will encounter during its lifetime. This one is called the *Apgar test series,* in which muscle tone, breathing, reflexes, and heart rate are evaluated. The obstetrician then checks for skin lesions and evidence of hernias. If the infant is a boy, it is checked to see

175 whether the testes have properly descended into the scrotum. A footprint is then recorded as a means of identification, since the new individual, despite the protestations of proud parents, does not yet have many other distinctive features that would be apparent to the casual observer. And there have been more than a few cases of

180 accidental baby-switching.

Skill Development: Outlining

Review your outline without referring to the text before answering the comprehension questions.

Comprehension Questions

Mark each statement with *T* for true or *F* for false.

_____   1. Babies are footprinted as a means of identification.

_____   2. The fetus is most susceptible to measles during the last trimester.

_____   3. During fertilization, the mother can feel the sperm and the egg touch.

_____   4. During the first trimester, changes in the facial expression of the fetus occur.

_____   5. During the second trimester, the fetus can have the hiccups.

_____   6. During the third trimester, the fetus floats freely with room to move in the uterus.

_____   7. The author implies that the mother's body works the hardest during the third trimester.

_____   8. The baby is forced to breathe when the cervix dilates.

_____   9. Sperm can live for several hours in the genital tract.

_____ 10. During the third trimester, the mother's antibodies confer immunity to the fetus.

Connecting and Reflecting

Consider for a moment that you are a guidance counselor in a large public high school, and your job includes more than registration and college placement. You counsel battered teens, substance abusers, and teens who are faced with the heartbreak of early pregnancy. Your particular area of expertise is teenage pregnancy. You are developing a list called "Kids Raising Kids," which contains ten compelling reasons for not wanting to be a teenage parent. You will discuss this list with both girls and boys who seem to be in danger. Read the following passage for more information and complete your list of ten reasons for avoiding teenage pregnancy.

Teenage Pregnancy

A phenomenon which is hardly new, but which has attained tremendous proportions in the last several decades, is that of out-of-wedlock, and particularly teenage, pregnancies. Some 30,000 girls under the age of 15 become pregnant every year, and if present trends continue an estimated 40 percent of 14-year-old girls will become pregnant at least once before the age of 20. In addition, about 18 percent of American women will have had at least one abortion before their twentieth birthday. In fact, abortions among teenagers account for more than a quarter of all the abortions performed in this country. It is feared that in the aftermath of the Supreme Court decision that gave states new leeway to regulate abortion, state laws will be passed that will force teenagers to have babies by default—babies they are ill prepared to care for (Greenhouse 1989).

Teen pregnancy is problematic for two generations, that of the parent and that of the child. Teen mothers are as likely as other women with young children to live below the poverty level (only half of those who give birth before age 18 complete high school). They are also more likely to be dependent on welfare: 71 percent of females under 30 who receive Aid to Families with Dependent Children had their first child when they were teenagers. Their offspring tend to experience high rates of illness and mortality and later in life are heirs to educational and emotional problems. Children of teenage parents are more likely to be abused by immature parents and unfortunately tend to repeat their parents' experience: 82 percent of girls who give birth at 15 or younger were daughters of teenage mothers (*Time* 1985).

John A. Perry and Erna K. Perry, *Contemporary Sociology*

Selection

2

HISTORY

© 1993 HarperCollins College Publishers

Stage 1

Preview

The pattern of organization in the first part of the selection is

_____

After reading this selection, I will need to know Sojourner Truth's feelings on the weakness of women.

agree ☐   *disagree* ☐

Activate Schema

Why did the Civil War throw women into many leadership roles?

Learning Strategy

Look at the historical trend toward altering the image of women and note the contributions to this change made by individuals and groups.

Word Knowledge
  Review the ten vocabulary items that follow the selection. Seek an understanding of unfamiliar words.

Stage 2: Integrate Knowledge While Reading
  As you read, use the thinking strategies discussed in Chapter 2.
  1. Predict 2. Picture 3. Relate 4. Monitor 5. Fix up

Skill Development: Notetaking

  Use the Cornell Method of notetaking to organize material in this selection for future study.

WOMEN IN HISTORY

From Leonard Pitt, *We Americans**

Three Radical Women
Amelia Bloomer (1818–1894) published the first newspaper issued expressly for women. She called it *The Lily*. Her fame, however, rests chiefly in dress reform. For six or eight years she wore an outfit composed of a knee-length skirt over full pants gathered at the ankle,
5 which were soon known everywhere as "bloomers." Wherever she went, this style created great excitement and brought her enormous audiences—including hecklers. She was trying to make the serious point that women's fashions, often designed by men to suit their own tastes, were too restrictive, often to the detriment of the health of
10 those who wore them. Still, some of her contemporaries thought she did the feminist movement as much harm as good.
  Very few feminists hoped to destroy marriage as such. Most of them had husbands and lived conventional, if hectic, lives. And many of the husbands supported their cause. Yet the feminists did challenge
15 certain marital customs. When Lucy Stone married Henry Blackwell, she insisted on being called "Mrs. Stone," a defiant gesture that brought her a lifetime of ridicule. Both she and her husband signed a marriage contract, vowing "to recognize the wife as an independent, rational being." They agreed to break any law which brought the
20 husband "an injurious and unnatural superiority." But few of the radical feminists indulged in "free love" or joined communal marriage experiments. The movement was intended mainly to help women gain control over their own property and earnings and gain better legal guardianship over their children. Voting also interested them,

*From Pitt, *We Americans*. Copyright 1987 Kendall/Hunt Publishing Company. Reprinted with permission.

25 but women's suffrage did not become a central issue until later in the century.

Many black women were part of the movement, including the legendary Sojourner Truth (1797–1883). Born a slave in New York and forced to marry a man approved by her owner, Sojourner Truth was
30 freed when the state abolished slavery. After participating in religious revivals, she became an active abolitionist and feminist. In 1851 she saved the day at a women's rights convention in Ohio, silencing hecklers and replying to a man who had belittled the weakness of women:

35 The man over there says women need to be helped into carriages and lifted over ditches, and to have the best place everywhere. Nobody ever helps me into carriages or over puddles, or gives me the best place—and ain't I a woman? . . . Look at my arm! I have ploughed and planted and gathered into barns, and no man could head me—and ain't I a woman? I could work as
40 much and eat as much as a man—when I could get it—and bear the lash as well! And ain't I a woman? I have borne thirteen children, and seen most of 'em sold into slavery, and when I cried out my mother's grief, none but Jesus heard me—and ain't I a woman?

Changing the Image and the Reality

The accomplishments of a few women who dared pursue professional
45 careers had somewhat altered the image of the submissive and brainless child-woman. Maria Mitchell of Nantucket, whose father was an astronomer, discovered a comet at the age of twenty-eight. She became the first woman professor of astronomy in the U.S. (at Vassar in 1865). Mitchell was also the first woman elected to the American
50 Academy of Arts and Sciences and a founder of the Association for the Advancement of Women. Elizabeth Blackwell applied to twenty-nine medical schools before she was accepted. She attended all classes, even anatomy class, despite the sneers of some male students. As a physician, she went on to make important contributions in sanitation
55 and hygiene.

By about 1860 women had effected notable improvements in their status. Organized feminists had eliminated some of the worst legal disadvantages in fifteen states. The Civil War altered the role—and the image—of women even more drastically than the feminist
60 movement did. As men went off to fight, women flocked into government clerical jobs. And they were accepted in teaching jobs as never before. Tens of thousands of women ran farms and businesses while the men were gone. Anna Howard Shaw, whose mother ran a pioneer farm, recalled:

65 It was an incessant struggle to keep our land, to pay our taxes, and to live. Calico was selling at fifty cents a yard. Coffee was one dollar a pound. There were no men left to grind our corn, to get in our crops, or to care for our livestock; and all around us we saw our struggle reflected in the lives of our neighbors.

Women took part in crucial relief efforts. The Sanitary Commission,
the Union's volunteer nursing program and a forerunner of the Red
Cross, owed much of its success to women. They raised millions of
dollars for medicine, bandages, food, hospitals, relief camps, and
convalescent homes.

North and South, black and white, many women served as nurses,
some as spies and even as soldiers. Dorothea Dix, already famous as a
reformer of prisons and insane asylums, became head of the Union
army nurse corps. Clara Barton and "Mother" Bickerdyke saved
thousands of lives by working close behind the front lines at
Antietam, Chancellorsville, and Fredericksburg. Harriet Tubman led a
party up the Combahee River to rescue 756 slaves. Late in life she was
recognized for her heroic act by being granted a government pension
of twenty dollars per month.

Southern white women suffered more from the disruptions of the
Civil War than did their northern sisters. The proportion of men who
went to war or were killed in battle was greater in the South. This
made many women self-sufficient during the war. Still, there was
hardly a whisper of feminism in the South.

The Civil War also brought women into the political limelight. Anna
Dickson skyrocketed to fame as a Republican speaker, climaxing her
career with an address to the House of Representatives on abolition.
Stanton and Anthony formed the National Woman's Loyal League to
press for a constitutional amendment banning slavery. With Anthony's
genius for organization, the League in one year collected 400,000
signatures in favor of the Thirteenth Amendment.

Once abolition was finally assured in 1865, most feminists felt
certain that suffrage would follow quickly. They believed that women
had earned the vote by their patriotic wartime efforts. Besides, it
appeared certain that black men would soon be allowed to vote. And
once black men had the ballot in hand, how could anyone justify
keeping it from white women—or black women? Any feminist who
had predicted in 1865 that women would have to wait another
fifty-five years for suffrage would have been called politically naive.

Stage 3: Recall for Self-Testing

Stop and self-test. Recall *what you have read. Do not allow gaps of
knowledge to exist. Review your use of the thinking strategies. Did you
use all five?*

Skill Development: Notetaking

Review your notes before answering the following comprehension
questions.

Comprehension Questions

1. Who or what is the topic? _____

   What is the main idea the author is trying to convey about the topic?

   _____

   _____

After reading the selection, answer the following questions with *a, b, c,* or *d.*

_____ 2. In originating "bloomers," Amelia Bloomer's greatest concern was
   a. fashion.
   b. principle.
   c. expense.
   d. good taste.

_____ 3. The major purpose of Sojourner Truth's quoted speech was to
   a. prove that women are stronger than men.
   b. reprimand men for social courtesy.
   c. dramatize the strengths of women.
   d. praise childbearing as a womanly virtue.

_____ 4. Lucy Stone's major motive in retaining the name "Mrs. Stone" after marriage was to
   a. condone "free love" without marriage.
   b. de-emphasize the responsibilities of marriage.
   c. purchase property in her own name.
   d. be recognized as an independent person equal to her husband.

_____ 5. The article explicitly states that women worked during the Civil War in all of the following except
   a. farms and businesses.
   b. the military.
   c. government clerical jobs.
   d. the Red Cross.

_____ 6. The author implies that the eventual assumption of responsible roles by large numbers of women was primarily due to
   a. the feminist movement.
   b. the determination and accomplishments of female professionals.
   c. a desire to give women a chance.
   d. economic necessity.

_____ 7. The author believes that the Civil War showed southern women to be
   a. as capable but less vocal than northern women.
   b. more capable than their northern sisters.
   c. capable workers and eager feminists.
   d. less able to assume responsible roles than northern women.

_____ 8. The author's main purpose in mentioning the accomplishments of Maria Mitchell is to point out that
   a. she discovered a comet.

   b. her professional achievements in astronomy were exceptional and thus somewhat improved the image of women.

   c. she was the first woman professor of astronomy in the U.S.

   d. she was a founder of the Association for the Advancement of Women.

9. The article states or implies that all of the following women worked to abolish slavery except

   a. Anna Howard Shaw.

   b. Harriet Tubman.

   c. Anna Dickson.

   d. Stanton and Anthony.

10. In the author's opinion, the long wait by women after the Civil War for suffrage

   a. was predictable in 1865.

   b. would not have been expected in 1865.

   c. was due to the vote of black men.

   d. was justified.

Answer the following with *T* (true) or *F* (false).

11. Women were granted the right to vote in 1920.

12. Sojourner Truth had been a southern slave.

13. The author implies that feminist leaders were more concerned with their own right to vote than with the abolition of slavery.

14. From the very beginning, the right to vote was the focal point of the women's movement.

15. Sojourner Truth had thirteen children.

Vocabulary

According to the way the italicized word was used in the selection, indicate *a, b, c,* or *d* for the word or phrase that gives the best definition.

1. "were too *restrictive*" (9)
   a. showy
   b. expensive
   c. complicated
   d. confining

2. "to the *detriment* of" (9)
   a. harm
   b. anger
   c. apology
   d. objection

3. "a *defiant* gesture" (16)
   a. unlucky
   b. resistive
   c. admirable
   d. ignorant

4. "*communal* marriage experiments" (21)
   a. permanent
   b. living together in groups
   c. illegal
   d. uncommon

____ 5. "silencing *hecklers*" (33)
    a. soldiers
    b. rioters
    c. disciples
    d. verbal harassers

____ 6. "*pursue* professional careers" (44)
    a. strive for
    b. abandon
    c. acknowledge
    d. indicate

____ 7. "sanitation and *hygiene*" (54)
    a. garbage disposal
    b. biology
    c. health care
    d. mental disorders

____ 8. "an *incessant* struggle" (65)
    a. earlier
    b. final
    c. novel
    d. unceasing

____ 9. "*convalescent* homes" (73)
    a. sanitary
    b. government
    c. reclaimed
    d. recuperating

____ 10. "called politically *naive*" (102)
    a. unsophisticated
    b. well informed
    c. dishonest
    d. unfortunate

Written Response

Use information from the text to answer the following question:

How did the actions of many early women "somewhat alter the image of the submissive and brainless child-woman"?

Writing Suggestion: List the women mentioned in the text and discuss how each changed stereotypical thinking. (Use your own paper.)

Connecting and Reflecting

In the following article, Gloria Steinem, an early leader in the women's liberation movement, states her observations on age and female activism. You may or may not agree. To investigate the matter, conduct a telephone interview with a working woman who is over 30 years of age. Ask questions about equality on the job, in the home, and in social situations. Write a paragraph for each of the three areas of inquiry to summarize her most significant comments and share the summaries in class. Read the following passage for Gloria Steinem's opinion.

Why Young Women Are More Conservative

If you had asked me a decade or more ago, I certainly would have said the campus was the first place to look for the feminist or any other revolution. I also would have assumed that student-age women, like student-age men, were much more likely to be activist and open to change than their parents.

It has taken me many years of traveling as a feminist speaker and organizer to understand that I was wrong about women; at least, about women acting on their own behalf. In activism, as in so many other things, I had been educated to assume that men's cultural pattern was the natural or the only one. If student years were the peak time of rebellion and openness to change for men, then the same must be true for women. In fact, a decade of listening to every kind of women's group—from brown-bag lunchtime lectures organized by office workers to all-night rap sessions at campus women's centers, from housewives' self-help groups to campus rallies—has convinced me that the reverse is more often true. Women may be the one group that grows more radical with age. Though some students are big exceptions to this rule, women in general don't begin to challenge the politics of our own lives until later.

As students, women are probably treated with more equality than we ever will be again. For one thing, we're consumers. The school is only too glad to get the tuition we pay, or that our families or government grants pay on our behalf. With population rates declining because of women's increased power over childbearing, that money is even more vital to a school's existence. Yet more than most consumers, we're too transient to have much power as a group. If our families are paying our tuition, we may have even less power.

As young women, whether students or not, we're still in the stage most valued by male-dominant cultures: we have our full potential as workers, wives, sex partners, and childbearers.

That means we haven't yet experienced the life events that are most radicalizing for women: entering the paid labor force and discovering how women are treated there; marrying and finding out that it is not yet an equal partnership; having children and discovering who is responsible for them and who is not; and aging, still a greater penalty for women than for men.

Young women have a big task of resisting pressures and challenging definitions. Their increasing success is a miracle of foresight and courage that should make us all proud. But they should know that they, too, may grow more radical with age.

Gloria Steinem, "Why Young Women Are More Conservative"

Selection **3**

PSYCHOLOGY

Stage 1:

Preview

>The author's main purpose is to teach techniques that will help you think creatively.

agree ☐   disagree ☐

>After reading this selection, I will need to know the difference between creative thinking and a critical attitude.

agree ☐   disagree ☐

Activate Schema
>Why are people afraid to express new ideas?

Learning Strategy
>Be able to describe the factors involved in both creative and critical thinking and explain how the two interact.

Word Knowledge
>Review the ten vocabulary items that follow the selection. Seek an understanding of unfamiliar words.

Stage 2: Integrate Knowledge While Reading

   1. Predict 2. Picture 3. Relate 4. Monitor 5. Fix up

Skill Development: Annotating

Annotate the following selection as if you were organizing the material to study for a quiz. Remember, do not annotate as you read, but wait until you finish a section and then mark the important points.

CREATIVE THINKING AND CRITICAL THINKING

From Gardner Lindzey et al., *Psychology**

Creative thinking is thinking that results in the discovery of a new or improved solution to a problem. *Critical thinking* is the examination and testing of suggested solutions to see whether they will work. Creative thinking leads to the birth of new ideas, while critical
5 thinking tests ideas for flaws and defects. Both are necessary for effective problem-solving, yet they are incompatible—creative thinking interferes with critical thinking, and vice versa. To think creatively we must let our thoughts run free. The more spontaneous the process, the more ideas will be born and the greater the
10 probability that an effective solution will be found. A steady stream of ideas furnishes the raw material. Then critical judgment selects and refines the best ideas, picking the most effective solution out of the available possibilities. Though we must engage in the two types of thinking separately, we need both for efficient problem-solving.

Inhibitions of Creative Thinking
15 *Conformity*—the desire to be like everyone else—is the foremost barrier to creative thinking. A person is afraid to express new ideas because he thinks he will make a fool of himself and be ridiculed. This feeling may date back to his childhood, when his spontaneous and imaginative ideas may have been laughed at by parents or older
20 people. During adolescence, conformity is reinforced because young people are afraid to be different from their peers. Then, too, history teaches us that innovators often are laughed at and even persecuted.

---

*From *Psychology* by Gardner Lindsey, Calvin Hall, and Richard F. Thompson, pp. 291-295. Copyright © 1975 by Werth Publishers, Inc. Reprinted by permission.

Censorship—especially self-imposed censorship—is a second significant barrier to creativity. External censorship of ideas, the
25 thought-control of modern dictatorships, is dramatic and newsworthy; but internal censorship is more effective and dependable. External censorship merely prevents public distribution of proscribed thoughts; the thoughts may still be expressed privately. But people who are frightened by their thoughts tend to react passively, rather than think
30 of creative solutions to their problems. Sometimes they even repress those thoughts, so that they are not aware they exist. Freud called this internalized censor the *superego*.

A third barrier to creative thinking is the rigid *education* still commonly imposed upon children. Regimentation, memorization, and
35 drill may help instill the accepted knowledge of the day, but these classroom methods cannot teach students how to solve new problems or how to improve upon conventional solutions. On the other hand, the progressive movement in education often has been criticized on the ground that its emphasis on creative thinking also encourages
40 intellectual nonconformity and radicalism. Such critics fear that new ideas may threaten the established order. Others simply believe that creative thinking must be balanced by critical thinking if it is to be useful.

A fourth barrier to creative thinking is the great *desire to find an answer quickly.* Such a strong motivation often narrows one's
45 consciousness and encourages the acceptance of early, inadequate solutions. People tend to do their best creative thinking when they are released from the demands and responsibilities of everyday living. Inventors, scientists, artists, writers, and executives often do their most creative thinking when they are not distracted by routine work.
50 The value of a vacation is not that it enables a person to work better on his return but rather that it permits new ideas to be born during the vacation.

The daydreamer often is criticized for wasting his time. Yet without daydreams, society's progress would be considerably slower, since
55 daydreaming often leads to the discovery of original ideas. This is not to suggest that all daydreaming or leisurely contemplation results in valid and workable ideas—far from it. But somewhere, among the thousands of ideas conceived, one useful idea will appear. Finding this one idea without having to produce a thousand poor ones would
60 achieve a vast saving in creative thinking. But such a saving seems unlikely, especially since creative thinking is generally enjoyable whether its results are useful or not.

Critical Thinking

Creative thinking must be followed by critical thinking if we want to sort out and refine those ideas that are potentially useful. Critical
65 thinking is essentially an idea-testing operation. Will it work? What is

wrong with it? How can it be improved? These are questions to be answered by a critical examination of newly hatched ideas. You may be highly creative, but if you cannot determine which ideas are practical and reasonable, your creativity will not lead to many fruitful

70 consequences. In order to make such distinctions, you must maintain some distance and detachment, so that you can appraise your own ideas objectively.

Critical thinking requires some criteria by which to judge the practicality of the ideas. For example, if a community wants to do

75 something about crime, it must decide what limitations are to be imposed upon the measures that are suggested. One limitation is the amount of money available; many proposals for curbing crime cost more than the community is willing or able to pay. Critical thinking must always take such realities into account.

80 What barriers stand in the path of critical thinking? One is the *fear of being aggressive and destructive.* We learn as children not to be critical, not to differ with what someone says, especially an older person. To criticize is to be discourteous.

A closely related barrier is the *fear of retaliation.* If I criticize your

85 ideas, you may turn about and criticize mine. This often involves yet another barrier, the *overevaluation* of one's own ideas. We like what we have created, and often we are reluctant to let others take apart our creation. By and large, those who are least secure hang on most tenaciously to their original ideas.

90 Finally, we should note again that if too much emphasis is placed upon being creative, the critical faculty may remain underdeveloped. In their zeal to stimulate creativity in their pupils, teachers often are reluctant to think critically. This is unfortunate, since for most people life requires a balance between creative and critical thinking.

95 **Critical Attitudes.**   There is an important distinction between critical thinking and a *critical attitude.* Critical thinking tries to arrive at a valid and practical solution to a problem. However much it may reject and discard, its final goal is constructive. A critical attitude, on the other hand, is destructive in intent. A person with a critical

100 attitude tends to criticize solely for the sake for criticizing. Such an attitude is emotional rather than cognitive.

The Creative Person

In recent years, psychologists have studied creativity intensively. The first challenge they faced was how to define and recognize creativity. One common solution to this problem is to ask knowledgeable

105 people to name the most creative individuals in their own field. Architects are asked to identify the most creative members of their profession or authors are asked to name the most creative writers.

These highly creative people then are studied by means of interviews, questionnaires, tests, and other devices to see how they differ from less creative members of the same profession. These studies show
110 that exceptionally creative people are characteristically:

1. flexible
2. intuitive
3. perceptive
4. original
5. ingenious
6. dedicated
7. hardworking
8. persistent
9. independent

10. unconventional
11. courageous
12. uninhibited
13. moody
14. self-centered
15. self-assertive
16. dominant
17. eccentric

Creative people often have vivid and sometimes even flamboyant personalities. They prefer complexity to simplicity. And those who are males accept the feminine side of their nature without being effeminate (Barron 1959).
115 Isolating such characteristics of highly creative people may be useful. If these traits are related to creativity, child training and educational procedures may be tailored to produce more creative people. Still, we are only assuming that these traits have anything to do with being creative. They may merely be associated with creativity,
120 rather than being determinants of it. Or, they may be necessary but not sufficient conditions for being creative. Flexibility, originality, and hard work, for example, may be requirements for creativity but they certainly are not sufficient to insure it. The creative genius displayed by Shakespeare, Leonardo da Vinci, Einstein, and Beethoven remains
125 a mystery that has so far eluded scientific analysis.

Stage 3: Recall for Self-Testing

Stop and recall what you have read. Review your use of the thinking strategies. Did you use all five?

Skill Development: Mapping

Review your annotations on this selection and condense the ideas into a map spatially representing the main ideas and significant subpoints to use as a quick overview for this selection.

Comprehension Questions

1. Who or what is the topic of this selection? _____

   What is the main idea the author is trying to convey about the topic?

   _____

   _____

After reading the selection, answer the following questions with *a, b, c,* or *d.*

_____ 2. According to the author, creative thinking includes all of the following except
   a. improved solutions to old problems.
   b. the birth of new ideas.
   c. a spontaneous flow of free thoughts.
   d. an evaluation of effective alternatives.

_____ 3. The author implies that critical thinking could be characterized as all of the following except
   a. selective.
   b. judgmental.
   c. spontaneous.
   d. organized.

_____ 4. Of the following barriers to creative thinking, an individual would probably have the most control over
   a. conformity.
   b. external censorship.
   c. education.
   d. the desire for a quick answer.

_____ 5. Of the following statements, the author would agree that
   a. in general, today's educational system encourages creativity.
   b. creative people must dare to be different.
   c. dictatorships encourage creative ideas.
   d. daily duties do not interfere with creativity.

_____ 6. The author believes that daydreaming
   a. is a waste of time.
   b. slows society's progress.
   c. fosters creative thinking.
   d. saves time in problem solving.

_____ 7. The author would agree with all of the following statements except
   a. creative thinking comes before critical thinking.
   b. critical thinking requires guidelines for evaluating ideas.
   c. critical thinking must be realistic.
   d. creative thinking should be done by one person and critical thinking by another.

_____ 8. All of the following are barriers to critical thinking except
      a. the threat of returned criticism.
      b. the chance of offending someone.
      c. an aggressive desire for improvement.
      d. the possible destruction of cherished ideas.

_____ 9. The author feels that a critical attitude is
      a. desirable.
      b. cognitive.
      c. unintentional.
      d. destructive.

_____ 10. The author believes that highly creative people
      a. cannot isolate the determinants of creativity.
      b. tend to be effeminate.
      c. make simple solutions complicated.
      d. do not need to work hard.

Answer the following with _T_ (true) or _F_ (false).

_____ 11. The author believes that rest is the most important result of a vacation.

_____ 12. The author feels that memorization cannot teach students to solve new problems.

_____ 13. The author implies that a teacher's constructive criticism helps students develop critical thinking.

_____ 14. The author views critical thinking as an idea-testing process.

_____ 15. The author feels that creative thinking is fun.

Vocabulary

According to the way the italicized word was used in the selection, indicate _a, b, c,_ or _d_ for the word or phrase that gives the best definition.

____ 1. "yet they are _incompatible_" (06)
    a. untouched
    b. not understood
    c. similar in nature
    d. unsuitable together

____ 2. "The more _spontaneous_ the process" (08)
    a. demanding
    b. momentarily impulsive
    c. reliable
    d. advantageous

____ 3. "_Inhibitions_ of Creative Thinking" (14)
    a. variations
    b. objections
    c. motivators
    d. restraints

____ 4. "_innovators_ often are laughed at" (22)
    a. clowns
    b. introducers of the new
    c. people who fail
    d. adventurers

____ 5. "nonconformity and
   radicalism" (40)
   a. conservatism
   b. extremism
   c. isolationism
   d. romanticism

____ 6. "leisurely *contemplation*"
   (56)
   a. relaxation
   b. conversation
   c. meditation
   d. manipulation

____ 7. "maintain some distance and
   detachment" (70)
   a. outside advice
   b. separation
   c. sophistication
   d. emotional involvement

____ 8. "hang on most *tenaciously*"
   (88)
   a. strongly
   b. loosely
   c. quickly
   d. quietly

____ 9. "in their *zeal* to stimulate"
   (92)
   a. attempt
   b. goal
   c. rush
   d. eagerness

____ 10. "*flamboyant* personalities"
   (111)
   a. annoying
   b. likable
   c. showy
   d. intelligent

Written Response

Use the information from the text to answer the following question:
Is it true that in the American classroom some time is spent on critical thinking but very little emphasis is placed on creative thinking?
Response Approach: First define critical thinking and relate the characteristics to the classroom. Then define creative thinking and discuss how inhibitions operate in the average American classroom.

Connecting and Reflecting

Thinking creatively often means thinking about something in a different way, taking a new perspective. The following problem illustrates this notion. Collaborate with another classmate and together explore solutions to the nine-dot problem. Do not be hesitant to break out of your predictable mental set and visualize the problem differently.

How Mental Set Affects Problem Solving
The concept of **mental set** is also very relevant in problem solving. A mental set is defined as a tendency to perceive or respond to something in a given (set) way. We often form expectations or set tendencies when we go about problem solving, and these often interfere with what we're doing.

The following problem provides another example of how an inappropriate mental set can interfere with problem solving. Most subjects when first presented with this problem make an assumption (form a mental set). They assume that the nine dots form a square and that their lines somehow must stay within that square. Only when this mental set is "broken" can the problem be solved.

The classic "nine-dot problem." The task is to connect all nine dots with just four straight lines, without removing your pen or pencil from the paper. (From Scheerer 1963.)

Josh Gerow, *Psychology: An Introduction*

WORD BRIDGE
Dictionary

Do you have an excellent collegiate dictionary such as *Webster's New Collegiate Dictionary?* Every college student needs two dictionaries: a small one for class and a large one to keep at home. In class you may use a small paperback dictionary for quick spelling or word meaning checks. The paperback is easy to carry but does not provide the depth of information needed for college study and found in the larger collegiate editions. Good dictionaries contain not only the definitions of words, but also provide the following additional information for each word:

Guide Words. The two words at the top of each dictionary page are the first and last entries on the page. They help guide your search for a particular entry by indicating what is covered on that page.

guide words

pronunciation

origin

single meaning

flagrante delicto ● flappy

fla·min·go \flə-'miŋ-(,)gō\ *n, pl* -gos *also* -goes
[Pg, fr. Sp *flamenco,* prob. fr. OProv *flamenc,* fr. *flama* flame (fr. L *flamma*) + -enc
'-ing] (1565) : any of several aquatic birds
(family Phoenicopteridae) with long legs
and neck, webbed feet, a broad lamellate bill
resembling that of a duck but abruptly bent
downward, and usu. rosy-white, plumage
with scarlet wing coverts and black wing
quills

part of speech

plural spelling

flamingo

By permission. From *Webster's Ninth New Collegiate Dictionary;* © 1991 by Merriam-Webster Inc., publisher of the Merriam-Webster® Dictionaries.

\ə\ abut	\ᵊ\ kitten, F table	\ər\ **further**	\a\ **ash**	\ā\ ace	\ä\ cot, cart					
\aú\ **out**	\ch\ **chin**	\e\ bet	\ē\ easy	\g\ go	\i\ hit	\ī\ ice	\j\ job			
\ŋ\ sing	\ō\ go	\o\ **law**	\oi\ **boy**	\th\ thin	\th\ the	\ü\ loot	\ú\ foot			
\y\ yet	\zh\ vision	\á, k̲, ⁿ, œ, œ̄, ʉ, ʉ̄, ʸ\ *see* Guide to Pronunciation								

Flagrante delicto is the first entry on the page of the dictionary on which *flamingo* appears, and *flappy* is the last entry.

Pronunciation.

The boldface main entry divides the word into sounds, using a dot between each syllable. In parentheses after the entry, letters and symbols show the pronunciation. A diacritical mark (′) at the end of a syllable indicates stress on that syllable. A heavy mark means major stress; a lighter one shows minor stress.

A key explaining the symbols and letters appears at the bottom of the dictionary page. For example, a word like *ragweed* (rag′ wēd) would be pronounced with a short *a* as in *ash* and a long *e* as in *easy.*

The *a* in *flamingo* sounds like the *a* in *abut,* and the final *o* has a long sound as in *go.* The stress is on the first syllable.

Parts of Speech.

The part of speech is indicated in an abbreviation for each meaning of a word. A single word, for example, may be a noun with one definition and a verb with another. The noun *flamingo* can be used as only one part of speech, but *sideline* can be both a noun and a verb.

Spellings.

Spellings are given for the plural of the word and for special forms. This is particularly useful in determining whether letters are added or dropped to form the new words. The plural of flamingo can be spelled correctly in two different ways. Both *flamingos* and *flamingoes* are acceptable.

Origin. For many entries, the foreign word and language from which the word was derived will appear after the pronunciation. For example, *L* stands for a Latin origin and *G* for Greek. A key for the many dictionary abbreviations usually appears at the beginning of the book.

The word *flamingo* has a rich history. It is Portuguese (*Pg*) and comes from the Spanish (*fr Sp*) word *flamenco*. It is derived ultimately from the Old Provençal (*fr OProv*) *flamenc*, from *flama* for *flame*, which comes from the Latin (*fr L*) word *flamma*.

Multiple Meanings. A single word can have many shades of meaning or several completely different meanings. Different meanings are numbered.

The word *flamingo* has only one meaning. The word *sideline*, however, has several, as shown in the entry.

A sideline can be a business, a product, or a designated area. In addition, it can mean to move something out of the action.

¹side·line \-ˌlin\ *n* (1862) **1 :** a line at right angles to a goal line or end line and marking a side of a court or field of play for athletic games **2 a :** a line of goods sold in addition to one's principal line **b :** a business or activity pursued in addition to one's regular occupation **3 a :** the space immediately outside the lines along either side of an athletic field or court **b :** the standpoint of persons not immediately participating — usu. used in pl.
²sideline *vt* (1943) **:** to put out of action **:** put on the sidelines

By permission. From *Webster's Ninth New Collegiate Dictionary*; © 1988 by Merriam-Webster Inc., publisher of the Merriam-Webster® Dictionaries.

Exercise 5: Using the Dictionary

Answer the following questions, using page 684 from *Webster's Ninth New Collegiate Dictionary*, with *T* (true), *F* (false), and *CT* (can't tell).

1. *Lent* is eight weekends before Easter.
2. *Lentils* can be eaten.
3. The word *leotard* is derived from *leopard*.
4. A convex *lense* lets in more light than a concave lense.
5. *Lenient* can be both an adjective and a noun.
6. The plural of *leone* can be either *leones* or *leone*.
7. One of the origins of *lemur* is the Latin word *lemures*, meaning *ghosts*.
8. The word *lemures* can be correctly pronounced in two different ways.
9. When the words *lend* and *lease* are used together to mean a transfer of goods, no hyphen is required.
10. A legitimate word can be formed by adding the suffix *-esque* to the first part of Leonardo da Vinci's name.

lemon yellow *n* (1807) : a variable color averaging a brilliant greenish yellow

lem·pi·ra \lem-'pir-ə\ *n* [AmerSp, fr. *Lempira*, 16th cent. Indian chief] (ca. 1934) — see MONEY table

le·mur \'lē-mər\ *n* [L *lemures*, pl., ghosts; akin to Gk *lamia* devouring monster] (1795) : any of numerous arboreal chiefly nocturnal mammals that were formerly widespread but are now largely confined to Madagascar, are related to the monkeys but are usu. regarded as constituting a distinct superfamily (Lemuroidea), and usu. have a muzzle like a fox, large eyes, very soft woolly fur, and a long furry tail

le·mu·res \'lem-ə-,rās, 'lem-yə-,rēz\ *n pl* [L] (ca. 1555) : spirits of the unburied dead exorcised from homes in early Roman religious observances

lend \'lend\ *vb* **lent** \'lent\; **lend·ing** [ME *lenen, lenden*, fr. OE *lǣnan*, fr. *lǣn* loan — more at LOAN] *vt* (bef. 12c) **1 a** : to give for temporary use on condition that the same or its equivalent be returned **b** : to let out (money) for temporary use on condition of repayment with interest **2 a** : to give the assistance or support of : AFFORD, FURNISH ⟨a dispassionate and scholarly manner which ~*s* great force to his criticisms — *Times Lit. Supp.*⟩ **b** : to adapt or apply (oneself) : ACCOMMODATE ⟨a topic that ~*s* itself admirably to class discussion⟩ ~ *vi* : to make a loan — **lend·able** \'len-də-bəl\ *adj* — **lend·er** *n*

lending library *n* (1708) : RENTAL LIBRARY

lend–lease \'len-'dlēs\ *n* [U.S. *Lend-Lease* Act (1941)] (1941) : the transfer of goods and services to an ally to aid in a common cause with payment being made by a return of the original items or their use in the common cause or by a similar transfer of other goods and services — **lend–lease** *vt*

length \'leŋ(k)th, 'len(t)th\ *n, pl* **lengths** \'leŋ(k)ths, 'len(t)ths, 'leŋ(k)s\ [ME *lengthe*, fr. OE *lengthu*, fr. *lang* long] (bef. 12c) **1 a** : the longer or longest dimension of an object **b** : a measured distance or dimension ⟨10-inch ~⟩ — see METRIC SYSTEM table, WEIGHT table **c** : the quality or state of being long **2 a** : duration or extent in time **b** : relative duration or stress of a sound **3 a** : distance or extent in space **b** : the length of something taken as a unit of measure ⟨his horse led by a ~⟩ **4** : the degree to which something (as a course of action or a line of thought) is carried — often used in pl. ⟨went to great ~*s* to learn the truth⟩ **5 a** : a long expanse or stretch **b** : a piece constituting or usable as part of a whole or of a connected series : SECTION ⟨a ~ of pipe⟩ **6** : a vertical dimension of an article of clothing — **at length 1** : FULLY, COMPREHENSIVELY **2** : at last : FINALLY

length·en \'leŋ(k)-thən, 'len(t)-\ *vb* **length·ened; length·en·ing** \'leŋ(k)th-(ə-)niŋ, 'len(t)th-\ *vt* (14c) : to make longer ~ *vi* : to grow longer ***syn*** see EXTEND — **length·en·er** \'leŋ(k)th-(ə-)nər, 'len(t)th-\ *n*

length·ways \'leŋ(k)th-,wāz, 'len(t)th-\ *adv* (1599) : LENGTHWISE

length·wise \-,wīz\ *adv* (1580) : in the direction of the length : LONGITUDINALLY — **lengthwise** *adj*

lengthy \'leŋ(k)-thē, 'len(t)-\ *adj* **length·i·er; -est** (1689) **1** : protracted excessively : OVERLONG **2** : EXTENDED, LONG — **length·i·ly** \-thə-lē\ *adv* — **length·i·ness** \-thē-nəs\ *n*

le·nience \'lē-nyən(t)s, -nē-ən(t)s\ *n* (1796) : LENIENCY

le·nien·cy \'lē-nē-ən-sē, -nyən-sē\ *n, pl* **-cies** (1780) **1** : the quality or state of being lenient **2** : a lenient disposition or practice

le·nient \'lē-nē-ənt, -nyənt\ *adj* [L *lenient-, leniens*, prp. of *lenire* to soften, soothe, fr. *lenis* soft, mild — more at LET] (1652) **1** : exerting a soothing or easing influence : relieving pain or stress **2** : of mild and tolerant disposition; *esp* : INDULGENT — **le·nient·ly** *adv*

Leni–Le·nape *or* **Len·ni–Le·nape** \,len-ē-lə-'näp-ē, ,len-ē-'len-ə-pē, ,len-ē-lə-'näp\ *n* [Delaware] (1781) : DELAWARE 1

Le·nin·ism \'len-ə-,niz-əm\ *n* (1918) : the political, economic, and social principles and policies advocated by Lenin; *esp* : the theory and practice of communism developed by or associated with Lenin — **Le·nin·ist** \-nəst\ *n or adj* — **Le·nin·ite** \-,nīt\ *n or adj*

le·nis \'lē-nəs, 'lā-\ *adj* [NL, fr. L, mild, smooth] (ca. 1897) : produced with relatively lax articulation and weak expiration ⟨\d\ in *doe* is ~, \t\ in *toe* is fortis⟩

len·i·tive \'len-ət-iv\ *adj* [ME *lenitif*, fr. MF, fr. ML *lenitivus*, fr. L *lenitus*, pp. of *lenire*] (15c) : alleviating pain or harshness : SOOTHING — **lenitive** *n* — **len·i·tive·ly** *adv*

len·i·ty \'len-ət-ē\ *n* (1548) : the quality or state of being lenient : CLEMENCY ***syn*** see MERCY

le·no \'lē-(,)nō\ *n* [perh. fr. F *linon* linen fabric, lawn, fr. MF *lin* flax, linen, fr. L *linum* flax] (1821) **1** : an open weave in which pairs of warp yarns cross one another and thereby lock the filling yarn in position **2** : a fabric made with a leno weave

[1]**lens** *also* **lense** \'lenz\ *n* [NL *lent-, lens*, fr. L, lentil; fr. its shape — more at LENTIL] (1693) **1 a** : a piece of transparent material (as glass) that has two opposite regular surfaces either both curved or one curved and the other plane and that is used either singly or combined in an optical instrument for forming an image by focusing rays of light **b** : a combination of two or more simple lenses **2** : a device for directing or focusing radiation other than light (as sound waves, radio microwaves, or electrons) **3** : something shaped like a double-convex optical lens ⟨~ of sandstone⟩ **4** : a highly transparent biconvex lens-shaped or nearly spherical body in the eye that focuses light rays (as upon the retina) — see EYE illustration — **lensed** \'lenzd\ *adj* — **lens·less** \'lenz-ləs\ *adj*

[2]**lens** *vt* (1942) : to make a motion picture of : FILM

Lent \'lent\ *n* [ME *lente* springtime, Lent, fr. OE *lencten*; akin to OHG *lenzin* spring] (13c) : the 40 weekdays from Ash Wednesday to Easter observed by the Roman Catholic, Eastern, and some Protestant churches as a period of penitence and fasting

len·ta·men·te \,lent-ə-'men-(,)tā\ *adv or adj* [It, fr. *lento* slow] (1724) : LENTO

len·tan·do \len-'tän-(,)dō\ *adv or adj* [It] (ca. 1847) : becoming slower — used as a direction in music

Lent·en \'lent-ᵊn\ *adj* (bef. 12c) : of, relating to, or suitable for Lent; *esp* : MEAGER ⟨~ fare⟩

len·tic \'lent-ik\ *adj* [L *lentus* sluggish] (ca. 1930) : of, relating to, or living in still waters (as lakes, ponds, or swamps) — compare LOTIC

len·ti·cel \'lent-ə-,sel\ *n* [NL *lenticella*, dim. of L *lent-, lens* lentil] (ca. 1864) : a pore in the stems of woody plants through which gases are exchanged between the atmosphere and the stem tissues

len·tic·u·lar \len-'tik-yə-lər\ *adj* [L *lenticularis* lentil-shaped, fr. *lenticula* lentil] (15c) **1** : having the shape of a double-convex lens **2** : of or relating to a lens **3** : provided with or utilizing lenticules ⟨a ~ screen⟩

len·tic·u·late \-lət\ *vt* **-lat·ed; -lat·ing** (1925) : to provide with lenticules (as by embossing, molding, or coating) ⟨*lenticulated* film⟩ — **len·tic·u·la·tion** \-,tik-yə-'lā-shən\ *n*

len·ti·cule \'lent-ə-,kyü(ə)l\ *n* [L *lenticula*] (1942) **1** : any of the minute lenses on the base side of a film used in stereoscopic or color photography **2** : any of the tiny corrugations or grooves molded or embossed into the surface of a projection screen

len·til \'lent-ᵊl\ *n* [ME, fr. OF *lentille*, fr. L *lenticula*, dim. of *lent-, lens*; akin to Gk *lathyros* vetch] (13c) **1** : a widely cultivated Eurasian annual leguminous plant (*Lens culinaris*) with flattened edible seeds and leafy stalks used as fodder **2** : the seed of the lentil

len·tis·si·mo \len-'tis-ə-,mō\ *adv or adj* [It, superl. of *lento*] (ca. 1903) : in a very slow manner — used as a direction in music

len·to \'len-(,)tō\ *adv or adj* [It, fr. *lento*, adj., slow, fr. L *lentus* pliant, sluggish, slow — more at LITHE] (1724) : in a slow manner — used as a direction in music

Leo \'lē-(,)ō\ *n* [L (gen. *Leonis*), lit., lion — more at LION] **1** : a northern constellation east of Cancer **2 a** : the 5th sign of the zodiac in astrology — see ZODIAC table **b** : one born under this sign — **Le·o·nine** \'lē-ə-,nīn\ *adj*

le·one \lē-'ōn\ *n, pl* **leones** *or* **leone** [*Sierra Leone*] (ca. 1964) — see MONEY table

Leo·nid \'lē-ə-nəd\ *n, pl* **Leo·nids** *or* **Le·on·i·des** \lē-'än-ə-,dēz\ [L *Leon-, Leo*; fr. their appearing to radiate from a point in Leo] (1876) : one of the shooting stars constituting the meteoric shower that recurs near the 15th of November

le·o·nine \'lē-ə-,nīn\ *adj* [ME, fr. L *leoninus*, fr. *leon-, leo*] (14c) : of, relating to, suggestive of, or resembling a lion

leop·ard \'lep-ərd\ *n* [ME, fr. OF *leupart*, fr. LL *leopardus*, fr. Gk *leopardos*, fr. *leōn* lion + *pardos* leopard] (13c) **1** : a large strong cat (*Felis pardus*) of southern Asia and Africa that is usu. tawny or buff with black spots arranged in broken rings or rosettes — called also *panther* **2** : a heraldic representation of a lion passant guardant — **leop·ard·ess** \-ərd-əs\ *n*

leopard 1

leopard frog *n* (1839) : a common American frog (*Rana pipiens*) that is bright green with large black white-margined blotches on the back; *also* : a similar frog (*R. sphenocephala*) of the southeastern U.S.

le·o·tard \'lē-ə-,tärd\ *n* [Jules *Léotard*, †1870 Fr. aerial gymnast] (1920) : a close-fitting one-piece garment worn by dancers, acrobats, and aerialists; *also* : TIGHTS

Lep·cha \'lep-chə\ *n, pl* **Lepcha** *or* **Lepchas** (1819) **1** : a member of a Mongoloid people of Sikkim, India **2** : the Tibeto-Burman language of the Lepcha people

lep·er \'lep-ər\ *n* [ME, fr. *lepre* leprosy, fr. MF, fr. LL *lepra*, fr. Gk, fr. *lepein* to peel; akin to OE *lǣfer* reed] (14c) **1** : a person affected with leprosy **2** : a person shunned for moral or social reasons

lepid- *or* **lepido-** *comb form* [NL, fr. Gk, fr. *lepid-, lepis* scale, fr. *lepein*] : flake : scale ⟨*Lepido*ptera⟩

le·pid·o·lite \li-'pid-ᵊl-,īt\ *n* [G *lepidolith*, fr. *lepid-* + *-lith*] (ca. 1796) : a variable mineral typically $K(Li,Al)_3(Si,Al)_4O_{10}(F,OH_2)$ that consists of a mica containing lithium and is used esp. in glazes and enamels

lep·i·dop·tera \,lep-ə-'däp-tə-rə\ *n pl* (1773) : insects that are lepidopterans

lep·i·dop·ter·an \-rən\ *n* [NL *Lepidoptera*, fr. *lepid-* + Gk *pteron* wing — more at FEATHER] (ca. 1902) : any of a large order (Lepidoptera) of insects comprising the butterflies, moths, and skippers that as adults have four broad or lanceolate wings usu. covered with minute overlapping and often brightly colored scales and that as larvae are caterpillars — **lepidopteran** *adj* — **lep·i·dop·ter·ous** \-tə-rəs\ *adj*

lep·i·dop·ter·ist \-tə-rəst\ *n* (1826) : a specialist in lepidopterology

lep·i·dop·ter·ol·o·gy \-,däp-tə-'räl-ə-jē\ *n* (1899) : a branch of entomology concerned with lepidopterans — **lep·i·dop·ter·o·log·i·cal** \-tə-rə-'läj-i-kəl\ *adj* — **lep·i·dop·ter·ol·o·gist** \-tə-'räl-ə-jəst\ *n*

lep·i·dote \'lep-ə-,dōt\ *adj* [Gk *lepidōtos* scaly, fr. *lepid-, lepis*] (ca. 1836) : covered with scurf or scurfy scales ⟨~ rhododendrons⟩

lep·re·chaun \'lep-rə-,kän, -,kȯn\ *n* [IrGael *leipreachān*] (1604) : a mischievous elf of Irish folklore usu. believed to reveal the hiding place of treasure if caught — **lep·re·chaun·ish** \-ish\ *adj*

le·pro·ma·tous \lə-'präm-ət-əs, -'prō-mət-\ *adj* [NL *lepromat-, leproma* leprous lesion, fr. LL *lepra*] (1898) : characterized by, exhibiting, or being leprosy with infective superficial granulomatous nodules

lep·ro·sar·i·um \,lep-rə-'ser-ē-əm\ *n, pl* **-i·ums** *or* **-ia** \-ē-ə\ [ML, fr. LL *leprosus*] (1846) : a hospital for leprosy patients

lep·ro·sy \'lep-rə-sē\ *n* [*leprous* + *-y*] (15c) **1** : a chronic disease caused by a bacillus (*Mycobacterium leprae*) and characterized by the formation of nodules or of macules that enlarge and spread accompanied by loss of sensation with eventual paralysis, wasting of muscle, and production of deformities and mutilations **2** : a morally or spiritually harmful influence — **lep·rot·ic** \le-'prät-ik\ *adj*

lep·rous \'lep-rəs\ *adj* [ME, fr. LL *leprosus* leprous, fr. *lepra* leprosy — more at LEPER] (13c) **1 a** : infected with leprosy **b** : of, relating to, or resembling leprosy or a leper **2** : SCALY, SCURFY — **lep·rous·ly** *adv* — **lep·rous·ness** *n*

-lep·sy \,lep-sē\ *n comb form* [MF *-lepsie*, fr. LL *-lepsia*, fr. Gk *-lēpsia*, fr. *lēpsis*, fr. *lambanein* to take, seize — more at LATCH] : taking : seizure ⟨nympho*lepsy*⟩

lep·to·ceph·a·lus \,lep-tə-'sef-ə-ləs\ *n, pl* **-li** \-,lī, -,lē\ [NL, fr. Gk *leptos* + *kephalē* head — more at CEPHALIC] (1769) : a long thin small-headed transparent pelagic first larva of various eels

[1]**lep·ton** \lep-'tän\ *n, pl* **lep·ta** \-'tä\ [NGk, fr. Gk, a small coin, fr. neut. of *leptos* peeled, slender, small, fr. *lepein* to peel — more at LEPER] (ca. 1727) — see *drachma* at MONEY table

[2]**lep·ton** \'lep-,tän\ *n* [Gk *leptos* + E [2]*-on*] (ca. 1948) : any of a family of particles (as electrons, muons, and neutrinos) that have spin quantum

By permission. From *Webster's Ninth New Collegiate Dictionary*; © 1991 by Merriam-Webster Inc., publisher of the Merriam-Webster® Dictionaries.

Exercise 6: Using Your Dictionary

Use your own dictionary to answer the following questions about words in this chapter.

1. *Naive* is derived from what language?
2. What is the meaning of the root word in *convalescent?*
3. Give three synonyms for *zeal.*
4. How is *flamboyant* connected with architecture?
5. What is *spontaneous combustion?*

CHAPTER 5

RATE FLEXIBILITY

- What is your reading rate?
- How fast should you read?
- What are some techniques for faster reading?
- Why skim?
- Why scan?

WHY IS RATE IMPORTANT?

Professors of college reading are far more concerned with comprehension than with a student's rate of reading. They would say that you should not attempt to "speed read" textbooks, and they would be right.

Most students, however, when asked what they would like to change about their reading, say, "I read too slowly. I would like to improve my reading speed." Whether or not this perception is accurate, rate is definitely a concern of college students. Whether you are reading a magazine or a textbook, reading 150 words per minute takes twice as long as reading 300 words per minute. Understanding the factors that contribute to rate can both quell anxiety and help increase reading efficiency.

WHAT IS YOUR READING RATE?

Do you know how many words you read on the average each minute? To find out, read the following selection at your usual reading rate, just as you would have read it before you started thinking about speed. Time your reading of the selection so that you can calculate your rate. Read carefully enough to answer the ten comprehension questions that follow the selection.

Exercise 1: Assessing Rate

Directions: Time your reading of this selection so that you can compute your words-per-minute rate. To make the calculations easier, try to begin reading on the exact minute, with zero seconds. In other words, begin when the second hand points to twelve. Record your starting time in minutes and seconds and, when you have finished reading, record your finishing time in minutes and seconds. Then answer the questions that follow. Remember, read the selection at your normal rate.

Starting time: _____ minutes _____ seconds

Sea Lions
"Hey, you guys, hurry up! They're gonna feed the seals!" No visit to the zoo or the circus would be complete without the playful antics of the trained "seal." However, the noisy animal that barks enthusiastically while balancing a ball on its nose is not really a seal at all. In reality, it is a small species of sea lion.

Like all mammals, seal lions are air breathers. Nevertheless, they spend most of their lives in the ocean and are skilled and graceful swimmers. Two species live off the Pacific coast of North America. The California sea lion is the smaller and more southerly. This is the circus "seal." An adult male may measure over seven feet in length and weigh more than 500 pounds. Females are considerably smaller, with a length of six feet and a weight of 200 pounds.

The larger northern, or Steller, sea lion lives off the Alaskan shore in summer and off the California coast in winter. Bulls may weigh over a ton and reach a length of more than eleven feet. Cows weigh some 750 pounds and are about nine feet long. The northern sea lion is generally not as noisy as the California sea lion, but it can bellow loudly when it wants to make its presence known.

At one time, sea lions were hunted almost to extinction for their hides, meat, and oil. Eskimos even stored the valuable oil in pouches made from the sea lion's stomach. Today, sea lions are protected by law, but many fall prey to their natural enemies, the shark and the killer whale. Sea lions are often disliked and sometimes killed by fishermen who accuse them of eating valuable fish and damaging nets. For the most part, the accusations are untrue. The northern sea lion eats mostly "trash fish," which are of little commercial value. The California sea lion prefers squid. Although sea lions do eat salmon, they also eat lampreys, a snake-like parasitic fish that devours salmon in great numbers. By controlling the lamprey population, the sea lion probably saves more salmon than it eats.

Sea lions come ashore in early summer to give birth and to mate. First to arrive are the bulls, which immediately stake out individual territories along the beach. The cows follow and soon give birth to the single pup that each has been carrying since the previous summer. The newborn pup has about a dozen teeth. Its big blue eyes are open from birth and will turn brown after a few weeks.

The pup is born into a tumultuous world of huge, bellowing adults, and it must mature quickly to avoid being trampled by the teeming mob around it. It can move about within an hour, and can be seen scrambling nimbly among its elders within a few days. It doubles its weight in the first month or two. The quick weight gain is largely attributable to the extremely rich milk of the sea lion mother. Low in water and high in protein, the milk is almost 50 percent fat, whereas cow's milk is about 4 percent fat. Zookeepers have found it difficult to provide sea lion pups with adequate nourishment in the absence of the mother. At Marineland of the Pacific, an orphaned pup was successfully raised on a diet of whipping cream, liquified mackerel muscle, calcium caseinate, and a multivitamin syrup. Not a very delectable-sounding menu, perhaps, but the pup loved it.

Throw a human infant into the ocean and it would drown. So would a sea lion baby. The only mammals that are known to swim from birth are whales and manatees. Although it will spend most of its twenty-year life in the ocean, the sea lion pup is at first terrified of water. The mother must spend about two months teaching it to swim.

Mating is no quiet affair among the sea lions. Almost immediately after the birth of the pups the huge bulls begin to wage bloody battles, trying to keep control of their harems of about a dozen cows. Using their long canine teeth as weapons, they fight with great ferocity for possession of the females. Fighting and mating consume so much of the bulls' time and energy during this period that little time is left for sleeping or eating.

At the end of the summer, the sea lions return to the ocean. The bulls, thin and scarred after a busy breeding season, regain their lost weight with several months of active feeding. As the weather grows colder, the huge northern sea lions begin their southward migration; leaving deserted the northern beaches which in warm weather were covered with their massive dark bodies.

The sea lion has to adapt to a considerable range of climate conditions. Its thick blubber and rapid metabolism are assets in the cold northern waters. But the California sea lion ranges as far south as the Gálapagos Islands off the coast of South America. How does it adapt to a hot and dry environment?

The most important thing that the sea lion does to stay cool is to sleep in the daytime and take care of business during the cooler night hours. Sea lions in warm climates spend a great deal of time sleeping on the wet sand. Their bodies are designed in such a way that a large surface of the torso comes in contact with the cool ground when the animal lies down. About 10 percent of body heat can be lost in this way. Furthermore, the animal produces nearly 25 percent less heat while it sleeps than it does when awake and active.

Unfortunately, none of the sea lion's cooling mechanisms are highly effective. Ultimately, the animal relies on immersion in the ocean to keep itself cool.

Victor A. Greulach and Vincent J. Chiappetta, *Biology*

958 words

Finishing time: _____ minutes _____ seconds

Reading time in seconds _____

Words per minute _____ (see chart below)

TIME (MIN.)	WORDS PER MINUTE	TIME (MIN.)	WORDS PER MINUTE
3:00	319	5:10	185
3:10	303	5:20	180
3:20	287	5:30	174
3:30	274	5:40	169
3:40	261	5:50	164
3:50	250	6:00	160
4:00	240	6:10	155
4:10	230	6:20	151
4:20	221	6:30	147
4:30	213	6:40	144
4:40	205	6:50	140
4:50	198	7:00	137
5:00	190		

Mark each statement with *T* for true or *F* for false.

_____ 1. The author focuses mainly on the sea lion's insatiable appetite for high-protein food.

_____ 2. The larger northern sea lion is the circus "seal."

_____ 3. Sea lions eat lampreys, which eat salmon.

_____ 4. Sea lions both give birth and get pregnant in the summer.

_____ 5. Sea lion milk contains a higher percentage of fat than cow's milk.

_____ 6. Baby sea lions, like whales and manatees, are natural swimmers.

_____ 7. Male sea lions mate with more than one female.

_____ 8. The cool ground provides the sea lion with a greater release of body heat than the ocean water.

_____ 9. In warm climates sea lions sleep more at night than during the day.

_____ 10. Sea lions are able to stay under water because they have gills.

Comprehension (% correct) _____%

HOW FAST SHOULD YOU READ?

Reading specialists say that the average adult reading speed on relatively easy material is approximately 250 words per minutes at 70 percent comprehension. The rate for college students tends to be a little higher, averaging about 300 words per minute on the same type of material with 70 percent comprehension. However, these figures are misleading for a number of reasons.

Anyone who says to you, "My reading rate is 500 words per minute" is not telling the whole story. The question that immediately comes to mind is, "Is that the rate for reading the newspaper or for the physics textbook?" For an efficient reader, no one reading rate serves for all purposes for all materials. Efficient readers demonstrate their flexibility by varying their rate according to their own purpose for reading or according to their prior knowledge of the material being read.

Rate Varies According to Prior Knowledge

One reason textbooks usually require slower reading than newspapers is that textbooks are more difficult; the vocabulary and ideas are new, and prior knowledge is limited. If you already have a lot of knowledge on a topic, you can usually read about it at a faster rate than if you are exploring a totally new subject. For example, a student who is already involved in advertising will probably be able to work through the advertising chapter in the business textbook at a faster rate than the chapter on a less familiar topic, like supply-side economics. The student may need to slow to a crawl at the beginning of the economics chapter in order to understand the new concepts, but as the new ideas become more familiar, the student can perhaps read at a faster rate toward the end of the chapter.

The "difficulty level" of a textbook is primarily measured by you according to your own prior knowledge of the subject. Another measure combines the length of the sentences and the number of syllables in the words. The longer sentences and words indicate a more difficult level of reading. Freshman textbooks vary greatly in difficulty from field to field and from book to book. Some are written at levels as high as 16th grade level (senior in college), whereas others may be on the 11th or 12th grade level. Even within a single textbook the levels vary from one section or paragraph to another. Unfamiliar technical vocabulary can bring a reader to a complete stop. Complex sentences are more difficult to read than simple, concise statements. Sometimes the difficulty is caused by the complexity of the ideas expressed and sometimes, perhaps unnecessarily, by the complexity of the author's writing style.

Before starting on the first word and moving automatically on to the second, third, and fourth at the same pace, take a minute to ask yourself, "Why am I reading this material?" and, based on your answer, vary your speed according to your purpose. Do you want 100 percent, 70 percent, or 50 percent comprehension? In other words, figure out what you want to know when you finish and read accordingly. If you are studying for an examination, you probably need to read slowly and carefully, taking time to monitor your comprehension as you progress. Because 100 percent comprehension is not always your goal, be willing to switch gears and move faster over low-priority material even though you may sacrifice a few details. If you are reading only to get an overview or to verify a particular detail, read as rapidly as possible to achieve your specific purpose.

TECHNIQUES FOR FASTER READING

Concentrate

Fast readers, like fast race car drivers, concentrate on what they are doing; they try to think fast while they take in the important aspects of the course before them. Although we use our eyes, we actually read with our minds. If our attention is veering off course, we lose some of that cutting-edge quickness necessary for success. Slow readers tend to become bored because ideas are coming too slowly to keep their minds alert. Fast readers are curious to learn, mentally alert, and motivated to achieve.

Distractions that interfere with concentration, as mentioned in Chapter 1, fall into two categories: external and internal. External distractions, the physical happenings around you, are fairly easy to control with a little assertiveness. You can turn the television off or get up and go to another room. You can ask people not to interrupt or choose a place to read where interruptions will be at a minimum. Through prior planning, set yourself up for success and create a physical environment over which you have control.

Internal distractions, the irrelevant ideas that pop into your head while reading, are more difficult to control. As mentioned in Chapter 1, a to-do list will help. Write down your nagging concerns as a reminder for action. Spend less time worrying and more time doing, and you will clear your head for success.

Visualize as you read so that you will become wrapped up in the material. Imagine the goslings following you around and see the bird in the nest that did not learn to fly. Use your five senses to increase your involvement with the material.

Stop Regressing

During your initial reading of material, have you ever realized halfway down the page that you have no idea what you have read? Your eyes were engaged, but your mind was not. Do you ever go back and reread sentences or paragraphs? Were you rereading because the material is difficult to understand, because you were tired and not concentrating, or because you were daydreaming? This type of rereading is called a **regression.**

Regression can be a crutch that allows you to make up for wasted time. If this is a problem for you, analyze when and why you are regressing. If you discern that your regression is due to thinking of something else, start denying yourself the privilege in order to break the habit. Say, "OK, I missed that paragraph because I was thinking of something else, but I'm going to keep on going and start paying close attention."

Rereading because you did not understand is a legitimate fix-up strategy used by good readers who monitor their own comprehension. Rereading because your mind was asleep is a waste of time and a habit of many slow readers.

Daydreaming is a habit caused by lack of involvement with the material. Be demanding on yourself and expect 100 percent attention to the task. Visualize the incoming ideas, and relate the new material to what you already know. Don't just read the words; think the ideas.

Expand Fixations

Your eyes must stop in order to read. These stops, called **fixations,** last a fraction of a second. On the average, 5 to 10 percent of the time is spent on fixations. Thus, reading more than one word per fixation will reduce your total reading time.

Research on vision shows that the eye is able to see about one-half inch on either side of a fixation point. This means that a reader can see two or possibly three words per fixation. To illustrate, read the following phrase.

in the car

Did you make three fixations, two, or one? Now read the following word.

entertainment

You can read this word automatically with one fixation. As a beginning reader, however, you probably stopped for each syllable for a total of four fixations. If you can read *entertainment,* which has thirteen letters, with one fixation, you can certainly read the eight-letter phrase *in the car* with only one fixation.

Use your peripheral vision on either side of the fixation point to help you read two or three words per fixation. In expanding your fixations, take in phrases or thought units that seem to go together automatically. To illustrate, the following sentence has been grouped into thought units with fixation points.

After lunch,   I studied   in the library   at a table.

By expanding your fixations, the sentence can easily be read with four fixations rather than ten and thus reduce your total reading time.

Monitor Subvocalization

Subvocalization is the little voice in your head that reads for you. Some experts say that subvocalization is necessary for difficult material, and others say that fast readers are totally visual and do not need to hear the words. Good college readers will probably experience some of both. On easy reading you may find yourself speeding up to the point that you are not hearing every word, particularly the unimportant filler phrases. However, on more difficult textbook readings, your inner voice may speak every word. The voice seems to add another sensory dimension to help you comprehend. Because experts say that the inner voice can read up to about 400 words per minute, many college students can make a considerable improvement in speed while still experiencing the inner voice.

Vocalizers, on the other hand, move their lips while reading to pronounce each word. This is an immature habit and should be stopped. Putting a slip of paper or a pencil in your mouth while reading will alert you to lip movement and inspire you to stop.

Preview

Size up your reading assignment before you get started. If it is a chapter, glance through the pages and read the subheadings. Look at the pictures and notice the italicized words and boldface print. Make predictions about what you think the chapter will cover. Activate your schema or prior knowledge on the subject. Pull out your computer chip on acupuncture, for example, and prepare to bring something to the printed page.

Use Your Pen as a Pacer

The technique of using your pen or fingers as a pacer means pointing under the words in a smooth, flowing motion, moving back and forth from line to line. Although as a child you were probably told never to point to words, it is a very effective technique for improving reading speed. The technique seems to have several benefits. After you overcome the initial distraction, the physical act of pointing tends to improve concentration by drawing your attention directly to the words. The forward motion of your pen tends to keep you from regressing because rereading would interrupt your established rhythm. By pulling your eyes down the page, the pen movement helps set a rapid, steady pace for reading and tends to shift you out of word-by-word reading and move you automatically into phrase reading. Obviously, you cannot read a whole book using your pen as a pacer, but you can start out with this technique. Later, if you feel yourself slowing down, use your pen again to get back on track.

The technique is demonstrated in the following passage. Your pen moves in a Z pattern from one side of the column to the other. Because you are trying to read several words at each fixation, your pen does not have to go to the extreme end of either side of the column.

> Rapid reading requires quick thinking and intense concentration. The reader must be alert and aggressive. Being interested in the subject helps to improve speed.

As you begin to read faster and become more proficient with the *Z* pattern, you will notice the corners starting to round into an *S*. The *Z* pattern is turning into a more relaxed *S* swirl. When you get to the point of using the *S* swirl, you will be reading for ideas and not be reading every word. You are reading actively and aggressively, with good concentration. Use the *Z* pattern until you find your pen or hand movement has automatically turned into an *S*. The following illustration compares the two.

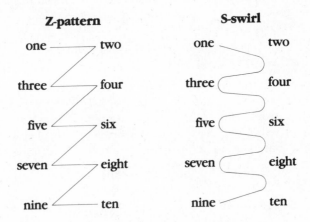

Push and Pace

Be alert and aggressive and try to read faster. Sit up straight and attack the text. Get uncomfortable and force yourself to hurry. Changing old habits is difficult. You will never read faster unless you try to read faster.

Set goals and pace yourself. Count the number of pages in your homework assignments and estimate according to your reading rate how many pages you can read in thirty minutes. Use a paper clip or an index card to mark the page you are trying to reach. Push yourself to achieve your goal.

Exercise 2: Pacing

The following passages are written in columns with approximately six words on each line. Using your pen as a pacer, read each passage, and try to make only two fixations per line. A dashed line has been placed down the middle of the column to help you with the fixations. Record your time for reading each passage and then answer the comprehension questions.

Determine your rate from the rate chart at the end of the passage. Before reading, use the title and any clues in the passage to predict organization: Is it definition or description?

© 1993 HarperCollins College Publishers

Skunks

Skunks are small, omnivorous animals found throughout most of the United States. Striped skunks are at home in practically every habitat in every state, living in dens and often beneath abandoned buildings. They can be seen wandering around on cloudy days and at sunset. They eat a variety of fruits, berries, insects, earthworms, other small invertebrates, and some rodents. They sport many color variations, from almost black to almost white.

Spotted skunks are also found throughout a good portion of the country, but they are not common in some of the more northerly states and the northern part of the East Coast. They eat a variety of invertebrates, eggs, and sometimes small birds. The hognose skunk and the hooded skunk are found in the Pacific Southwest and extend down into Mexico and parts of Central America.

In a country where millions of dollars are spent every year on human deodorants, it is not to be wondered that the skunk is not favored. Then, too, the animal can carry rabies. Thus, removal procedures are the order of the day when skunks invade suburban areas or campgrounds in large numbers. They can be kept away from buildings by repellents—moth balls (paradichlorobenzene) are effective. Screens can prevent them from getting under buildings. Proper fencing will keep them from chicken coops or

apiaries (skunks like honeybees).
Removal of insects from golf-
course grasses is useful.

Despite their bad reputation,
skunks do help keep small rodent
and insect populations in check.

Stanley Anderson, *Managing Our Wildlife Resources*

245 words

Time _____

Words per minute _____

Mark each statement with *T* for true or *F* for false.

_____   1. Skunks eat rats and insects.
_____   2. Skunks are repelled by moth balls.

TIME (MIN.)	WORDS PER MINUTE	TIME (MIN.)	WORDS PER MINUTE
0:10	1470	0:40	368
0:20	735	0:50	294
0:30	490	1:00	245

Exercise 3: Pacing

Predict organization: Is it simple listing or comparison?

Special Solutions to the Water Problem

Some insects are able to survive
for years enclosed in jars of dry
pepper. They do this by utilizing
metabolic water and excreting
almost dry uric acid.

A camel can tolerate dry
conditions by adopting a number

of tactics. At night it drops its body temperature several degrees so that bodily processes slow down. In the heat of the day it doesn't begin to sweat until its body temperature reaches about 105°F. In addition, the camel can lose twice as much of its body water (40 percent) without ill effect than can most other mammals. Peculiarly, the thick coat of a camel acts as insulation to keep the heat out. Also when the camel does drink, it may hold prodigious amounts of water.

Some seabirds and turtles have salt removal glands. The huge tears that may appear in the eyes of sea turtles have nothing to do with the turtle's realization that we are poisoning the oceans. They are merely the result of specialized salt-removing glands. These glands, however, remove only sodium chloride from the blood.

The tiny kangaroo rat doesn't drink at all and it lives on dry plant material. It survives because it doesn't sweat and is active only in the cool of night. Its feces are dry and its urine is highly concentrated. Most of its water loss is through the lungs. Fats produce more metabolic water than other foods, so it prefers fatty foods. On the other hand, soybeans are high in protein and thus produce a lot of nitrogenous waste for which a lot of water is needed—so if a kangaroo rat is fed only soybeans it will die of thirst.

Robert Wallace, *Biology: The World of Life*

278 words

TIME (MIN.)	WORDS PER MINUTE	TIME (MIN.)	WORDS PER MINUTE
0:10	1668	0:40	417
0:20	834	0:50	334
0:30	556	1:00	278

Time _____

Words per minute _____

Mark each statement with *T* for true or *F* for false.

_____ 1. A camel will die if its body temperature rises above 105°F.

_____ 2. The kangaroo rat drinks no water.

Exercise 4: Pacing

Predict organization: Is it sequence or description?

Can Humans Regenerate Missing Parts?

A few years ago a young boy was admitted to the Children's Hospital in Sheffield, England. He had accidentally cut off the end of his finger. Ordinarily the part would have been reattached by a plastic surgeon in the hope that it would grow back and that the feeling would be restored. However, due to a clerical error, the stub was simply bandaged and the boy was ignored for several days. When the error was discovered, anxious physicians unwrapped the finger to see how extensive the damage had become. They were stunned to see that the missing part was regenerating. They carefully monitored the progress of the finger over the next few weeks until the damage had, for all practical purposes, repaired itself. The technique is now routinely used for young children. There are several instances of regrown fingers, complete with nails and fingerprints. But how? This was contrary to all medical expectations. Should it have been? After all,

identical twins are formed when a developing
human breaks apart at the two-cell stage, each part
regenerating whatever was lost. But these enormous
powers reside in embryos, and the regrown finger
occurred on a young boy. It has not been found in
adults, other than to a limited degree in wound
healing. Subsequent research has shown that
age does, in fact, have something to do with
regeneration. It seems that children under the age
of eleven have marked powers of regeneration, and
these rapidly dissipate after this time. In the early
1970s it was demonstrated that electrical charges
surrounding the tissues become reversed at about
the time that regenerative powers dissipate.
Research attention is now focusing on maintaining
particular (young) electrical fields around those
areas in which regeneration is being attempted.
The time when humans can regenerate lost limbs is
probably not near, but scientists have new reasons
for optimism.

Robert Wallace, *Biology: The World of Life*

309 words

TIME (MIN.)	WORDS PER MINUTE	TIME (MIN.)	WORDS PER MINUTE
0:20	927	1:00	309
0:30	618	1:10	265
0:40	464	1:20	232
0:50	371	1:30	206

Time _____

Words per minute _____

Mark each statement with *T* for true or *F* for false.

_____ 1. The young boy's finger was sewn back on by the surgeon.

_____ 2. The regenerative powers seem to wane at age eleven.

Exercise 5: Pacing

Predict organization: Is it simple listing or description?

Shy People

The shy person does not seem to take full advantage of social opportunities to meet new persons and cultivate friendships. In public, shy persons are usually silent. They avoid eye contact and speak quietly when they speak at all. They avoid others whenever possible and take refuge in a private project such as reading.

Privately, shy persons are supersensitive about what other people think about them. They worry about unpleasant aspects of social situations and about leaving others with a negative impression. Increased pulse rate, blushing, perspiration, and rapid heart rate are pronounced in people who are shy in public. But the major problem for shy persons, which distinguishes them from others who have only occasional bouts of shyness, is that they label themselves as being shy. If persons believe they are shy, then they are likely to be especially sensitive to social situations that might produce shyness.

Probably the key to overcoming shyness involves practicing new forms of behavior designed to provide the person with rewarding experiences when meeting others. The chronically shy person has developed a self-defeating pattern of behavior: "I am a shy person, so I am going to be silent and withdrawn when I meet other people. I meet other people and keep silent, and no one talks to me. Therefore, I must be odd and basically shy."

Valerian J. Derlega and Louis H. Janda, *Personal Adjustment**

222 words

© 1993 HarperCollins College Publishers

TIME (MIN.)	WORDS PER MINUTE	TIME (MIN.)	WORDS PER MINUTE
0:10	1332	0:40	333
0:20	666	0:50	266
0:30	444	1:00	222

*From *Personal Adjustment,* Second Edition, by Valerian J. Derlega and Louis H. Janda, pp. 100-102. Copyright © 1981 by Scott, Foresman and Company, HarperCollinsCollege Publishers.

Time _____

Words per minute _____

Mark each statement with *T* for true or *F* for false.

_____ 1. Shy people tend to worry about what others think of them.
_____ 2. Shy people do not usually think of themselves as shy.

SKIMMING

Skimming is a technique of selectively reading for the gist or the main idea. Because it involves processing material at rates of around 900 words per minute, it is not defined by some experts as reading. Skimming involves skipping words, sentences, paragraphs, and even pages. It is a method of quickly overviewing material to answer the question, "What is this about?"

Skimming and previewing are very similar in that both involve getting an overview. Previewing sets the stage for later careful reading, whereas skimming is a substitute for a complete reading. Skimming is useful for material that you want to know about but don't have the time to read. For example, you might want to skim some of the supplemental articles for a course that have been placed on reserve in the library because you know your professor is interested only in your understanding the main idea of each article and a complete reading would be unnecessary. Sometimes you may want to pick up a book and just "get the idea" but not read it completely. Skimming is a useful tool. The technique is as follows:

1. Read the title, subheadings, italics, and boldface print to get an idea of what the material is about.
2. Try to get an insight into the organization of the material to help you anticipate where the important points will be located. Some of the organizational patterns and their functions are:
   a. Listing: explains items of equal value.
   b. Definition and examples: defines a term and gives examples to help the reader understand the term.
   c. Time order or sequence: presents items in chronological order.
   d. Comparison-contrast: items are compared for their similarities and differences.
   e. Description: characteristics of an item are explained.
   f. Cause and effect: one item is shown to have produced another.
   g. Problem-solution: explains the problem, causes, and effects as well as suggests a solution.
   h. Opinion-proof: gives an opinion and then supports it with proof.
3. If the first paragraph is introductory, read it. If not, skip to a paragraph that seems to introduce the topic.

4. Move rapidly, letting your eyes float over the words. Try to grasp the main ideas and the significant supporting details.
5. Notice first sentences in paragraphs and read them if they seem to be summary statements.
6. Skip words that seem to have little meaning, like *a, an,* and *the.*
7. Skip sentences or sections that seem to contain the following:
   a. Familiar ideas.
   b. Unnecessary details.
   c. Superfluous examples.
   d. Restatements or unneeded summaries.
   e. Material irrelevant to your purpose.
8. If the last paragraph of a section is a summary, read it if you need to check your understanding.

SCANNING

Because scanning is a process of searching for a single bit of information, it is more of a locating skill than a reading skill. A common use of scanning is looking up a number in a telephone book. When scanning for information, you do not need to understand the meaning of the material, but instead you merely need to pinpoint a specific detail. For example, you might find that after reading a chapter on pricing in your marketing textbook that you cannot recall the definition of *price lining.* To locate the information, you would not reread, but scan the chapter to find the key phrase *price lining* and then review the definition.

A combination of skimming and scanning is used by researchers. If you are working on a research paper on paranoia, you might have a list of thirty books and articles to read. A complete reading of each reference is probably unnecessary. Instead, you can scan to locate the information relevant to your topic and skim to get the main idea.

The techniques of scanning are:

1. Figure out the organization of the material. Get an overview of which section will probably contain the information you are looking for.
2. Know specifically what you are looking for. Decide on a key expression that will signal your information, but be ready to switch to a related idea if that doesn't work.
3. Repeat the phrase and hold the image in your mind. Concentrate on the image so that you will recognize it when it comes into view.
4. Move quickly and aggressively. Remember, you are scanning, not reading.
5. Verify through careful reading. After locating your information, read carefully to make sure you have really found it.

SUMMARY

The average adult reading speed on relatively easy material is approximately 250 words per minute at 70 percent comprehension. This rate should vary according to purpose and the difficulty of the material.

Reading faster requires effort. Faster readers concentrate on what they are doing; they are curious to learn, mentally alert, and motivated to achieve. They try to stop regressions. Regressing because of inattention is a crutch that allows the reader to make up for wasted time. Faster readers use peripheral vision and read two or three words per fixation. Before reading, they make predictions and activate schema. Both before and during reading, they anticipate the organization. Using the pen as a pacer is an important technique that can improve both concentration and rate.

Skimming and scanning are specialized methods of getting information. Skimming is a technique for getting an overview, and scanning is the process of searching for a single bit of information.

Selection

SOCIOLOGY

Skill Development: Skimming

Skim the selection and mark the following statements with T *for true or* F *for false.*

_____ *1. The author works for a Chinese newspaper.*
_____ *2. The author discusses restrictions in China.*
_____ *3. The author seems to want to return to China.*

Skill Development: Scanning

Scan to find each of the following details.

1. Before college in China students complete _____ years of schooling.

2. Sometimes "connections" are used to influence _____.

3. The old Chinese saying, "Those who are content are forever happy,"

refers to workers who _____.

Skill Development: Rate

Now read the selection in order to answer ten true-false items. Use your pen as a pacer and time your reading.

Starting time: _____ minutes _____ seconds

A Chinese Reporter on Cape Cod

From Guan Keguang, *The Cape Cod Times,* March 14, 1987

Next to the newsroom in the *Cape Cod Times* main office building there is a "lunchroom." My colleagues and I sometimes go there to buy something to eat or drink from the vending machines.

The experience has been quite a novelty for me. I put in some coins, push a button, and out comes what I want.

The machines offer a variety of food and drinks. Many of them are new to me and the labels don't tell me much about what's inside. The operation is simple and automatic. But so many decisions!

Such a process epitomizes what I have experienced while struggling hard to adapt my traditional ways of thinking and doing things to an American environment, which demands constantly considering alternatives and making decisions.

This has been no easy job for me.

For almost half a century I have lived in a culture where choices and decisions are made by authorities and circumstances rather than by individuals and personal preferences.

It's OK for young children to have things arranged for them by their parents, because they are inexperienced in life and not wise enough to make important decisions. But when they reach their late teens they don't like to be treated that way—even in China. They yearn for independence and freedom, as the recent demonstrations have shown. They are frustrated when things don't go their way and they find themselves helpless and unable to do anything about their fate.

When the time comes to enter the work force, however, reality sets in. They are assigned a job, and that's it. Moreover, the job assignment determines where you must live.

If you have completed twelve years' schooling, but you fail in the college entrance examination and are not admitted, the government will assign you a job—perhaps as a factory worker, a store clerk, or a bus driver. Very likely that will be your lifelong job, because you can't freely pick and choose or change your job. Once you are in a job you will have to stick to it, unless the authorities want to transfer you to another job. You could negotiate with the authorities, but the government always has the final say.

Students do have an opportunity to state their preference among university and courses of study—and if you pass your exams with flying colors, with scores much higher than others, you will be admitted into a department of a university of your own choice. But once you get into a university you stay in your major for four or five years without a break. You do not change your major. You take the courses given to you, pass all the exams, behave well and toe the party line, earn your bachelor's degree and graduate.

Then, you just wait until a job is assigned to you. During the waiting period, students with "connections" seek to influence the decision. A few succeed. In any event, until the decision is made, you will not know where you will go and what your lifelong career will be.

Your job assignment notice is more than a certificate with which you report for duty. It is also a certificate for your residence registration and your daily necessity rations. If you don't like the job assigned to you and refuse to take it, you are jobless. Because you don't have an official permission to live in any place other than where the job is, you won't get your ration coupons.

Your choice, therefore, is very simple: to eat or not to eat.

Every graduate is guaranteed a job. Each job affords the same starting salary. Engineer, schoolteacher, office clerk, truck driver, scientist—the difference in salary is negligible. That is the socialist way.

No matter if you like it or not, you stay with your job.

If you are not very ambitious, life can be very easy for you. Its pace won't be so maddeningly fast as it is here in America. You don't have to worry about choosing alternatives or making decisions. You don't have to worry about getting laid off.

Since you don't have much to choose from and everything is planned and arranged for you, you will be better off if you take things easy. As an old Chinese saying goes: "Those who are content are forever happy."

People like that—who have been content to let their decisions be made for them—would find it hard to get used to the American lifestyle, to keep their eyes open to opportunities, to be searching constantly for a better job, a better place to live. Such a way of life would be too risky, too precarious, too challenging.

Our old tradition taught us to be humble, modest, unassuming, moderate, and passive. Even when a Chinese host treats a guest to a dinner consisting of twelve courses and costing half of his monthly salary, he still apologizes repeatedly to the guest between the courses for the "inadequate" meal he has prepared for his honorable guest. Meanwhile, the guest politely and humbly refuses to accept the food his host keeps piling up on his dish, because he feels he shouldn't assume that he deserves so much good food and he should leave more good stuff for the host family, even though he is very hungry at the moment and he likes the food immensely.

The other day while I was going through the classified ads in the magazine *Editor & Publisher,* I came across ads placed by publications in search of "aggressive, talented, hungry" reporters.

What could I do if I wanted such a position?

If I were hungry, I would try every face-saving means not to admit it.

If I were talented, I would (or should) be modest enough not to advertise it.

Even if I were desperately in need of the position, I still wouldn't know how to be aggressive.

I wonder if I should take a crash course, teaching me how to be aggressive, talented, and hungry.

1003 words

Finishing time: _____ minutes _____ seconds

TIME (MIN.)	WORDS PER MINUTE	TIME (MIN.)	WORDS PER MINUTE	TIME (MIN.)	WORDS PER MINUTE
2:50	354	4:00	251	5:10	194
3:00	334	4:10	241	5:20	188
3:10	317	4:20	232	5:30	182
3:20	301	4:30	223	5:40	177
3:30	287	4:40	215	5:50	172
3:40	274	4:50	208	6:00	167
3:50	262	5:00	201	6:10	163

Comprehension Questions

Mark each statement with *T* for true or *F* for false.

_____ 1. The author is approximately 50 or more years of age.

_____ 2. In China, the government assigns jobs according to individual talents.

_____ 3. Students entering universities in China can choose their major course of study.

_____ 4. University graduates in China select a city of residence and then apply for a job.

_____ 5. A university student in China can change his or her major in the second year.

_____ 6. Every university graduate in China is guaranteed a job.

_____ 7. The starting salary for an engineer in China is much higher than for a truck driver.

_____ 8. In China, you are moved to another job if your boss does not like you.

_____ 9. According to the author, the system in China encourages people to be aggressive.

_____ 10. The author seems to prefer the Chinese system over the American.

Comprehension (% correct) _____%

Selection **2**

ESSAY

Skill Development: Skimming

Skim the selection and mark the following statements with T *for true or* F *for false.*

_____ 1. *The author is expressing his opinion.*

_____ 2. *The overall pattern of organization is cause and effect.*

_____ 3. *The author seems to condemn failure.*

Skill Development: Scanning

Scan to find each of the following details.

1. *The movie,* A Man for All Seasons, *was directed by* _____.

2. *The domestic form of the Peace Corps is called* _____.

3. *A Gallup survey shows that many college students* _____.

Skill Development: Rate

Now read the selection in order to answer ten true-false items. Use your pen as a pacer and time your reading.

Starting time: _____ minutes _____ seconds

The Right to Fail

From William Zinsser, *The Lunacy Boom*

I like "dropout" as an addition to the American language because it's brief and it's clear. What I don't like is that we use it almost entirely as a dirty word.

We only apply it to people under twenty-one. Yet an adult who spends his days and nights watching mindless TV programs is more of a dropout than an eighteen-year-old who quits college, with its frequently mindless courses, to become, say, a VISTA volunteer. For the young, dropping out is often a way of dropping in.

To hold this opinion, however, is little short of treason in America. A boy or girl who leaves college is branded a failure—and the right to fail is one of the few freedoms that this country does not grant its citizens. The American dream is a dream of "getting ahead," painted in strokes of gold wherever we look. Our advertisements and TV commercials are a hymn to material success, our magazine articles a toast to people who made it to the top. Smoke the right cigarette or drive the right car—so the ads imply—and girls will be swooning into your deodorized arms and caressing your expensive lapels. Happiness goes to the man who has the sweet smell of achievement. He is our national idol, and everybody else is our national fink.

I want to put in a word for the fink, especially the teen-age fink, because if we give him time to get through his finkdom—if we release him from the pressure of attaining certain goals by a certain age—he has a good chance of becoming our national idol, a Jefferson or a Thoreau, a Buckminster Fuller or an Adlai Stevenson, a man with a mind of his own. We need mavericks and dissenters and dreamers far more than we need junior vice-presidents, but we paralyze them by insisting that every step be a step up to the next rung of the ladder. Yet in the fluid years of youth, the only way for boys and girls to find their proper road is often to take a hundred side trips, poking out in different directions, faltering, drawing back, and starting again.

"But what if we fail?" they ask, whispering the dreadful word across the Generation Gap to their parents, who are back home at the Establishment, nursing their "middle-class values" and cultivating their "goal-oriented society." The parents whisper back: "Don't!"

What they should say is "Don't be afraid to fail!" *Failure isn't fatal.* Countless people have had a bout with it and come out stronger as a result. Many have even come out famous. History is strewn with eminent dropouts, "loners" who followed their own trail, not worrying about its odd twists and turns because they had faith in their own sense of direction. To read their biographies is always exhilarating, not only because they beat the system, but because their system was better than the one that they beat.

Luckily, such rebels still turn up often enough to prove that individualism, though badly threatened, is not extinct. Much has been written, for instance, about the fitful scholastic career of Thomas P. F. Hoving, New York's former Parks Commissioner and now director of the Metropolitan Museum of Art. Hoving was a dropout's dropout, entering and leaving schools as if they were motels, often at the request of the management. Still, he must have learned something during those unorthodox years, for he dropped in again at the top of his profession.

I'm not encouraging everyone to go out and fail just for the sheer therapy of it, or to quit college just to coddle some vague discontent. Obviously it's better to succeed than to flop, and in general a long education is more helpful than a short one. (Thanks to my own education, for example, I can tell George Eliot from T. S. Eliot, I can handle the pluperfect tense in French, and I know that Caesar beat the Helvetii because he had enough frumentum.) I only mean that failure isn't bad in itself, or success automatically good.

Fred Zinnemann, who has directed some of Hollywood's most honored movies, was asked by a reporter, when *A Man for All Seasons* won every prize, about his previous film *Behold a Pale Horse,* which was a box-office disaster. "I don't feel any obligation to be successful," Zinnemann replied. "Success can be dangerous—you feel you know it all. I've learned a great deal from my failures." A similar point was made by Richard Brooks about his ambitious money loser, *Lord Jim.* Recalling the three years of his life that went into it, talking almost with elation about the troubles that befell his unit in Cambodia, Brooks told me that he learned more about his craft from this considerable failure than from his many earlier hits.

It's a point, of course, that applies throughout the arts. Writers, playwrights, painters, and composers work in the expectation of periodic defeat, but they wouldn't keep going back into the arena if they thought it was the end of the world. It isn't the end of the world. For an artist—and perhaps for anybody—it is the only way to grow.

Today's younger generation seems to know that this is true, seems willing to take the risks in life that artists take in art. "Society," needless to say, still has the upper hand—it sets the goals and condemns as a failure everybody who won't play. But the dropouts and the hippies are not as afraid of failure as their parents and grandparents. This could mean, as their elders might say, that they are just plumb lazy, secure in the comforts of an affluent state. It could also mean, however, that they just don't buy the old standards of success and are rapidly writing new ones.

Recently it was announced, for instance, that more than two hundred thousand Americans have inquired about service in VISTA (the domestic Peace Corps) and that, according to a Gallup survey, "more than three million American college students would serve VISTA in some capacity if given the opportunity." This is hardly the road to riches or to an executive suite. Yet I have met many of these young volunteers, and they are not pining for traditional success. On the contrary, they appear more fulfilled than the average vice-president with a swimming pool.

Who is to say, then, if there is any right path to the top, or even to say what the top consists of? Obviously the colleges don't have more than a partial answer—otherwise the young would not be so disaffected with an education that they consider vapid. Obviously business does not have the answer—otherwise the young would not be so scornful of its call to be an organization man.

The fact is, nobody has the answer, and the dawning awareness of this fact seems to me one of the best things happening in America today. Success and failure are again becoming individual visions, as they were when the country was younger, not rigid categories. Maybe we are learning again to cherish this right of every person to succeed on his own terms and to fail as often as necessary along the way.

1202 words

Finishing time: _____ minutes _____ seconds

TIME (MIN.)	WORDS PER MINUTE	TIME (MIN.)	WORDS PER MINUTE	TIME (MIN.)	WORDS PER MINUTE
3:30	343	4:40	258	5:50	206
3:40	328	4:50	249	6:00	200
3:50	314	5:00	240	6:10	195
4:00	300	5:10	233	6:20	190
4:10	288	5:20	225	6:30	185
4:20	277	5:30	218	6:40	180
4:30	267	5:40	212	6:50	176

Comprehension Questions

Mark each statement with *T* for true or *F* for false.

_____ 1. The author supports becoming a VISTA volunteer.

_____ 2. The author suggests that VISTA workers do not make much money.

_____ 3. The author thinks dropping out can be positive.

_____ 4. The author believes that the American culture does not grant its citizens the right to fail.

_____ 5. The author feels that young people are more afraid of failure than their parents.

_____ 6. The author feels that all students should drop out of college for a while.

_____ 7. The author mentions the two movie failures to emphasize the embarrassment from failure.

_____ 8. The author believes that failure can result in growth.

_____ 9. The author believes that Thoreau was a junior vice-president type.

_____ 10. The author is encouraged by the spirit he sees in young people.

Comprehension (% correct) _____%

WORD BRIDGE
Glossary

The first shock in a new subject area, like sociology or geology, is the vocabulary. Each subject seems to have a language, or jargon, of its own. Words like *sociocultural* or *socioeconomic* crop up again and again in a sociology text. In truth, these words are somewhat unique to the subject-matter area—they are made-up words to describe sociological phenomena. The best explanation of such words and their relation to the subject area can usually be found in the textbook itself rather than in the dictionary. Often, textbooks have definitions inserted in a corner or at the bottom of a page, or more frequently, in a glossary of terms at the end of the book or at the end of a chapter. The glossary defines the words as they are used in the textbook.

Notice the following examples from the glossary of a psychology text. The terms using "learning" are part of the jargon of psychology and would probably not be found in the dictionary.

latent learning   hidden learning that is not demonstrated in performance until that performance is reinforced (p. 203)
learned helplessness   a condition in which a subject does not attempt to escape from a painful or noxious situation after learning in a previous, similar situation that escape is not possible (p. 193)
learning   demonstrated by a relatively permanent change in behavior that occurs as the result of practice or experience (p. 168)
learning set   an acquired strategy for learning or problem solving; learning to learn (p. 201)

Exercise 6: Using Your Glossary

Turn to the glossary at the end of this text for help in defining the following terms. Write a definition for each in your own words.

1. schema
2. bias
3. context clues
4. metacognition
5. inference

CHAPTER 6

INFERENCE

- What is an inference?
- What is the connotation of a word?
- What is figurative language?
- How do you draw conclusions?

WHAT IS AN INFERENCE?

The first and most basic level of reading is the literal level, that is, what are the facts? In reacting to a literal question, you can actually point to the words on the page that answer the question. Reading, however, progresses beyond this initial stage. A second and more sophisticated level of reading deals with motives, feelings, and judgments; this is the **inferential level.** At this level you no longer can point to the answer, but instead must form the answer from suggestions within the selection. In a manner of speaking, the reader must read **between the lines** for the implied meaning.

Rather than directly stating, authors often subtly suggest and thus manipulate the reader. Suggestion can be a more effective method of getting the message across than a direct statement. Suggestion requires greater writing skill, and it is also usually more artistic, creative, and entertaining. The responsible reader searches beyond the printed word for insights into what was left unsaid.

For example, in cigarette advertisements the public is enticed through suggestion, not facts, into spending millions of dollars on a product that is stated to be unhealthful. Depending on the brand, smoking offers the refreshment of a mountain stream or the sophisticated elegance of the rich and famous. Never in the ads is smoking directly praised or pleasure promised; instead, the positive aspects are *implied.* A lawsuit for false advertising is avoided because nothing tangible has been put into print. The emotionalism of the full-page advertisement is so overwhelming that the consumer hardly notices the warning peeking from the bottom of the page— "Warning: The Surgeon General Has Determined That Cigarette Smoking Is Dangerous to Your Health."

Exercise 1: Implied Meaning in Advertisements

Look through magazines and newspapers to locate advertisements for (1) cigarettes, (2) alcoholic beverages, and (3) fragrances. What characteristics do all three types of advertisements have in common? Select one advertisement for each product and answer the following questions about each of your three selections:

1. What is directly stated about the product?
2. What does the advertisement say about the product?
3. Who seems to be the potential customer for the product?

Authors and advertisers have not invented a new comprehension skill; they are merely capitalizing on an already highly developed skill of daily life. When asked by a co-worker, "How do you like your boss?" the employee might answer, "I think she wears nice suits," rather than "I don't like my boss." A lack of approval has been suggested, while the employee has avoided making a direct negative statement. In everyday life, we make inferences about people by examining what people say, what they do, and what others say about them. The intuition of everyday life applied to the printed word is the inferential level of reading.

CONNOTATION OF WORDS

Notice the power of suggested meaning in responding to the following questions:

1. If you read an author's description of classmates, which student would you assume is smartest?
   a. A student annotating items on a computer printout.
   b. A student with earphones listening to the radio.
   c. A student talking with classmates about soap operas.

2. Which would you find in a small town?
   a. Movies.
   b. Flickers.
   c. Picture shows.

3. Who probably earns the most money?
   a. A businessperson in a dark suit, white shirt, and tie.
   b. A businessperson in slacks and a sport shirt.
   c. A businessperson in a pale blue uniform.

Can you prove your answers? It's not the same as proving when the Declaration of Independence was signed, yet you still have a feeling for how each question should be answered. Even though a right or wrong answer is difficult to explain in this type of question, certain answers can still be defended as most accurate—they are *a, c,* and *a.* The answers are based on feelings, attitudes, and knowledge commonly shared by society.

A seemingly innocent tool, word choice is the first key to implied meaning. For example, if a person is skinny, he is unattractive, but if he is slender or slim he must be attractive. All three words might refer to the same underweight person, but *skinny* communicates a negative feeling while *slender* or *slim* communicates a positive one. This feeling or emotionalism surrounding a word is called **connotation. Denotation** is the specific meaning of a word, but the connotative meaning goes beyond this to reflect certain attitudes and prejudices of society. Even though it may not seem premeditated, writers select words, just as advertisers select symbols and models, to manipulate the reader's opinions.

Exercise 2: Connotation of Words

In each of the following word pairs, write the letter of the word that connotes the more positive feeling:

_____	1. (a) guest	(b) boarder
_____	2. (a) surplus	(b) waste
_____	3. (a) conceited	(b) proud
_____	4. (a) buzzard	(b) robin
_____	5. (a) heavyset	(b) obese
_____	6. (a) explain	(b) brag
_____	7. (a) house	(b) mansion
_____	8. (a) song	(b) serenade
_____	9. (a) calculating	(b) clever
_____	10. (a) neglected	(b) deteriorated
_____	11. (a) colleague	(b) accomplice
_____	12. (a) ambition	(b) greed
_____	13. (a) kitten	(b) cat
_____	14. (a) courageous	(b) audacious
_____	15. (a) contrived	(b) designed
_____	16. (a) flower	(b) orchid
_____	17. (a) distinctive	(b) peculiar
_____	18. (a) baby	(b) kid
_____	19. (a) persuasion	(b) propaganda
_____	20. (a) gold	(b) tin
_____	21. (a) slump	(b) decline
_____	22. (a) lie	(b) misrepresentation
_____	23. (a) janitor	(b) custodian
_____	24. (a) offering	(b) collection
_____	25. (a) soldiers	(b) mercenaries

Exercise 3: Connotation in Textbooks

For each of the underlined words in the following sentences, indicate the meaning of the word and reasons why the connotation is positive or negative. Note the example.

While the unions fought mainly for better wages and hours, they also championed various social reforms.

Leonard Pitt, *We Americans*

Means "supported"; suggests heroes and thus a positive cause

1. The ad was part of the oil companies' program to sell their image rather than their product to the public. In the ad they <u>boasted</u> that they were reseeding all the disrupted areas with a newly developed grass that grows five times faster than the grass that normally occurs there.

   Robert Wallace, *Biology: The World of Life*

   _____

2. Old Henry Reifsneider and his wife Phoebe were a loving couple. You perhaps know how it is with simple natures that fasten themselves like <u>lichens</u> on the stones of circumstance and weather their days to a <u>crumbling</u> conclusion.

   Theodore Dreiser, *The Lost Phoebe*

   _____

   _____

3. Tinbergen, like Lorenz and von Frisch, entered retirement by continuing to work. Tinbergen was a hyperactive child who, at school, was allowed to periodically dance on his desk to let off steam. So in "<u>retirement</u>" he entered a new arena, stimulating the use of ethological methods in autism.

   Robert Wallace, *Biology: The World of Life*

   _____

4. The cities were <u>garbage-filled</u> and <u>overrun</u> with rats. The <u>stench</u> was devastating. Life in the country was not much better, with the scattered hamlets being little more than isolated slums inhabited by people of <u>numbing</u> ignorance.

   Robert Wallace, *Biology: The World of Life*

   _____

   _____

   _____

5. Not since Wilson had tried to <u>ram</u> the League of Nations through the Senate had any president put more on the line.

   Leonard Pitt, *We Americans*

   _____

FIGURATIVE LANGUAGE

Figurative language requires readers to make inferences about comparisons that are not literally true and sometimes not logically related. What does it mean to say, "She worked like a dog"? To most readers it means that she worked hard, but since few dogs work, the comparison is not literally true or particularly logical. **Figurative language** is, in a sense, another language because it is a different way of using "regular language" words so that they take on new meaning. For example, "It was raining buckets" or "raining cats and dogs" are lively, figurative ways of describing a heavy rain. New speakers of English, however, who comprehend on a literal level, might look up in the sky for the descending pails or animals. The two expressions give an exaggerated, humorous effect, but, on the literal level, they do not make sense.

When first used, "works like a dog" and "raining cats and dogs" were probably very clever. Now the phrases have lost their freshness, but still convey meaning for those who are "in the know." Such phrases are called **idioms,** or expressions that do not make literal sense but have taken on a new generally accepted meaning over many years of use.

Examples:

She tried to *keep a stiff upper lip* during the ordeal.
His eyes were *bigger than his stomach.*

What do the following idioms mean?

a sacred cow? _____

a Dutch treat? _____

a red herring? _____

sleeping like a log? _____

the eleventh hour? _____

fitting like a glove? _____

Authors using figurative language try to move beyond familiar idioms and create original expressions. They use devices called similes, metaphors, and personifications to paint vivid images and to add zest, surprise, and beauty to our language. Readers may be caught off guard because such expressions are not literally true. Sophisticated readers use clues within the passage, as well as prior knowledge, to figure out meaning for these imaginative uses of language.

A **simile** is a comparison of two unlike things using the words *like* or *as.*

Examples:

The spring flower pushed up its bloom *like a lighthouse* beckoning on a gloomy night.

> And every soul, it passed me by,
> *Like the whizz* of my crossbow!
>
> Samuel Coleridge, The Ancient Mariner

A **metaphor** is a direct comparison of two unlike things (without using *like* or *as*).

Examples:

The corporate accountant is a computer from nine to five.

Miss Rosie was a wet brown bag of a woman who used to be the best looking gal in Georgia.

Lucille Clifton, Good Times

Personification is attributing human characteristics to nonhuman things.

Examples:

The *birds speak* from the forest.
Time marches on.

Exercise 4: Figurative Language in Textbooks

The figurative expressions in the following sentences are underlined. Identify the figurative type, define each expression, and suggest, if possible, the reason for its use.

Example:

As a trained nurse working in the immigrant slums of New York, she knew that table-top abortions were common among poor women, and she had seen some of the tragic results.

Leonard Pitt, We Americans

It is a metaphor, which may now be an idiom, and means illegal. The connection suggests the reality of where the operations probably occurred.

1. He <u>cast his lot</u> with the British, who at one point gave him command over a <u>redcoat army.</u>

Leonard Pitt, We Americans

_____

_____

2. Parker's wife was sitting on the front porch floor, snapping beans. Parker was sitting on the step, some distance away, watching her sullenly. She was plain, plain. The skin on her face was thin and drawn as tight <u>as the skin on an onion</u> and her eyes were grey and sharp <u>like the points of two icepicks.</u>

Flannery O'Connor, "Parker's Back"

_____

_____

3. The government urged women to fill the gaps in the assembly line as well as the empty desk chairs in the offices. Millions responded. <u>Rosie-the-Riveter</u> was welcomed into every plant.

Leonard Pitt, We Americans

_____

4. Then she screamed an extremely fierce "I said, preach it" and stepped up on the altar. The Reverend kept on throwing out phrases <u>like home-run balls</u> and Sister Monroe made a quick break and grasped for him. For just a second, everything and everyone in the church except Reverend Taylor and Sister Monroe hung loose <u>like stockings on a washline.</u>

Maya Angelou, "Sister Monroe"

_____

_____

5. The <u>Moving Finger</u> writes; and, having writ,
   Moves on; nor all <u>your Piety nor</u> Wit
   Shall lure it back <u>to cancel half a Line,</u>
   Nor all your <u>Tears wash out a Word of it.</u>

The Rubáiyát of Omar Khayyám

_____

_____

_____

IMPLIED MEANING

Reading would be rather dull if the author stated every idea, never giving you a chance to figure things out for yourself. For example, in a mystery novel you carefully weigh each word, each action, each conversation, each description, and each fact in an effort to identify the villain and solve the crime before it is revealed at the end. Although textbook material may not have the Sherlock Holmes spirit of high adventure, authors use the same techniques to imply meaning.

Note the inferences in the following example:

Johnson in Action

Lyndon Johnson suffered from the inevitable comparison with his young and stylish predecessor. LBJ was acutely aware of his own lack of polish; he sought to surround himself with Kennedy advisers and insiders, hoping that their learning and sophistication would rub off on him. Johnson's assets were very real—an intimate knowledge of Congress, an incredible energy and determination to succeed, and a fierce ego. When a young marine officer tried to direct him to the proper helicopter, saying, "This one is yours," Johnson replied, "Son, they are all my helicopters."

LBJ's height and intensity gave him a powerful presence; he dominated any room he entered, and he delighted in using his physical power of persuasion. One Texas politician explained why he had given in to Johnson: "Lyndon got me by the lapels and put his face on top of mine and he talked and talked and talked. I figured it was either getting drowned or joining."

Robert A. Divine et al., America Past and Present

Answer the following with *T* (true) or *F* (false).

_____ 1. Johnson was haunted by the style and sophistication of John F. Kennedy.
(True. He "suffered from the inevitable comparison," and he went so far as to maintain the Kennedy advisors.)

_____ 2. Johnson could be both egotistical and arrogant about his presidential power.
(True. The anecdote about the helicopters proves that.)

_____ 3. Even if he did not mentally persuade, Johnson could physically overwhelm people into agreement.
(True. His delight in "using his physical power of persuasion" and the anecdote about the Texas politician support that.)

The following examples, factual and fictitious, show how authors use suggestion, and from the clues given, how you can deduce the facts.

Exercise 5: Inference from Description

Looking back on the Revolutionary War, one cannot say enough about Washington's leadership. While his military skills proved less than brilliant and he and his generals lost many battles, George Washington was the single most important figure of the colonial war effort. His original appointment was partly political, for the rebellion that had started in Massachusetts needed a commander from the South to give geographic balance to the cause. The choice fell to Washington, a wealthy and respectable Virginia planter with military experience dating back to the French and Indian War. He had been denied a commission in the English army and had never forgiven the English for the insult. During the war he shared the physical suffering of his men, rarely wavered on important questions, and always used his officers to good advantage. His correspondence with Congress to ask for sorely needed supplies was tireless and forceful. He recruited several new armies in a row, as short-term enlistments gave out.

Leonard Pitt, *We Americans*[*]

Answer the following with *T* (true) or *F* (false).

_____ 1. The author regards George Washington as the most brilliant military genius in American history.
_____ 2. A prime factor in Washington's becoming president of the United States was a need for geographic balance.
_____ 3. Washington resented the British for a past injustice.
_____ 4. The Revolutionary War started as a rebellion in the Northeast.
_____ 5. The author feels that Washington's leadership was courageous and persistent even though not infallible.

Exercise 6: Inference from Action

When he came to the surface he was conscious of little but the noisy water. Afterward he saw his companions in the sea. The oiler was ahead in the race. He was swimming strongly and rapidly. Off to the correspondent's left, the cook's great white and corked back bulged out of the water, and in the rear the captain was hanging with his one good hand to the keel of the overturned dinghy.

There is a certain immovable quality to a shore, and the correspondent wondered at it amid the confusion of the sea.

Stephen Crane, *The Open Boat*

[*]From Pitt, *We Americans*. Copyright © 1987 by Kendall/Hunt Publishing Company. Reprinted with permission.

Answer the following with *a, b, c,* or *d.*

_____ 1. The reason that the people are in the water is because of
  a. a swimming race.
  b. an airplane crash.
  c. a capsized boat.
  d. a group decision.

_____ 2. In relation to his companions, the correspondent is
  a. closest to the shore.
  b. the second or third closest to the shore.
  c. farthest from the shore.
  d. in a position that is impossible to determine.

_____ 3. The member of the group that had probably suffered a previous injury is the
  a. oiler.
  b. correspondent.
  c. cook.
  d. captain.

_____ 4. The member of the group that the author seems to stereotype negatively as least physically fit is the
  a. oiler.
  b. correspondent.
  c. cook.
  d. captain.

_____ 5. The story is being told through the eyes of the
  a. oiler.
  b. correspondent.
  c. cook.
  d. captain.

Exercise 7: Inference from Factual Material

Except for some minor internal disturbances in the nineteenth century, Switzerland has been at peace inside stable boundaries since 1815. The basic factors underlying this long period of peace seem to have been (1) Switzerland's position as a buffer between larger powers, (2) the comparative defensibility of much of the country's terrain, (3) the relatively small value of Swiss economic production to an aggressive state, (4) the country's value as an intermediary between belligerents in wartime, and (5) Switzerland's own policy of strict and heavily armed neutrality. The difficulties which a great power might encounter in attempting to conquer Switzerland have often been popularly exaggerated since the Swiss Plateau, the heart of the country, lies open to Germany and France, and even the Alps have frequently been traversed by strong military forces in past times. On the other hand, resistance in the mountains might well be hard to thoroughly extinguish. In World War II Switzerland was able to hold a club over the head of Germany by mining the tunnels through which Swiss rail lines avoid the crests of Alpine passes. Destruction of these tunnels would have been very costly to Germany, as well as to its military partner, Italy, since the Swiss railways were depended on to carry much traffic between them.

Jesse H. Wheeler et al., *Regional Geography of the World*

Answer the following with *T* (true) or *F* (false).

———————— 1. The author implies that Switzerland is rich with raw materials for economic production.

———————— 2. The most important economic area of Switzerland is protected from its neighbors by the Alps.

———————— 3. In World War II Germany did not invade Switzerland primarily because of the fear of the strong Swiss army.

———————— 4. The maintenance of a neutral Swiss position in World War II was due in part to a kind of international blackmail.

———————— 5. The Swiss have avoided international war on their soil for over one hundred years.

PRIOR KNOWLEDGE AND IMPLIED MEANING

Have you ever considered what makes a joke funny? Why is it no longer funny when you have to explain the meaning of a joke to someone who didn't get it? The answer is that jokes are funny because of implied connections. The meaning that you may have to reluctantly explain is the inference or **implied meaning.** If the listener does not share the background knowledge to which the joke refers, your hilarious comic attempt will fall flat because the listener cannot understand the implied meaning. Listeners cannot connect with something they don't know, so you must choose the right joke for the right audience.

College reading may not be filled with comedy, but **prior knowledge** is expected and specifics are frequently implied rather than directly spelled out. For example, if a sentence began, "Previously wealthy investors were leaping from buildings in the financial district," you would know that the author was referring to the Stock Market Crash of 1929 on Wall Street in New York City. Although the specifics are not directly stated, you have used prior knowledge and have "added up" the details that are meaningful to you to infer time and place.

Exercise 8: Inferring Time and Place

Read the following passages and indicate *a, b,* or *c* for the suggested time or place. Underline the clues that helped you arrive at your answer.

Passage A

As women strove to maintain a semblance of home on the trail, they often experienced a profound sense of loss. The Sabbath, which had been ladies' day back home and an emblem of women's moral authority, was often spent working or traveling, especially once the going got rough. "Oh dear me I did not think we would have abused the sabbath in such a manner," wrote one guilt-stricken female emigrant. Women also felt the lack of close companions, to whom they could turn for comfort. One woman, whose husband separated their wagon from the train after a dispute, sadly watched the other wagons pull away: "I felt that indeed I had left all my friends to journey over the dreaded plains without one female acquaintance even for a companion—of course I wept and grieved about it but to no purpose."

James Davidson et al., *Nation of Nations*

_____ 1. The time when this takes place is probably in the
  a. 1920s.
  b. 1770s.
  c. 1840s.

_____ 2. The section of the United States is most likely the
  a. west.
  b. south.
  c. north.

3. Underline the clues to your answers.

Passage B

Looking eastward from Sharpsburg into the mountains, General Robert E. Lee uttered the fateful words: "We will make our stand." Behind him was the Potomac River, and to his front was Antietam Creek. Now he issued orders for his troops to regather with all haste at Sharpsburg. A major battle was in the making. General George B. McClellan's Army of the Potomac, numbering nearly 100,000 soldiers, was rapidly descending upon Lee's position.

James Martin et al., *America and Its People*

_____ 4. The time is probably
  a. 1812.
  b. 1862.
  c. 1889.

5. The place is most likely
   a. Virginia.
   b. Georgia.
   c. Ohio.
6. Underline the clues to your answers.

Passage C

If natives struck whites as starkly underdressed, Europeans seemed, by the Indians' standards, grotesquely overdressed. Indeed, European fashion was ill-suited to the environment between the Chesapeake and the Caribbean. Elizabethan gentlemen strutted in silk stockings attached with garters to padded, puffed knee breeches, topped by long-sleeved shirts and tight quilted jackets called "doublets." Men of lesser status wore coarse woolen hose, canvas breeches, shirts, and fitted vests known as "jerkins"; when at work, they donned aprons of dressed leather. Women wore gowns with long, full skirts, low-cut bodices, aprons, and hosiery held up by garters. Both sexes favored long hair, and men sported mustaches and beards. Such fashions complicated life in the American environment, especially since heavy clothing and even shoes rotted rapidly from sweat and humidity. The pungent aroma of Europeans also compounded the discomfort of natives who came in contact with them. For despite sweltering heat, the whites who swaddled themselves in woolens and brocades also disdained regular bathing and regarded Indian devotion to daily washing as another uncivilized oddity.

It would have been natural for Indians to wonder why the barbaric newcomers did not adapt their dress to a new setting. The answer may be that for Europeans—entering an alien environment inhabited by peoples whom they identified as "naked savages"—the psychological risk of shedding familiar apparel was simply too great. However inappropriate or even unhealthy, heavy, elaborate dress afforded the comfort of familiarity and distinguished "civilized" newcomer from "savage" native in America.

James Davidson et al., *Nation of Nations*

7. The time is probably in the early
   a. 1600s.
   b. 1500s.
   c. 1400s.
8. The place is most likely
   a. Massachusetts.
   b. Virginia.
   c. Indiana.
9. Underline the clues to your answers.

DRAWING CONCLUSIONS

To arrive at a conclusion, the reader must make a logical deduction from both stated and unstated ideas. Using the hints as well as the facts, the reader relies on prior knowledge and experience to interpret motives, actions, and outcomes. Conclusions are drawn on the basis of perceived evidence, and because perceptions differ, conclusions can vary from reader to reader. Generally, however, the author attempts to direct the reader to a preconceived conclusion. Read the following example and look for a basis for the stated conclusion.

Underground Conductor

Harriet Tubman was on a northbound train when she overheard her name spoken by a white passenger. He was reading aloud an ad which accused her of stealing $50,000 worth of property in slaves, and which offered a $5000 reward for her capture. She lowered her head so that the sunbonnet she was wearing hid her face. At the next station she slipped off the train and boarded another that was headed south, reasoning that no one would pay attention to a black woman traveling in that direction. She deserted the second train near her hometown in Maryland and bought two chickens as part of her disguise. With her back hunched over in imitation of an old woman, she drove the chickens down the dusty road, calling angrily and chasing them with her stick whenever she sensed danger. In this manner Harriet Tubman was passed by her former owner who did not even notice her. The reward continued to mount until it reached $40,000.

Leonard Pitt, *We Americans*

Conclusion: Harriet Tubman was a clever woman who became a severe irritant to white slave owners.
What is the basis for this conclusion?

_____

_____

(Her disguise and subsequent escape from the train station provides evidence for her intelligence. The escalating amount of the reward, finally $40,000, proves the severity of the sentiment against her.)

Exercise 9: Drawing Conclusions

Read the following passages and indicate evidence for the conclusions that have been drawn.

© 1993 HarperCollins College Publishers

Passage A

A tragic counterpoint to the voluntary movement of American workers in search of jobs was the forced relocation of 120,000 Japanese-Americans from the West Coast. Responding to racial fears in California after Pearl Harbor, President Roosevelt approved an army order in February 1942 to move both the Issei (Japanese-Americans who had emigrated from Japan) and the Nisei (people of Japanese ancestry born in the United States and therefore American citizens) to concentration camps in the interior. Forced to sell their farms and businesses at distress prices, the Japanese-Americans lost not only their liberty but also most of their worldly goods. Herded into ten hastily built detention centers in seven western states, they lived as prisoners in tar-papered barracks behind barbed wire, guarded by armed troops.

Robert Divine et al., America Past and Present

Conclusion: After Pearl Harbor many Japanese-Americans were treated unfairly by the American government.
What is the basis for this conclusion?

_____

_____

Passage B

Pesticides are biologically rather interesting substances. They have no known counterpart in the natural world, and most of them didn't even exist thirty years ago. Today, however, a metabolic product of DDT, called DDE, may be the most common and widely distributed man-made chemical on earth. It has been found in the tissues of living things from the polar regions to the remotest parts of the oceans, forests, and mountains. Although the permissible level of DDT in cow's milk, set by the U.S. Food and Drug Administration, is 0.05 parts per million, it often occurs in human milk in concentrations as high as 5 parts per million and in human fat at levels of more than 12 parts per million.

Robert Wallace, Biology: The World of Life

Conclusion: DDT accumulates in the environment far beyond the areas where it was directly applied.
What is the basis for this conclusion?

_____

_____

Exercise 10: Building a Story with Inferences

The following story unfolds as the reader uses the clues to predict and make inferences. To make sense out of the story, the reader is never told—but must figure out—who the man is, what he is doing, and why he is doing it. Like a mystery, the story is fun to read because you are actively involved. Use your inferential skills to figure it out.

Caged

Emphatically, Mr. Purcell did not believe in ghosts. Nevertheless, the man who bought the two doves, and his strange act immediately thereafter, left him with a distinct sense of the eerie.

Purcell was a small, fussy man; red cheeks and a tight, melon stomach. He owned a pet shop. He sold cats and dogs and monkeys; he dealt in fish food and bird seed, and prescribed remedies for ailing canaries. He considered himself something of a professional man.

There was a bell over the door that jangled whenever a customer entered. This morning, however, for the first time Mr. Purcell could recall, it failed to ring. Simply he glanced up, and there was the stranger, standing just inside the door, as if he had materialized out of thin air.

The storekeeper slid off his stool. From the first instant he knew instinctively, unreasonably, that the man hated him; but out of habit he rubbed his hands briskly together, smiled and nodded.

"Good morning," he beamed. "What can I do for you?"

The man's shiny shoes squeaked forward. His suit was cheap, ill-fitting, but obviously new. A gray pallor deadened his pinched features. He had a shuttling glance and close-cropped hair. He stared closely at Purcell and said, "I want something in a cage."

"Something in a cage?" Mr. Purcell was a bit confused. "You mean—some kind of pet?"

"I mean what I said!" snapped the man. "Something alive that's in a cage."

"I see," hastened the storekeeper, not at all certain that he did. "Now let me think. A white rat, perhaps."

"No!" said the man. "Not rats. Something with wings. Something that flies."

"A bird!" exclaimed Mr. Purcell.

"A bird's all right." The customer pointed suddenly to a suspended cage which contained two snowy birds. "Doves? How much for those?"

"Five-fifty. And a very reasonable price."

"Five-fifty?" The sallow man was obviously crestfallen. He hesitantly produced a five-dollar bill. "I'd like to have those birds. But this is all I got. Just five dollars."

Mentally, Mr. Purcell made a quick calculation, which told him that at a fifty-cent reduction he could still reap a tidy profit. He smiled magnanimously. "My dear man, if you want them that badly, you can certainly have them for five dollars."

"I'll take them." He laid his five dollars on the counter. Mr. Purcell teetered on tiptoe, unhooked the cage, and handed it to his customer. The man cocked his head to one side, listening to the constant chittering, the rushing scurry of the shop. "That noise!" he blurted. "Doesn't it get you? I mean all this caged stuff. Drives you crazy, doesn't it?"

Purcell drew back. Either the man was insane, or drunk.

"Listen." The staring eyes came closer. "How long d'you think it took me to make that five dollars?"

The merchant wanted to order him out of the shop. But he heard himself dutifully asking, "Why—why, how long *did* it take you?"

The other laughed. "Ten years! At hard labor. Ten years to earn five dollars. Fifty cents a year."

It was best, Purcell decided, to humor him. "My, my! Ten years—"

"They give you five dollars," laughed the man, "and a cheap suit, and tell you not to get caught again."

Mr. Purcell mopped his sweating brow. "Now, about the care and feeding of—"

"Bah!" The sallow man swung around, and stalked abruptly from the store.

Purcell sighed with sudden relief. He waddled to the window and stared out. Just outside, his peculiar customer had halted. He was holding the cage shoulder-high, staring at his purchase. Then, opening the cage, he reached inside and drew out one of the doves. He tossed it into the air. He drew out the second and tossed it after the first. They rose like wind-blown balls of fluff and were lost in the smoky grey of the wintry city. For an instant the liberator's silent and lifted gaze watched after them. Then he dropped the cage. A futile, suddenly forlorn figure, he shoved both hands deep in his trouser pockets, hunched down his head and shuffled away. . . .

The merchant's brow was puckered with perplexity. "Now why," Mr. Purcell muttered, "did he do that?" He felt vaguely insulted.

Lloyd Eric Reeve, *Household Magazine*

1. Where had the man been?
2. How do you know for sure? Underline the clues.
3. When did you figure it out? Circle the clincher.
4. Why does he want to set the birds free?
5. Why should the shopkeeper feel insulted?
6. After freeing the birds, why is the stranger "a futile, suddenly forlorn figure," rather than happy and excited?

SUMMARY

The **inferential level** of reading deals with motives, feelings, and judgments. The reader must read between the lines and look for the implied meaning in words and actions.

The author's choice of words can manipulate the reader. The feeling or emotionalism surrounding a word is its **connotation.** The connotation of a word reflects certain attitudes and prejudices of society than can be positive or negative.

Figurative language creates images to suggest attitudes. It is a different way of using "regular language" words so that the words take on a new meaning.

Readers use **implied meaning** to draw conclusions. Based on hints, facts, and prior knowledge, readers interpret motives, actions, and outcomes. Suggested meaning is powerful and can be a more effective method of getting the message across than a direct statement.

Selection **1**

LITERATURE

Stage 1

Preview

The author's main purpose is to tell a story.

agree ☐ *disagree* ☐

This selection is narrative rather than expository.

agree ☐ *disagree* ☐

After reading this, I will need to explain a theory.

agree ☐ *disagree* ☐

Learning Strategy

Use the action and the characters to develop a conclusion or a theme about human qualities.

Word Knowledge

Review the ten vocabulary items that follow the selection. Seek an understanding of unfamiliar words.

Activate Schema

What lies have you read about celebrities in the tabloid newspapers? Have you read two other short stories by De Maupassant entitled "The Necklace" and "Gift of the Magi"?

Stage 2: Integrate Knowledge While Reading

Use the thinking strategies as you read.

1. Predict 2. Picture 3. Relate 4. Monitor 5. Fix up

THE PIECE OF STRING

From Guy de Maupassant, *Short Stories of De Maupassant*

Along all the roads around Goderville the peasants and their wives were coming toward the burgh because it was market day. The men were proceeding with slow steps, the whole body bent forward at each movement of their long twisted legs; deformed by their hard
5   work, by the weight on the plow which, at the same time, raised the left shoulder and swerved the figure, by the reaping of the wheat

which made the knees spread to make a firm "purchase," by all the slow and painful labors of the country. Their blouses, blue, "stiff-starched," shining as if varnished, ornamented with a little
10 design in white at the neck and wrists, puffed about their bony bodies, seemed like balloons ready to carry them off. From each of them a head, two arms and two feet protruded.

Some led a cow or a calf by a cord, and their wives, walking behind the animal, whipped its haunches with a leafy branch to hasten its
15 progress. They carried large baskets on their arms from which, in some cases, chickens and, in others, ducks thrust out their heads. And they walked with a quicker, livelier step than their husbands. Their spare straight figures were wrapped in a scanty little shawl pinned over their flat bosoms, and their heads were enveloped in a white
20 cloth glued to the hair and surmounted by a cap.

Then a wagon passed at the jerky trot of a nag, shaking strangely, two men seated side by side and a woman in the bottom of the vehicle, the latter holding onto the sides to lessen the hard jolts.

In the public square of Goderville there was a crowd, a throng of
25 human beings and animals mixed together. The horns of the cattle, the tall hats, with long nap, of the rich peasant and the headgear of the peasant women rose above the surface of the assembly. And the clamorous, shrill, screaming voices made a continuous and savage din which sometimes was dominated by the robust lungs of some
30 countryman's laugh or the long lowing of a cow tied to the wall of a house.

All that smacked of the stable, the dairy and the dirt heap, hay and sweat, giving forth that unpleasant odor, human and animal, peculiar to the people of the field.
35 Maître Hauchecome of Breaute had just arrived at Goderville, and he was directing his steps toward the public square when he perceived upon the ground a little piece of string. Maître Hauchecome, economical like a true Norman, thought that everything useful ought to be picked up, and he bent painfully, for he suffered
40 from rheumatism. He took the bit of thin cord from the ground and began to roll it carefully when he noticed Maître Malandain, the harness maker, on the threshold of his door, looking at him. They had heretofore had business together on the subject of a halter, and they were on bad terms, both being good haters. Maître Hauchecome was
45 seized with a sort of shame to be seen thus by his enemy, picking a bit of string out of the dirt. He concealed his "find" quickly under his blouse, then in his trousers' pocket; then he pretended to be still looking on the ground for something which he did not find, and he went toward the market, his head forward, bent double by his pains.
50 He was soon lost in the noisy and slowly moving crowd which was

busy with interminable bargainings. The peasants milked, went and came, perplexed, always in fear of being cheated, not daring to decide, watching the vender's eye, ever trying to find the trick in the man and the flaw in the beast.

55 The women, having placed their great baskets at their feet, had taken out the poultry which lay upon the ground, tied together by the feet, with terrified eyes and scarlet crests.

They heard offers, stated their prices with a dry air and impassive face, or perhaps, suddenly deciding on some proposed reduction,
60 shouted to the customer who was slowly going away: "All right, Maître Authirne, I'll give it to you for that."

Then little by little the square was deserted, and the Angelus ringing at noon, those who had stayed too long scattered to their shops.

At Jourdain's the great room was full of people eating, as the big
65 court was full of vehicles of all kinds, carts, gigs, wagons, dumpcarts, yellow with dirt, mended and patched, raising their shafts to the sky like two arms or perhaps with their shafts in the ground and their backs in the air.

Just opposite the diners seated at the table the immense fireplace,
70 filled with bright flames, cast a lively heat on the backs of the row on the right. Three spits were turning on which were chickens, pigeons and legs of mutton, and an appetizing odor of roast beef and gravy dripping over the nicely browned skin rose from the hearth, increased the jovialness and made everybody's mouth water.

75 All the aristocracy of the plow ate there at Maître Jourdain's, tavern keeper and horse dealer, a rascal who had money.

The dishes were passed and emptied, as were the jugs of yellow cider. Everyone told his affairs, his purchases and sales. They discussed the crops. The weather was favorable for the green things
80 but not for the wheat.

Suddenly the drum beat in the court before the house. Everybody rose, except a few indifferent persons, and ran to the door or to the windows, their mouths still full and napkins in their hands.

After the public crier had ceased his drumbeating he called out in a
85 jerky voice, speaking his phrases irregularly:

"It is hereby made known to the inhabitants of Goderville, and in general to all persons present at the market, that there was lost this morning on the road to Benzeville, between nine and ten o'clock, a black leather pocketbook containing five hundred francs and some
90 business papers. The finder is requested to return same with all haste to the mayor's office or to Maître Fortune Houlbreque of Manneville; there will be twenty francs reward."

Then the man went away. The heavy roll of the drum and the crier's voice were again heard at a distance.

95　　　They began to talk of this event, discussing the chances that Maître Houlbreque had of finding or not finding his pocketbook.

And the meal concluded. They were finishing their coffee when a chief of the gendarmes appeared upon the threshold.

He inquired:

100　"Is Maître Hauchecome of Breaute here?"

Maître Hauchecome, seated at the other end of the table, replied:

"Here I am."

And the officer resumed:

105　"Maître Hauchecome, will you have the goodness to accompany me to the mayor's office? The mayor would like to talk to you."

The peasant, surprised and disturbed, swallowed at a draught his tiny glass of brandy, rose and, even more bent than in the morning, for the first steps after each rest were specially difficult, set out,

110　repeating: "Here I am, here I am."

The mayor was awaiting him, seated on an armchair. He was the notary of the vicinity, a stout, serious man with pompous phrases.

"Maître Hauchecome," said he, "you were seen this morning to pick up, on the road to Benzeville, the pocketbook lost by Maître

115　Houlbreque of Manneville."

The countryman, astounded, looked at the mayor, already terrified by this suspicion resting on him without his knowing why.

"Me? Me? Me pick up the pocketbook?"

"Yes, you yourself."

120　"Word of honor, I never heard of it."

"But you were seen."

"I was seen, me? Who says he saw me?"

"Monsieur Malandain, the harness maker."

The old man remembered, understood and flushed with anger.

125　"Ah, he saw me, the clodhopper, he saw me pick up this string here, M'sieu the Mayor." And rummaging in his pocket, he drew out the little piece of string.

But the mayor, incredulous, shook his head.

"You will not make me believe, Maître Hauchecome, that Monsieur

130　Malandain, who is a man worthy of credence, mistook this cord for a pocketbook."

The peasant, furious, lifted his hand, spat at one side to attest his honor, repeating:

"It is nevertheless the truth of the good God, the sacred truth,

135　M'sieu the Mayor. I repeat it on my soul and my salvation."

The Mayor resumed:

"After picking up the object you stood like a stilt, looking a long while in the mud to see if any piece of money had fallen out."

The good old man choked with indignation and fear.

140 "How anyone can tell—how anyone can tell—such lies to take away an honest man's reputation! How can anyone—"

There was no use in his protesting; nobody believed him. He was confronted with Monsieur Malandain, who repeated and maintained his affirmation. They abused each other for an hour. At his own

145 request Maître Hauchecome was searched; nothing was found on him.

Finally the mayor, very much perplexed, discharged him with the warning that he would consult the public prosecutor and ask for further orders.

The news had spread. As he left the mayor's office the old man was

150 surrounded and questioned with a serious or bantering curiosity in which there was no indignation. He began to tell the story of the string. No one believed him. They laughed at him.

He went along, stopping his friends, beginning endlessly his statement and his protestations, showing his pockets turned inside out

155 to prove that he had nothing.

They said:

"Old rascal, get out!"

And he grew angry, becoming exasperated, hot and distressed at not being believed, not knowing what to do and always repeating himself.

160 Night came. He must depart. He started on his way with three neighbors to whom he pointed out the place where he had picked up the bit of string, and all along the road he spoke of his adventure.

In the evening he took a turn in the village of Breaute in order to tell it to everybody. He only met with incredulity.

165 It made him ill at night.

The next day about one o'clock in the afternoon Marius Paumelle, a hired man in the employ of Maître Breton, husbandman at Ymanville, returned the pocketbook and its contents to Maître Houlbreque of Manneville.

170 This man claimed to have found the object in the road, but not knowing how to read, he had carried it to the house and given it to his employer.

The news spread through the neighborhood. Maître Hauchecome was informed of it. He immediately went the circuit and began to

175 recount his story completed by the happy climax. He was in triumph.

"What grieved me so much was not the thing itself as the lying. There is nothing so shameful as to be placed under a cloud on account of a lie."

He talked of his adventure all day long; he told it on the highway to

180 people who were passing by, in the wineshop to people who were drinking there and to persons coming out of church the following Sunday. He stopped strangers to tell them about it. He was calm now, and yet something disturbed him without his knowing exactly what it

was. People had the air of joking while they listened. They did not
185 seem convinced. He seemed to feel that remarks were being made
behind his back.

On Tuesday of the next week he went to the market at Goderville,
urged solely by the necessity he felt of discussing the case.

Malandain, standing at his door, began to laugh on seeing him pass.
190 Why?

He approached a farmer from Crequetot who did not let him finish
and, giving him a thump in the stomach, said to his face:

"You big rascal."

Then he turned his back on him.

195 Maître Hauchecome was confused; why was he called a big rascal?

When he was seated at the table in Jourdain's tavern he
commenced to explain "the affair."

A horse dealer from Monvilliers called to him:

"Come, come, old sharper, that's an old trick; I know all about your
200 piece of string!"

Hauchecome stammered:

"But since the pocketbook was found."

But the other man replied:

"Shut up, papa, there is one that finds and there is one that reports.
205 At any rate you are mixed with it."

The peasant stood choking. He understood. They accused him of
having had the pocketbook returned by a confederate, by an accomplice.

He tried to protest. All the table began to laugh.

He could not finish his dinner and went away in the midst of jeers.

210 He went home ashamed and indignant, choking with anger and
confusion, the more dejected that he was capable, with his Norman
cunning, of doing what they had accused him of and ever boasting of
it as a good turn. His innocence to him, in a confused way, was
impossible to prove, as his sharpness was known. And he was stricken
215 to the heart by the injustice of the suspicion.

Then he began to recount the adventures again, prolonged his
history every day, adding each time new reasons, more energetic
protestations, more solemn oaths which he imagined and prepared in
his hours of solitude, his whole mind given up to the story of the
220 string. He was believed so much the less as his defense was more
complicated and his arguing more subtle.

"Those are lying excuses," they said behind his back.

He felt it, consumed his heart over it and wore himself out with
useless efforts. He wasted away before their very eyes.

225 The wags now made him tell about the string to amuse them, as
they make a soldier who has been on a campaign tell about his
battles. His mind, touched to the depth, began to weaken.

Toward the end of December he took to his bed.

He died in the first days of January, and in the delirium of his death
230 struggles he kept claiming his innocence, reiterating:

"A piece of string, a piece of string—look—here it is, M'sieu the
Mayor."

Recall for self-testing.

_____

_____

Skill Development: Implied Meaning

According to the implied meaning in the selection, answer the following
with *T* (true) or *F* (false).

_____ 1. The author begins the story by appealing to the reader's senses to paint a
picture.

_____ 2. The author focuses on the bad rather than the good in people.

_____ 3. The author implies that only a small group of neighbors supported
Hauchecome in his time of need.

_____ 4. The phrase that describes blouses, "like balloons ready to carry them
off," is a simile.

_____ 5. The phrase, "their heads were enveloped in a white cloth glued to the
hair," contains a metaphor.

Comprehension Questions

1. Who or what is this selection about? _____

   What is the main point the author is trying to convey about the topic?

   _____

Answer the following with *a, b, c,* or *d.*

_____ 2. The reader can conclude that the setting for this story is
   a. England.
   b. France.
   c. Spain.
   d. Italy.

3. Because of previous encounters, the relationship between Hauchecome and Malandain was
   a. indifferent.
   b. warm.
   c. trusting.
   d. hostile.

4. The manner in which Hauchecome picked up and pocketed the string suggested
   a. innocence.
   b. guilt.
   c. openness.
   d. self-confidence.

5. The author suggests that Hauchecome was known by his neighbors to be
   a. honest.
   b. unintelligent.
   c. shrewd.
   d. religious.

6. After listening to Hauchecome and Malandain, the Mayor
   a. believed Hauchecome's story.
   b. let Hauchecome go free for lack of evidence.
   c. told Malandain to find more witnesses.
   d. requested a trial.

7. People listened to Hauchecome's story with all of the following except
   a. ridicule.
   b. suspicion.
   c. laughter.
   d. sympathy.

8. The one person who could have stopped the nightmare and restored Hauchecome's reputation was
   a. Paumelle.
   b. Malandain.
   c. Houlbreque.
   d. the Mayor.

9. Hauchecome's protestations and explanations seemed to make people
   a. increasingly suspicious.
   b. sensitive to his needs.
   c. hopeful of his recovery.
   d. frightened of his anger.

10. The author suggests that
    a. lies breed more lies.
    b. the truth is stronger than a lie.
    c. lies can be overcome by good people.
    d. truth always wins.

Answer the following with *T* (true) or *F* (false).

_____ 11. The author portrays the peasants as stout and robust as they come to market.

_____ 12. Items sold in the marketplace had a fixed price.

_____ 13. The tavern in which the peasants ate was owned by a horse dealer.

_____ 14. People began to treat Hauchecome like a fool.

_____ 15. Hauchecome learned that his friends were not really his friends.

Vocabulary

According to the way the italicized word was used in the selection, indicate *a, b, c,* or *d* for the word or phrase that gives the best definition.

_____ 1. "coming toward the *burgh*" (2)
   a. town
   b. street
   c. festival
   d. market

_____ 2. "*scanty* little shawl" (18)
   a. handmade
   b. embroidered
   c. skimpy
   d. dusty

_____ 3. "with *interminable* bargainings" (51)
   a. endless
   b. dishonest
   c. skillful
   d. angry

_____ 4. "*impassive* face" (58)
   a. knowing
   b. smiling
   c. eager
   d. emotionless

_____ 5. "with *pompous* phrases" (111)
   a. pretentious
   b. meaningful
   c. insightful
   d. helpful

_____ 6. "*rummaging* in his pocket" (126)
   a. resting
   b. hiding
   c. looking
   d. searching

_____ 7. "worthy of *credence*" (130)
   a. respect
   b. admiration
   c. belief
   d. love

_____ 8. "choked with *indignation*" (139)
   a. sympathy
   b. anger
   c. terror
   d. remorse

_____ 9. "his Norman *cunning*" (211)
   a. craftiness
   b. upbringing
   c. instinct
   d. behavior

_____ 10. "*reiterating*: A piece of string" (230)
   a. shouting
   b. demanding
   c. pleading
   d. repeating

Written Response

Refer to the information in this text to write a letter to Hauchecome or Malandain explaining how you feel about his actions.

Connecting and Reflecting

The account of Kitty Genovese's death is a classic example of bystander apathy. Psychologists have conducted many experiments to try to understand why onlookers allowed the tragedy to occur. What do you feel are the reasons for people not to intervene? Why did the 38 neighbors do nothing to help Kitty Genovese, not even to call 911? Why did so many subjects in Darley and Latané's experiment fail to respond? Discuss these questions with others and then create a tragic situation at your college that calls for intervention. Write a psychological description of two people who witness the tragedy: (1) a person who intervenes and (2) a person who does not intervene. Describe each person in detail and explain why you think they respond as they do.

Bystander Apathy

What would you do if, late some dark night, you heard screams outside your place? Would you rush out at once, or would you first go to the window to see what was happening? If you saw a man with a knife attacking one of your neighbors, how would you react? Might you call the police, or go to the neighbor's aid? Or would you remain **apathetic** and unresponsive? And if you failed to assist the neighbor in any way, how would you respond if someone later on asked why you didn't help?

Before you answer, consider the following facts. Early one morning in 1964, a young New York woman named Kitty Genovese was returning home from work. As she neared her front door, a man jumped out of the shadows and attacked her. She screamed and attempted to defend herself. Because she screamed loudly, 38 of her neighbors came to their windows to see what was happening. And because she fought valiantly, it took the man almost 30 minutes to kill Kitty Genovese. During this period of time, not one of those 38 neighbors came to her aid—and not one of them even bothered to call the police (Cunningham 1984; Shotland 1985; Darley & Latané 1968; Takooshian & O'Connor 1984).

The Darley-Latané Studies   Kitty Genovese's death so distressed scientists John Darley and Bibb Latané, they began a study of why people refuse to help others in similar situations.

In one experiment, the subjects heard a loud crash from the next room, and a woman began moaning loudly that she had fallen and was badly hurt and needed help.

Now, how many of the subjects do you think came to her rescue?

The answer is—it depends. Some of the subjects were exposed to this little drama when they were all by themselves in the testing room. About 70 percent of the "alone" subjects offered help. Another 40 subjects faced this apparent emergency in pairs. Only 8 of these 40 people responded by going to the woman's aid. The other 32 subjects simply sat there listening to the moans and groans.

James V. McConnell, *Understanding Human Behavior*

Selection

2

ESSAY

Stage 1

Preview

The author's main purpose is to change the school system.

agree ☐   disagree ☐

The overall pattern of organization is definition-example.

agree ☐   disagree ☐

After reading this selection, I will need to explain how to teach Spanish.

agree ☐   disagree ☐

Learning Strategy

Read to understand what the author means by a public and a private language.

Word Knowledge

Review the ten vocabulary items that follow the selection. Seek an understanding of unfamiliar words.

Activate Schema

How do parents who speak English as a second language keep their first language alive for their children?

Stage 2: Integrate Knowledge While Reading

Use the thinking strategies as you read:

1. Predict 2. Picture 3. Relate 4. Monitor 5. Fix up

BILINGUAL EDUCATION

From Richard Rodriguez, *Hunger of Memory*

Supporters of bilingual education today imply that students like me miss a great deal by not being taught in their family's language. What they seem not to recognize is that, as a socially disadvantaged child, I considered Spanish to be a private language. What I needed to learn
5   in school was that I had the right—and the obligation—to speak the public language of *los gringos.*
  Without question, it would have pleased me to hear my teachers address me in Spanish when I entered the classroom. I would have felt much less afraid. I would have trusted them and responded with
10 ease. But I would have delayed—for how long postponed?—having to learn the language of public society. I would have evaded—and for how long could I have afforded to delay?—learning the great lesson of school, that I had a public identity.
  Fortunately, my teachers were unsentimental about their
15 responsibility. What they understood was that I needed to speak a public language. So their voices would search me out, asking me

questions. Each time I'd hear them, I'd look up in surprise to see a nun's face frowning at me. I'd mumble, not really meaning to answer. The nun would persist, "Richard, stand up. Don't look at the floor.
20 Speak up. Speak to the entire class, not just to me!" But I couldn't believe that the English language was mine to use.

Three months. Five. Half a year passed. Unsmiling, ever watchful, my teachers noted my silence. They began to connect my behavior with the difficult progress my older sister and brother were making.
25 Until one Saturday morning three nuns arrived at the house to talk to our parents. Stiffly, they sat on the blue living room sofa. From the doorway of another room, spying the visitors, I noted the incongruity—the clash of two worlds, the faces and voices of school intruding upon the familiar setting of home. I overhead one voice
30 gently wondering, "Do your children speak only Spanish at home, Mrs. Rodriguez?" While another voice added, "That Richard especially seems so timid and shy."

That Rich-heard!

With great tact the visitors continued, "Is it possible for you and
35 your husband to encourage your children to practice their English when they are home?" Of course, my parents complied. What would they not do for their children's well-being? And how could they have questioned the Church's authority which those women represented? In an instant, they agreed to give up the language (the sounds) that
40 had revealed and accentuated our family's closeness. The moment after the visitors left, the change was observed. "*Ahora,* speak to us *en inglés,*" my father and mother united to tell us.

At first, it seemed a kind of game. After dinner each night, the family gathered to practice "our" English. (It was still then *inglés,* a
45 language foreign to us, so we felt drawn as strangers to it.) Laughing, we would try to define words we could not pronounce. We played with strange English sounds, often overanglicizing our pronunciations. And we filled the smiling gaps of our sentences with familiar Spanish sounds. But that was cheating, somebody shouted. Everyone laughed.
50 In school, meanwhile, like my brother and sister, I was required to attend a daily tutoring session. I needed a full year of special attention. I also needed my teachers to keep my attention from straying in class by calling out, *Rich-heard*—their English voices slowly prying loose my ties to my other name, its three notes,
55 *Ri-car-do.* Most of all I needed to hear my mother and father speak to me in a moment of seriousness in broken—suddenly heartbreaking—English. The scene was inevitable: One Saturday morning I entered the kitchen where my parents were talking in Spanish. I did not realize that they were talking in Spanish however
60 until, at the moment they saw me, I heard their voices change to speak English. Those *gringo* sounds they uttered startled me. Pushed

me away. In that moment of trivial misunderstanding and profound insight, I felt my throat twisted by unsounded grief. I turned quickly and left the room. But I had no place to escape to with Spanish. (The spell was broken.) My brother and sisters were speaking English in another part of the house.

Again and again in the days following, increasingly angry, I was obliged to hear my mother and father: "Speak to us *en inglés.*" (*Speak.*) Only then did I determine to learn classroom English.

Weeks after, it happened: One day in school I raised my hand to volunteer an answer. I spoke out in a loud voice. And I did not think it remarkable when the entire class understood. That day, I moved very far from the disadvantaged child I had been only days earlier. The belief, the calming assurance that I belonged in public, had at last taken hold.

Shortly after, I stopped hearing the high and loud sounds of *los gringos.* A more and more confident speaker of English, I didn't trouble to listen to *how* strangers sounded, speaking to me. And there simply were too many English-speaking people in my day for me to hear American accents anymore.

At last, seven years old, I came to believe what had been technically true since my birth: I was an American citizen.

But the special feeling of closeness at home was diminished by then. Gone was the desperate, urgent, intense feeling of being at home; rare was the experience of feeling myself individualized by family intimates. We remained a loving family, but one greatly changed. No longer so close; no longer bound tight by the pleasing and troubling knowledge of our public separateness. Neither my older brother nor sister rushed home after school anymore. Nor did I. When I arrived home there would often be neighborhood kids in the house. Or the house would be empty of sounds.

Following the dramatic Americanization of their children, even my parents grew more publicly confident. Especially my mother. She learned the names of all the people on our block. And she decided we needed to have a telephone installed in the house. My father continued to use the word *gringo.* But it was no longer charged with the old bitterness or distrust. (Stripped of any emotional content, the word simply became a name for those Americans not of Hispanic descent.) Hearing him, sometimes, I wasn't sure if he was pronouncing the Spanish word *gringo* or saying gringo in English.

Matching the silence I started hearing in public was a new quiet at home. The family's quiet was partly due to the fact that, as we children learned more and more English, we shared fewer and fewer words with our parents. Sentences needed to be spoken slowly when a child addressed his mother or father. (Often the parent wouldn't understand.) The child would need to repeat himself. (Still the parent misunderstood.) The young voice, frustrated, would end up saying, "Never mind"—the subject was closed. Dinners would be noisy with the clinking of knives and forks against dishes. My mother would smile softly between her remarks; my father at the other end of the table would chew and chew at his food, while he stared over the heads of his children.

My *mother!* My *father!* After English became my primary language, I no longer knew what words to use in addressing my parents. The old Spanish words (those tender accents of sound) I had used earlier—*mamá* and *papá*—I couldn't use anymore. They would have been too painful reminders of how much had changed in my life. On the other hand, the words I heard neighborhood kids call *their* parents seemed equally unsatisfactory. *Mother* and *Father; Ma, Papa, Pa, Dad, Pop* (how I hated the all-American sound of that last word especially)—all these terms I felt were unsuitable, not really terms of address for *my* parents. As a result, I never used them at home. Whenever I'd speak to my parents, I would try to get their attention with eye contact alone. In public conversations, I'd refer to "my parents" or "my mother and father."

My mother and father, for their part, responded differently, as their children spoke to them less. She grew restless, seemed troubled and anxious at the scarcity of words exchanged in the house. It was she who would question me about my day when I came home from school. She smiled at small talk. She pried at the edges of my sentences to get me to say something more. (What?) She'd join conversations she overheard, but her intrusions often stopped her children's talking. By contrast, my father seemed reconciled to the new quiet. Though his English improved somewhat, he retired into silence. At dinner he spoke very little. One night his children and even his wife helplessly giggled at his garbled English pronunciation of the Catholic Grace before Meals. Thereafter he made his wife recite the prayer at the start of each meal, even on formal occasions, when there were guests in the house. Hers became the public voice of the family. On official business, it was she, not my father, one would usually hear on the phone or in stores, talking to strangers. His children grew so accustomed to his silence that, years later, they would speak routinely of his shyness. (My mother would often try to explain: Both his parents died when he was eight. He was raised by an uncle who treated him like little more than a menial servant. He was never encouraged to speak. He grew up alone. A man of few words.) But my father was not shy, I realized, when I'd watch him speaking Spanish with relatives. Using Spanish, he was quickly effusive. Especially when talking with other men, his voice would

150 spark, flicker, flare alive with sounds. In Spanish, he expressed ideas and feelings he rarely revealed in English. With firm Spanish sounds, he conveyed confidence and authority English would never allow him.

I would have been happier about my public success had I not sometimes recalled what it had been like earlier, when my family had
155 conveyed its intimacy through a set of conveniently private sounds. Sometimes in public, hearing a stranger, I'd hark back to my past. A Mexican farmworker approached me downtown to ask directions to somewhere. "¿*Hijito*. . . ?" he said. And his voice summoned deep longing. Another time, standing beside my mother in the visiting
160 room of a Carmelite convent, before the dense screen which rendered the nuns shadowy figures, I heard several Spanish-speaking nuns—their busy, singsong overlapping voices—assure us that yes, yes, we were remembered, all our family was remembered in their prayers. (Their voices echoed faraway family sounds.)

165 Today I hear bilingual educators say that children lose a degree of "individuality" by becoming assimilated into public society. (Bilingual schooling was popularized in the seventies, that decade when middle-class ethnics began to resist the process of assimilation—the American melting pot.) But the bilingualists simplistically scorn the
170 value and necessity of assimilation. They do not seem to realize that there are *two* ways a person is individualized. So they do not realize that while one suffers a diminished sense of *private* individuality by becoming assimilated into public society, such assimilation makes possible the achievement of *public* individuality.

175 The bilingualists insist that a student should be reminded of his difference from others in mass society, his heritage. But they equate mere separateness with individuality. The fact is that only in private—with intimates—is separateness from the crowd a prerequisite for individuality. (An intimate draws me apart, tells me
180 that I am unique, unlike all others.) In public, by contrast, full individuality is achieved, paradoxically, by those who are able to consider themselves members of the crowd. Thus it happened for me: Only when I was able to think of myself as an American, no longer an alien in *gringo* society, could I seek the rights and opportunities
185 necessary for full public individuality. The social and political advantages I enjoy as a man result from the day that I came to believe that my name, indeed, is *Rich-heard Road-ree-guess*.

I celebrate the day I acquired my new name.

My awkward childhood does not prove the necessity of bilingual
190 education. My story discloses instead an essential myth of childhood—inevitable pain. If I rehearse here the changes in my private life after my Americanization, it is finally to emphasize the public gain. The loss implies the gain: The house I returned to each

195 afternoon was quiet. Intimate sounds no longer rushed to the door to greet me. There were other noises inside. The telephone rang. Neighborhood kids ran past the door of the bedroom where I was reading my schoolbooks—covered with shopping-bag paper. Once I learned public language, it would never again be easy for me to hear intimate family voices. More and more of my day was spent hearing
200 words. But that may only be a way of saying that the day I raised my hand in class and spoke loudly to an entire roomful of faces, my childhood started to end.

Skill Development: Implied Meaning

According to the implied meaning in the selection, answer the following with *T* (true) or *F* (false).

_____ 1. The author feels a sense of loss along with the gain in his final victory over the English language.

_____ 2. The author suggests that constant happiness is a myth of childhood.

_____ 3. The author could understand spoken English before he could speak it himself.

_____ 4. The author believes that assimilation is necessary for success.

_____ 5. The author views the proponents of bilingual education as unrealistic.

Comprehension Questions

1. Who or what is this selection about? _____

What is the main idea the author is trying to convey about the topic?

_____

_____

Answer the following with *a, b, c,* or *d.*

_____ 2. The author is addressing the issue of bilingual education in American schools and is taking a position against
   a. learning two languages.
   b. speaking two languages at school.
   c. using only English to teach Spanish-speaking students.
   d. using only Spanish to teach Spanish-speaking students.

_____ 3. In looking back the author believes that his teachers
   a. should have taught him in Spanish.
   b. were afraid to speak to him in Spanish.

     c. did not know how to speak in Spanish.

     d. were correct in not speaking to him in Spanish.

4. The author's view of the nuns who came to his house is that

     a. they were wrong to intrude upon his family life.

     b. they were kind and ultimately changed his language perspective.

     c. they did not care about him or his family.

     d. they were too strict and demanding.

5. When the author says, "I celebrate the day I acquired my new name," that "day" probably refers to

     a. the day the nuns came to his house.

     b. the day he started school.

     c. the day he first volunteered to answer a question in class.

     d. the day he felt the loss of Spanish in his home.

6. After he learned to speak English in public, the author

     a. focused more on what was said rather than how it was said.

     b. listened to sounds to distinguish among different American accents.

     c. listened for the tone of voice that went with the words.

     d. noticed the high and low sounds of English as well as Spanish.

7. Before his family began speaking English at home, the author believed the family shared a closeness that

     a. was a result of a separation they all felt in public.

     b. gave each of them a public identity.

     c. encouraged them to assimilate into the melting pot.

     d. eventually made him ashamed of his childhood.

8. The author feels that his father was silent because

     a. his father was raised by an uncle after his parents died.

     b. his father lacked confidence with the English language.

     c. the children were frustrated at having to speak slowly to the parents.

     d. his mother became more assertive and dominated conversations.

9. The author feels that those who support bilingual education

     a. do not realize the ultimate danger of the social isolation of language.

     b. do not sympathize with the disadvantaged.

     c. are not willing to resist the process of assimilation.

     d. do not recognize differences in heritage in a mass society.

10. The author believes that in order to achieve "full individuality," a person must

     a. resist the characteristics that are common to the crowd.

     b. focus on differences rather than similarities.

     c. be comfortable as a member of the crowd.

     d. have a private rather than a public language.

Answer the following with *T* (true) or *F* (false).

11. The author was born in Mexico.

12. The author's father had been orphaned at an early age.

_____ 13. The author did not speak English as his public language until he was in fifth grade.

_____ 14. The author began to view English as a predominately public language because it was used in class to make oneself understood by others.

_____ 15. The author suggests that the authentic sounds of the Spanish language bring back warm memories of childhood.

Vocabulary

According to the way the italicized word was used in the selection, indicate *a, b, c,* or *d* for the word or phrase that gives the best definition.

___ 1. "noted the *incongruity*" (27)
   a. emotions
   b. lack of fit
   c. anger
   d. argument

___ 2. "With great *tact*" (34)
   a. force
   b. conviction
   c. courage
   d. diplomacy

___ 3. "*accentuated* our family's closeness" (40)
   a. emphasized
   b. denied
   c. aggravated
   d. controlled

___ 4. "*trivial* misunderstanding" (62)
   a. honest
   b. petty
   c. important
   d. conflicting

___ 5. "*profound* insight" (62)
   a. unhappy
   b. false
   c. deeply felt
   d. quick

___ 6. "*pried* at the edges" (130)
   a. laughed
   b. stopped
   c. asked questions
   d. listened

___ 7. "was quickly *effusive*" (148)
   a. conservative
   b. bubbling
   c. aware
   d. nervous

___ 8. "his *garbled* English" (136)
   a. slow
   b. confused
   c. confident
   d. abundant

___ 9. "*menial* servant" (145)
   a. helpful
   b. loyal
   c. lowly
   d. honest

___ 10. "essential *myth* of childhood" (190)
   a. truth
   b. fictitious story
   c. concern
   d. difficult limitation

Written Response

Use the information from the text to answer the following question:
Why is Rodriguez opposed to using the family language of school children for teaching them in school?

Connecting and Reflecting

In the United States, students who must learn English as a second language enter public schools in which instruction is given only in English. Many students are lost and intimidated. What can teachers do to help new students make this difficult transition?

Collaborate in a small group to discuss the needs of elementary school students who speak English as a second language. Devise a list of at least eight daily reminders that your group believe are important for teachers in assisting students with their language transition. Explain why you think each is important. Read the following passage to gain additional insight into the problem.

The Misery of Silence

When I went to kindergarten and had to speak English for the first time, I became silent. A dumbness—a shame—still cracks my voice in two, even when I want to say "hello" casually, or ask an easy question in front of the check-out counter, or ask directions of a bus driver. I stand frozen, or I hold up the line with the complete, grammatical sentence that comes squeaking out at impossible length. "What did you say?" says the cab driver, or "Speak up," so I have to perform again, only weaker the second time. A telephone call makes my throat bleed and takes up that day's courage. It spoils my day with self-disgust when I hear my broken voice come skittering out into the open. It makes people wince to hear it. I'm getting better, though.

During the first silent year I spoke to no one at school, did not ask before going to the lavatory, and flunked kindergarten. My sister also said nothing for three years, silent in the playground and silent at lunch. There were other quiet Chinese girls not of our family, but most of them got over it sooner than we did. I enjoyed the silence. At first it did not occur to me I was supposed to talk or to pass kindergarten. I talked at home and to one or two of the Chinese kids in class. I made motions and even made some jokes. I drank out of a toy saucer when the water spilled out of the cup, and everybody laughed, pointing at me, so I did it some more. I didn't know that Americans don't drink out of saucers.

© 1993 HarperCollins College Publishers

It was when I found out I had to talk that school became a misery, that the silence became a misery. I did not speak and felt bad each time that I did not speak. I read aloud in first grade, though, and heard the barest whisper with little squeaks come out of my throat. "Louder," said the teacher, who scared the voice away again. The other Chinese girls did not talk either, so I knew the silence had to do with being a Chinese girl.

From Maxine Hong Kingston, *The Noman Warrior: Memoirs of a Girlhood among Ghosts*

C H A P T E R ▪ 7

POINT OF VIEW

- Are textbooks influenced by the author's point of view?
- What is the author's point of view?
- What is the reader's point of view?
- What is a fact?
- What is an opinion?
- What is the author's purpose?
- What is the author's tone?

ARE TEXTBOOKS INFLUENCED BY THE AUTHOR'S POINT OF VIEW?

How many of the following statements are true?

_____ 1. Textbooks contain facts rather than opinions.

_____ 2. The historical account of an incident is based on fact and thus does not vary from one author to another.

_____ 3. Except for the style of the author, freshman biology textbooks do not vary in their informational content.

_____ 4. Textbooks are supposed to be free from an author's interpretation.

Unfortunately, too many students tend to answer "*true*" to *all of the above*. Paying big money for a thick history book with lots of facts and an authoritative title does not mean, contrary to student belief, that the text is a cleansed chronicle of the nation's past. No purity rule applies to textbook writing. In the case of history, the author portrays the past from a personal and unique perspective. The name of the first president of the United States does not vary from one text to another, but, depending on the point of view of the author, the emphasis on the importance of Washington's administration might vary.

WHAT IS THE AUTHOR'S POINT OF VIEW?

Authors of factual material, like authors of fiction, have opinions and theories that influence their presentation of the subject matter. For example, would a British professor's account of American history during the revolutionary period be the same as the version written by a U.S.-born scholar from Philadelphia? Because of national loyalties, the two scholars might look at the events from two different angles—the first as a colonial uprising on a distant continent and the second as a struggle for personal freedom and survival. The two authors would write from different **points of view** and express particular opinions because they have different ways of looking at the subject.

Recognizing the author's point of view is part of understanding what you read. Sophisticated readers seek to identify the beliefs of the author in order to "know where he or she is coming from." When the point of view is not directly stated, the author's choice of words and information provide clues for the reader.

The terms **point of view** and **bias** are very similar and are sometimes used interchangeably. When facts are slanted, though not necessarily distorted, toward the author's personal beliefs, the written material is said to reflect the author's bias. Thus, a **bias** is simply an opinion or position on a subject. As commonly used, however, *bias has a negative connotation* suggesting narrowmindedness and prejudice, whereas *point of view* seems more thoughtful and open. Perhaps you would like to refer to your own opinion as point of view and to that of others, particularly if they disagree with you, as biases!

Read the following passage and use the choice of information and words to identify the author's point of view on whaling.

Our own species is providing us with clear examples of how density-dependent regulation can fail. The great whales have been hunted to the brink of oblivion over the past few decades as modern whaling methods have reduced personal risk while increasing profits. Although there is nothing that whales provide that can't be obtained elsewhere, the demand for whale products (and their price) hasn't diminished, especially in Japan. Thus, instead of the human predators relaxing their pressure and allowing the whale population to recover, whaling fleets continue to exert their depressing effect on populations of the great mammals. . . . Then, as whales decrease in number, the price of whale products goes up, and the hunt becomes still more avid. If humans actually starved when they couldn't catch whales (which might once have been the case among the Eskimos) both populations might eventually stabilize (or cycle). But the current decline in whale numbers has had no effect on the growth of the human population.

Robert Wallace et al., *Biology: Science of Life*

What is the author's point of view? Underline clues that suggest your answer.

_____

_____

(The author is against commercial whaling because the whale population is severely declining. Whaling is for profit and seemingly unlimited greed and not for products that cannot be obtained elsewhere.)

Exercise 1: Comparing Authors' Points of View

Read the following two descriptions of Mary of Scotland from two different history books. While both include positive and negative comments, the second author obviously finds the subject more engaging and has chosen to include more positive details.

Passage A

Mary Stuart returned to Scotland in 1561 after her husband's death. She was a far more charming and romantic figure than her cousin Elizabeth, but she was no stateswoman. A convinced Catholic, she soon ran head-on into the granitelike opposition of Knox and the Kirk. In 1567 she was forced to abdicate, and in the following year she fled from Scotland and sought protection in England from Elizabeth. No visitor could have been more unwelcome.

Joseph R. Strayer et al., *The Mainstream of Civilization*

Passage B

Mary Stuart was an altogether remarkable young woman, about whom it is almost impossible to remain objectively impartial. Even when one discounts the flattery that crept into descriptions of her, one is inclined to accept the contemporary evidence that Mary was extraordinarily beautiful, though tall for a girl—perhaps over six feet. In addition to beauty, she had almost every other attractive attribute in high degree: courage, wit, resourcefulness, loyalty, and responsiveness, in short everything needful for worldly greatness save discretion in her relations with men and a willingness to compromise, if need be, on matters of religion. She was a thoroughgoing Roman Catholic, a good lover, and a magnificent hater.

Shepard B. Clough et al., *A History of the Western World*

1. How are the two descriptions alike? _____

   _____

   _____

2. How do the two descriptions differ? _____

   _____

   _____

3. Which do you like better, and why? _____

   _____

   _____

4. What clues signal that the author of the second description is more biased than the first? _____

   _____

   _____

WHAT IS THE READER'S POINT OF VIEW?

To recognize a point of view, you have to know enough about the subject to realize that there is another opinion beyond the one being expressed. Thus, prior knowledge and a slightly suspicious nature open the mind to countless other views and alternative arguments.

On the other hand, prior knowledge can also lead to a closed mind and rigid thinking. Our existing opinions affect how much we accept or reject of what we read. If our beliefs are particularly strong, sometimes we refuse to hear what is said or we hear something that is not said. Research has shown that readers will actually "tune out" new material that is drastically different from their own views. For example, if you were reading that the AIDS virus should not be a concern for most middle-class Americans, would you be "tuned in" or "tuned out"?

Read the following passage on smoking first from the point of view of a nonsmoker and second from the point of view of a smoker, and then answer the questions.

Smoke can permanently paralyze the tiny cilia that sweep the breathing passages clean and can cause the lining of the respiratory tract to thicken irregularly. The body's attempt to rid itself of the smoking toxins may produce a deep, hacking cough in the person next to you at the lunch counter. Console yourself with the knowledge that these hackers are only trying to rid their bodies of nicotines, "tars," formaldehyde, hydrogen sulfide, resins, and who knows what. Just enjoy your meal.

Robert Wallace, *Biology: The World of Life*

1. Is the author a smoker? Underline the clues suggesting your answer. _____

_____

2. What is your view on smoking? _____

3. Reading this passage in the guise of nonsmoker, what message is

   conveyed to you? _____

4. Assuming the role of smoker, what message is conveyed to you from

   reading this passage? _____

(While it is possible that both the smoker and nonsmoker would get exactly the same message, it is more likely that the nonsmoker would be disgusted by the health risks, whereas the smoker would claim exaggeration and discrimination.)

Exercise 2: Identifying Points of View

Read the following passages and answer the questions about point of view.

Passage A. Columbus

On August 3, 1492, Columbus and some ninety mariners set sail from Palos, Spain, in the *Niña, Pinta,* and *Santa Maria.* Based on faulty calculations, the Admiral estimated Asia to be no more than 4500 miles to the west (the actual distance is closer to 12,000 miles). Some 3000 miles out, his crew became fearful and wanted to return home. But he convinced them to keep sailing west. Just two days later, on October 12, they landed on a small island in the Bahamas, which Columbus named San Salvador (holy savior).

A fearless explorer, Columbus turned out to be an ineffective administrator and a poor geographer. He ended up in debtor's prison, and to his dying day in 1506 he never admitted to locating a world unknown to Europeans. Geographers overlooked his contribution and named the Western continents after another mariner, Amerigo Vespucci, a merchant from Florence who participated in a Portuguese expedition to South America in 1501. In a widely reprinted letter, Vespucci claimed that a new world had been found, and it was his name that caught on.

James Martin et al., *America and Its People*

1. Which paragraph sounds more like the Columbus you learned about in elementary school? _____

2. What is the author's position on Columbus? Underline clues for your answer. _____

3. What is your view of Columbus? What has influenced your view?

_____

_____

Passage B

The tragedy of the Mexican cession is that most Anglo-Americans have not accepted the fact that the United States committed an act of violence against the Mexican people when it took Mexico's northwestern territory. Violence was not limited to the taking of the land; Mexico's territory was invaded, her people murdered, her land raped, and her possessions plundered. Memory of this destruction generated a distrust and dislike that is still vivid in the minds of many Mexicans, for the violence of the United States left deep scars. And for Chicanos—Mexicans remaining within the boundaries of the new United States territories—aggression was even more insidious, for the outcome of the Texas and Mexican-American wars made them a conquered people. Anglo-Americans were the conquerors, and they evinced all the arrogance of military victors.

In material terms, in exchange for 12,000 lives and more than $100,000,000 the United States acquired a colony two and a half times as large as France, containing rich farm lands and natural resources such as gold, silver, zinc, copper, oil, and uranium which would make possible its unprecedented industrial boom. It acquired ports on the Pacific which generated further economic expansion across that ocean. Mexico was left with its shrunken resources to face the continued advances of the expanding capitalist force on its border.

Rodolfo Acuña, *Occupied America: A History of Chicanos*

1. What is the author's point of view? Underline clues. _____

_____

2. How does this author's view differ from what you would expect in most
American history texts? _____

3. What is your point of view on the subject? _____

_____

Passage C. Surviving in Vietnam

Vietnam ranks after World War II as America's second most expensive
war. Between 1950 and 1975, the United States spent $123 billion on
combat in Southeast Asia. More importantly, Vietnam ranks—after our
Civil War and World Wars I and II—as the nation's fourth deadliest
war, with 57,661 Americans killed in action.

Yet, when the last U.S. helicopter left Saigon, Americans suffered
what historian George Herring terms "collective amnesia." Everyone,
even those who had fought in 'Nam, seemed to want to forget
Southeast Asia. It took nearly ten years for the government to erect a
national monument to honor those who died in Vietnam.

Few who served in Vietnam survived unscathed, whether
psychologically or physically. One of the 303,600 Americans wounded
during the long war was 101st Airborne platoon leader James
Bombard, first shot and then blown up by a mortar round during the
bitter Tet fighting at Hue in February 1968. He describes his traumatic
experience as

> *feeling the bullet rip into your flesh, the shrapnel tear the flesh from your
> bones and the blood run down your leg. . . . To put your hand on your chest
> and to come away with your hand red with your own blood, and to feel it run-
> ning out of your eyes and out of your mouth, and seeing it spurt out of your
> guts, realizing you were dying. . . . I was ripped open from the top of my head
> to the tip of my toes. I had forty-five holes in me.*

Somehow Bombard survived Vietnam.

Withdrawing U.S. forces from Vietnam ended only the combat.
Returning veterans fought government disclaimers concerning the
toxicity of the defoliant Agent Orange. VA hospitals across the nation
still contain thousands of para- and quadriplegic Vietnam veterans, as
well as the maimed from earlier wars. Throughout America the
"walking wounded" find themselves still embroiled in the
psychological aftermath of Vietnam.

James Divine et al., *America: Past and Present*

1. **What is the author's own view of the war? Underline clues for your**

answer. _____

2. What is your own position on the Vietnam War?

_____

3. What is the purpose of Bombard's quotation?

_____

4. How do you feel about war after reading this passage?

_____

WHAT IS A FACT AND WHAT IS AN OPINION?

For both the reader and the writer, a point of view is a position or belief that logically evolves through time with knowledge and experience and is usually based on both facts and opinions. For example, what is your position on city curfews for youth, on helping the homeless, on abortion? Are your views on these issues supported solely by facts? Do you recognize the difference between the facts and the opinions employed in your thinking?

Both fact and opinion are used persuasively to support positions. You have to determine which is which and then judge the issue accordingly. A fact is a statement based on actual evidence or personal observation. It can be checked objectively with empirical data and proved to be either true or false. On the other hand, an opinion is a statement of personal feeling or a judgment. It reflects a belief or an interpretation rather than an accumulation of evidence, and it cannot be proved true or false. Adding the quoted opinion of a well-known authority to a few bits of evidence does not improve the data, yet this is an effective persuasive technique. Even though you may feel an opinion is valid, it is still an opinion.

Authors mix facts and opinions, sometimes in the same sentence, in order to win you over to a particular point of view. Persuasive tricks include factually quoting sources who then voice opinions or hedging a statement with "It is a fact that" and attaching a disguised opinion. Recognize that both facts and opinions are valuable but be able to distinguish between the two.

Examples:

Fact: Freud developed a theory of personality.

Fact: Freud believed that the personality is divided into three parts.

Opinion: Freud constructed the most complete theory of personality development.

Opinion: The personality is divided into three parts: the id, the ego, and the superego.

Exercise 3: Fact or Opinion

Read each of the following and indicate *F* for fact and *O* for opinion.

_____ 1. For women locked into socioeconomic situations that cannot promise financial independence, liberation is relatively meaningless and sometimes suggests the denial of femininity as a goal.

Reece McGee et al., *Sociology: An Introduction*

_____ 2. The territorial base from which Soviet ambitions proceed is the largest country area on the globe.

Jesse H. Wheeler, Jr., et al., *Regional Geography of the World*

_____ 3. Company sources attribute Coors' success to product quality, boasting that it "is the most expensively brewed beer in the world."

Louis Boone and David L. Kurtz, *Contemporary Business*

_____ 4. If you wish to "break the hunger habit" in order to gain better control over your own food intake, you might be wise to do so slowly—by putting yourself on a very irregular eating schedule.

James V. McConnell, *Understanding Human Behavior*

_____ 5. The first step in running for the nomination is to build a personal organization, because the party organization is supposed to stay neutral until the nomination is decided.

James M. Burns et al., *Government by the People*

_____ 6. It is true that American politics often rewards with power those who have proved that they can direct the large institutions of commerce and business, of banking, and of law, education, and philanthropy.

Kenneth Prewitt and Sidney Verba, *An Introduction to American Government*

_____ 7. Precipitation is not uniform, and neither is the distribution of population.

Robert J. Foster, *Physical Geology*

_____ 8. Massively built, with eyes so piercing they seemed like the headlights of an onrushing train, J. P. Morgan was the most powerful figure in American finance.

Robert Divine et al., *American Past and Present*

_____ 9. At least 10 percent of the world's available food is destroyed by pests, waste, and spoilage somewhere between the marketplace and the stomach of the consumer.

Robert Wallace, *Biology: The World of Life*

_____ 10. Women, young girls, and even mere children were tortured by driving needles under their nails, roasting their feet in the fire, or crushing their legs under heavy weights until the marrow spurted from their bones, in order to force them to confess to filthy orgies with demons.

Edward M. Burns, Western Civilization

Exercise 4: Fact and Opinion in Textbooks

The following passage from a history text describes Franklin D. Roosevelt. Notice the mixture of facts and opinions in developing a view of Roosevelt. Mark the items that follow as fact (F) or opinion (O).

Franklin D. Roosevelt won the Democratic nomination in June 1932. At first glance he did not look like someone who could relate to suffering people; he had spent his entire life in the lap of luxury.

Handsome and outgoing, Roosevelt had a bright political future. Then disaster struck. In 1921, he developed polio. The disease left him paralyzed from the waist down and confined to a wheelchair for the rest of his life. Instead of retiring, however, Roosevelt threw himself into a rehabilitation program and labored diligently to return to the public life. "If you had spent two years in bed trying to wiggle your toe," he later observed, "after that anything would seem easy."

Few intellectuals had a high opinion of him. Walter Lippmann described Roosevelt as "a pleasant man who, without any important qualifications for the office, would very much like to be President."

The people saw Roosevelt differently. During the campaign, he calmed their fears and gave them hope. Even a member of Hoover's administration had to admit: "The people seem to be lifting eager faces to Franklin Roosevelt, having the impression that he is talking intimately to them." Charismatic and utterly charming, Roosevelt radiated confidence. He even managed to turn his lack of a blueprint into an asset. Instead of offering plans, he advocated the experimental method. "It is common sense to take a method and try it," he declared, "if it fails, admit it frankly and try another."

James Martin et al., America and Its People

_____ 1. He won the Democratic nomination in June 1932.
_____ 2. He was handsome and outgoing.
_____ 3. He developed polio in 1921.
_____ 4. Few intellectuals thought highly of him.
_____ 5. During the campaign he calmed fears and gave hope.
_____ 6. Roosevelt radiated confidence.

WHAT IS THE AUTHOR'S PURPOSE?

Be aware that a textbook author can shift from an objective and factual explanation of a topic to a subjective and opinionated treatment of the facts. Recognizing the author's purpose does not mean that you won't buy the product; it just means that you are a more cautious, well-informed consumer.

An author always has a purpose in mind when putting words on paper. The reader of a textbook expects that the author's purpose will be to inform or explain and, in general, this is true. At times, however, texts can slip from factual explanation to persuasion. The sophisticated reader recognizes this shift in purpose and thus is more critical in evaluating the content. A persuasive paragraph for or against birth control alerts the reader to be more skeptical and less accepting than a paragraph explaining how birth control methods work.

The purpose of the author can be a single one or a combination of the following:

to inform	to argue	to entertain
to explain	to persuade	to narrate
to describe	to condemn	to describe
to enlighten	to ridicule	to shock

Read the following passage to determine the author's purpose.

love, *n.* A temporary insanity curable by marriage or by removal of the patient from the influences under which he incurred the disorder. This disease, like caries and many other ailments, is prevalent only among civilized races living under artificial conditions; barbarous nations breathing pure air and eating simple food enjoy immunity from its ravages. It is sometimes fatal, but more frequently to the physician than to the patient.

Ambrose Bierce, *The Devil's Dictionary*

(The author defines love in a humorous and exaggerated manner for the purpose of entertaining the reader.)

Exercise 5: Determining the Author's Purpose

Read the following passage and answer the questions about the author's purpose.

Isabella Katz and the Holocaust: A Living Testimony
No statistics can adequately render the enormity of the Holocaust, and its human meaning can perhaps only be understood through the experience of a single human being who was cast into the nightmare

of the Final Solution. Isabella Katz was the eldest of six children—Isabella, brother Philip, and sisters Rachel, Chicha, Cipi, and baby Potyo—from a family of Hungarian Jews. She lived in the ghetto of Kisvarda, a provincial town of 20,000 people, where hers was a typical Jewish family of the region—middle-class, attached to Orthodox traditions, and imbued with a love of learning.

In 1938 and 1939 Hitler pressured Hungary's regent, Miklós Horthy, into adopting anti-Jewish laws. By 1941 Hungary had become a German ally, and deportations and massacres were added to the restrictions. Isabella's father left for the United States, where he hoped to obtain entry papers for his family, but after Pearl Harbor, Hungary was at war with America and the family was trapped. In the spring of 1944, when Hitler occupied Hungary, the horror of the Final Solution struck Isabella. On March 19 Adolf Eichmann, as SS officer in charge of deportation, ordered the roundup of Jews in Hungary, who numbered some 650,000. On May 28, Isabella's nineteenth birthday, the Jews in Kisvarda were told to prepare for transportation to Auschwitz on the following morning. Isabella recalled:

> And now an SS man is here, spick-and-span, with a dog, a silver pistol, and a whip. And he is all of sixteen years old. On his list appears the name of every Jew in the ghetto.... "Teresa Katz," he calls—my mother. She steps forward.... Now the SS man moves toward my mother. He raises his whip and, for no apparent reason at all, lashes out at her.

En route to Auschwitz, crammed into hot, airless boxcars, Isabella's mother told her children to "stay alive":

> Out there, when it's all over, a world's waiting for you to give it all I gave you. Despite what you see here . . . believe me, there is humanity out there, there is dignity.... And when this is all over, you must add to it, because sometimes it is a little short, a little skimpy.

Isabella and her family were among more than 437,000 Jews sent to Auschwitz from Hungary.

When they arrived at Auschwitz, the SS and camp guards divided the prisoners into groups, often separating family members. Amid the screams and confusion, Isabella remembered:

> We had just spotted the back of my mother's head when Mengele, the notorious Dr. Josef Mengele, points to my sister and me and says, "Die Zwei" [those two]. This trim, very good-looking German, with a flick of his thumb and a whistle, is selecting who is to live and who is to die.

Isabella's mother and her baby sister perished within a few days.

> The day we arrived in Auschwitz, there were so many people to be burned that the four crematoriums couldn't handle the task. So the Germans built big open fires to throw the children in. Alive? I do not know. I saw the flames. I heard the shrieks.

Isabella was to endure the hell of Auschwitz for nine months.

The inmates were stripped, the hair on their heads and bodies was shaved, and they were herded into crude, overcrowded barracks. As if starvation, forced labor, and disease were not enough, they were subjected to unspeakable torture, humiliation, and terror, a mass of living skeletons for whom the difference between life and death could be measured only in an occasional flicker of spirit that determined to resist against impossible odds. Isabella put it this way:

> Have you ever weighed 120 pounds and gone down to 40? Something like that—not quite alive, yet not quite dead. Can anyone, can even I, picture it? . . . Our eyes sank deeper. Our skin rotted. Our bones screamed out of our bodies. Indeed, there was barely a body to house the mind, yet the mind was still working, sending out the messages "Live! Live!"

In November, just as Isabella and her family were lined up outside a crematorium, they were suddenly moved to Birnbäumel, in eastern Germany—the Russians were getting nearer and the Nazis were closing down their death camps and moving the human evidence of their barbarism out of reach of the enemy. In January, as the Russians and the frigid weather closed in, the prisoners were forced to march through the snows deeper into Germany, heading toward the camp at Bergen-Belsen. Those who could not endure the trial fell by the side, shot or frozen to death. On January 23, while stumbling through a blizzard with the sound of Russian guns in the distance, Isabella, Rachel, and Chicha made a successful dash from the death march and hid in an abandoned house. Two days later Russian soldiers found them. Philip had been sent to a labor camp, and Cipi made it to Bergen-Belsen, where she died.

Isabella later married and had two children of her own, making a new life in America. Yet the images of the Holocaust remain forever in her memory. "Now I am older," she says, "and I don't remember all the pain. . . . That is not happiness, only relief, and relief is blessed. . . . And children someday will plant flowers in Auschwitz, where the sun couldn't crack through the smoke of burning flesh."

Richard L. Greaves et al., Civilizations of the World

1. What is the author's purpose for including this story in the history textbook?
2. What does the author mean by "its human meaning can perhaps only be understood through the experience of a single human being"?
3. Why does the author include Isabella's quote?
4. Why does the author include Isabella's quote about the SS man?
5. What is Isabella's purpose in relating her story?
6. Is the passage predominately developed through facts or opinions? Give an example of each.
7. How does the passage influence your thinking about the Holocaust?

WHAT IS THE AUTHOR'S TONE?

The tone of an author's writing is similar to the tone of a speaker's voice. For listeners, it is fairly easy to tell the difference between an angry tone and a romantic tone by noticing the speaker's voice. Distinguishing among humor, sarcasm, and irony, however, may be more difficult. **Humorous** remarks are designed to be comical and amusing, while **sarcastic** remarks are designed to cut or give pain. **Ironic** remarks, on the other hand, express something other than the literal meaning and are designed to show the incongruity between the actual and the expected. Making such precise distinctions requires more than just listening to sounds; it requires a careful evaluation of what is said. Because the sound of the voice is not heard in reading, clues to the tone must come from the writer's presentation of the message. The reader's job is to look for clues to answer the question, "What is the author's attitude toward the topic?"

The following is a list of some of the words that can be used to describe the author's tone. Can you imagine an example for each?

angry	hateful	ironic	professional
bitter	hopeful	jovial	respectful
cynical	horrifying	lonely	sarcastic
defensive	hostile	loving	satirical
depressing	humorous	miserable	scornful
enthusiastic	hypocritical	nostalgic	subjective
fearful	hysterical	objective	sincere
gloomy	insulting	optimistic	sympathetic
happy	intellectual	pessimistic	threatening

As an example of tone, pretend that your friend is already a half-hour late for a meeting. You can wait no longer but you can leave a note. On your own paper, write your friend three different notes—one in a sympathetic tone, one in an angry tone, and one in a sarcastic tone. Notice in doing this how your tone reflects your purpose. Which note would you really leave and to which friend?

Read the following passage and note that the overall tone is informative and educational. However, the author sees a certain aspect to the subject matter that brings out another tone. What is that tone?

Some plants depend upon fire to maintain high densities. The most famous example is the giant sequoia *(Sequoiadendron giganteum)* of California. These magnificent trees are replaced by other conifers, but only in the absence of fire. Conservation attempts to protect the sequoia forests by stopping all forest fires have, in effect, almost doomed these trees to disappear, and attempts to restore fire to a useful place in forest management are currently under way in the National Parks Service of the United States.

Large sequoia trees have a thick, fire-resistant bark and so they are not damaged by ground fires that are fatal to many other conifers, such as white fir and sugar pine. Sequoia seedlings also germinate best on bare mineral soil, and ground fires provide a good environment for seedling establishment by removing the litter on the forest floor. Thus organisms as different as blue grouse, moose, and sequoia trees may all depend upon habitat changes brought on by fire in order to keep their numbers high. Good habitats are not necessarily those that are never disturbed.

Charles Krebs, *The Message of Ecology*

(There is an underlying tone of irony as the author points out that fire, which is deadly to most, is essential for the life of the giant sequoias. Irony is the opposite of the expected. In fiction or life, it is the twist or surprise ending that no one anticipates. Irony can make us laugh, but usually it is a bittersweet and somewhat cruel chuckle.)

Exercise 6: Determining the Author's Tone

Read the following passages to determine the author's tone and attitude toward the subject.

Passage A. Water Pollution
In many locales the water is not safe to drink, as evidenced by the recent outbreaks of infectious hepatitis in the United States. Infectious hepatitis is believed to be caused by a virus carried in human waste, usually through a water supply that is contaminated by sewage. There is some disturbing evidence that this virus may be resistant to chlorine, especially in the presence of high levels of organic material. Despite our national pride in indoor plumbing and walk-in bathrooms, sewage treatment for many communities in the United States is grossly inadequate, and waste that has been only partially treated is discharged into waterways. Recently the news services carried a story announcing that the New Orleans water supply may be dangerous to drink. However, we have been assured that there is no cause for alarm—a committee has been appointed to study the problem!

Robert Wallace, *Biology: The World of Life*

1. What is the author's attitude toward the water supply? _____

_____

2. What tone comes through in the last two sentences? _____

_____

Passage B. Educating Black Athletes

For decades, student athletes, usually seventeen-to-nineteen-year-old freshmen, have informally agreed to a contract with the universities they attend: athletic performance in exchange for an education. The athletes have kept their part of the bargain; the universities have not. Universities and athletic departments have gained huge gate receipts, television revenues, national visibility, donors to university programs, and more, as a result of the performances of gifted basketball and football players, of whom a disproportionate number of the most gifted and most exploited have been black.

While blacks are not the only student athletes exploited, the abuses usually happen to them first and worst. The black athlete who blindly sets out today to fill the shoes of Dr. J., Reggie J., Magic J., Kareem Abdul-J., or O. J. may well end up with "No J."—no job that he is qualified to do in our modern, technologically sophisticated society.

Harry Edwards, *The Atlantic Monthly*, August 1983

1. What is the author's tone?
2. What is the author's point of view?
3. What is your own point of view on the subject?

POLITICAL CARTOONS

Political cartoons vividly illustrate how an author or an artist can effectively communicate point of view without making a direct verbal statement. Through their drawings, cartoonists have great freedom to be extremely harsh and judgmental. For example, they take positions on local and national news events and frequently depict politicians as crooks, thieves, or even murderers. Because the accusations are implied rather than directly stated, the cartoonist communicates a point of view but is still safe from libel charges.

To illustrate, study the cartoon on political campaign advertisements to determine what the cartoonist feels and is saying about the subject. Use the following steps to help you analyze the implied meaning and point of view.

1. Glance at the cartoon for an overview and then read the dialogue.
2. Answer the question, "What is this about?" to determine the general topic.
3. Study the details for symbolism. What do the man, the character, and the door represent?
4. Why is Pinocchio used in the cartoon?
5. With all the information in mind, answer the question, "What is the main point the cartoonist is trying to get across?"
6. Taking the message into consideration, answer "What is the cartoonist's purpose?"
7. What is the tone of the cartoon?

DICK WRIGHT reprinted by Permission of UNITED FEATURES SYNDICATE, INC.

8. What is the cartoonist's point of view or position on the subject? What is your point of view?

To summarize, the cartoonist feels that political campaign advertisements are not honest. The tone is sarcastic, the purpose is to ridicule, and the point of view is strongly against the credibility of campaign ads.

Exercise 7: Political Cartoons

Use the same steps to analyze the message and answer the questions on the next cartoon.

1. What is the general topic of this cartoon?
2. What do the people and objects represent?

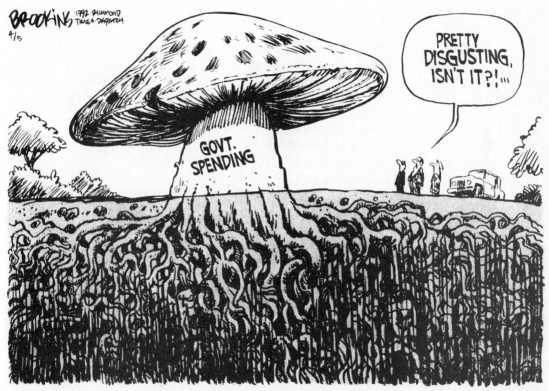

Gary Brookins, *Richmond Times-Dispatch*

3. Why is the mushroom used?
4. What is the main point the cartoonist is trying to convey?
5. What is the cartoonist's purpose?
6. What is the tone of the cartoon?
7. What is the cartoonist's point of view?
8. What is your point of view on the subject?

Cartoons are fun but challenging, because they require prior knowledge for interpretation. For current news cartoons, you have to be familiar with the latest happening in order to make connections and understand the message. Look on the editorial page of your newspaper to enjoy world events from a cartoonist's point of view.

As stated in the beginning of the chapter, even in college textbooks the authors' attitudes and biases slip through. It is the reader's responsibility to be alert for signs of manipulation and to be ready to question interpretations and conclusions. Sophisticated readers are aware and draw their own conclusions based on their own interpretation of the facts.

SUMMARY

Authors have opinions, theories, and prejudices that influence their presentation of material. When facts are slanted, though not necessarily distorted, the material is biased toward the author's beliefs. A bias is a prejudice, a mental leaning, or an inclination. The bias, in a sense, creates the point of view, the particular angle from which the author views the material.

Both fact and opinion are used persuasively to support positions. A fact is a statement that can be proved to be either true or false. An opinion, on the other hand, is a statement of feeling or a judgment.

When putting thoughts into words, an author always has a purpose in mind. A sophisticated reader should recognize that purpose. Recognizing the purpose does not mean you won't buy the product; it means you are a well-informed consumer.

The tone of an author's writing is similar to the tone of a speaker's voice. The reader's job is to look for clues to determine the author's attitude about the subject.

Selection

EDUCATION

Stage 1

Preview

Does the title of this selection surprise you? Why?
Is the author a teacher?

Activate Schema
Do you like to read?
If you had a free hour this afternoon, what would you choose to read?

Learning Strategy
Read to find out why the author feels that teachers make children hate reading.

Skill Development: Group Discussion

Before reading, form a team of three volunteers to lead the class in discussing this selection. Volunteers will meet or plan by phone prior to class to organize the class discussion.

Stage 2

1. Predict 2. Picture 3. Relate 4. Monitor 5. Fix up

HOW TEACHERS MAKE CHILDREN HATE READING

From John Holt, *Redbook,* November 1967

When I was teaching English at the Colorado Rocky Mountain School, I used to ask my students the kinds of questions that English teachers usually ask about reading assignments—questions designed to bring out the points that *I* had decided *they* should know. They, on their
5　part, would try to get me to give them hints and clues as to what I wanted. It was a game of wits. I never gave my students an opportunity to say what they really thought about a book.

I gave vocabulary drills and quizzes too. I told my students that every time they came upon a word in their book they did not
10　understand, they were to look it up in the dictionary. I even devised special kinds of vocabulary tests, allowing them to use their books to see how the words were used. But looking back, I realize that these tests, along with many of my methods, were foolish.

My sister was the first person who made me question my
15　conventional ideas about teaching English. She had a son in the seventh grade in a fairly good public school. His teacher had asked the class to read Cooper's *The Deerslayer.* The choice was bad enough in itself; whether looking at man or nature, Cooper was superficial, inaccurate and sentimental, and his writing is ponderous

20 and ornate. But to make matters worse, this teacher had decided to give the book the microscope and x-ray treatment. He made the students look up and memorize not only the definitions but the derivations of every big word that came along—and there were plenty. Every chapter was followed by close questioning and testing to make
25 sure the students "understood" everything.

Being then, as I said, conventional, I began to defend the teacher, who was a good friend of mine, against my sister's criticisms. The argument soon grew hot. What was wrong with making sure that children understood every thing they read? My sister answered that
30 until this year her boy had always loved reading, and had read a lot on his own; now he had stopped. (He was not really to start again for many years.)

Still I persisted. If children didn't look up the word they didn't know, how would they ever learn them? My sister said, "Don't be silly!
35 When you were little you had a huge vocabulary, and were always reading very grown-up books. When did you ever look up a word in a dictionary?"

She had me. I don't know that we had a dictionary at home; if we did, I didn't use it. I don't use one today. In my life I doubt that I
40 have looked up as many as fifty words, perhaps not even half that.

Since then I have talked about this with a number of teachers. More than once I have said, "According to tests, educated and literate people like you have a vocabulary of about twenty-five thousand words. How many of these did you learn by looking them up in a
45 dictionary?" They usually are startled. Few claim to have looked up even as many as a thousand. How did they learn the rest?

They learned them just as they learned to talk—by meeting words over and over again, in different contexts, until they saw how they fitted.

Unfortunately, we English teachers are easily hung up on this
50 matter of understanding. Why should children understand everything they read? Why should anyone? Does anyone? I don't, and I never did. I was always reading books that teachers would have said were "too hard" for me, books full of words I didn't know. That's how I got to be a good reader. When about ten, I read all the D'Artagnan stories
55 and loved them. It didn't trouble me in the least that I didn't know why France was at war with England or who was quarreling with whom in the French court or why the Musketeers should always be at odds with Cardinal Richelieu's men. I didn't even know who the Cardinal was, except that he was a dangerous and powerful man that
60 my friends had to watch out for. This was all I needed to know.

Having said this, I will now say that I think a big, unabridged dictionary is a fine thing to have in any home or classroom. No book is more fun to browse around in—*if* you're not made to. Children, depending on their age, will find many pleasant and interesting

65 things to do with a big dictionary. They can look up funny-sounding words which they like, or long words, which they like, or forbidden words, which they like best of all. At a certain age, and particularly with a little encouragement from parents or teachers, they may become very interested in where words came from and when they

70 came into the language and how their meanings have changed over the years. But exploring for the fun of it is very different from looking up words out of your reading because you're going to get into trouble with your teacher if you don't.

While teaching fifth grade two years or so after the argument with

75 my sister, I began to think again about reading. The children in my class were supposed to fill out a card—just the title and author and a one-sentence summary—for every book they read. I was not running a competition to see which child could read the most books, a competition that almost always leads to cheating. I just wanted to

80 know what the children were reading. After a while it became clear that many of these very bright kids, from highly literate and even literary backgrounds, read very few books and deeply disliked reading. Why should this be?

At this time I was coming to realize, as I described in my book

85 *How Children Fail,* that for most children school was a place of danger, and their main business in school was staying out of danger as much as possible. I now began to see also that books were among the most dangerous things in school.

From the very beginning of school we make books and reading a

90 constant source of possible failure and public humiliation. When children are little we make them read aloud, before the teacher and other children, so that we can be sure they "know" all the words they are reading. This means that when they don't know a word, they are going to make a mistake, right in front of everyone. Instantly they are

95 made to realize that they have done something wrong. Perhaps some of the other children will begin to wave their hands and say, "Ooooh! O-o-o-oh!" Perhaps they will just giggle, or nudge each other, or make a face. Perhaps the teacher will say, "Are you sure?" or ask someone else what he thinks. Or perhaps, if the teacher is kindly, she will just

100 smile a sweet, sad smile—often one of the most painful punishments a child can suffer in school. In any case, the child who has made the mistake knows he has made it, and feels foolish, stupid, and ashamed, just as any of us would in his shoes.

Before long many children associate books and reading with

105 mistakes, real or feared, and penalties and humiliation. This may not seem sensible, but it is natural. Mark Twain once said that a cat that sat on a hot stove lid would never sit on one again—but it would never sit on a cold one either. As true of children as of cats. If they, so to speak, sit on a hot book a few times, if books cause them

110 humiliation and pain, they are likely to decide that the safest thing to
do is to leave all books alone.

    After having taught fifth-grade classes for four years I felt quite sure
of this theory. In my next class were many children who had had
great trouble with schoolwork, particularly reading. I decided to try at
115 all costs to rid them of their fear and dislike of books, and to get
them to read oftener and more adventurously.

    One day soon after school had started, I said to them, "Now I'm
going to say something about reading that you have probably never
heard a teacher say before. I would like you to read a lot of books
120 this year, but I want you to read them only for pleasure. I am not
going to ask you questions to find out whether you understand the
books or not. If you understand enough of a book to enjoy it and
want to go on reading it, that's enough for me. Also I'm not going to
ask you what words mean.

125   "Finally," I said, "I don't want you to feel that just because you start
a book, you have to finish it. Give an author thirty or forty pages or so
to get his story going. Then if you don't like the characters and don't
care what happens to them, close the book, put it away, and get
another. I don't care whether the books are easy or hard, short or
130 long, as long as you enjoy them. Furthermore I'm putting all this in a
letter to your parents, so they won't feel they have to quiz and heckle
you about books at home."

    The children sat stunned and silent. Was this a teacher talking? One
girl, who had just come to us from a school where she had had a very
135 hard time, and who proved to be one of the most interesting, lively,
and intelligent children I have every known, looked at me steadily for
a long time after I had finished. Then, still looking at me, she said
slowly and solemnly, "Mr. Holt, do you really mean that?" I said just
as solemnly, "I mean every word of it."

140   Apparently she decided to believe me. The first book she read was
Dr. Seuss's *How the Grinch Stole Christmas,* not a hard book even for
most third graders. For a while she read a number of books on this
level. Perhaps she was clearing up some confusion about reading that
her teachers, in their hurry to get her up to "grade level," had never
145 given her enough time to clear up. After she had been in the class six
weeks or so and we had become good friends, I very tentatively
suggested that, since she was a skillful rider and loved horses, she
might like to read National Velvet. I made my sell as soft as possible,
saying only that it was about a girl who loved and rode horses, and
150 that if she didn't like it, she could put it back. She tried it, and
though she must have found it quite a bit harder than what she had
been reading, finished it and liked it very much.

    During the spring she really astonished me, however. One day, in
one of our many free periods, she was reading at her desk. From a

155 glimpse of the illustrations I thought I knew what the book was. I said to myself, "It can't be," and went to take a closer look. Sure enough, she was reading *Moby Dick,* in the edition with woodcuts by Rockwell Kent. When I came close to her desk she looked up. I said, "Are you really reading that?" She said she was. I said, "Do you like

160 it?" She said, "Oh, yes, it's neat!" I said, "Don't you find parts of it rather heavy going?" She answered, "Oh, sure, but I just skip over those parts and go on to the next good part."

This is exactly what reading should be and in school so seldom is—an exciting, joyous adventure. Find something, dive into it, take

165 the good parts, skip the bad parts, get what you can out of it, go on to something else. How different is our mean-spirited, picky insistence that every child get every last little scrap of "understanding" that can be dug out of a book.

Skill Development: Class Discussion

After collaborating to devise a format for interaction, volunteers will lead the class in a group discussion of this selection. Use the following questions to explore your own thinking about the issues in preparation for this discussion.

Exploring Your Point of View

1. What do you read regularly?
2. What are your two favorite books of all time?
3. What kind of books did you read for pleasure in the fifth grade?
4. Why do you think some kids hate to read?
5. Do you like to look up words in the dictionary?
6. How do you learn new words?
7. How can kids read material that is "too hard" for them?
8. Is it "better" to read a best-selling novel or a classic? Why?
9. Who encouraged you to read? How? Did it work?
10. What do you hate to read? Why?
11. Have you ever read aloud to a child? Is it important?
12. Do you read when you have to wait for an appointment or a ride?
13. Do you feel that teachers make children hate reading?

Exploring the Author's Point of View

1. Why does the author say that "books were among the most dangerous things in school"?
2. What would the author say about reading as an interaction between the reader and the material? Is the reader "an empty bucket"?
3. What facts does the author use to support his position? What opinions?

4. What is the author's tone?
5. What is the author's purpose?
6. What do we know about the author's background?
7. Why does the author feel it was important for the girl to read the Dr. Seuss book?
8. Does the author feel that students should read *Moby Dick?*
9. How does the author feel teachers can encourage reading?

Exploring Other Points of View

1. Why do teachers teach dictionary skills?
2. How do comprehension quizzes help students?
3. Why do teachers give vocabulary tests?
4. Why do teachers ask students to read aloud?
5. Do you like to discuss what you have read?
6. Why do teachers require book reports? What formats for the reports have you used?
7. Why is the bookstore business profitable?
8. How do reading goals differ in fifth grade and in college?
9. Do teachers want students to love reading?

Connecting and Reflecting

The following passage introduces a study of excellent teachers at a community college in the Southeast. Reflect on the subheadings in the three categories of performance: **motivation, interpersonal, and intellectual.** From your own experiences, predict what you think the research indicated. **Write a paragraph for each of the three categories describing the characteristics that would apply to excellent teachers in each.** Use the subheads as guides, but not limits, for your thinking and **include examples** that illustrate your points about excellence.

Excellent Teachers

What distinguishes a great teacher? Most of us can recall great teachers we've known, although we may not be able to explain precisely why they were "great." This is what researchers study: What makes these teachers different? What sets them apart? The literature on teaching effectiveness and the results of our study confirm that there is a core of characteristics which are central to excellent teaching. These characteristics are exemplified by the excellent teachers we studied at Miami-Dade Community College.

© 1993 HarperCollins College Publishers

Excellent teachers have every intention of making a difference in their students' lives. Of course, they mean to affect students through their subject matter, but they are quite aware that they hold the power to have a profound impact on the students assigned to them. This belief that they can teach assumes that students can learn, for a teacher can have no impact unless the learner also chooses to be influenced. Excellent teachers believe in their own efficacy (Farrar, Neufeld, & Milse, 1984).

Using Klemp's categories for grouping the characteristics of superior performance from people in all career fields, the thirteen themes were divided into three divisions: motivation, interpersonal skills, and intellectual skills. These divisions served to organize the general teaching themes.

John Roueche and George Baker, *Access and Excellence*

Teaching for Success

MOTIVATION

1. Commitment
2. Goal orientation
3. Integrated perception
4. Positive action
5. Reward orientation

INTERPERSONAL

6. Objectivity
7. Active listening
8. Rapport
9. Empathy

INTELLECTUAL

10. Individualized perception
11. Teaching strategies
12. Knowledge
13. Innovation

G. O. Klemp, Jr., "Three Factors of Success," in D. W. Vermilye, ed., *Current Issues in Higher Education* (San Francisco: Jossey-Bass, 1977).

Selection **2**

LITERATURE

Stage 1

Preview

What is eugenics?
Is the author for or against genetic engineering?

Activate Schema

What is Down syndrome?
Will new laws be needed to protect humans from genetic engineering?

Learning Strategy

Read to understand the author's concerns about genetic screening.

Skill Development: Your Point of View

Answer the following questions about your point of view.

1. Would you marry a person if you knew your offspring would be at high risk for a genetic disease? Why or why not?
2. Would you take a test to know if you are susceptible to Alzheimer's disease or manic-depression? Why or why not?
3. If you were a geneticist, would you perform a test if you knew the parents would abort for gender selection? Why or why not?
4. Would you abort a fetus that was sure to die by age five? Why or why not?

MADE TO ORDER BABIES

From Geoffrey Cowley, *Newsweek*

For centuries, Jewish communities lived Job-like with the knowledge that many of their babies would thrive during infancy, grow demented and blind as toddlers and die by the age of 5. Joseph Ekstein, a Hasidic rabbi in Brooklyn, lost four children to Tay-Sachs disease over
5 three decades, and his experience was not unusual. Some families were just unlucky.

Today, the curse of Tay-Sachs is being lifted—not through better treatments (the hereditary disease is as deadly as ever) but through a new cultural institution called Chevra Dor Yeshorim, the "Association
10 of an Upright Generation." Thanks largely to Rabbi Ekstein's efforts, Orthodox teenagers throughout the world now line up at screening centers to have their blood tested for evidence of the Tay-Sachs gene. Before getting engaged, prospective mates simply call Chevra Dor Yeshorim and read off the code numbers assigned to their tests results.

15 If the records show that neither person carries the gene, or that just one does, the match is judged sound. But if both happen to be carriers (meaning any child they conceive will have a one-in-four chance of suffering the fatal disease), marriage is virtually out of the question. Even if two carriers wanted to wed, few rabbis would abet
20 them. "It's a rule of thumb that engagements won't occur until compatibility is established," says Rabbi Jacob Horowitz, codirector of the Brooklyn-based program. "Each day, we could stop many marriages worldwide."

Marriage isn't the only institution being reshaped by modern
25 genetics; a host of new diagnostic tests could soon change every aspect of creating a family. Physicians can now identify some 250 genetic defects, not only in the blood of a potential parent but in the tissue of a developing fetus. The result is that, for the first time in history, people are deciding, rather than wondering, what kind of
30 children they will bear.

Choosing to avoid a horrible disease may be easy, at least in
principle, but that's just one of many options 21st century parents
could face. Already, conditions far less grave than Tay-Sachs have been
linked to specific genes, and the science is still exploding.

35 Researchers are now at work on a massive $3 billion project to
decipher the entire human genetic code. By the turn of the century,
knowledge gained through this Human Genome Initiative could
enable doctors to screen fetuses—even test-tube embryos—for traits
that have nothing to do with disease. "Indeed," says Dr. Paul Berg,

40 director of the Beckman Center for Molecular and Genetic Medicine
at Stanford, "we should be able to locate which [gene] combinations
affect kinky hair, olive skin and pointy teeth."

How will such knowledge be handled? How should it be handled?
Are we headed for an age in which having a child is morally

45 analogous to buying a car? There is already evidence that couples are
using prenatal tests to identify and abort fetuses on the basis of sex,
and there is no reason to assume the trend will stop there. "We
should be worried about the future and where this might take us,"
says George Annas, a professor of health law at Boston University's

50 School of Medicine. "The whole definition of normal could well be
changed. The issue becomes not the ability of the child to be happy
but rather our ability to be happy with the child."

So far, at least, the emphasis has been on combating serious
hereditary disorders. Everyone carries four to six genes that are

55 harmless when inherited from one parent but can be deadly when
inherited from both. Luckily, most of these mutations are rare enough
that carriers are unlikely to cross paths. But some have become
common within particular populations. Five percent of all whites carry
the gene for cystic fibrosis, for example, and one in 2,000 is born

60 with the disease. Seven percent of all blacks harbor the mutation for
sickle-cell anemia, and one in 500 is afflicted. Asian and
Mediterranean people are particularly prone to the deadly blood
disease thalassemia, just as Jews are to Tay-Sachs.

When accommodating the disability means watching a toddler die

65 of Tay-Sachs or thalassemia, few couples hesitate to abort, and only
the most adamant pro-lifer would blame them. But few of the defects
for which fetuses can be screened are so devastating. Consider
Huntington's disease, the hereditary brain disorder that killed the folk
singer Woody Guthrie. Huntington's relentlessly destroys its victim's

70 mind, and anyone who inherits the gene eventually gets the disease.
Yet Huntington's rarely strikes anyone under 40, and it can remain
dormant into a person's 70s. What does a parent do with the
knowledge that a fetus has the gene? Is some life better than none?
Most carriers think not. . . .

© 1993 HarperCollins College Publishers

75　　As more abnormalities are linked to genes, the dilemmas can only get stickier. Despite all the uncertainties, a positive test for Down or Huntington's leaves no doubt that the condition will set in. But not every disease-related gene guarantees ill health. Those associated with conditions like alcoholism, Alzheimer's disease and manic-depressive
80　illness signal only a susceptibility. Preventing such conditions would thus require aborting kids who might never have suffered. And because one gene can have more than one effect, the effort could have unintended consequences. There is considerable evidence linking manic-depressive illness to artistic genius, notes Dr. Melvin
85　Konner, an anthropologist and nonpracticing physician at Emory University. "Doing away with the gene would destroy the impetus for much human creativity."

　　The future possibilities are even more troubling when you consider that mere imperfections could be screened for as easily as serious
90　diseases. Stuttering, obesity and reading disorders are all traceable to genetic markers, notes Dr. Kathleen Nolan of The Hastings Center, a biomedical think tank in suburban New York. And many aspects of appearance and personality are under fairly simple genetic control. Are we headed for a time when straight teeth, a flat stomach and a
95　sense of humor are standards for admission into some families? It's not inconceivable. "I see people in my clinic occasionally who have a sort of new-car mentality," says Dr. Francis Collins, a University of Michigan geneticist who recently helped identify the gene for cystic fibrosis. "It's got to be perfect, and if it isn't you take it back to the
100　lot and get a new one."

　　At the moment, gender is the only nonmedical condition for which prenatal tests are widely available. There are no firm figures on how often people abort to get their way, but physicians say many patients use the tests for that purpose. The requests have traditionally come
105　from Asians and East Indians expressing a cultural preference for males. But others are now asking, too. "I've found a high incidence of sex selection coming from doctors' families in the last two years," says Dr. Lawrence D. Platt, a geneticist at the University of Southern California—"much higher than ethnic requests. Once there is public
110　awareness about the technology, other people will use the procedure as well."

　　Those people will find their physicians increasingly willing to help. A 1973 survey of American geneticists found that only 1 percent considered it morally acceptable to help parents identify and abort
115　fetuses of the undesired sex. Last year University of Virginia ethicist John C. Fletcher and Dr. Mark I. Evans, a geneticist at Wayne State University, conducted a similar poll and found that nearly 20 percent approved. Meanwhile, 62 percent of the geneticists questioned in a

1985 survey said they would screen fetuses for a couple who had four
healthy daughters and wanted a son.

Right or wrong, the new gender option has set an important
precedent. If parents will screen babies for one nonmedical
condition, there is no reason to assume they won't screen them for
others. Indeed, preliminary results from a recent survey of 200 New
England couples showed that while only 1 percent would abort on
the basis of sex, 11 percent would abort to save a child from obesity.
As Dr. Robin Dawn Clark, head of clinical genetics at Loma Linda
Medical Center observes, the temptation will be to select for "other
features that are honored by society."

The trend toward even greater control could lead to bizarre, scifi
scenarios. But it seems unlikely that prenatal swimsuit competitions
will sweep the globe anytime soon: most of the globe has yet to reap
the benefits of 19th-century medicine. Even in America, many
prospective parents are still struggling to obtain basic health
insurance. If the masses could suddenly afford cosmetic screening
tests, the trauma of abortion would remain a powerful deterrent. And
while [geneticist] John Buster's dream of extracting week-old embryos
for a quick gene check could ease the trauma, it seems a safe bet
many women would still opt to leave their embryos alone.

The more immediate danger is that the power to predict children's
medical futures will diminish society's tolerance for serious defects.
Parents have already sued physicians for "wrongful life" after giving
birth to disabled children, claiming it was the doctor's responsibility
to detect the defect in the womb. The fear of such suits could prompt
physicians to run every available test, however remote the possibility
of spotting a medical problem. Conversely, parents who are content to
forgo all the genetic fortune-telling could find themselves stigmatized
for their backward ways. When four-cell embryos can be screened for
hereditary diseases, failing to ensure a child's future health could
become the same sort of offense that declining heroic measures for a
sick child is today.

In light of all the dangers, some critics find the very practice of
prenatal testing morally questionable. "Even at the beginning of the
journey the eugenics question looms large," says Jeremy Rifkin, a
Washington activist famous for his opposition to genetic tinkering.
"Screening is eugenics." Perhaps, but its primary effect so far has been
to bring fewer seriously diseased children into the world. In Britain's
Northeast Thames region, the number of Indian and Cypriot children
born with thalassemia fell by 78 percent after prenatal tests became
available in the 1970s. Likewise, carrier and prenatal screening have
virtually eliminated Tay-Sachs from the United States and Canada.

Failing to think, as a society, about the appropriate uses of the new
tests would be a grave mistake. They're rife with potential for abuse,

and the coming advances in genetic science will make them more so.
165 But they promise some control over diseases that have caused
immense suffering and expense. Society need only remember that
there are no perfect embryos but many ways to be a successful human
being.

Comprehension Questions

Answer the following with *T* (true) or *F* (false).

_____ 1. Geneticists have discovered a cure for Tay-Sachs disease.
_____ 2. Genetic defects can be detected from testing fetal tissue.
_____ 3. According to the passage everyone carries deadly genes.
_____ 4. The author feels that we are not in immediate danger of massive fetal
screening.
_____ 5. The author suggests that some doctors are allowing patients to abort for
gender selection.

Skill Development: Investigating Points of View

Respond to the following questions on your own paper.

1. Why does the author state that marriage is "being reshaped by modern
genetics"?
2. What does Annas mean by saying, "The issue becomes not the ability of
the child to be happy but rather our ability to be happy with the child"?
3. What does Collins mean by people "who have a sort of new-car mentality"?
4. What does the author mean by, "The more immediate danger is that the
power to predict children's medical futures will diminish society's
tolerance for serious defects"?
5. What is the author's point of view on genetic screening? What is the
purpose and tone of the article? Give two examples of how both facts
and opinions are used to develop the thought.

Connecting and Reflecting

Genetic engineering is a relatively new field with great promise and
also great danger. Form a collaborative group to discuss the moral and
ethical concerns surrounding genetic engineering. Decide on your position. Do you support the work of the geneticists? As a group **develop
a list of five "great promises" and five potential "dangers" that
you foresee in the near future of genetic engineering.** Read the
following passage for more information.

Advances in Genetics

The field of genetics is presently undergoing sweeping changes largely because of a simple introduction: Madison Avenue has met the microbe. Already we find that the most conservative of financiers are interested in the mating habits of a lowly bacterium that is found in the bowels of everyone (including their employees). How did this all come to be?

Genetic engineering, as the name implies, involves manipulating genes to achieve some particular goal. Already you can see what sorts of objections might arise. But it doesn't take much imagination to see what new achievements might be on the horizon.

Perhaps the greatest threat of recombinant techniques, some would say, lies in its very promise. The possibilities of such genetic manipulation seem limitless. For example, we can mix the genes of anything, say, for example, an ostrich and a German shepherd. This may only bring to mind images of tall dogs, but what would happen if we inserted cancer-causing genes into the familiar E. *coli* that is so well adapted to living in our intestines? What if the gene that makes botulism toxin, one of the deadliest poisons known, were inserted into the DNA of friendly E. *coli* and then released into some human population? One might ask, "But who would do such a terrible thing?" Perhaps the same folks who brought us napalm and nerve gas.

Another, less cynical, concern is that well-intended scientists could mishandle some deadly variant and allow it to escape from the laboratory. Some variants have been weakened to prevent such an occurrence, but we should remember that even after smallpox was "eradicated" from the earth, there were two minor epidemics in Europe caused by cultured experimental viruses that had escaped from a lab. One person died of a disease that technically didn't exist.

There were people who feared the results of gene splicing, but no one could deny that the promise was great and that the successes of the technique were beginning to mount.

Take, for example, insulin. Insulin has traditionally been harvested from human tissue, or from slaughtered pigs and cows (which yielded a similar kind of insulin that worked in most humans, but caused allergic reactions in others). Unfortunately, very little insulin could be extracted by such methods. Now, though, the gene that clones for human insulin has been isolated, inserted into a plasmid and cloned, so authentic human insulin is essentially unlimited. Thus, great quantities of insulin are now available that can be used by anyone.

Robert Wallace, *Biology: The World of Life*

Selection **3**

HISTORY

Stage 1

Preview

> *Who are some of the heroes mentioned?*
> *When did the Civil Rights Movement begin?*

Activate Schema

> *How did Martin Luther King die?*
> *Who is Cesar Chavez?*

Learning Strategy

> *Read to learn the significance of each leader's contribution to the Civil Rights Movement.*

Stage 2

1. Predict 2. Picture 3. Relate 4. Monitor 5. Fix up

HEROES FOR CIVIL RIGHTS

From James Martin et al., *America and Its People*

On a cold afternoon in Montgomery, Alabama, Rosa Parks, a
well-respected black seamstress, who was active in the NAACP, took a
significant stride toward equality. She boarded a bus and sat in the
first row of the "colored" section. The white section of the bus
5   quickly filled, and according to Jim Crow rules, blacks were expected
to give up their seats rather than force whites—male or female—to
stand. The time came for Mrs. Parks to give up her seat. She stayed
seated. When told by the bus driver to get up or he would call the
police, she said, "You may do that." Later she recalled that the act of
10   defiance was "just something I had to do." The bus stopped, the
driver summoned the police, and Rosa Parks was arrested.

Black Montgomery rallied to Mrs. Parks's side. Like her, they were
tired of riding in the back of the bus, tired of giving up their seats to
whites, tired of having their lives restricted by Jim Crow. Local black
15   leaders decided to organize a boycott of Montgomery's white-owned
and white-operated bus system. They hoped that economic pressure
would force changes which court decisions could not. For the next
381 days, more than ninety percent of Montgomery's black citizens
participated in an heroic and successful demonstration against racial
20   segregation. The common black attitude toward the protest was
voiced by an elderly black woman when a black leader offered her a
ride. "No," she replied, "my feets is tired, but my soul is rested."

To lead the boycott, Montgomery blacks turned to the new minister
of the Dexter Avenue Baptist Church, a young man named Martin
25   Luther King, Jr. Reared in Atlanta, the son of a respected and
financially secure minister, King had been educated at Morehouse
College, Crozier Seminary, and Boston University, from which he
earned a doctorate in theology. King was an intellectual, excited by
ideas and deeply influenced by the philosophical writings of Henry
30   David Thoreau and Mahatma Gandhi as well as the teachings of
Christ. They believed in the power of nonviolent, direct action.

King's words as well as his ideas stirred people's souls. At the start
of the Montgomery boycott he told his followers:

There comes a time when people get tired. We are here this evening to say to
35   those who have mistreated us so long that we are tired—tired of being segregated and humiliated, tired of being kicked about by the brutal feet of oppression.... We've come here tonight to be saved from the patience that makes us
patient with anything less than freedom and justice.... If you protest coura-
geously and yet with dignity and Christian love, in the history books that are
40   written in future generations, historians will have to pause and say "there
lived a great people—a black people—who injected a new meaning and dignity into the veins of civilization."

Dr. Martin Luther King, Jr., gave voice to the new mood: "We're
through with tokenism and gradualism and see-how-far-you've-
45   comeism. We're through with we've-done-more-for-your-people-
than-anyone-else-ism, We can't wait any longer. Now is the time."

Sit-ins

On Monday, February 1, 1960, four black freshmen at North Carolina
Agricultural and Technical College—Ezell Blair, Jr., Franklin McClain,
Joseph McNeill, and David Richmond—walked into the F. W.
50   Woolworth store in Greensboro, North Carolina, and sat down at the
lunch counter. They asked for a cup of coffee. A waitress told them
that she would only serve them if they stood.

Instead of walking away, the four college freshmen stayed in their
seats until the lunch counter closed. The next morning, the four
55   college students reappeared at Woolworth's accompanied by
twenty-five fellow students. On Wednesday, student protesters filled
sixty-three of the lunch counter's sixty-six seats. The sit-in movement
had begun.

In April, 142 student sit-in leaders from eleven states met in
60   Raleigh, North Carolina, and voted·to set up a new group to
coordinate the sit-ins, the Student Non-Violent Coordinating
Committee (SNCC). Martin Luther King told the students that their
willingness to go to jail would "be the thing to awaken the dozing
conscience of many of our white brothers." The president of Fisk
65   University echoed King's judgment: "This is no student panty raid. It
is a dedicated universal effort, and it has cemented the Negro
community as it has never been cemented before."

College Registration

Civil rights activists' next major aim was to open state universities to
black students. Although many southern states opened their
70   universities to black students without incident, others were stiff-
backed in their opposition to integration. A major breakthrough
occurred in September 1962, when a federal court ordered the state
of Mississippi to admit James Meredith—a nine-year veteran of the Air
Force—to the University of Mississippi in Oxford. Ross Barnett, the
75   state's governor, promised on statewide television that he would "not
surrender to the evil and illegal forces of tyranny" and would go to
jail rather than permit Meredith to register for classes. Barnett flew
into Oxford, named himself special registrar of the university, and
ordered the arrest of federal officials who tried to enforce the court order.
80   James Meredith refused to back down. A "man with a mission and a
nervous stomach," Meredith was determined to get a higher
education. "I want to go to the university," he said. "This is the life I
want. Just to live and breathe—that isn't life to me. There's got to be

something more." Meredith arrived at the campus in the company of
85 police officers, federal marshals, and lawyers. Angry white students
waited, chanting, "Two, four, six, eight—we don't want to integrate."

Four times James Meredith tried unsuccessfully to register. He
finally succeeded on the fifth try, escorted by several hundred federal
marshals. The ensuing riot left two people dead and 375 injured,
90 including 166 marshals. Ultimately, President Kennedy sent 16,000
troops to put down the violence.

"Boomingham"

It was in Birmingham, Alabama, that civil rights activists faced the
most determined resistance. A sprawling steel town of 340,000 known
as the "Pittsburgh of the South," Birmingham had a long history of
95 racial acrimony.

Day after day, well dressed and neatly groomed men, women and
children marched against segregation—only to be jailed for
demonstrating without a permit. On April 12, King himself was
arrested—and while in jail wrote a scathing attack on those who
100 asked black Americans to wait patiently for equal rights. A group of
white clergymen had publicly criticized King for staging "unwise and
untimely" demonstrations.

For two weeks, all was quiet, but in early May demonstrations
resumed with renewed vigor. On May 2 and again on May 3, more
105 than a thousand of Birmingham's black children marched for equal
rights. In response, Birmingham's police chief, Theophilus Eugene
"Bull" Connor, unleashed police dogs on the children and sprayed
them with 700 pounds of water pressure—shocking the nation's
conscience. Tension mounted as police arrested 2,543 blacks and
110 whites between May 2 and May 7, 1963. Under intense criticism, the
Birmingham Chamber of Commerce reached an agreement on May 9
with black leaders to desegregate public facilities in ninety days, hire
blacks as clerks and salespersons in sixty days, and release
demonstrators without bail in return for an end to the protests.

The March on Washington

115 The violence that erupted in Birmingham and elsewhere in 1961 and
1962 alarmed many veteran civil rights leaders. In December 1962,
two veteran fighters for civil rights—A. Philip Randolph and Bayard
Rustin—met at the office of the Brotherhood of Sleeping Car Porters
in Harlem. Both men were pacifists, eager to rededicate the civil
120 rights movement to the principle of nonviolence. Both men wanted to
promote passage of Kennedy's civil rights bill, school desegregation,
federal job training programs, and a ban on job discrimination.
Thirty-two years before, Randolph had threatened to lead a march on
Washington unless the federal government ended job discrimination

125 against black workers in war industries. Now Rustin revived the idea
of a massive march for civil rights and jobs.

On August 28, 1963, more than 200,000 people gathered around the
Washington Monument and marched eight-tenths of a mile to the
Lincoln Memorial. As they walked, the marchers carried placards
130 reading: "Effective Civil Rights Laws—Now! Integrated Schools—Now!
Decent Housing—Now!" and sang the civil rights anthem, "We Shall
Overcome."

The Civil Rights Act of 1964
For seven months, debate raged in the halls of Congress. In a futile
effort to delay the Civil Rights Bill's passage, opponents proposed
135 more than 500 amendments and staged a protracted filibuster in the
Senate. On July 2, 1964—a year and a day after President Kennedy
had sent it to Congress—the Civil Rights Act was enacted into law. As
finally passed, the act prohibited discrimination in voting,
employment, and public facilities such as hotels and restaurants, and
140 it established the Equal Employment Opportunity Commission
(EEOC) to prevent discrimination in employment on the basis of
race, religion, or sex. Ironically, the provision barring sex
discrimination had been added by opponents of the civil rights act in
an attempt to kill the bill.

Skill Development

Answer the following questions to review the material from your own point
of view and that of a historian. Use your own paper for responses.

Exploring Your Point of View

1. Would you have participated in the civil rights sit-ins? Why or why not?
2. Would you have the courage to make a single stand like Rosa Parks or
   James Meredith? Why or why not?
3. What modern issues are drawing protesters to demonstrate?
4. Have you ever participated in a demonstration? About what?
5. Name a modern hero for individual rights.

Exploring the Historian's Point of View

1. Are the heroes in this selection the only heroes in the Civil Rights
   Movement? Who selected the heroes?
2. Why does the author begin the selection with Rosa Parks?
3. Why do historians compare King and Gandhi?

4. Why does the author quote part of King's Montgomery boycott speech, as well as his list of "isms"?
5. How were college students heroes?
6. What is the "nation's conscience"? Why does the author feel that shocking it was of historical importance?
7. Why was the march on Washington historically significant?
8. What is the author's purpose and tone?
9. Does the author include mostly facts or opinions in this selection? Why?
10. Why does the author begin the last sentence with "Ironically"? What does the word mean in the sentence?

Connecting and Reflecting

Read the following letter, in which a mother expresses her concerns and feelings to her daughter. **Pretend that you are the daughter and write a letter of response back to the mother.** Address the concerns of the mother and explain how you feel about things and why she should not worry about you.

Is My "Post-Integration" Daughter Black Enough?

My dearest Daughter:

Something's been troubling me for the past two years. I jokingly call it the "Post-Integration Blues." Actually, it's no laughing matter.

I get it every time something happens like last month when I said to you, "Martin Luther King's birthday is coming up and we're going to do something special like attend a memorial service." You looked at me with total disdain and said, "Momma, that's the only day I'll get to sleep late."

When you say things like that, I take them personally. I know that I shouldn't, but I hurt. I take it as rejection of all that my generation of Blacks fought for, yet I know that is not how you intended it.

We've discussed this. You told me just recently, "Just because we don't march doesn't mean we don't know it's Dr. King's birthday." Still, I hurt, and wonder: What happened to my little girl who could barely print, but wrote the governor of North Carolina to ask him to "free the Wilmington 10"?

See, at 35, I come from a generation of marchers. I do not understand inaction. In fact, it frightens me. I do not trust it. You think my distrust is paranoia; I understand. It is because you have not seen what I have seen.

You have never known such. You ride a shiny school bus to a nine-year-old school that is thoroughly integrated. "Momma, we just don't put the emphasis on Black and White that you do," you told me the other day, adding, "But when we are in school, I do end up hanging with my friends, who just happen to be Black."

You would probably say I am overreacting. I wonder if what I want isn't impossible. You think that you don't "act White," and mostly you're right. But changes can creep up so slowly and in such small ways. . . .

. . . I am torn. I don't want you to live on the razor's edge as I did in South Carolina, when I couldn't enter certain doors, drink from certain water fountains or eat a meal sitting down at any restaurant downtown. But I don't want you to forget either. I'm afraid if you haven't lived on the razor's edge you forget you can bleed.

I am encouraged by incidents like the one when you came home a couple of weeks ago and in a disgusted voice said, "My history teacher didn't even know who Louis Farrakhan is, momma."

Maybe my words aren't just flying around your head. You have caught some of what I've been saying. Anyway, it's not just you who triggers my blues, but a lot of Black children.

For instance, remember when I took my friend's 12-year-old son, David-Askia, to the movie? Well, while we were sitting there waiting for the film to begin, I started telling him about how when I lived in Beaufort, S.C., in 1962, Black people could only sit in the balcony of the theater.

"We used to throw popcorn and ice from our sodas down on the White kids," I said.

"There would always be two empty rows just under the edge of the balcony, since none of the White kids wanted to sit there and have to duck all the time."

"That was dumb, to throw things down on people," David-Askia said.

"It seems dumb now but it wasn't dumb if that was the only way you could get back at them," I said.

"Anyway," he said, turning to give me a puzzled look, "You can see better in the balcony."

"True," I told him. "But you only know that if you have had the chance to sit everywhere in the theater." He's so young, I'm not sure he understood what I was saying.

I hope you do.

With Love,
Momma

Patrice Gaines-Carter, *Ebony,* September 1985

CRITICAL THINKING

- What is critical thinking?
- How do you identify issues?
- What are the parts of an argument?
- What are the types of evidence?
- How do you evaluate an argument for relevance, believability, and consistency?
- What is creative thinking?

WHAT IS CRITICAL THINKING?

Do you accept the thinking of others or do you think for yourself? Do you examine and judge? Can you identify important questions and systematically search for answers? Can you justify what you believe? If so, you are thinking critically. For example, if each of the following represented a textbook portrayal of Christopher Columbus, which would you tend to accept most readily and why?

A courageous hero _____

_____

A despot who enslaved the Indians _____

_____

A hapless explorer who failed to find India or gold _____

_____

Rather than answer immediately, most students would say, "I need more information. I want to consider the arguments, weigh the facts, and draw my own conclusions." From a metacognitive perspective, such students want to think critically about the available information about Columbus before "labeling" the explorer and filing the Columbus "computer chip" back into their knowledge networks.

Thinking critically means deliberating in a purposeful, organized manner in order to assess the value of information, both old and new. Critical thinkers search, compare, analyze, clarify, evaluate, and conclude. Critical thinkers do not start from scratch; they build on previous knowledge or schemata to forge new relationships. They recognize both sides of an issue and supply reasons and examples to support their own position.

Some professors speak of critical thinking as if it were a special discipline rather than an application of many known skills. Frank Smith, an educator who has written eleven books on thinking, says that thinking critically refers simply to the manner in which thinking is done.[1] It is merely an approach to thinking, in the same sense that thinking impulsively or thinking seriously are approaches, and the approach can be practiced and learned.

Both reading and writing promote thinking. Reading offers an unlimited pool of new ideas, and writing provides a medium for adjusting and blending those ideas. Writing helps us to probe our thoughts, organize our insights, and make discoveries. Our writing first shows us—and then others—what we think. Clear writing reveals clear thinking.

[1]F. Smith, *To Think* (New York: Teachers College Press, 1990).

CHARACTERISTICS OF CRITICAL THINKERS

Critical thinkers dare to question, to challenge the status quo, and to evaluate. In a book entitled *Thought and Knowledge,* Diane Halpern lists four characteristics of critical thinkers which are presented in the box below.[2]

Characteristics of Critical Thinkers

1. Willingness to plan
   They think first and write later. They refrain from being impulsive and develop a habit of planning.
2. Flexibility
   They are open to new ideas and willing to consider new solutions for old problems.
3. Persistence
   They keep on working on a difficult task even when they get tired and discouraged. Good thinking is hard work.
4. Willingness to self-correct
   They are not defensive about their errors. They figure out what went wrong and learn from their mistakes.

COURTROOM ANALOGY

Thinking critically is the method of thinking that jurors use in deciding court cases. Clever lawyers argue conflicting versions of the truth before the jury. Each presents reasons and selected evidence to support the case of the client. Needless to say, in the summation to the jury, each attorney interprets the truth in the client's best interest. The jury is left to decide between two logical arguments. Through critical thinking, the jurors systematically answer the following questions:

1. What is the issue?
2. What are the arguments?
3. What is the evidence?
4. What is the verdict?

[2]D. Halpern, *Thought and Knowledge,* 2nd ed. (Hillsdale, NJ: Lawrence Erlbaum Associates, 1989), pp. 29–30.

College students can apply the jury's critical thinking approach to textbook reading. The same four questions are as relevant in weighing information about Christopher Columbus, genetic engineering, or manic depression as they are to making life-or-death courtroom decisions. The following steps explain how these four questions can be used to guide your thinking and help you make decisions about what you read.

STEP 1: IDENTIFY THE ISSUE

In the courtroom, the judge instructs the jury on the issue and the lawyers provide the arguments. In reading, however, the issues may not be as clearly defined. The reader must first recognize the argument in order to identify the underlying issue. Use the following strategy.

Recognize the Argument

Ask yourself, "What opinion or point of view is the author trying to convince me to accept?" The answer is usually the main idea of the passage. The following key words are sometimes used to signal this claim, conclusion, or point of view:

in summary consequently
therefore for these reasons
thus we can conclude
it follows that

Find the Issue

After recognizing the argument, seek an opposing point of view and ask, "What seems to be the debatable question or issue?"

Some issues are highly controversial and thus easy to identify. An article advocating either pro-life or pro-choice decisions is obviously about the central issue of abortion. Nevertheless, the specific issue addressed may vary from "Should abortion be legal?" to "Is abortion ethical?" to "Should the government pay for abortions?"

Writers are under no obligation to explain, or even admit, opposing points of view. Knowledgeable readers, however, sense possible biases and look for the hidden agenda. They ask, "Am I being manipulated or persuaded?" They are "tuned in" and looking for issues that have opposing points of view. As readers and writers, modern pressures have made us become "tuned in" to racism and sexism. Other biased thinking, however, more easily escapes our critical attention.

No Wrong Issues.   In critical thinking there is no "I'm right, and you are wrong." Instead, there are many different ways of logically looking at problems. Readers with different knowledge and past experiences are likely to view problems from slightly different perspectives. Readers from Portugal and San Salvador may have grown up with different views of Columbus, but both views, when reflecting logical thought and analysis, can be equally worthwhile. Thus, the author may have one issue in mind, while the reader sees another.

Make Analogies

Polya, a pioneer in mathematical problem solving, said we cannot imagine or solve a problem that is totally new and absolutely unlike any problem we have ever known.[3] We seek connections and look for similarities to previous experiences. Such comparisons are called **analogies.**

Analogies are most easily made on a personal level. We think about how the issue has or could affect us or someone we know. For example, if high school principals were seeking your input on the issue of declining mathematics scores, you would first relate the problem to your own experience. How did you score in math? Why do you think you did or did not do well? What about your friends? From your memory of high school, what would you identify as the key reasons for the declining scores? The problem now has a personal meaning and is linked to prior knowledge.

Analogies can also be formed with seemingly *unconnected* subject areas, depending on the thinker's knowledge and creativity. Comparing the new problem to familiar problems in other fields of study is usually more difficult than forming a personal analogy. Alexander Graham Bell created the idea for the telephone by drawing a comparison with the human ear. Perhaps the decline in mathematics scores in the United States could be compared to air pollution or the decline of the Roman Empire.

Linking new knowledge with personal and expanded comparisons applies past experience to new situations. Two researchers tested the importance of analogies by asking students to read technical passages with and without analogies to familiar topics.[4] The students who read the material containing the analogies scored higher on tests of comprehension and recall than students who did not have the benefit of the familiar comparisons.

Read the following passage. Identify the opinion, the opposing point of view, and the issue, and form analogies.

[3]G. Polya, *How to Solve It,* 2nd ed. (Princeton, N.J.: Princeton University Press, 1957).

[4]C.C. Hansen and D.F. Halpern, *Using analogies to improve comprehension and recall of scientific passages.* Paper presented at the 28th Annual Meeting of the Psychonomic Society (Seattle, WA, 1987).

Exercise 1

Kids and Television

No one can doubt that society is becoming more career-oriented with time, for more adults than ever are now devoting their lives to a specific career. Despite their heavy workloads, however, many of these people are also maintaining a family at home. This accounts for the fact that more and more students of all ages have become "latch-key" kids—kids who come home to an empty house and don't see their parents until late at night. So, what does a kid do at home while his parents are at work making millions? Television is usually the answer. Television has definitely become an integral part of most students' lives, and ours has become known as the "video" generation. Recent studies even indicate that typical American students watch an average of 26 hours of television a week. What are the consequences of spending so much time in front of the tube? Certainly, the programs aired on television today are distorting the minds and actions of today's youth by providing them with a false sense of reality and by limiting their imaginations.

1. What is the opinion? _____

2. What is an opposing point of view? _____

3. What is the issue? _____

4. What is a personal comparison? Other comparisons? _____

_____

Tom Paradis, "A Child's Other World"

The author feels, as stated in the last sentence, that television is limiting and distorting the minds of our children. An opposing point of view might be that television offers stimulating and educational programming that is preferable to an empty room.

When it comes to identifying issues, you may see one or you may see ten. Possible issues raised by this passage include, but are not limited to, the following questions: Is television harmful to kids? Are we missing a golden opportunity to educate kids through television? Why do television executives fail to respond to the needs of society? Should kids be home alone after school? Should public schools provide after-school care? How can children thrive in a dual-career family? Each issue is relevant and your choice may depend on your own experience.

To draw personal comparisons, you may recall programs you watched as a child or think about programs kids watch now. Comparisons to other domains are unlimited but might include similarities with potential for programming television and programming a computer. In critical thinking, both the questions and the answers are limited only by your own knowledge and imagination.

STEP 2: FIND SUPPORT FOR THE ARGUMENT

The argument is the support for the opinion. The support comes in two forms: reasons and evidence. In a perfect argument, the claim, opinion, or conclusion would be supported by several reasons, with supporting evidence for each reason. Few arguments, however, come close to such perfection.

Both the reasons and the evidence are intended to persuade the reader that the conclusion is true. The strength of the argument depends on the acceptability of the reasons and evidence. Often the reasons are obvious, especially when they are strong and convincing. At other times, the reasons are confusing and difficult to identify. A writer might put four reasons in one paragraph and later use five paragraphs to explain a single reason. The following key words often signal that the author is presenting a reason:

because	first. . .second. . .finally
assuming that	since
given that	if

Types of Evidence

As support for arguments readers would probably prefer the simplicity of a smoking gun with fingerprints on it, but such conclusive evidence is usually hard to find. Evidence comes in many different forms, and it is usually tainted by opinion. The list below contains some categories of "evidence" typically used to support the reasons in an argument. However, each type has its pitfalls and should be immediately tested with an evaluative question.

Categories of Evidence for Arguments

1. Facts: objective truths
   Ask: How were the facts gathered, and are they true?
2. Examples: anecdotes to demonstrate the truth
   Ask: Are the examples true and relevant?
3. Analogies: comparisons to similar cases
   Ask: Are the analogies accurate and relevant?
4. Authority: words from a recognized expert
   Ask: What are the credentials and biases of the expert?
5. Causal relationship: saying one thing caused another
   Ask: Is it an actual cause or merely an association?
6. Common knowledge claim: assertion of wide acceptance
   Ask: Is it relevant and does everyone really believe it?

Exercise 2: Find Support

Read the following passage and identify the opinion, the issue, the reasons, and the evidence. Label and evaluate the evidence according to the categories listed above.

No Smoking

On-the-job smoking is a hot issue for both smokers and nonsmokers, and many managers now see smoking as a productivity problem. Although opponents question whether smoking affects one's productivity, it has, in fact, been proven that a smoker costs a company, both medically and in productivity, more than a nonsmoker. According to William Weis, an associate professor in the Albers School of Business at Seattle University, a "smoking employee costs his or her employer an estimated $5,740 more annually than a non-smoking employee" (Collison 1988: 80). These costs include absenteeism (which is 50 percent greater for smokers), medical care, lost earnings, insurance, damages, and the health impact (Collison 1988: 80). Absenteeism, and absence due to smoking breaks, is but one of the productivity problems, yet it accounts for a great deal of employer costs.

When discussing the issue of smoking at the workplace, perhaps the most important aspect is the health risk smoking causes to both smokers and nonsmokers. It was proven in 1964 that smoking is, in fact, linked to lung cancer, and in 1986 Surgeon General C. Everett Koop warned further that involuntary smoking can cause lung cancer and other illnesses in healthy nonsmokers ("Involuntary Risk": 64). Involuntary smoking can be defined as simply breathing in the vicinity of people with lit cigarettes in enclosed areas ("Involuntary Risk": 64). Anyone who has been with a smoker indeed knows that in addition to lung cancer, their smoke can also cause eye irritation, coughing, headaches, and throat soreness. While eye irritation may seem trivial to some smokers, it nonetheless is a problem that occurs on a daily basis in offices and break rooms and can, eventually, lead to greater health problems. Employees who do not smoke should not be subjected to the risks of involuntary smoking and need to be able to work in a safe environment. Surgeon General Koop states that "the right of the smoker stops at the point where his or her smoking increases the disease risk of those occupying the same environment ("Involuntary Risk": 64).

Teresa Schmidt

1. What is the author's opinion? _____

2. What is the issue? _____

3. List the reasons and supporting evidence given to back the claim. _____

_____

Reason: _____

Evidence: _____

Reason: _____

Evidence: _____

To support the ban of smoking in the workplace, the author gives two reasons: reduced productivity and an unhealthy working environment. Health costs and time away from the desk are offered as factual evidence to back the claim of reduced productivity. Surgeon Koop's message, as well as generally accepted health hazards, are used as authority and common-knowledge proof of an unhealthy environment. What additional reasons and evidence would you add to strengthen the argument?

STEP 3: EVALUATE THE ARGUMENT

As a reader, you will decide to accept or reject the author's opinion. Strong arguments are supported by well-crafted reasons and evidence, but clever arguments can be supported by the crafty use of reason and evidence. To evaluate an argument, consider the three following factors: relevance, believability, and consistency. Ask questions to test the significance or abuse of "evidence" in each area.

1. Relevance: Is the Support Relevant?   Does the evidence support the claim or is it unrelated?

Common Abuses

Testimonials: opinions of agreement from respected celebrities who are not actually experts

Transfer: an association with a positively or negatively regarded person or thing in order to lend the same association to the argument

Personal attack: an attack on the person rather than the issue in hopes that if the person is opposed, the idea will be opposed

Bandwagon: the idea that everybody is doing it and you will be left out if you do not quickly join the crowd

Straw person: a setup in which a distorted form of the opponent's argument is introduced and knocked down as if to represent a totally weak opposition

Misleading analogy: a comparison of two things suggesting that they are similar when they are, in fact, distinctly different

2. Believability: Is the Support Believable?   Is the evidence acceptable or highly suspicious?

Common Abuses

   Incomplete facts: omission of factual details in order to misrepresent reality

   Misinterpreted statistics: numerical data misapplied to unrelated populations which they were never intended to represent

   Overgeneralizations: examples and anecdotes asserted to apply to all cases rather than a select few

   Questionable authority: testimonial suggesting authority from people who are not experts

3: Consistency: Is the Support Consistent?   Does the argument hold together or does it fall apart and contradict itself?

Common Abuses

   Appeals to pity: pleas to support the underdog, the person or issue that needs your help

   Appeals to emotions: highly charged language used for emotional manipulation

   Oversimplification: reduction of an issue to two simple choices, without consideration of other alternatives or "gray areas" in between

   Circular reasoning: support for the conclusion which is merely a restatement of it

Exercise 3: Evaluate Support

Read the following passage to identify the opinion, the issue, the reasons, and the evidence, as well as to evaluate the quality of the support.

Why Justice Fails
Anyone who claims it is impossible to get rid of the random violence of today's mean streets may be telling the truth, but is also missing the point. Street crime may be normal in the U.S., but it is not inevitable at such advanced levels, and the fact is that there are specific reasons for the nation's incapacity to keep its street crime down. Almost all these reasons can be traced to the American criminal justice system. It is not that there are no mechanisms in place to deal with American crime, merely that the existing ones are impractical, inefficient, anachronistic, uncooperative, and often lead to as much civic destruction as they are meant to curtail.

   Why does the system fail? For one thing, the majority of criminals go untouched by it. The police learn about one quarter of the thefts committed each year, and about less than half the robberies, burglaries and rapes. Either victims are afraid or ashamed to report crimes, or they may conclude gloomily that nothing will be done if they do. Murder is the crime the police do hear about, but only 73% of the nation's murders lead to arrest. The arrest rates for lesser crimes are astonishingly low—59% for aggravated assault in 1979, 48% for rape, 25% for robbery, 15% for burglary.

Even when a suspect is apprehended, the chances of his getting punished are mighty slim. In New York State each year there are some 130,000 felony arrests; approximately 8,000 people go to prison. There are 94,000 felony arrests in New York City; 5,000 to 6,000 serve time.

A study of such cities as Detroit, Indianapolis and New Orleans produced slightly better numbers, but nothing to counteract the exasperation of New York Police Commissioner Robert McGuire: "The criminal justice system almost creates incentives for street criminals." . . .

Roger Rosenblatt, Time, March 23, 1981

1. What is the opinion? _____

2. What is the issue? _____

3. What are the reasons? _____

4. What is the evidence? _____

5. Evaluate the quality of the support, and identify the fallacies.

_____

_____

The issue is crime, and the opinion is that crime goes unpunished. The reason offered, however, that many crimes are unreported, is not believable because you cannot report on the unreported. The statistics support the failure to arrest and convict, but the source of the data is not given. The commissioner is quoted as an authority, but his quote is an unclear opinion. The author may be speaking the truth, but the argument is flawed.

What Is Missing?

Arguments are written to persuade, and thus include the proponent's version of the convincing reasons. Writers do not usually supply the reader with many points that could be made by the other side. In analyzing an argument, ask yourself, "What is left out?" Be an advocate for the opposing point of view and guess at the evidence that would be presented. Was evidence consciously omitted because of its adverse effect on the conclusion? In the previous passage on crime, would you like to know why so few of the arrested people serve time in prison? Are they convicted or are they given other sentences?

Exercise 4: Evaluating an Argument

Read the following passages and determine the issue, the opinion, the quality of the reasons and evidence, and the missing information.

Passage A. The J. B. Factor

J.B. was a street kid from South St. Louis, a nice-looking, bright kid with a drive to be somebody. But he was impatient. Working for a living took too much time. He wanted some money immediately. One night he and a friend walked into a tavern to rob it. A cop came in and went for his gun. J.B. shot him. The cop died, and J.B. was sentenced to life imprisonment.

J.B. was tough and became a minor legend in prison. He tried to escape, and his status rose among the convicts. For a while he was poor, so he robbed other convicts of their cigarettes and commissary books. Then a friend got out of prison and started sending dope to him through a guard. He was getting amphetamine in by the ounce and selling it to other convicts. That made him a king. He used this income to start poker games and lending operations. He eventually was making more than $1,000 a month, a staggering sum in a world where the average convict might have $15 a month to spend. The average guard's salary then was only a third of what J.B. was making.

He began to feed the officials tidbits of information to convince them he was rehabilitated. J.B. would even tell the warden where to find a gallon of hooch, that sort of thing—never anything that would get another convict in trouble. He probably planted the hooch himself, then told the prison officials where to find it.

Finally he convinced them he had changed, and he was paroled.

In the free world he quickly learned there is no market for a consummate prison hustler. He may have had the brains, but he lacked the education to get a high-paying job. Instead he took a menial job and scraped by. He probably stared wistfully at the people driving Mercedes and wearing Brooks Brothers suits.

Here was a man who had everything in prison and nothing outside of it. The only people who respected him were ex-convicts.

Prison was on his mind. He periodically called the warden, probably sensing he would be going back, and wanting to ensure a job and good treatment when he did. No one expressed it better than Milton when he wrote, "Better to reign in hell than serve in heav'n."

Not long after his release, J.B. was shot and killed while attempting a robbery.

J.B. is a classic example of what is wrong with American prisons. For him, prison became an acceptable alternative, as it does for the young convicts who aspire to be like him.

J. J. Maloney, *Saturday Review,* Nov./Dec. 1983

1. What is the opinion? _____

2. What is the issue? _____

3. What are the reasons? _____

4. What is the evidence? _____

5. Evaluate the quality of the support, and identify the fallacies.

_____

_____

Passage B. Are Criminals Made or Born?

A revolution in our understanding of crime is quietly overthrowing some established doctrines. Until recently, criminologists looked for the causes of crime almost entirely in the offenders' social circumstances. There seemed to be no shortage of circumstances to blame: weakened, chaotic or broken families, ineffective schools, antisocial gangs, racism, poverty, unemployment.

Today, many learned journals and scholarly works draw a different picture. Sociological factors have not been abandoned, but increasingly it is becoming clear to many scholars that crime is the outcome of an interaction between social factors and certain biological factors, particularly for the offenders who, by repeated crimes, have made public places dangerous.

The most compelling evidence of biological factors for criminality comes from two studies—one of twins, the other of adopted boys. Since the 1920's it has been understood that twins may develop from a single fertilized egg, resulting in identical genetic endowments—identical twins—or from a pair of separately fertilized eggs that have about half their genes in common—fraternal twins. A standard procedure for estimating how important genes are to a trait is to compare the similarity between identical twins with that between fraternal twins. When identical twins are clearly more similar in a trait than fraternal twins, the trait probably has high heritability.

There have been about a dozen studies of criminality using twins. More than 1,500 pairs of twins have been studied in the United States, the Scandinavian countries, Japan, West Germany, Britain and elsewhere, and the result is qualitatively the same everywhere. Identical twins are more likely to have similar criminal records than fraternal twins. For example, the late Karl O. Christiansen, a Danish criminologist, using the Danish Twin Register, searched police, court and prison records for entries regarding twins born in a certain region of Denmark between 1881 and 1910. When an identical twin had a criminal record, Christiansen found his or her co-twin was more than

© 1993 HarperCollins College Publishers

twice as likely to have one also than when a fraternal twin had a criminal record.

James Q. Wilson and Richard J. Herrnstein, *Crime and Human Nature*

1. What is the opinion? _____

2. What is the issue? _____

3. What are the reasons? _____

4. What is the evidence? _____

5. Evaluate the quality of the support, and identify the fallacies.

_____

_____

Making Connections

The three preceding passages are about crime, each from a different perspective. After considering all three opinions, do any other issues come to mind that were not identified by you or the authors? What are these issues?

1. _____

2. _____

3. _____

Discuss these issues with your classmates.

STEP 4: MAKE A DECISION

Important decisions are rarely quick or easy. A span of incubation time is often needed for deliberating among alternatives. Allow yourself time to go over and over the arguments, and their advantages and disadvantages, from different perspectives. Good critical thinkers are persistent in seeking solutions.

At some point the reader takes a position, puts the computer chip back in storage, and moves on. The reader's decision can be *"I agree," "I disagree,"* or *"I can't tell."* For example, after considering all the arguments and evidence about Columbus, you might decide to go with a modified version of your old schema such as "He had his faults but at least he was adventurous enough to sail west to a new world."

Diane Halpern expresses the difficulty of decision making by saying, "There is never just one war fought. Each side has its own version, and rarely do

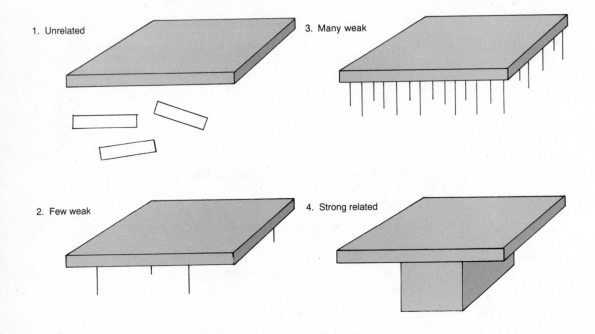

1. Unrelated
2. Few weak
3. Many weak
4. Strong related

they agree."[5] The reader must consider carefully in seeking the truth. Halpern uses a picture of a table to present four different degrees of support for a conclusion:

1. Unrelated reasons give no support.
2. A few weak reasons do not adequately support.
3. Many weak reasons can support.
4. Strong related reasons support.

Remember, in critical thinking there is no "I'm right, and you are wrong." There are, however, strong and weak arguments. Be able to list your reasons, give supporting evidence, and justify your decision.

Now that you are familiar with the critical thinking process, analyze your own thinking in making an important recent decision. The issue is choosing a college, and the question is, "Why did you decide to attend the college where you are now enrolled?" No college is perfect; many factors must be considered. Why did you decide on your particular institution? List five of your reasons and then give the support that you viewed as evidence.

1. Reason: _____

   Evidence: _____

[5]Halpern, *Thought and Knowledge,* p. 191.

2. Reason: _____

   Evidence: _____

3. Reason: _____

   Evidence: _____

4. Reason: _____

   Evidence: _____

5. Reason: _____

   Evidence: _____

How would you evaluate your own critical thinking in making a choice of colleges? Perhaps you relied heavily on information from others. Were those sources credible?

Inductive and Deductive Reasoning

In choosing a college, did you follow an inductive or deductive reasoning process? Did you collect extensive information on several colleges and then weigh the advantages and disadvantages of each? **Inductive** reasoners start by gathering data, and then, after considering all available material, they formulate a conclusion. Textbooks written in this manner give details first and lead you into the main idea or conclusion. They strive to put the parts into a logical whole and thus reason "up" from particular details to a broad generalization.

Deductive reasoners, on the other hand, follow the opposite pattern. Deductive reasoning starts with the conclusion of a previous experience and applies it to a new situation. Perhaps your college choice is a family tradition, your parents are graduates, and you have always expected to attend. Although your thinking may have begun with this premise for your choice, you may then have discovered many reasons why the college is right for you. When writers use a deductive pattern, they first give a general statement and then enumerate the reasons.

Despite this formal distinction between induction and deductive reasoning, in real life we switch back and forth as we think. Our everyday observations lead to conclusions which we then reuse and modify to form new conclusions.

Exercise 5: Deciding Positions

Read the following passages to determine the issue, evaluate the argument, and make a decision. Answer the questions which follow.

Passage A. Asian Discrimination

I especially appreciate the efforts made by many universities to increase opportunities for able people from educationally disadvantaged backgrounds. In this regard, Asian applicants have posed some complex new questions for universities. Asians, though clearly a separate and minority ethnic group, do not fit into traditional categories. Indeed, a number of universities do not regard Asian-Americans as "minority" for many reasons.

What we must deal with is how to handle the large number of Asian-Americans applying—and being admitted—to universities. These numbers often exceed by far the comparable proportion of Asian-Americans in the total national or regional college-age population. The success of such students is usually attributed to cultural factors that stress education, discipline, and achievement.

Asian-American communities are worried that de facto quotas or other limitations on admissions have been or might be established. They want assurances that Asian-American applicants are not denied admission simply because an above-average number of such applicants may be qualified.

Universities deny that they discriminate against Asian-Americans, or that they use racial quotas in any form. On the other hand, some California studies have suggested that Asian-American applicants have been accepted at a somewhat lower rate than whites. Some universities could conceivably worry that enrolling too large a concentration of Asian-Americans might harm their educational efforts by decreasing diversity, or might lead to political problems, especially in public institutions.

Questions concerning discrimination—we are speaking here, after all, about discrimination and not about affirmative action—can be answered directly and readily. At the level of fundamental principle, there cannot be disagreement: No person should suffer any disadvantage because of race.

At the practical level, there should also be no controversy. In the normal admissions process, applicants should be accepted on the basis of merit. In any case, the definition of merit and the criteria and process by which applicants are accepted should be clearly and publicly spelled out. All are entitled to know the rules of the game, and to attempt to measure performance against the stated norms.

Victor Hao Li, *The College Board Review*, Fall 1988

1. What is the opinion? _____

2. What is the issue? _____

3. What is an analogy? _____

4. What are the reasons and supporting evidence?

_____

5. Is the support relevant, believable, and consistent? Explain.

_____

6. Do you agree, disagree, or can't tell, and why?

_____

Passage B. My Life as a "Twofer"

So what's my problem? Why not take advantage of every opportunity that comes my way? The answer is: I've been in this situation before and I don't like the way it makes me feel. There's something almost insulting about these well-meaning affirmative-action searches. In the past I'd always rationalized my participation partly because I needed the break and even more because I needed the money. And as fate would have it, whenever a film- or TV-production company saw fit to round up minorities for a head count, I always came out on top. But the truth is that I've never felt good about it.

I've asked myself the obvious questions. Am I being picked for my writing ability, or to fulfill a quota? Have I been selected because I'm a "twofer"—a female Hispanic, or because they were enthralled with my deftly drawn characters and strong, original story line? My writing career, it appears, has taken a particularly tortuous course. I've gone from being a dedicated writer to dedicated *minority* writer, which seems limiting for someone who was first inspired by Woody Allen.

Truth is, that even with the aid of special programs, job assignments for writers who fit the "minority" category are inexplicably few and far between. The sad employment statistics reveal that ethnic minorities comprise less than 3 percent of our guild. Those who work do so less frequently and for a lot less money, yet the publicity harvested by the special programs creates the illusion of equal opportunity where very little exists. I don't want to seem overly gloomy. Nevertheless, my work's almost always seen on shows that have a minority star like "The Facts of Life," "What's Happening Now!" and "Punky Brewster."

Except for "The Cosby Show," minorities are not being taken seriously enough to write about their real lives outside of the ghetto. Though few of us will admit to it—for fear of speaking out or being tagged as ungrateful—we're reminded of our status in not-so-subtle ways. I remember the time I was waiting for a story meeting where I wanted to pitch several ideas. As I chatted with the production secretary, an aspiring writer herself, I could hear laughter coming from inside the conference room. Finally, the executive in charge stepped outside, followed by five young men. Judging by the look of satisfaction on their faces, it had probably been a profitable session. The executive greeted me effusively by saying, as he turned to the rest of the group, "Meet M-I-G-D-I-A V-A-R-R-R-R-E-L-A. She's one of our minority writers."

Migdia Chinea-Varela, Newsweek, December 26, 1988

1. What is the opinion? _____

2. What is the issue? _____

3. What is an analogy? _____

4. What are the reasons and supporting evidence?

   _____

5. Is the support relevant, believable, and consistent? Explain.

   _____

6. Do you agree, disagree, or can't tell, and why?

   _____

Passage C. Racism 101

At the University of California at Berkeley, Asian-American students are engaged in a different kind of struggle with the administration.

Enrollment by Asians has not declined, but in the last few years it has leveled off. Students charge that some admissions policies are deliberately designed to keep them out. Berkeley awards extra points, for example, to students who pass achievement tests in European foreign languages, but no points are awarded to students who know Chinese or Vietnamese. Asian students, like Hispanics and blacks, also say they feel alienated and receive inadequate support while at the university.

Chancellor Ira Michael Heyman denies that the university's admissions policies are discriminatory, but he recently made a public apology for not responding "more openly and less defensively" to Asian students' concerns.

One major bone of contention is the English-language program. More than half of the Asian students at Berkeley are recent immigrants, and they represent 80 percent of those enrolled in the three-semester English as a Second Language sequence. As with all the university's remedial programs, a student who fails more than one ESL course flunks out, regardless of grade-point average. Many Asian immigrants who pass their other classes do not graduate because of the English requirement.

"U.C. Berkeley considers that there are too many Asians on campus in the first place, and not enough are flunking out to need help," says Richard Ehara, a tutor at Berkeley and a member of a committee protesting the university's Asian policies. "There are no Asian counselors and they are not considered a priority for tutoring."

Student activists claim the ESL program is culturally discriminatory.

"That's why a lot of Asians flunk out of Berkeley," says Nam Nguyen, a Vietnamese-American student, "not because they can't do the work. You have to write an essay on a subject that you don't understand because of cultural differences. For instance, they ask you to debate a point in the Constitution. First of all, if you're a recent immigrant, you might not know the Constitution as well. And secondly, if it's someone from an Asian culture, most people don't debate in Asian culture. When you write a paper, it's more of a discussion. You use a lot of philosophy and a lot of quotes and stuff. And teachers don't understand why the students are writing this way."

Ruth Conniff, *The Progressive,* December 1988

1. What is the opinion? _____

2. What is the issue? _____

3. What is an analogy? _____

4. What are the reasons and supporting evidence?

   _____

5. Is the support relevant, believable, and consistent? Explain.

   _____

6. Do you agree, disagree, or can't tell, and why?

   _____

Making Connections

The three preceding passages were about discrimination. After considering all three opinions, what other issues come to mind?

1. _____

2. _____

3. _____

Discuss these issues with your classmates.

CREATIVE AND CRITICAL THINKING

A chapter on critical thinking would not be complete without an appeal for creative thinking. You may ask, "Are critical thinking and creative thinking different?" Creative thinking refers to the ability to generate many possible solutions to a problem, whereas critical thinking refers to the examination of those solutions for the selection of the best of all possibilities. Both ways of thinking are essential for good problem solving.

Diana Halpern uses the following story to illustrate creative thinking:[6]

Many years ago when a person who owed money could be thrown into jail, a merchant in London had the misfortune to owe a huge sum to a money-lender. The money-lender, who was old and ugly, fancied the merchant's beautiful teenage daughter. He proposed a bargain. He said he would cancel the merchant's debt if he could have the girl instead.

Both the merchant and his daughter were horrified at the proposal. So the cunning money-lender proposed that they let Providence decide the matter. He told them that he would put a black pebble and a white pebble into an empty money-bag and then the girl would have to pick out one of the pebbles. If she chose the black pebble she would become his wife and her father's debt would be cancelled. If she chose the white pebble she would stay with her father and the debt would still be cancelled. But if she refused to pick out a pebble her father would be thrown into jail and she would starve.

Reluctantly the merchant agreed. They were standing on a pebble-strewn path in the merchant's garden as they talked and the money-lender stooped down to pick up two pebbles. As he picked up the pebbles the girl, sharp-eyed with fright, noticed that he picked up two black pebbles and put them into the money-bag. He then asked the girl to pick out the pebble that was to decide her fate and that of her father.

If you were the girl, what would you do? Think creatively, and, without evaluating your thoughts, list at least five possible solutions. Next think critically to evaluate and then circle your final choice.

1. _____
2. _____
3. _____
4. _____
5. _____

[6]Halpern, *Thought and Knowledge*, p. 408.

© 1993 HarperCollins College Publishers

In discussing the possible solutions to the problem, Halpern talks about two kinds of creative thinking, vertical thinking and lateral thinking. **Vertical thinking** is a straightforward and logical way of thinking that would typically result in a solution like, "Call his hand and expose the money-lender as a crook." The disadvantage of this solution is that the merchant is still in debt so the original problem has still not been solved. **Lateral thinking,** on the other hand, is a way of thinking *around* a problem or even redefining the problem. DeBono[7] suggests that a lateral thinker might redefine the problem from "What happens when I get the black pebble?" to "How can I avoid the black pebble?" Using this new definition of the problem and other seemingly irrelevant information, DeBono's lateral thinker came up with a winning solution. When the girl reaches into the bag, she should fumble and drop one of the stones on the "pebble-strewn path." The color of the pebble she dropped could then be determined by looking at the one left in the bag. Since the remaining pebble is black, the dropped one that is now mingled in the path must have been white. Any other admission would expose the money-lender as a crook. Probably the heroine thought of many alternatives, but thanks to her ability ultimately to generate a novel solution and evaluate its effectiveness, the daughter and the merchant lived happily free of debt.

DeBono[8] defines vertical thinking as "digging the same hole deeper" and lateral thinking as "digging the hole somewhere else (p. 195)." For example, after many years of researching a cure for smallpox, Dr. Edward Jenner stopped focusing on patients who were sick with the disease and instead began studying groups of people who never seemed to get the smallpox. Shortly thereafter, using this different perspective, Dr. Jenner discovered the clues that led him to the smallpox vaccine.

Creative and critical thinking enable us to see new relationships. We blend knowledge and see new similarities and differences, a new sequence of events, or a new solution for an old problem. We create new knowledge by using old learning differently.

SUMMARY

Thinking critically means deliberating in a purposeful, organized manner in order to assess the value of information, both old and new. Critical thinkers do not start from scratch, but build on previous knowledge or schemata to forge new relationships. They question, challenge, and evaluate in much the same way as a courtroom jury considers the relevance, believability, and consistency of the arguments and evidence in making a decision on an issue. Both critical and creative thinking help us see old relationships from a new perspective.

[7] E. DeBono, *New Think: The Use of Lateral Thinking in the Generation of New Ideas* (New York: Basic Books, 1968).

[8] E. DeBono, "Information Processing and New Ideas—Lateral and Vertical Thinking," in S. J. Parnes, R. B. Noller, and A. M. Biondi, eds., *Guide to Creative Action: Revised Edition of Creative Behavior Guidebook* (New York: Charles Scribner's Sons).

Selection **1**

LITERATURE

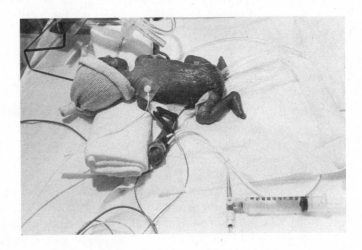

Stage 1

Preview

The author's main purpose is to argue for more police.

agree ☐   disagree ☐

This selection is narrative rather than expository.

agree ☐   disagree ☐

After reading this selection, I will need to know what happened to the child in the house.

agree ☐   disagree ☐

Activate Schema

Who is the youngest person you know who is taking drugs?
From what kind of environment did this person come?

Learning Strategy

Seek to understand the effects of the mother's drug addiction on the child and on society.

Stage 2: Integrate Knowledge While Reading

Use the thinking strategies as you read:

1. Predict 2. Picture 3. Relate 4. Monitor 5. Fix up

CHILD OF CRACK

From Michele L. Norris, *The Washington Post National Weekly Edition,* September 11–17, 1989

Dooney Waters, a thickset six-year-old missing two front teeth, sat hunched over a notebook, drawing a family portrait.

First he sketched a stick-figure woman smoking a pipe twice her size. A coil of smoke rose from the pipe, which held a white square he called a "rock." Above that, he drew a picture of himself, another stick figure with tears falling from its face.

"Drugs have wrecked my mother," Dooney said as he doodled. "Drugs have wrecked a lot of mothers and fathers and children and babies. If I don't be careful, drugs are going to wreck me too."

His was a graphic rendering of the life of a child growing up in what police and social workers have identified as a crack house, an apartment in Washington Heights, a federally subsidized complex in Landover, Maryland, where people congregated to buy and use drugs. Dooney's life was punctuated by days when he hid behind his bed to eat sandwiches sent by teachers who knew he would get nothing else. Nights when Dooney wet his bed because people were "yelling and doing drugs and stuff." And weeks in which he barely saw his thirty-two-year-old mother, who spent most of her time searching for drugs.

Addie Lorraine Waters, who described herself as a "slave to cocaine," said she let drug dealers use her apartment in exchange for the steady support of her habit. The arrangement turned Dooney's home into a modern-day opium den where pipes, spoons, and needles were in supply like ketchup and mustard at a fast-food restaurant. . . .

Addie's apartment was on Capital View Drive, site of more than a dozen slayings last year. Yet, the locks were removed from the front door to allow an unyielding tide of addicts and dealers to flow in and out. Children, particularly toddlers, often peered inside to ask: "Is my mommy here?"

While he was living in the crack house, Dooney was burned when a woman tossed boiling water at his mother's face in a drug dispute, and his right palm was singed when his thirteen-year-old half brother handed him a soft drink can that had been used to heat crack cocaine on the stove.

Teachers say that Dooney often begged to be taken to their homes, once asking if he could stay overnight in his classroom. "I'll sleep on the floor," Dooney told an instructor in Greenbelt Center Elementary School's after-school counseling and tutorial program. "Please don't make me go home. I don't want to go back there."

Dooney was painfully shy or exhaustively outgoing, depending largely on whether he was at home or in school—the one place where he could relax. In class, he played practical jokes on friends and passed out kisses and hugs to teachers. But his mood darkened when he boarded a bus for home.

On Saturday, April 29, Dooney was sitting in the living room near his mother when a fifteen-year-old drug dealer burst in and tossed a pan of boiling water, a weapon that anybody with a stove could afford. Dooney, his mother, and two neighbors recalled that the dealer then plopped down on a sofa and watched as Dooney's weeping mother soothed the burns on her shoulder and neck. Dooney also was at home when another adolescent enforcer leaned through an open window on Sunday, May 14 and pitched a blend of bleach and boiling water in the face of nineteen-year-old Clifford E. Bernard, a regular in the apartment, for ignoring a $150 debt.

"People around here don't play when you owe them money," said Sherry Brown, twenty-five, a friend of Addie Waters who frequented the apartment. Brown said she smokes crack every day and has given birth to two crack-addicted babies in the past three years. "These young boys around here will burn you in a minute if you so much as look at them the wrong way," she said. "I'm telling you sure as I'm sitting here, crack has made people crazy."

Almost everyone was welcome at "Addie's place." Her patrons included some unlikely characters, but as one said, "Addie don't turn nobody away." Not the fifteen-year-old who in May burned her furniture and clothing intentionally with a miniature blow torch. Not even the twenty-one-year-old man who "accidentally" shot her thirteen-year-old son, Frank Russell West, five inches above the heart last Dec. 16. Police ascribed the shooting to a "drug deal gone bad."

Dooney was sleeping when Russell, shot in the left shoulder, stumbled back into the apartment. Dooney will not talk about the night his half brother was shot except to say, "Russell was shot 'cause of drugs."

Waters did not press charges against Edward "June" Powell, the man police charged with shooting Russell. Powell, whose trial has been discontinued because he did not have an attorney, is out on bail. "He didn't mean to do it," said Waters, who referred to Powell as a close friend of the family. "It was an accident. He meant to kill someone else." . . .

Dooney's mother and others who congregated in her apartment were bound by a common desperation for drugs. The majority, in their late twenties or early thirties, described themselves as "recreational" drug users until they tried the highly addictive crack. Many said they had swapped welfare checks, food stamps, furniture,

85 and sexual favors to support their craving for crack. They had lost
jobs, spouses, homes, and self-respect. Nearly all were in danger of
losing children, too.

The Prince George's County Department of Social Services was
investigating charges of parental neglect against many of the people
90 who frequented Waters's apartment. But they rarely took the county's
investigations seriously. Some would joke about timid caseworkers
who were too "yellow" to visit Washington Heights or would pass
around letters in which officials threatened to remove children from
their custody. The problem, as in Dooney's case, was that the county's
95 threats lacked teeth. Caseworkers were usually so overloaded that they
rarely had time to bring cases to court, even after they had
corroborated charges of abuse and neglect.

Prince George's County police said they knew about Waters's
operation but never found enough drugs in the apartment to charge
100 her or others. "The problem is that drugs don't last long up there,"
said Officer Alex Bailey, who patrols the Washington Heights
neighborhood. "They use them up as soon as they arrive."

Such explanations seemed lost on Dooney.

"Everybody knows about the drugs at my house," he said with a
105 matter-of-fact tone not common to a first-grader. "The police know,
too, but they don't do nothing about it. Don't nobody do nothing
about it," he said.

Police did raid Dooney's apartment on Saturday, May 13, after they
were called there by neighbors who complained about noise. "They
110 were looking for the drugs," Dooney said two days later, as his eyes
grew full of tears. "They took all the clothes out of my mother's
closets. They threw it all on my mother. They called my mother names."

Dooney also said he was afraid of the police, and when asked why,
he inquired, "How do you spell the word 'shoot'?" Supplied with a
115 notebook and pen, he wrote the word slowly in large, shaky letters
and then repeatedly punched the pen into the paper to form a circle
of black marks. Pausing a minute, he drew a person holding a pipe, a
smiling face atop a body with a circle in her belly. "That's my
mother," Dooney said, pointing to the figure's face. He moved his
120 finger toward the circle. "And that's a bullet hole."

Since kindergarten, Dooney has pulled himself out of bed almost
every school morning without the help of adults or alarm clocks, said
his mother, who boasted about his independence. Asked how he got
himself up in the morning, Dooney tapped a finger to his forehead
125 and said, "My brain wakes me up. I get up when it gets light outside."

Dooney rarely bathed or brushed his hair before he went to school
while he was living with his mother. The bathroom was inoperable
during the period that a *Washington Post* reporter and photographer

regularly visited. The toilet overflowed with human waste. Stagnant
water stood in the bathtub. There was no soap, no shampoo, no toilet
paper or toothpaste.

The children's lives declined in step with their parents. Dooney's
thirteen-year-old half brother dropped out of the seventh grade last
fall and has been arrested six times in two years on charges ranging
from jumping trains to stealing cars.

Both of Waters's sons begged her to seek help. In the last three
years, addiction had whittled her body from a size 16 to a size 5. Her
eyes were sunken, underlined by tufts of purplish skin. Her
complexion, which she said was once "the envy" of her three sisters,
was lifeless, almost like vinyl.

Pictures in a blue photo album she kept in her living room show a
more attractive Addie L. Waters—a buxom woman with radiant eyes,
bright red lipstick, and a voluminous hairdo. Dooney paged through
the photo album one afternoon and said, "My mother used to be pretty."

Dooney comes from a family with a legacy of addiction. His mother
said she bought her first bag of drugs, a $5 sack of marijuana, from
her alcoholic father in the late seventies. Dooney's father said he
started smoking marijuana in high school and moved on to using PCP,
speed, and powder cocaine.

Dooney's father says he smoked his first hit of crack about two
years ago, when a girlfriend encouraged him to try the drug.
Dooney's mother also tried crack for the first time with a lover, a
boyfriend who said it "was the best high around."

When she first started smoking crack, Waters said, she would lock
herself in the bathroom to hide from her two sons. The charade
didn't last long. One evening Russell threw open the bathroom door
and discovered his mother with a plastic pipe in her mouth.

"I tried to hide it and he saw me," says Waters, who went on to
describe how Russell, then in the fifth grade, slapped her several
times and flushed the drugs down the toilet. "By him seeing me, it
really affected me," Waters says. "I left it alone for about an hour."

Eventually she says, Russell's reactions became less extreme, and he
got involved with the drug trade himself by selling soap chips on the
street to unsuspecting buyers.

Waters will take the blame for Russell, but she maintained that it
would not be her fault if Dooney started using or selling drugs.

"If he does, it won't be because of me," Waters said. "I learned with
Russell so I tell [Dooney] not to smoke or sell drugs. It's my fault that
I'm doing it but I think [Dooney] knows better. I tell him all the time
that he don't want to live like me."

Crack became such a part of Dooney's life that he could list the
steps for cooking it before he could tie his shoelaces. Perhaps that's

why he sometimes scoffed at school programs designed to teach
pupils to "just say no" to drugs.

175 Dooney's teachers began to suspect that his mother had a drug
problem shortly after he entered kindergarten.

"It was rather sudden," said Janet Pelkey, Dooney's kindergarten
teacher. "He wasn't bathed. He became very angry and started striking
out. He started gobbling down food whenever he got it, even candy
180 and snacks in the classroom. It was obvious that something was going
on at home."

Dooney's condition worsened when he entered first grade last
September, teachers said. He was given to fits of screaming and crying
and came to school wearing torn and filthy clothes. "It was almost
185 like he was shellshocked when he came to school . . . ," Field said.
"He is such a sad little boy. He walks around with his head down and
he's always sucking his little thumb."

"When I discovered what he was going through at home, I thought,
'My goodness, it's amazing that he even gets to school,' " Field said.

190 Acting on the advice of teachers, the Prince George's County
Department of Child Protective Services investigated Dooney's mother
in April 1988.

"Based on the provided investigative information, the allegations of
neglect have been indicated," child protective services worker
195 Conchita A. Woods wrote in a letter to Waters dated April 24, 1989, a
year after the investigation began. But a caseworker said that it would
be "months, maybe even years" before they could seek to remove
Dooney from his mother's custody.

Russell Brown, the investigator, said he had about twenty cases on
200 his desk just like Waters's.

"We have a lot of cases that are much worse than that," Brown said.
"There's probably not a whole lot I can do" for Dooney. Brown said
that he does not have time to go through the arduous process of
taking a child from a parent unless there is imminent danger.

Skill Development: Explore for Understanding

To explore your understanding of the passage, answer and discuss the following questions. Use your own paper.

1. What observations and evidence led the teachers to conclude that
   Dooney had severe problems at home?
2. Why was Addie's apartment the crack house?
3. What physical injuries did Dooney receive while in the crack house?

4. What violence did Dooney witness at the apartment?
5. Why was Dooney afraid of the police?
6. What happened to Dooney's half brother Russell?
7. What is the mother's view of her responsibility for Russell? What is your view?
8. How did the teachers try to help Dooney?
9. What do the case workers of the Child Protective Services do to help Dooney?
10. What future would you predict for Dooney? Why?

Skill Development: Think Critically

Answer the following questions in order to determine the issue, evaluate the argument, and make a decision. Discuss the answers with classmates.

1. What does the author see as the controversial issue in this article?
2. How have you encountered this issue on a personal basis? Draw a personal analogy.
3. What is the author's opinion on this issue?
4. What is the opposing point of view?
5. What reasons does the author give to support her opinion?
6. Are the reasons relevant, believable, and consistent, or do they contain tricks of persuasion? Explain.
7. What evidence supports the reasons?
8. Is the evidence relevant, believable, and consistent, or does it contain tricks of persuasion? Explain.
9. What additional information would you like to have on the subject?
10. What is your own opinion on the issue?
11. Give reasons and predict the evidence you might use to support your opinion.
12. What other issues come to mind on this subject?

Connecting and Reflecting

Child abuse is a topic of great concern with no easy answers. Parents argue that children should stay with the family although the home situation may be less than desirable and no family member is perfect. Critics say that the courts have not been innovative in responding to the needs of children, and that judges continue to return children to parents who have a history of abuse. What conditions do you feel merit removing a child from its biological parents? What are the rights of the child, the parent, and the state? Read the following passage for a historical perspective. Many people would say that what happened to Anna and Isabelle could not happen today, but others would argue that it happens every day, just in different ways. **In the last few years, what case of child abuse in the news has made you angry?** Describe the case as best as you can from your memory of past news reports, and **explain what you feel the state should have done.**

Anna and Isabelle

Anna was an "illegitimate" child born in a rural midwestern American setting after 1930. Anna's mother's father locked the infant in an upstairs room in his home. Here, Anna received only enough care from her mother to keep her alive. She had no communicative contact with other persons and was moved infrequently from one position to another and constantly lived in her own body wastes. When Anna was six years old, she was removed from her room by local law-enforcement authorities. Anna could not walk or talk and was reported to show no "intelligent" behavior. She was reported to be apathetic, emotionless, indifferent to the movement of other people, badly emaciated, and made no efforts to feed, dress, or care for herself. Kingsley Davis (1949), in describing Anna's behavior, noted that her condition at six years of age showed how little her purely biological resources alone contributed to her having a personality and an ability to act in meaningful cultural and social ways.

Anna died at 10½ years of age from hemorrhagic jaundice. However, in the four years following her removal from her grandfather's home, she made considerable progress in learning a variety of cultural and social behavior forms. At her death, Anna had learned to talk in simple phrases, to repeat words, and had tried to carry on conversations with the adults and other children in the "county home" setting where she lived. She could follow simple verbal directions, identify some colors, build with play blocks, and responded emotionally to attractive and unattractive pictures. Anna had learned to walk and could run without falling. She had also cared for herself in a rudimentary fashion. Anna cuddled a doll and was said to have a "pleasant disposition" in the time before her death. It is not possible to determine fully the amount of Anna's cultural and social learning in the 4½ years following her discovery in a situation of nearly complete cultural and social isolation. But it is clear that she made extraordinary progress in cultural and social learning in a very brief time. The specialists familiar with Anna's case have concluded that, at her death, she probably had the mental and social age of a "normal" 2½- to 3-year-old American child and probably was somewhat "retarded" at her birth in her capacity to learn.

Isabelle also was an "illegitimate" child, born after 1930 in a rural midwestern American setting. Following her birth, Isabelle was placed by her mother's father in a darkened room with her deaf and mute mother and was kept locked away from all contacts with other persons until she was six years old. Then, under court order, local law-enforcement officials moved her to a hospital. Isabelle suffered from rickets, a childhood disease characterized by softening of bone from lack of vitamin D or calcium or both, and was reported to have exhibited both "fear" and "hostility" to the medical and psychological specialists who first examined her. When she was admitted to the hospital, Isabelle was believed to be a "feebleminded child," and she was placed in a specially designed program to help her learn.

Initially, Isabelle showed no response to her special training program. Then, after several months, she began to use simple words and proceeded rapidly through each one of the stages of cultural and social learning said by psychologists to be typical of American infants and young children. Isabelle could use short sentences three months after first speaking. Thirteen months after using her first word, Isabelle could read words and sentences, write clearly, add to ten, and retell simple stories. Seventeen months after using her first words, Isabelle had an estimated vocabulary of between 1400 and 2000 words and could easily ask and answer complex questions. Isabelle's dramatic progress in learning can be summarized in this way: In approximately two years, Isabelle acquired many of the cultural and social skills it had been believed to take five to six years for most American children to learn.

Later, Isabelle was placed in a public school and, at fourteen years of age, was in the sixth grade, where her teachers, unaware of her earlier life, reported her to be a competent and emotionally well-adjusted student. Isabelle is said to have married and to have had her own normal children, raised without any special problems.

Thomas Williams, *Cultural Anthropology**

*From Thomas Rhys Williams, *Cultural Anthropology,* © 1990, pages 157-158. Reprinted by permission of Prentice Hall, Englewood Cliffs, New Jersey.

© 1993 HarperCollins College Publishers

Selection

2

BUSINESS

Stage 1

Preview

The author's main purpose is to criticize the Japanese.

agree ☐   disagree ☐

The overall pattern of organization is definition-example.

agree ☐   disagree ☐

After reading this selection, I will need to know how Japanese businesses improve productivity.

agree ☐   disagree ☐

Activate Schema

Why have the Japanese moved ahead of the Americans in the automobile industry?

Learning Strategy

Read to find out the success secrets of Japanese businesses and the impact Japanese ownership is having on American workers.

Stage 2: Integrate Knowledge While Reading

Use the thinking strategies as you read:

1. Predict 2. Picture 3. Relate 4. Monitor 5. Fix up

JAPAN'S INFLUENCE ON AMERICAN LIFE

From Stratford P. Sherman, *Fortune,* June 17, 1991

Remember when America was the greatest country in the whole wide world? After World War II a euphoric sense of supremacy—*No. 1, by God, and proud of it!*—seemed the birthright of U.S. citizens. But the feeling has faded, and even the whipping America gave Saddam
5 Hussein couldn't quite bring it back. The changed mood accompanies a new respect for the Japanese, who rose to mastery and power while Americans were horsing around with LBOs, credit cards, and cocaine.

Suddenly, all around the U.S., Japanese are settling in as neighbors, classmates, and employers—over 200,000 at last count, with more
10 coming all the time. Many are executives whose decisions affect thousands of workers. Unlike earlier arrivals on these shores, these people have no intention of becoming Americans. They come not as immigrants, but as expatriates—and conquerors.

Japan has much more to offer than the business ideas, such as
15 just-in-time manufacturing, that already have altered the habits of many U.S. corporations. What most Americans don't yet see is Japan's deeper effect on their society. The barriers of language and race are formidable, and Japanese expatriates often seem more eager to fit in than impose their culture on the U.S.

20 But buy a round of drinks for the patrons at Rumors, a dimly lit bar on the outskirts of Lexington, Kentucky, and they'll talk your ear off about Japan's growing influence. The bar is a few miles down the road from Toyota's Georgetown plant—where 68 Japanese, 3,650 Americans, and a whole lot of robots build the Camry sedans that J.D.
25 Power & Associates rates as the nation's top-quality auto.

When asked why Japan so often bests America in business, Buck Arnett, 31, doesn't flinch: "It's our own damn fault." The others all nod and raise their brewskies in agreement. "Hell, yes!" they say.

That recognition represents a turning point for grass-roots America.
30 Says David Halberstam, whose book *The Reckoning* explored U.S.-Japanese competition in autos: "It's the end of an illusion we've had since the Battle of Midway, that if America does it, it's the best." Now Americans are asking themselves why they can't do as well as the Japanese.

35 When folks in Kentucky and elsewhere first saw Japanese companies clobber their U.S. counterparts years ago, many reacted as if the Japanese had landed from Mars, equipped with some kind of extra-smart mutant genes. But as greater numbers of ordinary Americans meet Japanese face to face, many respond just like Barbara
40 Tinnell, 26, a team leader at the Toyota plant, who has spent six weeks in Japan on training tours. Says she: "From how good they're doing you almost expect the Japanese to be superior people—but

they're not different, really." Perceptions like hers are priceless
because they imply a responsibility to measure up.

45   But how? Americans like Tinnell are finding one answer in the
Japanese management practice of *kaizen,* or continuous improvement—
and in the enthusiasm for learning that is the real force behind it.
Japan's towering achievement in manufacturing is the sum of
countless small advances by individual workers and companies. For

50   Americans raised to regard learning as something that happens in
school, that is a profoundly new way of looking at things.

    "I don't think there's any question that the Japanese will change
America. I've seen a change right before my eyes," says Alan
Sugarman, Fort Lee's superintendent of schools. He is a fervent

55   believer in multiculturalism, the idea that ethnic groups can no longer
be expected to abandon their distinctiveness in the traditional melting
pot: "We can't stampede newcomers into being Americans anymore."
But that's okay, he says. The Asian kids' diligent study habits set the
standard for everyone else, leading American students to work harder.

60   Achievement scores in Fort Lee are rising, and 90% of high school
graduates go to college, vs. 75% in the mid-seventies.

    The Japanese are shrewd employers. In Kentucky, which lost many
sons in World War II—Harrodsburg has a memorial to victims of the
Bataan death march—the Japanese hire mostly young people with no

65   memory of that war and little chance of finding a better job anywhere
else. The Japanese can be more demanding than boot-camp drill
instructors, but they pay well and reward outstanding performance.
And the plants make products that sell, which translates into pride
and job security for workers.

70   Some become enthusiasts. Dean Lee has been promoted twice in
his three years at Hitachi; only 27, he manages the plant's production
planning. An intelligent man who holds a degree in industrial
technology from Morehead State University, Lee sounds like a Moonie
when he says, with conviction, "We're an American company"—as if

75   Japanese ownership and management counted for nothing.

    Working for Hitachi, he says, "has just changed me totally." Among
the lessons learned from his employers: patient deliberation in
making decisions. Instead of just buying a car this year, Lee pondered
his choices for four months before settling on a Mercury, which, he

80   notes, uses Hitachi parts. He recently sold his house but plans to rent
an apartment and carefully consider his options before buying again.

    John Beets, 35, a Toyota team leader, learned a lot by observing the
Japanese at play. "They know how to relax," he says, "but a party or a
golf game with them lasts two or three hours at the maximum—then

85   the schedule kicks in and they go off somewhere else. Now I tend to
set schedules for myself more. I make sure I have flexibility but also
try to get something done at certain points along the day."

For Karen Satterly, 24, a born-again Baptist who assembles circuitboards at Hitachi, the lesson is more personal. In her high
90 school she says many Americans felt inferior to their few Japanese schoolmates, the offspring of expatriate managers. When she joined Hitachi, she felt uncertain of her ability to meet the company's standards. "The Japanese are such particular people," she explains. In time Satterly learned how to make the parts the precise way her
95 employers want them. She's proud of her work now, and of herself. "I think a lot of people feel inferior, and that tends to make them a little mean," she says. "That's just something they have to overcome."

Experiences like these are the essence of Japan's influence in America: an accumulation of personal discoveries, small in
100 themselves, that could add up to something big.

Skill Development: Explore for Understanding

To explore your understanding of the passage, answer and discuss the following questions. Use your own paper.

1. Why do Americans no longer feel a euphoric sense of supremacy?
2. Why have American workers sometimes felt inferior to the Japanese?
3. How have Japanese companies surpassed American companies in achievement?
4. How have the Japanese influenced American thinking?
5. What do you think a Japanese worker in America would say about American workers?
6. What facts suggest that America is changing?

Skill Development: Think Critically

Answer the following questions in order to determine the issue, evaluate the argument, and make a decision. Discuss the answers with classmates.

1. What does the author see as the controversial issue in this article?
2. How have you encountered this issue on a personal basis? Draw a personal analogy.
3. What is the author's opinion on this issue?
4. What is the opposing point of view?
5. What reasons does the author give to support his opinion?
6. Are the reasons relevant, believable, and consistent, or do they contain tricks of persuasion? Explain.
7. What evidence supports the reasons?
8. Is the evidence relevant, believable, and consistent, or does it contain tricks of persuasion? Explain.

9. What additional information would you like to have on the subject?
10. What is your own opinion on the issue?
11. Give reasons and predict the evidence you might use to support your opinion.
12. What other issues come to mind on this subject?

Connecting and Reflecting

American companies are now studying Japanese businesses in order to learn how to improve our lagging position in the competitive world marketplace. Many workers say that American companies should also seek the advice of their own employees. If your own company or a previous employer were seeking such advice, what would you suggest? Begin by **giving a brief description of the mission and operation** of the company for which you now work or have previously worked. Then **explain five suggestions that you believe would lead to improved productivity and greater long-range success for the company.** Read the following passage to gain additional understanding.

Managing Better

The task of developing committed employees, never easy, may be even more difficult in the future than it has been in the past. For example, managing human resources in the future will present entirely different challenges for corporations and the old methods will be, for the most part, anachronistic. The traditional workforce of yesterday, whose main focus was salary and salary-equivalent benefits, who found strength as part of a collective group that rarely *intellectually* challenged management, has been replaced by a non-docile, individualist, provocative and creative body of mixed gender, mixed language, and mixed work objectives. Even to think of applying the quick fix remedy of emulating Japanese management techniques is nonsense.

We are not a homogeneous people similar to the Japanese, and our culture is in many instances in direct opposition to many of their business practices. The heterogeneity of the U.S. population is not a second-order effect, it is primary to our thinking and behavioral patterns. It must be an important aspect of our strategic planning of human resource management.

Sheldon Weinig, in D. Obey and P. Sarbance, *The Changing American Economy*

Selection

3
SCIENCE

"Hard to believe this was all rain forest just fifteen years ago."

Drawing by Dedini; © 1990
The New Yorker Magazine, Inc.

Stage 1

Preview

The author's main purpose is to heighten environmental awareness.

agree ☐   disagree ☐

The selection is expository rather than narrative.

agree ☐   disagree ☐

After reading this selection, I will need to know why the tropical forests should be saved.

agree ☐   disagree ☐

Activate Schema

How did the burning oil fields in Kuwait during the Persian Gulf War affect other nations?

Learning Strategy

Seek to understand how the tropical forests affect the well-being of the planet.

Stage 2: Integrate Knowledge While Reading

Use the thinking strategies as you read:

1. Predict 2. Picture 3. Relate 4. Monitor 5. Fix up

WHY SAVE TROPICAL FORESTS?

From *The New York Times,* November 8, 1986

Many Americans feel that saving the world's tropical forests warrant about as much concern as the snail darter. In Europe and the United States, they say, deforestation was the inevitable and desirable consequence of economic progress; why, therefore, should it be any

5   different in the largely underdeveloped nations where the world's tropical forests are to be found?

It *is* different, and our failure to appreciate the difference stems largely from our inability to distinguish between temperate and tropical conditions. The rich soils and relative biological simplicity of

10   the temperate world enhance forest conversion and eventual reforestation. In tropical forest regions, soils tend to be poor. Life supporting nutrients are stored not in soils but in the trees. Remove them and the whole fragile system collapses. History is littered with examples of failed efforts to convert large areas of tropical forest to

15   agriculture, cattle ranching or other "modern" uses.

People and nature both end up losers when the tropical forest is clumsily invaded. To begin with, such forests supply the world with goods—hardwoods, rubber, fruits and nuts, drugs and medicines and fragrances and spices—that often cannot be successfully raised in any

20   but natural conditions. Harvesting beyond sustainable limits has already brought some of the tropical forests' best hardwoods— Brazilian rosewood for example—close to extinction.

The tropical forest is also a biological warehouse. Estimates of the total number of species on the planet range up to 30 million, of

25   which only 1.6 million have been identified. It is further estimated that tropical forests, while occupying only 7 percent of the earth's surface, may contain as many as half of all the earth's forms of life. This means that only a tiny fraction of all tropical forest species has so far been studied, and despite the drug industry's increasing

30   reliance on computer modeling, genetic engineering and other laboratory devices, concerned biologists regard the heedless

squandering of the tropical forests' known and unknown resources as a major tragedy.

Similarly, we depend on a small group of plants—corn, rice, wheat
35 and the like—for a large part of our sustenance. From time to time, plant pathologists have found, the commonly used strains of these plants require genetic fortification from the wild to protect them from blight and disease. Since many such plants originated in tropical areas and only later were cultivated elsewhere, the primeval forests of the
40 tropics represent a vast genetic storehouse of great potential value to everyone.

Left untouched, tropical forests also contribute to the stability of the world's climate. But when the forests are burned, the carbon released plays an important role in the buildup of atmospheric gases
45 producing the "greenhouse effect," which is causing a warming trend on the planet. The consequences of this trend could be profound. America's corn belt could become a subtropical region, while the melting of the polar ice cap could cause sea levels to rise and lead to drastic losses of coastal land.

50 In view of all these factors, one might ask why the attack against the tropical forest continues so relentlessly. The answer is that even the infertile tropical forest is often capable of providing short-term economic benefits to individuals and corporations. Given the human propensity to enjoy one last meal if the alternative seems to be no
55 meal at all, the present defoliation will probably continue unless a revolution in public and official attitudes—equivalent to the dramatic change of the 1980's in how smoking is perceived and handled— comes to the rescue at the 11th hour.

Skill Development: Explore for Understanding

To explore your understanding of the passage, answer and discuss the following questions. Use your own paper.

1. How do tropical and temperate soils differ?
2. Why do scientists feel that squandering the resources of the tropical forest is a major tragedy?
3. Why is the tropical forest called a tropical warehouse?
4. How can plants in the tropical forest be used to fight against crop diseases elsewhere in the world?
5. How does the tropical forest relate to the world's climate?
6. Why does destruction of the tropical forest continue?

Skill Development: Think Critically

Answer the following questions in order to determine the issue, evaluate the argument, and make a decision. Discuss the answers with classmates.

1. What does the author see as the controversial issue in this article?
2. How have you encountered this issue on a personal basis? Draw a personal analogy.
3. What is the author's opinion on this issue?
4. What is the opposing point of view?
5. What reasons does the author give to support his opinion?
6. Are the reasons relevant, believable, and consistent or do they contain tricks of persuasion?
7. What evidence supports the reasons?
8. Is the evidence relevant, believable, and consistent, or does it contain tricks of persuasion?
9. What additional information would you like to have on the subject?
10. What is your own opinion on the issue?
11. Give reasons and predict the evidence you might use to support your opinion.
12. What other issues come to mind on this subject?

Connecting and Reflecting

Saving the planet cannot be accomplished merely through the conservation efforts of Americans. All nations share the same earth, use its air and oceans, and deplete each other's resources. Review recent history and **describe at least five abuses or disasters that have occurred in one nation and produced adverse effects in another.** Collaborate with classmates on this assignment. Read the following for additional information on the interconnected nature of our planet.

Will Earth Survive Man?
Oceans inevitably expand as they are heated. The global "warming" already under way could therefore push sea levels everywhere to more than six feet. One third of the world's population that lives within 60 kilometres of coastlines would be threatened.

A rise of less than two feet in sea level might inundate 27 percent of Bangladesh, displacing 25 million people. Egypt could lose 20 percent of its productive land, the United States, between 50 and 80 percent of its coastal wetlands. A six-foot rise could wipe out the 1,190-island Maldivian archipelago.

If the Arctic and the Antarctic glaciers were to melt, sea levels would rise nearly 300 feet, flooding many major world cities and all ports.

Average global temperatures may rise by 4.5 degrees centigrade by the year 2030. To understand the magnitude of this occurrence, one only must realize that the planet's climate has not varied by more than 2 degrees centigrade over the past 10,000 years and that during the last Ice Age global temperatures averaged some 5 degrees colder than now.

A six-foot sea level rise, dramatic as that might be, would be among the milder consequences of a global warming. Agriculture would be hardest hit. Wheat production would have to move north, where depleted soils could result in crop reduction. The production of rice—crucial to the diets of 60 percent of the world's population—
would suffer in a drier world. Dust bowls, dying forests, unbearably hot cities, more frequent storms, forest fires and outbreaks of pestilence and disease would also occur.

U.N. Chronicle, 1988

GRAPHIC ILLUSTRATIONS

- What do graphics do?
- How do you read a diagram?

  a table?

  a map?

  a pie graph?

  a bar graph?

  a line graph?

  a flowchart?

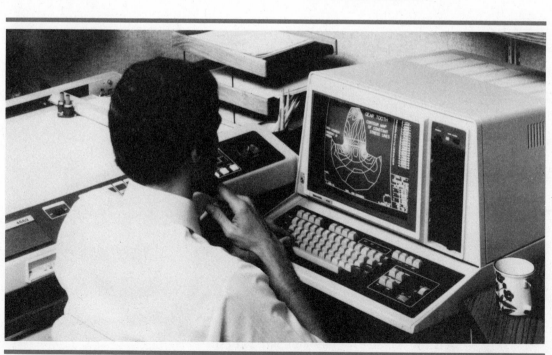

WHAT GRAPHICS DO

If a picture is worth a thousand words, a graphic illustration is worth at least several pages of facts and figures. Graphics express complex interrelationships in simplified form. Instead of plodding through repetitious data, you can glance at a chart, a map, or a graph and immediately see how everything fits together as well as how one part compares with another. Instead of reading several lengthy paragraphs and trying to visualize comparisons, you can study an organized design. The graphic illustration is a logically constructed aid for understanding many small bits of information.

Graphic illustrations are generally used for the following reasons.

1. **To condense.** Pages of repetitious, detailed information can be organized into one explanatory design.
2. **To clarify.** Processes and interrelationships can be more clearly defined through visual representations.
3. **To convince.** Developing trends and gross inequities can be forcefully dramatized.

There are five kinds of graphic illustrations: (1) diagrams, (2) tables, (3) maps, (4) graphs, and (5) flowcharts. All are used in textbooks, and the choice of which is best to use depends on the type of material presented. Study the following explanations of the different graphic forms.

HOW TO READ GRAPHIC MATERIAL

1. Read the title and get an overview. What is it about?
2. Look for footnotes and read italicized introductory material.
   Identify the who, where, and how.
   How and when were the data collected?
   Who collected the data?
   How many persons were included on the survey?
   Do the researchers seem to have been objective or biased?
   Considering the above information, does the study seem valid?
3. Read the labels.
   What do the vertical columns and the horizontal rows represent?
   Are the numbers in thousands or millions?
   What does the legend represent?
4. Notice the trends and find the extremes.
   What are the highest and lowest rates?
   What is the average rate?
   How do the extremes compare with the total?
   What is the percentage of increase or decrease?

5. Draw conclusions and formulate future exam questions.
   What does the information mean?
   What needs to be done with the information?
   What wasn't included?
   Where do we go from here?

   This chapter contains explanations and exercises for five types of graphic illustration. Read the explanations, study the illustrations, and respond to the statements as instructed.

Exercise 1: Diagrams

A *diagram* is an outline drawing or picture of an object or a process. It shows the labeled parts of a complicated form such as the muscles of the human body, the organizational makeup of a company's management and production teams, or the directional flow of a natural ecological system.

Read the following passage and refer to the diagram to aid your comprehension.

The Vertebrate Brain

Comparing the anatomical structures of the brain in five classes of vertebrates (cartilaginous fish, amphibian, reptile, bird, and mammal) reveals general evolutionary trends and specific trends in specialization. (a) Note the relatively large olfactory lobes in the shark's brain. It clearly reflects the importance of chemical detection to this predator. (b) The frog feeds by visual means, as does the chicken. Note the relative size of their optic lobes. The trend toward increasing dominance of the cerebrum in vertebrate evolution is also apparent, beginning with the alligator (c) and becoming more pronounced in the bird (d). (e) The trend is greatest in the mammal, with increased convolutions in the cortex. Convolutions, or foldings, are a way of increasing cerebral size without greatly increasing cranial size.

Robert Wallace et al., *Biology: The Science of Life*

The purpose of the diagram on the following page is to

_____

Referring to both the passage and the diagram, respond to the following items with *T* (true), *F* (false), or *CT* (can't tell).

_____ 1. The shark is a cartilaginous fish.

_____ 2. This diagram also reveals the digestive system.

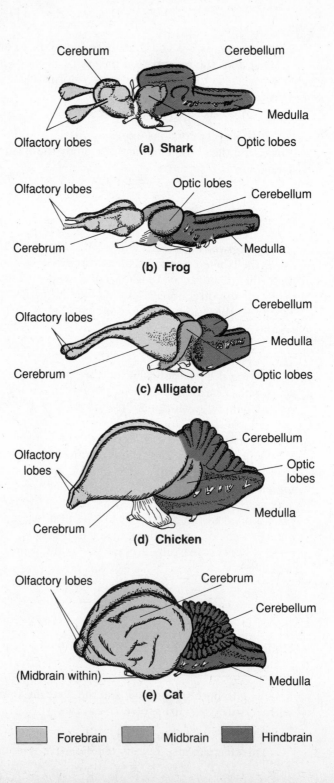

Cerebrum

Cerebellum

Medulla

Optic lobes

Olfactory lobes

(a) Shark

Olfactory lobes

Optic lobes

Cerebellum

Cerebrum

Medulla

(b) Frog

Olfactory lobes

Cerebellum

Medulla

Cerebrum

Optic lobes

(c) Alligator

Olfactory lobes

Cerebellum

Optic lobes

Cerebrum

Medulla

(d) Chicken

Olfactory lobes

Cerebrum

Cerebellum

(Midbrain within)

Medulla

(e) Cat

Forebrain   Midbrain   Hindbrain

_____ 3. The shark has the largest olfactory lobes of the five vertebrates compared.

_____ 4. The cerebrum of the chicken is larger than that of the frog.

_____ 5. Folds in the cerebrum are a way of increasing cerebral size.

_____ 6. The medulla of the alligator allows it to live on land and in the water.

_____ 7. The size of the optic lobes of the chicken reflects the need of vision for survival.

_____ 8. The cerebrum of the cat is larger than that of the chicken.

_____ 9. For the shark, vision is more important than smell for survival.

_____ 10. The cerebellum is considered a part of the hindbrain.

Exercise 2: Tables

A *table* is a listing of facts and figures in columns and rows for quick and easy reference. The information in the columns and rows is usually labeled in two different directions. First read the title for the topic and then read the footnotes to judge the source. Determine what each column represents and how they interact.

In the following table, note the categories on the horizontal row and the categories and subcategories on the vertical column. Be clear about which figures represent numbers of people and which represent percentages.

The purpose of the table on the following page is to

_____

Respond to the following items with *T* (true), *F* (false), or *CT* (can't tell).

_____ 1. Less than one thousand people were interviewed for this study.

_____ 2. The age at which the greatest number of people in the nation learned to read is six.

_____ 3. In this study there were 11 more males than females polled.

_____ 4. Hispanic females learn to read earlier than white males.

_____ 5. Among the three age groups, age 50 and older has the highest percent of individuals who did not learn to read until eight or older.

_____ 6. In this survey at least three people in the South reported learning to read by age three.

_____ 7. Most college graduates reported learning to read by at least five years old.

_____ 8. Individuals in this study who learned to read at one or two years old report higher incomes than those who learned to read later.

_____ 9. Approximately one fourth of the people surveyed read 16 or more books in the past year.

_____ 10. All Democrats listed their ideology as liberal.

Age Began Reading

QUESTION: AT WHAT AGE DID YOU FIRST START READING?

	ONE	TWO	THREE	FOUR	FIVE	SIX	SEVEN	EIGHT OR OLDER	NO OPINION	NO. OF INTERVIEWS
National	•	•	1%	6%	17%	29%	13%	25%	9%	1019
Sex										
Male	•	•	2	6	18	26	14	24	10	515
Female	0%	1%	1	5	16	32	12	25	8	504
Age										
18-29 years	0	1	2	8	22	27	13	20	7	215
30-49 years	•	0	1	5	18	30	13	24	9	464
50 & older	0	•	1	4	12	30	13	30	10	332
Region										
East	0	0	1	6	19	31	9	27	7	252
Midwest	0	1	1	7	18	31	14	20	8	256
South	0	0	1	5	14	29	12	29	10	302
West	1	1	2	5	18	25	16	22	10	206
Race										
White	•	•	1	6	16	30	13	25	9	875
Black	0	0	1	6	29	26	9	23	6	85
Other	0	4	2	1	11	26	20	33	3	49
Education										
College grads.	0	0	2	8	22	30	12	21	5	290
College Inc.	1	0	1	6	17	26	14	25	10	237
High school grads.	0	1	1	5	16	31	14	23	9	362
Not H.S. grads.	0	1	1	2	13	28	8	36	11	123
Politics										
Republicans	1	0	2	7	14	29	14	26	7	353
Democrats	0	0	1	4	20	31	11	25	8	360
Independents	0	1	1	6	17	28	13	24	10	267
Ideology										
Liberal	0	0	1	6	20	29	11	25	8	337
Moderate	0	0	6	6	23	31	16	16	2	72
Conservative	•	1	1	5	15	31	13	26	8	449
Income										
$50,000 & over	0	0	1	8	20	34	11	20	6	221
$30,000-49,999	0	0	2	6	17	28	14	22	11	271
$20,000-29,999	0	0	0	6	16	32	16	23	7	190
Under $20,000	1	1	1	4	16	28	11	29	9	267
Books Read in Past Year										
2 or less	0	•	1	3	13	34	12	23	14	287
3 to 5	0	0	2	3	23	24	15	25	8	179
6 to 15	0	0	2	8	17	30	13	25	5	255
16 or more	1	1	2	8	17	27	12	26	6	274

• Less than 1 percent   *The Gallup Poll Monthly, February 1991*

Exercise 3: Maps

A *map* shows a geographic area. It shows differences in physical terrain, direction, or variations over a specified area. The legend of a map, which usually appears in a corner box, explains the distance scale and the meanings of symbols and shading. Use the legend on the following map to help you answer the questions.

Geographical Review

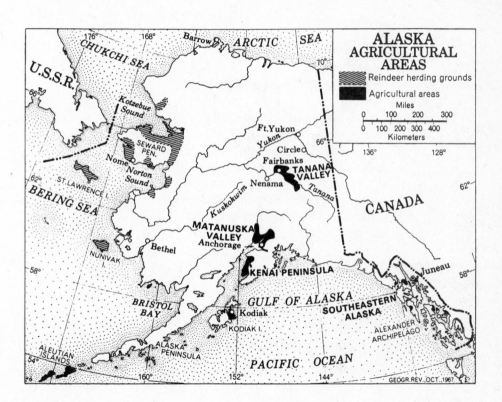

The purpose of this map is to

_____

Answer the following with *T* (true), *F* (false), or *CT* (can't tell).

1. The major concentration of reindeer-herding grounds in Alaska is on Seward Peninsula.

_____ 2. There are no major highways in Alaska north of Anchorage.

_____ 3. Bethel is the largest city in Alaska.

_____ 4. Anchorage is less than 300 miles from Juneau.

_____ 5. The Matanuska Valley and the Tanana Valley are two of the major agricultural areas in Alaska.

_____ 6. The Yukon River flows from Canada.

_____ 7. Eskimos live in the areas around Nome and Barrow.

_____ 8. Reindeer herding is more prevalent than agriculture on the islands in the Bering Sea.

_____ 9. No farming exists in southeastern Alaska.

_____ 10. The northernmost city in the United States is Fort Yukon.

Exercise 4: Pie Graphs

A *pie graph* is a circle that is divided into wedge-shaped slices. The complete pie or circle represents a total, or 100 percent. Each slice is a percent or fraction of that whole. Budgets, such as the annual expenditure of the federal or state governments, are frequently illustrated by pie graphs.

You can use a pie graph to illustrate your own monthly spending. First, estimate how much you spend each month and on what. Your figures do not need to be exact. Use the following categories to jog your memory; add additional categories if needed.

Total Monthly Expenditures: $_____ = 100%

Rent $_____ = _____% Utilities $_____ = _____%

Food $_____ = _____% Clothes $_____ = _____%

Transportation $_____ = _____% School $_____ = _____%

Entertainment $_____ = _____% Other $_____ = _____%

Each of your expense categories is a percentage of your total monthly expenditures. For example, if you spend $500 each month and your rent is $250, the rent is 50 percent of your total monthly expenditures. Calculate an approximate percentage for each of your expenses, and then illustrate and label your expenses on the pie graph.

The following graphs are slightly more complicated. Notice that the figures are percentages and not numbers of people. We cannot assume that the male and female populations are equal.

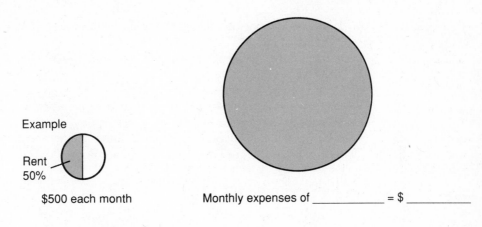

Example

Rent
50%

$500 each month

Monthly expenses of _____ = $ _____

Virginia in 1625: An age profile

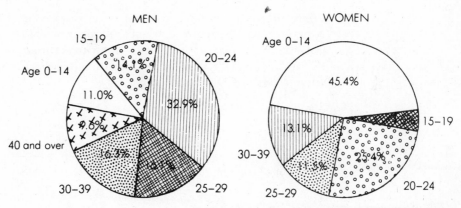

Keith Ian Polakoff et al., *Generations of Americans, Part 1*

The purpose of these pie graphs is to

_____

Answer the following with *T* (true), *F* (false), or *CT* (can't tell).

_____ 1. The majority of the children arriving in Virginia from England were females.

_____ 2. There were more men than women in Virginia in 1625.

_____ 3. Only approximately one quarter of the men in Virginia in 1625 were thirty years or more of age.

_____ 4. The population of Virginia in 1625 was thirty percent younger than Virginia's population today.

_____ 5. Almost half the women in Virginia in 1625 were under eighteen years of age.

_____ 6. A greater number of women than men in Virginia in 1625 were 20 to 24 years of age.

_____ 7. According to the graph there were no women in Virginia in 1625 over 40 years of age.

_____ 8. More women than men left the Virginia colony.

_____ 9. There was a greater number of men than women between the ages of 30 and 39 in Virginia in 1625.

_____ 10. Because of the availability of females, men married women much younger than themselves in the Virginia colony.

Exercise 5: Bar Graphs

A *bar graph* is a series of horizontal or vertical bars in which the length of each bar represents a particular amount or number of what is being discussed. A series of different items can be quickly compared by noting the different bar lengths. In the following graph, notice that the bars represent average salaries according to years of education.

How Education Raises Our Income

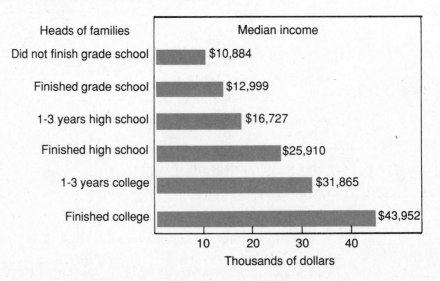

The purpose of this bar graph is to

_____

Respond to the following items with *T* (true), *F* (false), or *CT* (can't tell).

_____ 1. The graph indicates that no individual in the study who did not finish college could make more money than people who did complete college.

_____ 2. Individuals who finish high school make an average of two and a half times more than those who do not finish grade school.

_____ 3. The incomes reported in this graph reflect the incomes of dual-career families.

_____ 4. Approximately one million people were surveyed for this report.

_____ 5. The graphic information illustrates that education can improve earnings.

Exercise 6: Line Graphs

A *line graph* is a continuous curve or frequency distribution. The horizontal scale often measures time and the vertical scale measures amount. As the data fluctuate, the line will change direction and with extreme differences become very jagged. Notice that this graph shows past and projected school enrollment over a 35-year period.

The purpose of this line graph is to

_____

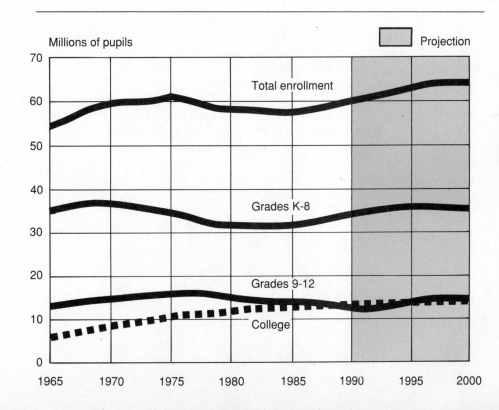

Respond to the following items with *T* (true), *F* (false), or *CT* (can't tell).

_____ 1. The total enrollment of 1990 matched the total enrollment of 1970.

_____ 2. The total enrollment is a combination of elementary school, high school, and college.

_____ 3. College enrollment is not expected to make a drastic rise in the next 20 years.

_____ 4. By the year 2000 all the students who graduate from high school are expected to go to college.

_____ 5. The total college enrollment in 1990 was approximately 130,000.

Exercise 7: Flowcharts

Flowcharts provide a diagram of the relationships and sequence of elements. They were first used in computer programming. Key ideas are stated in boxes, along with supporting ideas that are linked by arrows. Arrows pointing downward or to the right indicate sequence or mean "leads to," and arrows pointing upward or to the left mean "supports" or "relates to." For the following flow chart, note the path from a lower court to the U.S. Supreme Court.

Structure of the United States Judicial System
At the apex of the American judicial system is the United States Supreme Court, which has both original and appellate jurisdiction. Its **original jurisdiction** covers cases that come directly to it. These cases—involving foreign diplomats or one of the states, for example—are listed in Article III of the Constitution. Many more cases, however, come through **appellate jurisdiction**—the right to review decisions of lower courts. All cases originating in lower courts are concerned with constitutional issues.

Charles Dunn, *Constitutional Democracy in America*

The purpose of the flowchart on the following page is to

_____

Answer the following with *T* (true), *F* (false), or *CT* (can't tell).

_____ 1. The U.S. Supreme Court hears cases directly from the state trial courts.

_____ 2. Foreign diplomats can bypass local courts and be heard directly by the U.S. Supreme Court.

_____ 3. The U.S. Court of Appeals is a federal court.

_____ 4. Patent appeals are heard in state courts.

_____ 5. Each state has only one U.S. District Court.

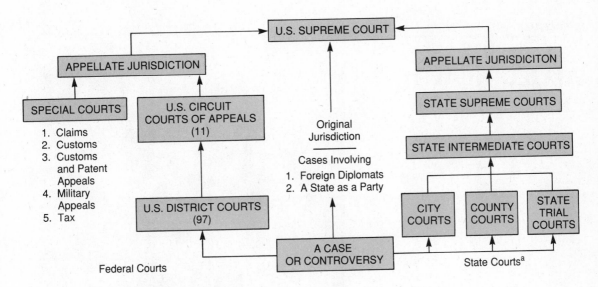

APPELLATE JURISDICTION

SPECIAL COURTS

1. Claims
2. Customs
3. Customs and Patent Appeals
4. Military Appeals
5. Tax

U.S. CIRCUIT COURTS OF APPEALS (11)

U.S. DISTRICT COURTS (97)

Federal Courts

U.S. SUPREME COURT

Original Jurisdiction
—————
Cases Involving
1. Foreign Diplomats
2. A State as a Party

A CASE OR CONTROVERSY

APPELLATE JURISDICITON

STATE SUPREME COURTS

STATE INTERMEDIATE COURTS

CITY COURTS

COUNTY COURTS

STATE TRIAL COURTS

State Courts[a]

[a]Although state court systems differ, they generally follow the basic pattern outlined above.

SUMMARY

Graphic illustrations condense, clarify, and convince. They express complex interrelationships in simplified form. The following kinds of graphic illustrations can be used to present information:

A *diagram* is an outline drawing or picture of an object or a process.

A *table* is a listing of facts and figures in columns for quick and easy reference.

A *map* shows a geographic area.

A *pie graph* is a circle that is divided into wedge-shaped slices. The whole circle represents 100 percent.

A *bar graph* is a series of horizontal bars in which the length of each bar represents a particular amount.

A *line graph* is a continuous curve or frequency distribution.

Flowcharts provide a diagram of the relationships and sequence of elements.

Selection

ALLIED HEALTH

Stage 1

Preview

The author's main purpose is to condemn alcohol.

agree ☐   disagree ☐

The different sections describe the cause-and-effect relationship of alcohol on the body.

agree ☐   disagree ☐

After reading this selection, I will need to know how alcohol affects the brain.

agree ☐   disagree ☐

Activate Schema

What is the legal limit for driving a car on a breathalyzer test?

Learning Strategy

Trace alcohol through the body and note the effects as it travels.

Word Knowledge

Review the ten vocabulary items that follow the selection. Seek an understanding of unfamiliar words.

Stage 2: Integrate Knowledge While Reading

Use the thinking strategies as you read:

1. Predict 2. Picture 3. Relate 4. Monitor 5. Fix up

ALCOHOL AND NUTRITION

From Eva May Nunnelley Hamilton et al., *Nutrition*

People naturally congregate to enjoy conversation and companionship, and it is natural, too, to offer beverages to companions. All beverages ease conversation whether or not they contain alcohol. Still, some people choose alcohol over cola, milk, or coffee, and they should know a few things about alcohol's short term and long term effects on health. One consideration is energy—alcohol yields energy to the body, and many alcoholic drinks are much more fattening than their nonalcoholic counterparts. Additionally, alcohol has a tremendous impact on the overall well-being of the body.

People consume alcohol in servings they call "a drink." However, the serving that some people consider one drink may not be the same as the standard drink that delivers 1/2 ounce pure ethanol:

3 to 4 ounces wine
10 ounces wine cooler
12 ounces beer
1 ounce hard liquor (whiskey, gin, brandy, rum, vodka)

The percentage of alcohol in distilled liquor is stated as *proof:* 100-proof liquor is 50 percent alcohol; 90-proof is 45 percent, and so forth. Compared with hard liquor, beer and wine have a relatively low percentage of alcohol.

Alcohol Enters the Body

From the moment an alcoholic beverage is swallowed, the body confers special status on it. Unlike foods, which require digestion, the tiny alcohol molecules are all ready to be absorbed; they can diffuse right through the walls of an empty stomach and reach the brain within a minute. A person can become intoxicated almost immediately when drinking, especially if the person's stomach is empty. When the stomach is full of food, molecules of alcohol have less chance of touching the walls and diffusing through, so alcohol affects the brain a little less immediately. (By the time the stomach contents are emptied into the small intestine, it doesn't matter that food is mixed with the alcohol. The alcohol is absorbed rapidly anyway.)

A practical pointer derives from this information. If a person wants to drink socially and not become intoxicated, the person should eat the snacks provided by the host (avoid the salty ones; they make you thirstier). Carbohydrate snacks are best suited for slowing alcohol absorption. High-fat snacks help too because they slow peristalsis, keeping the alcohol in the stomach longer.

If one drinks slowly enough, the alcohol, after absorption, will be collected into the liver and processed without much affecting other parts of the body. If one drinks more rapidly, however, some of the alcohol bypasses the liver and flows for a while through the rest of the body and the brain.

Figure R-1

Alcohol's Effects on the Brain

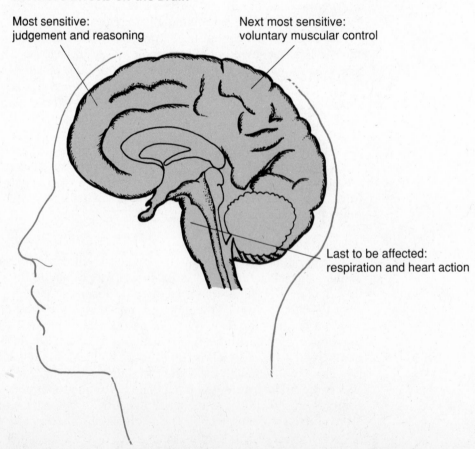

Most sensitive:
judgement and reasoning

Next most sensitive:
voluntary muscular control

Last to be affected:
respiration and heart action

Alcohol Arrives in the Brain

People use alcohol today as a kind of social anesthetic to help them
relax or to relieve anxiety. One drink relieves inhibitions, and this
50 gives people the impression that alcohol is a stimulant. Actually the
way it does this is by sedating *inhibitory* nerves, allowing excitatory
nerves to take over. This is temporary. Ultimately alcohol acts as a
depressant and sedates all the nerve cells. Figure R1 describes
alcohol's effects on the brain.

55   It is lucky that the brain centers respond to elevating blood alcohol
in the order described in Figure R1 because a person usually passes
out before managing to drink a lethal dose. It is possible, though, for
a person to drink fast enough so that the effects of alcohol continue
to accelerate after the person has gone to sleep. The occasional death
60 that takes place during a drinking contest is attributed to this effect.
The drinker drinks fast enough, before passing out, to receive a lethal
dose. Table R1 shows the blood alcohol levels that correspond with
progressively greater intoxication and Table R2 shows the brain
responses that occur at these blood levels.

65   Brain cells are particularly sensitive to excessive exposure to
alcohol. The brain shrinks, even in people who drink only
moderately. The extent of the shrinkage is proportional to the amount
drunk. Abstinence, together with good nutrition, reverses some of the
brain damage—possibly all of it if heavy drinking has not continued
70 for more than a few years—but prolonged drinking beyond an
individual's capacity to recover can cause severe and irreversible
effects on vision, memory, learning ability, and other functions.

     Anyone who has had an alcoholic drink knows that alcohol
increases urine output. This is because alcohol depresses the brain's

Table R1 Alcohol Doses and Blood Levels

Percent Blood Alcohol by Body Weight

NUMBER OF DRINKS[a]	100 LB	120 LB	150 LB	180 LB	200 LB
2	0.08	0.06	0.05	0.04	0.04
4	0.15	0.13	0.10	0.08	0.08
6	0.23	0.19	0.15	0.13	0.11
8	0.30	0.25	0.20	0.17	0.15
12	0.45	0.36	0.30	0.25	0.23
14	0.52	0.42	0.35	0.34	0.27

[a]Taken within an hour or so.

Table R2 Alcohol Blood Levels and Brain Responses

BLOOD LEVEL (%)	BRAIN RESPONSE
0.05	Judgment impaired
0.10	Emotional control impaired
0.15	Muscle coordination and reflexes impaired
0.20	Vision impaired
0.30	Drunk, totally out of control
0.35	Stupor
0.50–0.60	Total loss of consciousness, finally death

75 production of **antidiuretic hormone.** Loss of body water leads to thirst. The only fluid that will relieve dehydration is water, but if alcohol is the only drink available, the thirsty person may choose another alcoholic beverage and worsen the problem. The smart drinker, then, alternates alcoholic beverages with nonalcoholic 80 choices and when thirsty chooses the latter.

The water loss caused by hormone depression involves loss of more than just water. The water takes with it important minerals, such as magnesium, potassium, calcium, and zinc, depleting the body's reserves. These minerals are vital to the maintenance of fluid balance 85 and to nerve and muscle action and coordination.

Alcohol Arrives in the Liver
The capillaries that surround the digestive tract merge into veins that carry the alcohol-laden blood to the liver. Here the veins branch and rebranch into capillaries that touch every liver cell. The liver cells make nearly all of the body's alcohol-processing machinery, and the 90 routing of blood through the liver allows the cells to go right to work on the alcohol. The liver's location at this point along the circulatory system guarantees that it gets the chance to remove toxic substances before they reach other body organs such as the heart and brain.

The liver makes and maintains two sets of equipment for 95 metabolizing alcohol. One is an enzyme that removes hydrogens from alcohol to break it down; the name almost says what it does—**alcohol dehydrogenase (ADH).**[*] This handles about 80 percent or more of

[*]There are actually two ADH enzymes, each for a specific task in alcohol breakdown. Enzyme 1, alcohol dehydrogenase, converts alcohol to acetaldehyde. Enzyme 2, acetaldehyde dehydrogenase, converts acetaldehyde to a common body compound, acetyl CoA, identical to that derived from carbohydrate and fat during their breakdown.

body alcohol. The other alcohol-metabolizing equipment is a chain of enzymes (known as the **MEOS**) thought to handle about 10 to 20
100 percent of body alcohol. With high blood alcohol concentrations, the MEOS activity is enhanced, as will be shown later. But let us look at the ADH system first.

The amount of alcohol a person's body can process in a given time is limited by the number of ADH enzymes that reside in the liver.[†] If
105 more molecules of alcohol arrive at the liver cells than the enzymes can handle, the extra alcohol must wait. It enters the general circulation and is carried to all parts of the body, circulating again and again through the liver until enzymes are available to degrade it.

The number of ADH enzymes present is affected by whether or not
110 a person eats. Fasting for as little as a day causes degradation of body proteins, including the ADH enzymes in the liver, and this can reduce the rate of alcohol metabolism by half. Prudent drinkers drink slowly, with food in their stomachs, to allow the alcohol molecules to move to the liver cells gradually enough for the enzymes to handle the
115 load. It takes about an hour and a half to metabolize one drink, depending on a person's body size, on previous drinking experience, on how recently the person has eaten, and on general health at the time. The liver is the only organ that can dispose of significant quantities of alcohol, and its maximum rate of alcohol clearance is
120 fixed. This explains why only time will restore sobriety. Walking will not; muscles cannot metabolize alcohol. Nor will it help to drink a cup of coffee. Caffeine is a stimulant, but it won't speed up the metabolism of alcohol. The police say ruefully that a cup of coffee will only make a sleepy drunk into a wide-awake drunk.

125 As the ADH enzymes break alcohol down, they produce hydrogen ions (acid), which must be picked up by a compound that contains the B vitamin niacin as part of its structure. Normally this acid is disposed of through a metabolic pathway, but when alcohol is present in the system, this pathway shuts down. The niacin-containing
130 compound remains loaded with hydrogens that it cannot get rid of and so becomes unavailable for a multitude of other vital body processes for which it is required.

The synthesis of fatty acids also accelerates as a result of the liver's exposure to alcohol. Fat accumulation can be seen in the liver after a
135 single night of heavy drinking. **Fatty liver,** the first stage of liver deterioration seen in heavy drinkers, interferes with the distribution of nutrients and oxygen to the liver cells. If the condition lasts long

---

[†]Some ADH enzymes reside in the stomach, offering a protective barrier against alcohol entering the blood. Research shows that alcoholics make less stomach ADH, and so do women. Women may absorb about one-third more alcohol than men, even when they are the same size and drink the same amount of alcoholic beverage.

enough, the liver cells die, and fibrous scar tissue invades the area—the second stage of liver deterioration called **fibrosis.** Fibrosis
140 is reversible with good nutrition and abstinence from alcohol, but the next (last) stage—**cirrhosis**—is not. All of this points to the importance of moderation in the use of alcohol.

The presence of alcohol alters amino acid metabolism in the liver cells. Synthesis of some proteins important in the immune system
145 slows down, weakening the body's defenses against infection. Synthesis of lipoproteins speeds up, increasing blood triglyceride levels. In addition, excessive alcohol increases the body's acid burden and interferes with normal uric acid metabolism, causing symptoms like those of **gout.**
150 Liver metabolism clears most of the alcohol from the blood. However, about 10 percent is excreted through the breath and in the urine. This fact is the basis for the breathalyzer test that law enforcement officers administer when they suspect someone of driving under the influence of alcohol.

Alcohol's Long-Term Effects
155 By far the longest term effects of alcohol are those felt by the child of a woman who drinks during pregnancy. Pregnant women should not drink at all. For nonpregnant adults, however, what are the effects of alcohol over the long term?

A couple of drinks set in motion many destructive processes in the
160 body, but the next day's abstinence reverses them. As long as the doses taken are moderate, time between them is ample, and nutrition is adequate meanwhile, recovery is probably complete.

If the doses of alcohol are heavy and the time between them is short, complete recovery cannot take place, and repeated onslaughts
165 of alcohol gradually take a toll on the body. For example, alcohol is directly toxic to skeletal and cardiac muscle, causing weakness and deterioration in a dose-related manner. Alcoholism makes heart disease more likely probably because alcohol in high doses raises the blood pressure. Cirrhosis can develop after 10 to 20 years from the
170 additive effects of frequent heavy drinking episodes. Alcohol abuse also increases a person's risk of cancer of the mouth, throat, esophagus, rectum, and lungs. Women who drink even moderately may run an increased risk of developing breast cancer. Although some dispute these findings, a reliable source tentatively ranks daily human
175 exposure to ethanol as high in relation to other possible carcinogenic hazards. Other long-term effects of alcohol abuse include:

Ulcers of the stomach and intestines
Psychological depression
Kidney damage, bladder damage, prostate gland damage, pancreas
180 damage

Skin rashes and sores

Impaired immune response

Deterioration in the testicles and adrenal glands, leading to feminization and sexual impotence in men

185 Central nervous system damage

Malnutrition

Increased risk of violent death

This list is by no means all inclusive. Alcohol has direct toxic effects, independent of the effect of malnutrition, on all body organs.

190 The more alcohol a person drinks, the less likely that he or she will eat enough food to obtain adequate nutrients. Alcohol is empty calories, like pure sugar and pure fat; it displaces nutrients. In a sense, each time you drink 150 calories of alcohol, you are spending those calories on a luxury item and getting no nutritional value in

195 return. The more calories you spend this way, the fewer you have left to spend on nutritious foods. Table R3 shows the calorie amounts of typical alcoholic beverages.

Alcohol abuse not only displaces nutrients from the diet but also affects every tissue's metabolism of nutrients. Alcohol causes stomach

200 cells to oversecrete both acid and an agent of the immune system, histamine, that produces inflammation. These changes make the stomach and esophagus linings vulnerable to ulcer formation. Intestinal cells fail to absorb thiamin, folate, and vitamin B_{12}. Liver cells lose efficiency in activating vitamin D and alter their production

205 and excretion of bile. Rod cells in the retina, which normally process vitamin A alcohol (retinol) to the form needed in vision, find

---

Table R3 Calories in Alcoholic Beverages and Mixers

BEVERAGE	AMOUNT (OZ)	ENERGY (CAL)
Beer	12	150
Light beer	12	100
Gin, rum, vodka, whiskey (86 proof)	1 1/2	105
Dessert wine	3 1/2	140
Table wine	3 1/2	85
Tonic, ginger ale, other sweetened carbonated waters	8	80
Cola, root beer	8	100
Fruit-flavored soda, Tom Collins mix	8	115
Club soda, plain seltzer, diet drinks	8	1

themselves processing drinking alcohol instead. The kidneys excrete magnesium, calcium, potassium, and zinc.

Alcohol's intermediate products interfere with metabolism too.

210 They dislodge vitamin B_6 from its protective binding protein so that it is destroyed, causing a vitamin B_6 deficiency and thereby lowered production of red blood cells.

Most dramatic is alcohol's effect on folate. When alcohol is present, it is as though the body were actively trying to expel folate from all

215 its sites of action and storage. The liver, which normally contains enough folate to meet all needs, leaks folate into the blood. As the blood folate concentration rises, the kidneys are deceived into excreting it, as though it were in excess. The intestine normally releases and retrieves folate continuously, but it becomes damaged by

220 folate deficiency and alcohol toxicity, so it fails to retrieve its own folate and misses out on any that may trickle in from food as well. Alcohol also interferes with the action of what little folate is left, and this inhibits the production of new cells, especially the rapidly dividing cells of the intestine and the blood. Alcohol abuse causes a

225 folate deficiency that devastates digestive system function.

Nutrient deficiencies are thus a virtually inevitable consequence of alcohol abuse, not only because alcohol displaces food but also because alcohol directly interferes with the body's use of nutrients, making them ineffective even if they are present. Over a lifetime,

230 excessive drinking, whether or not accompanied by attention to nutrition, brings about deficits of all the nutrients mentioned in this discussion and many more besides.

Alcohol and Drugs

The liver's reaction to alcohol affects its handling of drugs as well as nutrients. In addition to the ADH enzymes, the liver possesses an

235 enzyme system that metabolizes *both* alcohol and drugs—any compounds that have certain chemical features in common. As mentioned earlier, at low blood alcohol concentrations, the MEOS handles about 10 to 20 percent of the alcohol consumed. However, at high blood alcohol concentrations, or if repeatedly exposed to

240 alcohol, the MEOS is enhanced.

As a person's blood alcohol concentration rises, the alcohol competes with—and wins out over—other drugs whose metabolism relies on the MEOS. If a person drinks and uses another drug at the same time, the drug will be metabolized more slowly and so will be

245 much more potent. The MEOS is busy disposing of alcohol, so the drug cannot be handled until later; the dose may build up to where its effects are greatly amplified—sometimes to the point of killing the user.

In contrast, once a heavy drinker stops drinking and alcohol is not
250   present to compete with other drugs, the enhanced MEOS
metabolizes those drugs much faster than before. This can make it
confusing and tricky to work out the correct dosages of medications.
The doctor who prescribes sedatives every four hours, for example,
unaware that the person has recently gone from being a heavy drinker
255   to an abstainer, expects the MEOS to dispose of the drug at a certain
predicted rate. The MEOS is adapted to metabolizing large quantities
of alcohol, however. It therefore metabolizes the drug extra fast. The
drug's effects wear off unexpectedly fast, leaving the client
undersedated. Imagine the doctor's alarm should a patient wake up
260   on the table during an operation! A skilled anesthesiologist always
asks the patient about his drinking pattern before putting him to sleep.

    This discussion has touched on some of the ways alcohol affects
health and nutrition. Despite some possible benefits of moderate
alcohol consumption, the potential for harm is great, especially with
265   excessive alcohol consumption. Consider that over 50 percent of all
fatal auto accidents are alcohol related. Translated to human lives,
more than 25,000 people die each year in alcohol-related traffic
accidents. The best way to avoid the harmful effects of alcohol is, of
course, to avoid alcohol altogether. If you do drink, do so with care—
270   for yourself and for others—and in moderation.

Skill Development: Reading Graphs

Refer to the designated graphic and answer the following items with *T*
(true) or *F* (false).

_____   1. According to Figure R1, alcohol first affects muscular control.

_____   2. According to Table R1, a person who has two drinks and weighs 120
        pounds would have 13% blood alcohol level.

_____   3. According to Table R2, a blood alcohol level of 0.35 will cause a stupor.

_____   4. According to Tables R1 and R2, a person weighing 150 pounds who has
        eight drinks would have impaired vision.

_____   5. According to Table R3, vodka has more calories than rum.

Comprehension Questions

1. What is this selection about?
  What is the main idea the author is trying to convey about the topic?

After reading the selection, answer the following questions with *a, b, c,* or *d.*

_____ 2. When the stomach is full of food, alcohol
   a. goes directly to the liver.
   b. bypasses the liver for the bloodstream.
   c. affects the brain less immediately.
   d. rapidly diffuses through the walls of the stomach.

_____ 3. The brain responds to elevated blood alcohol in all of the following ways except
   a. loss of consciousness.
   b. shrinking.
   c. sedating nerve cells.
   d. increasing production of antidiuretic hormones.

_____ 4. Most of the body's processing of alcohol is done by the
   a. liver.
   b. brain.
   c. stomach.
   d. blood.

_____ 5. Alcohol reaches the liver through
   a. direct absorption.
   b. vein and capillaries.
   c. the intestines.
   d. loss of body water.

_____ 6. When enzymes are not available to degrade the total amount of alcohol consumed, this extra alcohol that cannot be immediately processed by the liver
   a. waits in the liver for enzymes to become available.
   b. circulates to all parts of the body.
   c. is metabolized by the MEOS.
   d. is sent to the stomach for storage.

_____ 7. All of the following are true about ADH except
   a. its production can be accelerated to meet increased demand.
   b. it removes hydrogen from alcohol.
   c. the number of ADH enzymes is affected by the presence of food in the stomach.
   d. ADH enzymes can reside in the stomach.

_____ 8. The destruction of vitamin B6 by alcohol results in
   a. the excretion of bile.
   b. a reduction in the number of red blood cells.
   c. the oversecretion of acid and histamine.
   d. loss of retinol by the rod cells in the eye.

_____ 9. The negative influence of alcohol on the production of new cells is caused by
   a. folate excretion.
   b. ulcer formation.

© 1993 HarperCollins College Publishers

    c. esophagus inflammation.

    d. carcinogenic hazards.

_____ 10. If a doctor knows that the patient's MEOS has adapted to metabolizing large amounts of alcohol, the doctor's prescription should vary from the normal by calling for

    a. larger amounts with more time in between.

    b. larger amounts with less time in between.

    c. smaller amounts with less time in between.

    d. smaller amounts with more time in between.

Answer the following with *T* (true) or *F* (false).

_____ 11. The sentence in the first paragraph, "All beverages ease conversation whether or not they contain alcohol" is a statement of fact.

_____ 12. Carbohydrate snacks slow alcohol absorption.

_____ 13. Alcohol can bypass the liver and flow directly to the brain.

_____ 14. High doses of alcohol can raise blood pressure.

_____ 15. Men absorb alcohol faster than women.

Vocabulary

According to the way the italicized word was used in the selection, indicate *a, b, c,* or *d* for the word or phrase that gives the best definition.

____ 1. "their nonalcoholic *counterparts*" (13)

    a. duplicates

    b. sugars

    c. energy sources

    d. stimulants

____ 2. "*diffuse* right through the walls" (28)

    a. disappear

    b. weaken

    c. stick together

    d. spread widely

____ 3. "*sedating* inhibitory nerves" (51)

    a. soothing

    b. connecting

    c. closing

    d. exciting

____ 4. "receive a *lethal* dose" (61)

    a. complete

    b. large

    c. legal

    d. deadly

____ 5. "remove *toxic* substances" (93)

    a. inhibiting

    b. foreign

    c. poisonous

    d. digestive

____ 6. "MEOS activity is *enhanced*" (101)

    a. increased

    b. condensed

    c. redirected

    d. consolidated

_____ 7. "*Prudent* drinkers" (112)
  a. Older
  b. Wise
  c. Experienced
  d. Addicted

_____ 8. "police say *ruefully*" (123)
  a. happily
  b. angrily
  c. mournfully
  d. humorously

_____ 9. "next day's *abstinence*" (160)
  a. headache
  b. sickness
  c. repentance
  d. giving up drinking

_____ 10. "*devastates* digestive system function" (225)
  a. destroys
  b. divides
  c. follows
  d. loosens

Written Response

Use information from the selection to write a letter to a friend who drinks and drives. In a scientific manner explain to your friend why driving after having a few drinks is a danger.

Connecting and Reflecting

Read the following for information on the effects of alcohol on the unborn.

Drinking During Pregnancy

Drinking excess alcohol during pregnancy threatens the fetus with the irreversible brain damage and mental and physical retardation known as **fetal alcohol syndrome, or FAS.** The fetal brain is extremely vulnerable to a glucose or oxygen deficit, and alcohol causes both. In addition, alcohol itself crosses the placenta freely and is directly toxic to the fetal brain. FAS is not curable, only preventable.

Alcohol's Effects   Even before fertilization, alcohol may damage the ovum and so lead to abnormalities in offspring. In males the same is true—drinking before impregnation damages sperm and can also produce an infant of low birthweight.

Although the syndrome was named for damage evident at birth, it has been shown that children born with it remain damaged—they may live, but they never fully recover. About 1 to 3 in every 1000 children are victims of this preventable damage, making FAS the leading known cause of mental retardation in the world. Moreover, for every baby born with these symptoms, another may go undiagnosed until problems develop later in the preschool years. In addition, many others are born with **subclinical FAS.** The mothers of these children drank but not enough to cause visible, obvious effects. Even a child without external damage may have a lower IQ than peers.

Thus, apparently even moderate drinking can affect a fetus negatively. Oxygen is indispensable, on a minute-to-minute basis, to the development of the fetus's central nervous system, and a sudden dose of alcohol can halt the delivery of oxygen through the umbilical cord. During the first month of pregnancy, even a few minutes of such exposure can have a major effect on the fetal brain, which at that time is growing at the rate of 100,000 new brain cells a minute. Alcohol also interferes with placental transport of nutrients to the fetus.

Every container of beer, wine, or liquor for sale in the United States is now required to warn pregnant women of FAS. Before this, many women who would have ceased drinking during pregnancy had they known the danger unwittingly damaged their infants.

Experts' Advice   The editors of the *Journal of the American Medical Association* have taken the position that women should stop drinking as soon as they *plan* to become pregnant. The editors of *Nutrition Today* magazine have stated the following:

The pregnant woman who drinks is more likely to give birth to a baby with FAS defects.
The woman who is pregnant should not drink.
The woman who is addicted to alcohol should be advised to avoid pregnancy at all costs.

From Eva May Nunnelley Hamilton et al., *Nutrition*

Join in a collaborative group with two other classmates and **conduct a study on the extent to which alcohol's effects on the unborn are known.** Dividing work among group members, poll 15 women and 15 men, and ask each person the following questions:

1. Did you know that a pregnant woman can endanger the fetus by drinking alcohol?
2. Did you know that drinking before impregnation can damage sperm?
3. Did you know that drinking alcohol during pregnancy can affect the delivery of oxygen to the fetal brain?

Separately tally the responses for men and women on each of the three questions. Display your results on the following bar graph and share the information in a class discussion.

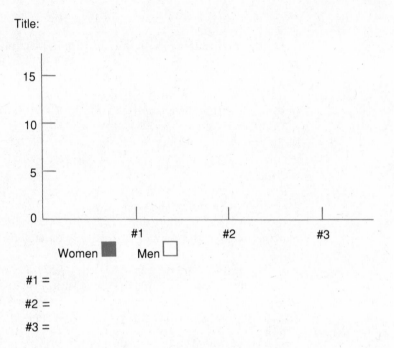

#1 =

#2 =

#3 =

© 1993 HarperCollins College Publishers

TEST TAKING

- Can testwiseness help?
- How should you prepare before the test?
- What should you notice during a test?
- What strategies should you use to read a comprehension passage?
- How can you recognize the major question types?
- What hints help with multiple-choice items?
- How do you answer an essay question?

TESTS IN COLLEGE

For college students, tests may seem at times to come from all directions and to fall into many areas, ranging from personality tests to blood tests. Although students and professors may joke about tests and bemoan the need for them, test taking is a serious part of the business of being a successful college student. In this chapter, two types of tests will be discussed: standardized reading tests and content area exams.

Standardized reading tests, like the reading portion of the SAT, have been developed and administered to large numbers of students in order to establish performance levels. When taking such a test, you are usually striving to perform at a certain level in order to demonstrate your ability to comprehend written material and your potential for college work. The SAT and the ACT are typically associated with college admission, but many colleges and states require additional standardized testing. Developmental studies students, for example, frequently find a statewide test to be part of their exit criteria. In addition, juniors in many states are required to pass a standardized test of reading proficiency in order to continue their work in college. Although the actual value of such testing programs can be questioned, the reality is that standardized reading tests exist and that students need to know how to perform well on them.

Content area exams, by contrast, are the midterms and final exams in courses like Psychology 101 and History 111. These tests are designed to measure how much psychology or history you know so that professors can assign your final course grades. Content exams may be multiple-choice, essay, or a combination of the two. For the multiple-choice portion, questions are usually taken from an item pool provided by a textbook publishing company. For short-answer and essay tests, professors usually make up their own questions to reflect both the text material and the class lectures.

Standardized reading tests and content exams have both similarities and differences. Although intensive studying has always been considered a prerequisite for content testing, research has shown that preparation and practice can also improve standardized test scores. Both types of test require you to be mentally and physically alert, aware of procedures, and aware of environmental factors that can affect your score. Both types of test also use multiple-choice items. While standardized reading tests are almost exclusively multiple-choice, content exams may also make heavy use of multiple-choice items, especially in introductory courses. Therefore, many general observations and suggestions for answering multiple-choice items apply to both types of testing.

CAN TESTWISENESS HELP?

Receiving a passing grade on a test should not be the result of a trick; your grade should be a genuine assessment of the mastery of a skill or the understanding of a body of information. High scores, therefore, should depend on preparation, both mental and physical, and not on schemes involving length of responses or the likelihood of *b* or *c* being the right answer. Research has proven many such gimmicks don't work.[1] Tricks will not get you through college. For a well constructed examination, the only magic formula is mastery of the skill and an understanding of the material being tested.

Insight into test construction and the testing situation, however, will help you achieve at your highest potential. You will perhaps discover answers that you know but didn't think you knew.

The purpose of this material is to help you gain points by being aware. You can improve your score by understanding how tests are constructed and what is needed for maximum performance. Study the following and do everything you can both mentally and physically to gain an edge.

STRATEGIES FOR MENTAL AND PHYSICAL AWARENESS

Before Taking a Test

Get Plenty of Sleep the Night Before. How alert can you be with inadequate sleep? Would you want a physician operating on you who had only a few hours sleep the night before? The mental alertness that comes from a good night's sleep could add two, four, or even six points to your score and mean the difference between passing or failing. Why take a chance by staying up late and gambling at such high stakes?

Arrive Five or Ten Minutes Early and Get Settled. If you run in flustered at the last second, you will spend the first five minutes of the test calming yourself rather than getting immediately to work. Do your nerves a favor and arrive early. Find a seat, get settled with pen or pencil and paper, and relax with some small talk about the weather to a neighbor.

Know What to Expect on the Test. Check beforehand to see if the test will be essay or multiple choice so that you can anticipate the format. Research has shown that studying for both types should stress main ideas, and that it is as difficult to get a good grade on one as it is on another.[2]

---

[1]W. G. Brozo, R. V. Schmelzer, and H. A. Spires, "A Study of Test-Wiseness Clues in College and University Teacher-Made Tests with Implications for Academic Assistance Centers," *College Reading and Learning Assistance,* Technical Report 84-01 (ERIC, 1984), ED 240928.

[2]P. M. Clark, "Examination Performance and Examination Set," in D. M. Wark, ed., *Fifth Yearbook of the North Central Reading Association* (Minneapolis: Central Reading Association, 1968), 114–122.

Have Confidence in Your Abilities. The best way to achieve self-confidence is to be well prepared. Be optimistic, and approach the test with a positive mental attitude. Lack of preparation breeds anxiety, but positive testing experiences tend to breed confidence. Research shows that students who have frequent quizzes during a course tend to do better on the final exam.[3]

Know How the Test Will Be Scored. If the test has several sections, be very clear on how many points can be earned from each section so that you can set priorities on your time and effort.

Find out if there is a penalty for guessing and, if so, what it is. Because most test scores are based on answering all of the questions, you are usually better off to guess than to leave items unanswered. Research shows that guessing can add points to your score.[4] Know the answers to the following questions and act accordingly:

Are some items worth more points than others?
Will the items omitted count against you?
Is there a penalty for guessing?

Plan Your Attack. Take an inventory at least a week before the test of what needs to be done and make plans to achieve your goals. Preparation can make a difference for both standardized tests and content area exams. Professors report that students gain awareness prior to content exams from truthfully writing answers to questions like the following:

1. How will the test look?
   How many parts to the test? What kind of questions will be asked? How will points be counted?
2. What material will be covered?
   What textbook pages are covered? What lecture notes are included? Is outside reading significant?
3. How will you study?
   Have you made a checklist or study guide? Have you read all the material? Will you study notes or annotations from your textbook? Will you write down answers to potential essay questions? Will you include time to study with a classmate?
4. When will you study?
   What is your schedule the week before the test? How long will you need to study? How much of the material do you plan to cover each day? What are your projected study hours?

---

[3]M. L. Fitch, A. J. Drucker, and J. A. Norton, "Frequent Testing as a Motivating Factor in Large Lecture Classes," *Journal of Educational Psychology* 42 (1951): 1–20.

[4]R. C. Preston, "Ability of Students to Identify Correct Responses Before Reading," *Journal of Educational Research* 58 (1964): 181–183.

5. What grade are you honestly working to achieve?
Are you willing to work for an *A,* or are you actually trying to earn a *B* or *C?*

During the Test

Concentrate.   Tune out both internal and external distractions and focus your attention on the material on the test. Visualize and integrate old and new knowledge as you work. Read with curiosity and an eagerness to learn something new. If you become anxious or distracted, close your eyes and take a few deep breaths to relax and get yourself back on track.

On a teacher-made test, you may have a few thoughts that you want to jot down immediately on the back of the test so that you don't forget them. Do so, and proceed with confidence.

Read and Follow Directions.   Find out what you are supposed to do by reading the directions. On a multiple-choice test, perhaps more than one answer is needed. Perhaps on an essay exam you are to respond to only three of five questions. Find out, and then do it.

Schedule Your Time.   Wear a watch and plan to use it. When you receive your copy of the test, look it over, size up the task, and allocate your time. Determine the number of sections to be covered and organize your time accordingly. As you work through the test, periodically check to see if you are meeting your time goals.

On teacher-made tests, the number of points for each item may vary. Do the easy items first, but spend the most time on the items that will yield you the most points.

Work Rapidly.   On a test every minute counts. Do not waste the time that you may need later by pondering at length over an especially difficult item. Mark the item with a check or a dot and move on to the rest of the test. If you have a few minutes at the end of the test, return to the marked items for further study.

Think.   Use knowledge, logic, and common sense in responding to the items. Be aggressive and alert in moving through the test.

If you are unsure, use a process of elimination to narrow down the options. Double-check your paper to make sure you have answered every item.

Don't Be Intimidated by Students Who Finish Early.   Early departures draw attention and can create anxiety for those still working, but calm yourself with knowing that students who finish early do not necessarily make the highest scores. Even though some students work more rapidly than others, fast students do not necessarily work more accurately. If you have time, review areas of the test where you felt a weakness. If your careful rethinking indicates another response, change your answer to agree with your new thoughts. Research shows that scores can be improved by making such changes.[5]

After the Test

Analyze Your Preparation.
Question yourself after the test, and learn from the experience. Did you study the right material? Do you wish you had spent more time studying any particular topic? Were you mentally and physically alert enough to function at your full capacity?

Analyze the Test.
Decide if the test was what you expected. If not, what was unexpected? Did the professor describe the test accurately or were there a few surprises? Why were you surprised? Use your memory of the test to predict the patterns of future tests.

Analyze Your Performance.
Most standardized tests are not returned, but you do receive scores and subscores. What do these scores tell you about your strengths and weaknesses? What can you do to improve?

Content area exams are usually returned and reviewed in class. Ask questions and seek a clear understanding of your errors. Find out why any weak responses that were not wrong did not receive full credit. Do you see any patterns in your performance? What are your strengths and weaknesses? Plan to use what you learn to make an even higher grade on the perpetual "next test."

Meet with your professor if you are confused or disappointed. Ask the professor to analyze your performance and suggest means of improvement. Find out if tutorial sessions or study groups are available for you to join. Formulate a plan with your professor for improved performance on the next test.

STRATEGIES FOR STANDARDIZING READING TESTS

Read to Comprehend the Passage as a Whole

While discussing test-taking strategies a student will usually ask, "Should I read the questions first and then read the passage?" Although the answer to this is subject to some debate, most reading experts would advise reading the passage first and then answering the questions. The reasoning behind this position is convincingly logical. Examining the questions first arms the reader with a confusing collection of key words and phrases. Rather than reading to compre-

[5]F. K. Berrien, "Are Scores Increased on Objective Tests by Changing the Initial Decision?," *Journal of Educational Psychology* 31 (1940): 64–67.

hend the author's message, the reader instead searches for many bits of information. Reading becomes fragmented and lacks focus. Few people are capable of reading with five or six purposes in mind. Not only is this method confusing, but it is also detail-oriented and does not prepare the reader for more general questions concerning the main idea and implied meanings.

Too many students muddle through test passages with only the high hopes that they will later be able to recognize answers. In other words, they passively watch the words go by with their fingers crossed for good luck. Get aggressive. Attack the passage to get the message. Predict the topic and activate your schema. Interact with the material as you read, and employ the thinking strategies of good readers. Monitor and self-correct. Function on a metacognitive level and expect success. Apply what you already know about the reading process to each test passage.

Read to understand the passage as a whole. Each passage has a central theme. Find it. If you understand the central theme or main idea, the rest of the ideas fall into place. The central theme may have several divisions that are developed in the different paragraphs. Attempt to understand what each paragraph contributes to the central theme. Don't worry about the details, other than understanding how they contribute to the central theme. If you find later that a minor detail is needed to answer a question, you can quickly use a key word to locate and reread for accuracy the sentence in which it appears.

Anticipate What Is Coming Next

Most test passages are untitled and thus offer no initial clue for content. Before reading, glance at the passage for a repeated word, name, or date. In other words, look for any quick clue to let you know whether the passage is about Queen Victoria, pit bulls, or chromosome reproduction.

Do not rush through the first sentence. The first sentence further activates your computer chip and sets the stage for what is to come. In some cases, the first sentence may give an overview or even state the central theme. Other times, it may simply pique your curiosity or stimulate your imagination. In any case, the first sentence starts you thinking, wondering, and anticipating. You begin to guess what will come next and how it will be stated.

Anticipating and guessing continues throughout the passage. Some guesses are proven correct and others wrong. When necessary, glance back in the passage to double-check a date, fact, or event that emerges differently than expected. Looking back does not signal weak memory but instead indicates skill in monitoring one's own comprehension.

Read Rapidly, But Don't Allow Yourself to Feel Rushed

Use your pen as a pacer to direct your attention both mentally and physically to the printed page. Using your pen will help you focus your attention, particularly at the times of the test when you feel more rushed.

That uneasy, rushed feeling tends to be with you at the beginning of the test when you have not yet fixed your concentration and become mentally involved with the work. During the middle of the test, you may feel anxious again if you look at your watch and discover you are only half finished and half your time is gone (which is where you should be). Towards the end of the test, when the first person finishes, you will again feel rushed if you have not yet finished. Check your time, keep your cool, and use your pen as a pacer. Continue working with control and confidence.

Read with Involvement to Learn and Enjoy

Reading a passage to answer five or six questions is reading with an artificial purpose. Usually you read to learn and enjoy, not for the sole purpose of quickly answering questions. Most test passages can be fairly interesting to a receptive reader. Try changing your attitude about reading the passages. Use the thinking strategies of a good reader to become involved in the material. Picture what you read and relate the ideas to what you already know. Think, learn, and enjoy—or at least, fake it.

Self-Test for the Main Idea

Pull it together before pulling it apart. At the end of a passage, self-test for the main idea. This is a final monitoring step that should be seen as part of the reading process. Work efficiently, with purpose and determination. Actively seek meaning rather than waiting for the questions to prod you. Take perhaps ten or fifteen seconds to pinpoint the focus of the passage and to tell yourself the point that the author is trying to make. Again, if you understand the main point, the rest of the passage will fall into place.

Pretend that the following passage is part of a reading comprehension test. Read it using the above suggestions. Note the handwritten reminders to make you aware of a few aspects of your thinking. *No title, so glance for key words. Dates? Names?*

Practice Passage A

great image! In January 1744 a coach from Berlin bumped its way eastward over ditches and mud toward Russia. It carried Sophia, a young German princess, on a bridal journey. At the Russian border she was met with pomp, appropriate for one chosen to be married to Peter, heir to the Russian throne. The wedding was celebrated in August 1745 with gaiety and ceremony. *Why wait 1½ years?*

Surprise! For Sophia the marriage was anything but happy because the seventeen-year-old heir was "physically less than a man and mentally little more than a child." The "moronic booby" played with dolls and toy soldiers in his leisure time. He neglected his wife and was *Will he* constantly in a drunken stupor. Moreover, Peter was strongly pro- *be tsar?* German and made no secret of his contempt for the Russian people, intensifying the unhappiness of his ambitious young wife. This dreary

[handwritten: How?]

[handwritten: What is that?]

[handwritten: What is she planning?]

period lasted for seventeen years, but Sophia used the time wisely. She set about "russifying" herself. She mastered the Russian language and avidly embraced the Russian faith; on joining the Orthodox church, she was renamed Catherine. She devoted herself to study, reading widely the works of Montesquieu, Voltaire, and other Western intellectuals.

[handwritten: Did she kill him?]

When Peter became tsar in January 1762, Catherine immediately began plotting his downfall. Supported by the army, she seized power in July 1762 and tacitly consented to Peter's murder. It was announced that he died of "hemorrhoidal colic." Quickly taking over the conduct of governmental affairs, Catherine reveled in her new power. For the next thirty-four years the Russian people were dazzled by their ruler's political skill and cunning and her superb conduct of tortuous diplomacy. Perhaps even more, they were intrigued by gossip concerning her private life.

[handwritten: Ironic, since she's not Russian]

[handwritten: What gossip? Lovers?]

[handwritten: crucial term.]

Long before she became empress, Catherine was involved with a number of male favorites referred to as her house pets. At first her affairs were clandestine, but soon she displayed her lovers as French kings paraded their mistresses. Once a young man was chosen, he was showered with lavish gifts; when the empress tired of him, he was given a lavish going-away present.

[handwritten: did she kill them?]

[handwritten: Now moving from personal info to accomplishments]

Catherine is usually regarded as an enlightened despot. She formed the Imperial Academy of Art, began the first college of pharmacy, and imported foreign physicians. Her interest in architecture led to the construction of a number of fine palaces, villas, and public buildings and the first part of the Hermitage in Saint Petersburg. Attracted to Western culture, she carried on correspondence with the French *philosophes* and sought their flattery by seeming to champion liberal causes. The empress played especially on Voltaire's vanity, sending him copious praise about his literary endeavors. In turn this *philosophe* became her most ardent admirer. Yet while Catherine discussed liberty and equality before the law, her liberalism and dalliance with the Enlightenment was largely a pose—eloquent in theory, lacking in practice. The lot of serfs actually worsened, leading to a bloody uprising in 1773. This revolt brought an end to all talk of reform. And after the French Revolution, strict censorship was imposed.

[handwritten: So, she did little towards human progress]

[handwritten: Double check years—not long]

[handwritten: Changes to foreign policy accomplishments]

In her conduct of foreign policy, the empress was ruthless and successful. She annexed a large part of Poland and, realizing that Turkey was in decline, waged two wars against this ailing power. As a result of force and diplomacy, Russian frontiers reached the Black Sea, the Caspian, and the Baltic. Well could this shrewd practitioner of power politics tell her adopted people, "I came to Russia a poor girl. Russia has dowered me richly, but I have paid her back with Azov, the Crimea, and Poland."

[handwritten: What was the point?]

T. Walter Wallbank et al., *Civilization Past and Present*

Certainly your reading of the passage contained many more thoughts than those indicated on the page. The gossip at the beginning of the passage humanizes the empress and makes it easier for the reader to relate emotionally to the historic figure. Did you anticipate Peter's downfall and Catherine's subsequent relationships? Did you note the shift from gossip to accomplishments, both national and then international? The shift signals the alert reader to a change in style, purpose, and structure.

Take a few seconds to regroup and think about what you have read before proceeding to the questions that follow a passage. Self-test by pulling the material together before you tear it apart. Think about the focus of the passage and then proceed to the questions.

RECOGNIZE MAJOR QUESTION TYPES

Learn to recognize the types of questions asked on reading comprehension tests. Although the phraseology may vary slightly, most tests will include one or more of each of the following types of comprehension questions.

Main Idea

Main idea questions test your ability to find the central theme, central focus, gist, controlling idea, main point, or thesis. The terms are largely interchangeable in asking the reader to identify the main point of the passage. Main idea items are stated in any of the following forms:

The best statement of the main idea is. . . .
The best title for this passage is. . . .
The author is primarily concerned with. . . .
The central theme of the passage is. . . .

Incorrect responses to main idea items tend to fall into two categories. Some responses will be too general and express more ideas than are actually included in the passage. Other incorrect items will be details within the passage that support the main idea. The details may be attention-getting and interesting, but they do not describe the central focus of the passage. If you are having difficulty with the main idea, reread the first and last sentences of the passage. Sometimes, though not always, one of the two sentences will give you an overview or focus.

The following main idea items apply to the passage on Catherine the Great. Notice the handwritten remarks reflecting the thinking involved in judging a correct or incorrect response.

The best statement of the main idea of this passage is
a. Peter lost his country through ignorance and drink. *(Important detail, but focus is on heir.)*

b. gossip of Catherine's affairs intrigued the Russian people. *(Very interesting, but a detail.)*

c. progress for the Russian people was slow to come. *(Too broad and general, or not really covered)*

d. Catherine came to Russia as a poor girl but emerged as a powerful empress and a shrewd politician. *(Yes, sounds great)*

———————— The best title for this passage is

a. Catherine Changes Her Name. *(Detail)*

b. Peter Against Catherine. *(Only part of the story, so detail)*

c. Catherine the Great, Empress of Russia. *(Sounds best)*

d. Success of Women in Russia. *(Too broad—this is only about one woman)*

Details

Detail questions check your ability to locate and understand explicitly stated material. Such items can frequently be answered correctly without a thorough understanding of the passage. To find the answer to such an item, note a key word in the question and then scan the passage for the word or a synonym. When you locate the term, reread the sentence to double-check your answer. Stems for detail questions fall into the following patterns:

The author states that. . . .
According to the author. . . .
According to the passage. . . .
All of the following are true except. . . .
A person, term, or place is. . . .

Incorrect answers to detail questions tend to be false statements. Sometimes the test maker will trick the unsophisticated reader by using a pompous or catchy phrase from the passage as a distractor. The phrase may indeed appear in the passage and sound authoritative, but on close inspection it means nothing. Read the detail question on Catherine the Great and note the handwritten remarks. *Look for the only false item as the answer*

———————— Catherine changed all of the following except

a. her religion. *(True, she joined the Orthodox church)*

b. her name. *(True, from Sophia to Catherine)*

c. Russia's borders. *(True, she gained seaports)*

d. the poverty of the serfs. *(The serfs were worse off, but still in poverty, so this is the best answer)*

Implied Meaning

Questions concerning implied meaning test your ability to look beyond what is directly stated and understand the suggested meaning.

Items testing implied meaning deal with attitudes and feelings, sarcastic comments, snide remarks, the motivation of characters, favorable and unfavorable descriptions, and a host of other hints, clues, and ultimate assumptions. Stems for such items include the following:

The author believes (or feels or implies). . . .
It can be inferred from the passage. . . .
The passage or author suggests. . . .
It can be concluded from the passage that. . . .

To answer inference items correctly, look for clues to help you develop logical assumptions. Base your conclusions on what is known and what is suggested. Incorrect inference items tend to be false statements. Study the following question.

The author implies that Catherine
a. did not practice the enlightenment she professed. *(Yes, "eloquent in theory but lacking practice")*
b. preferred French over Russian architecture. *(not suggested)*
c. took Voltaire as her lover. *(not suggested)*
d. came to Russia knowing her marriage would be unhappy. *(not suggested)*

Purpose

The purpose of a reading passage is not usually stated; it is implied. In a sense, the purpose is part of the main idea; you probably need to understand the main idea to understand the purpose. Generally, however, reading comprehension tests include three basic types of passages, and each type tends to dictate its own purpose. Study the following three types.

1. Factual
   Identification: gives the facts about science, history, or other subjects
   Strategy: If complex, do not try to understand each detail before going to the questions. Remember, you can look back.
   Example: textbook
   Purposes: to inform, to explain, to describe, or to enlighten
2. Opinion
   Identification: puts forth a particular point of view
   Strategy: The author states opinions and then refutes them. Sort out the opinions of the author and the opinions of the opposition.

Example: newspaper editorial
Purposes: to argue, to persuade, to condemn, or to ridicule
3. Fiction
    Identification: tells a story
    Strategy: Read slowly to understand the motivation and interrelationships
             of characters.
    Example: novel or short story
    Purposes: to entertain, to narrate, to describe, or to shock

_____ The purpose of the passage on Catherine is
a. to argue. *(No side is taken)*

b. to explain. *(Yes, because it is factual material)*

c. to condemn. *(Not judgmental)*

d. to persuade. *(No opinion is pushed)*

Vocabulary

Vocabulary items test your general word knowledge as well as your ability to use context to figure out word meaning. The stem of most vocabulary items on reading comprehension tests is as follows:

As used in the passage, the best definition of _____ is

Note that both word knowledge and context are necessary for a correct response. The item is qualified by "As used in the passage," and thus you must go back and reread the sentence (context) in which the word appears to be sure you are not misled by a multiple meaning. To illustrate, the word *sports* means *athletics* as well as *offshoots from trees*. As a test taker you would need to double-check the context to see which meaning appears in your test passage. In addition, if you knew only one definition of the word *sport,* rereading the sentence would perhaps suggest the alternate meaning to you and help you get the item correct. Note the following example.

_____ As used in the passage, the best definition of *dreary* is *(2ⁿᵈ paragraph)*
a. sad. *(Yes, unhappiness is used in the previous sentence)*

b. commonplace. *(Possible, but not right in the sentence)*

c. stupid. *(Not right in the sentence)*

d. neglected. *(True, but not the definition of the word)*

STRATEGIES FOR MULTIPLE-CHOICE ITEMS

Consider All Alternatives Before Choosing an Answer

Read all the options. Do not rush to record an answer without considering all the alternatives. Be careful, not careless, in considering each option. Multiple-choice test items usually ask for the best choice for an answer, not any choice that is reasonable.

_____ Peter was most likely called a "moronic booby" because
a. he neglected Catherine.
b. he drank too much.
c. he disliked German customs.
d. he played with dolls and toys.

Although the first three answers are true and reasonable, the last answer seems to be most directly related to that particular name.

Anticipate the Answer and Look for Something Close to It

As you read the beginning of a multiple-choice item, anticipate what you would write for a correct response. Develop an answer in your mind before you read the options, and then look for a response that corroborates your thinking.

_____ The author suggests that Catherine probably converted to the Russian Orthodox church because ··· *she wanted to rule the country and wanted the people to think of her as Russian, rather than German.*
a. she was a very religious person.
b. Peter wanted her to convert.
c. she was no longer in Germany.
d. she wanted to appear thoroughly Russian to the Russian people.

The last answer most closely matches the kind of answer you were anticipating.

Avoid Answers with 100 Percent Words

All and *never* mean 100 percent, without exceptions. A response containing either word is seldom correct. Rarely can a statement be so definitely inclusive or exclusive. Other 100 percent words to avoid are:

no	none	only
every	always	must

_____ Catherine the Great was beloved by all the Russian people.
Answer with *true* or *false*.

All means 100 percent and thus is too inclusive. Surely one or two Russians did not like Catherine, so the answer must be false.

Consider Answers with Qualifying Words

Words like *sometimes* and *seldom* suggest frequency but do not go so far as to say *all* or *none*. Such qualifying words can mean more than *none* and less than *all*. By being so indefinite, the words are difficult to dispute. Therefore, qualifiers are more likely to be included in a correct response. Other qualifiers are:

few	much	often	may
many	some	perhaps	generally

_____ Catherine was beloved by many of the Russian people.
Answer with *true* or *false*.

The statement is difficult to dispute, given Catherine's popularity. An uprising against her occurred, but it was put down, and she maintained the support of many of the Russian people. Thus the answer would be *true*.

Choose the Intended Answer Without Overanalyzing

Try to follow logically the thinking of the test writer rather than overanalyzing minute points. Don't make the question harder than it is. Use your common sense and answer what you think was intended.

_____ Catherine was responsible for Peter's murder.
Answer *true* or *false*.

This is false in that Catherine did not personally murder Peter. On the other hand, she did "tacitly consent" to his murder, which suggests responsibility. After seizing power, it was certainly in her best interest to get rid of Peter permanently. Perhaps without Catherine, Peter would still be playing with his toys, so the intended answer is *true*.

True Statements Must Be True Without Exception

A statement is either totally true or it is incorrect. Adding an incorrect *and, but,* or *because* phrase to a true statement makes the statement false and thus an unacceptable answer. If a statement is half true and half false, mark it false.

_____ Catherine was an enlightened despot who did her best to improve the lot of all of her people.
Answer with *true* or *false*.

It is true that Catherine was considered an enlightened despot, but she did very little to improve the lot of the serfs. In fact, conditions for the serfs worsened. The statement is half true and half false, so it must be answered *false*.

If Two Options Are Synonymous, Eliminate Both

If *both* is not a possible answer and two items say basically the same thing, then neither can be correct. Eliminate the two and spend your time on the others.

_____ The purpose of this passage is
a. to argue.
b. to persuade.
c. to inform.
d. to entertain.

Because *argue* and *persuade* are basically synonymous, you can eliminate both and move to the other options.

Study Similar Options to Figure Out the Differences

If two similar options appear, frequently one of them will be correct. Study the options to see the subtle difference intended by the test maker.

_____ Catherine was
a. unpopular during her reign.
b. beloved by all of the Russian people.
c. beloved by many of the Russian people.
d. considered selfish and arrogant by the Russians.

The first and last answers are untrue. Close inspection shows that the 100 percent *all* is the difference between the second and third answer that makes the second answer untrue. Thus, the third answer with the qualifying word is the correct response.

Use Logical Reasoning If Two Answers Are Correct

Some tests include the options *all of the above* and *none of the above*. If you see that two of the options are correct and you are unsure about a third choice, then *all of the above* would be a logical response.

_____ Catherine started
a. the Imperial Academy of Art.
b. the first college of pharmacy.
c. the Hermitage.
d. all of the above.

If you remembered that Catherine started the first two but were not sure about the Hermitage, *all of the above* would be your logical option because you know that two of the above *are* correct.

Look Suspiciously at Directly Quoted Pompous Phrases

In searching for distractors, test makers sometimes quote a pompous phrase from the passage that doesn't make much sense. Students read the phrase and think, "Oh yes, I saw that in the passage. It sounds good, so it must be right." Beware of such repetitions and make sure they make sense before choosing them.

_____ In her country Catherine enacted
a. few of the progressive ideas she championed.
b. the liberalism of the Enlightenment.
c. laws for liberty and equality.
d. the liberal areas of the philosophers.

The first response is correct because Catherine talked about progress but did little about it. The other three answers sound impressive and are quoted from the text, but are totally incorrect.

Simplify Double Negatives by Canceling Out Both

Double negatives are confusing to unravel and, in addition, time consuming to think through. Simplify a double negative statement by first canceling out both negatives. Then reread the statement without the confusion of the two negatives, which at this point have canceled each other out, and decide on the accuracy of the statement.

_____ Catherine's view of herself was not that of an unenlightened ruler.
Answer with *true* or *false*.

Cancel out the two negatives, the *not* and the *un* in the word *unenlightened.* Reread the sentence without the negatives and decide on its accuracy: Catherine's view of herself was that of an enlightened ruler. The statement is correct so the answer is *true.*

Can't-Tell Responses Contain Insufficient Clues

Mark an item *can't tell* only if you are not given clues on which to base an assumption. In other words, there is no evidence to indicate the statement is either true or false.

_____ Catherine the Great had no children.

From the information in this passage, which is the information on which your reading test is based, you do not have any clues to indicate whether she did or did not have children. Thus, the answer must be *can't tell*.

Validate True Responses on "All of the Following Except"

In this type of question, you must recognize several responses as correct and find the one that is incorrect. Corroborate each response and, by the process of elimination, find the one that does not fit.

Note Oversights on Hastily Constructed Tests

Reading tests developed by professional test writers are usually well constructed and do not contain obvious clues to the correct answers. However, some teacher-made tests are hastily constructed and contain errors in test making that can help a student find the correct answer. Do not, however, rely on these flaws to make a big difference in your score because they should not occur in a well-constructed test.

Grammar. Eliminate responses that do not have subject-verb agreement. The tense of the verb as well as modifiers such as *a* or *an* can also give clues to the correct response.

_____ Because of his described habits, it is possible that Peter was an
a. hemophiliac.
b. alcoholic.
c. Catholic.
d. barbarian.

The *an* suggests an answer that starts with a vowel. Thus *alcoholic* is the only possibility.

Clues from Other Parts of the Test. Because the test was hastily constructed, information in one part of the test may help you with an uncertain answer.

_____ Not only was Peter childlike and neglectful, but he was also frequently
a. abusive.
b. drunk.
c. dangerous.
d. out of the country.

The previous question gives this answer away by stating that he was possibly an alcoholic.

Length. On poorly constructed tests, longer answers are more frequently correct.

The word *cunning* used in describing Catherine suggests that she was
a. evil.
b. dishonest.
c. untrustworthy.
d. crafty and sly in managing affairs.

In an effort to be totally correct without question, the test maker has made the last answer so complete that its length gives it away.

Absurd Ideas and Emotional Words. Avoid distractors with absurd ideas or emotional words. The test maker probably got tired of thinking of distractors and in a moment of weakness included nonsense.

As used in the passage, the term *house pets* refers to
a. Peter's toys.
b. Catherine's favorite lovers.
c. the dogs and cats in the palace.
d. trained seals that performed for the empress.

Yes, the test maker has, indeed, become weary. The question itself has very little depth, and the last two answers are particularly flippant.

Pretend that the following selection is a passage on a reading comprehension test. Use what you have learned to read with understanding and answer the questions.

Practice Passage B
It seems odd that one of the most famous figures of antiquity—the founder of a philosophical movement—was a vagrant with a criminal record. Diogenes the Cynic began life as the son of a rich banker. This fact may not seem so strange when one remembers the rebellious young people of the late 1960s in America, many of whom also came from affluent families.
  The turning point in Diogenes' life came when his father, Hikesios, treasurer of the flourishing Greek commercial city of Sinope in Asia Minor, was found guilty of "altering the currency." Since Hikesios was a sound money man concerned about maintaining the high quality of the Sinopean coinage, this was obviously a miscarriage of justice. The Persian governor of nearby Cappadocia had issued inferior imitations of the Sinopean currency, and Hikesios, who realized that this currency was undermining the credit of Sinope, ordered the false coins to be defaced in order to put them out of circulation. But a faction of Sinopean citizens—it is not clear whether for economic or political reasons—successfully prosecuted Hikesios. Hikesios was

imprisoned, and Diogenes, who was his father's assistant, was exiled. He eventually settled in Athens.

The shock of this experience caused Diogenes to become a rebel against society—to continue "altering the currency," but in a different way. He decided to stop the circulation of all false values, customs, and conventions. To achieve this goal, he adopted the tactics that made him notorious—complete freedom in speaking out on any subject and a type of outrageous behavior that he called "shamelessness."

Diogenes called free speech "the most beautiful thing in the world" because it was so effective a weapon. He shocked his contemporaries with such statements as "Most men are so nearly mad that a finger's breadth would make the difference." He advocated free love, "recognizing no other union than that of the man who persuades with the woman who consents." He insisted that "the love of money is the mother of all evils"; when some temple officials caught someone stealing a bowl from a temple, he said, "The great thieves are leading away the little thief." He liked to point out that truly valuable things cost little, and vice versa. "A statue sells for three thousand drachmas, while a quart of flour is sold for two copper coins." And when he was asked what was the right time to marry, he replied, "For a young man not yet; for an old man never at all."

Diogenes' "shamelessness"—his eccentric behavior—was his second weapon against the artificiality of conventional behavior as well as his means of promoting what he called "life in accordance with nature," or self-sufficiency. He believed that gods are truly self-sufficient and that people should emulate them: "It is the privilege of the gods to want nothing, and of men who are most like gods to want but little." It was said that he "discovered the means of adapting himself to circumstances through watching a mouse running about, not looking for a place to lie down, not afraid of the dark, not seeking any of the things that are considered dainties." And he got the idea for living in a large pottery jar—his most famous exploit—from seeing a snail carrying its own shell. Above all, Diogenes admired and emulated the life-style of dogs because of their habit of "doing everything in public." For this reason he was called *Kynos,* "the Dog," and his disciples were called Cynics.

"We live in perfect peace," one Cynic wrote, "having been made free from every evil by the Sinopean Diogenes." Eventually the citizens of Sinope also came to honor their eccentric exile with an inscription in bronze:

> Even bronze grows old with time, but your fame, Diogenes, not all eternity shall take away. For you alone did point out to mortals the lesson of self-sufficiency, and the easiest path of life.
>
> T. Walter Wallbank et al., *Civilization Past and Present*

Identify each question type and answer with *a, b, c,* or *d.* Explain what is wrong with the incorrect distractors.

_____ 1. The best statement of the main idea of this passage is

(Question type _____)　　　　　　(Explain errors)

  a. the turning point in the life of Diogenes was the imprisonment of his father.　　　_____

  b. the eccentric Diogenes founded a philosophy and promoted self-sufficiency.　　　_____

  c. Diogenes became famous for living the life of a dog.　　　_____

  d. the Greek way of life and thought changed under the influence of Diogenes.　　　_____

_____ 2. The best title for this passage is

(Question type _____)　　　　　　(Explain errors)

  a. Diogenes Shocks Athens.　　　_____

  b. Great Greek Philosophers.　　　_____

  c. The Eccentric Behavior of a Philosopher.　　　_____

  d. Diogenes, the Self-Sufficient Cynic.　　　_____

_____ 3. Diogenes' father

(Question type _____)　　　　　　(Explain errors)

  a. was exiled from Athens.　　　_____

  b. destroyed conterfeit money.　　　_____

  c. stole from the treasury.　　　_____

  d. was treasurer of Sinope and Cappadocia.　　　_____

_____ 4. The author believes that Diogenes was all of the following except

(Question type _____)　　　　　　(Explain errors)

  a. uninhibited by tradition.　　　_____

  b. insincere in not practicing what he preached.　　　_____

  c. angered by his father's persecution.　　　_____

  d. vocal in advocating free speech.　　　_____

_____ 5. The author's purpose is to

    (Question type _____)   (Explain errors)

      a. argue.   _____

      b. inform.   _____

      c. ridicule.   _____

      d. persuade.   _____

_____ 6. As used in the passage, the best definition of *affluent* is

    (Question type _____)   (Explain errors)

      a. wealthy.   _____

      b. close-knit.   _____

      c. loving.   _____

      d. politically prominent.   _____

STRATEGIES FOR CONTENT AREA EXAMS

Almost all professors would say that the number one strategy for scoring high on content exams is to study the material. Although this advice is certainly on target, there are other suggestions that can help you gain an edge.

Multiple-Choice Items

Multiple-choice, true-false, or matching items on content area exams are written to evaluate the following three categories: factual knowledge, conceptual comprehension, and application skill. Factual questions tap your knowledge of names, definitions, dates, events, and theories. Conceptual comprehension questions evaluate your ability to see relationships, notice similarities and differences, and combine information from different parts of a chapter. Application questions provide the opportunity to generalize from a theory to a real-life illustration, and they are particularly popular in psychology and sociology. The following is an example of an application question from psychology.

An illustration of obsessive-compulsive behavior is

_____ a. Maria goes to the movies most Friday nights.
_____ b. Leon washes his hands over a hundred times a day.
_____ c. Pepe wants to buy a car.
_____ d. Sue eats more fish than red meat.

The second response is obviously correct, but such questions can be tricky if you have not prepared for them. To study for a multiple-choice test, make lists of key terms, facts, and concepts. Quiz yourself on recognition and general knowledge. Make connections and be sure you know similarities and differences. Lastly, invent scenarios that depict principles and concepts. Use your own knowledge, plus the previous suggestions for multiple-choice tests, to separate answers from distractors.

Short-Answer Items

Professors ask short-answer questions because they want you to use your own words to describe or identify. For such questions, be sure that you understand exactly what the professor is asking you to say. You do not want to waste time writing more than is needed, but on the other hand, you do not want to lose points for not writing enough. Study for short-answer items by making lists and self-testing, just as you do when studying for multiple-choice items.

Essay Questions

Essay answers demand more effort and energy from the test taker than multiple-choice items. Rather than simply recognizing correct answers, you must recall, create, and organize. On a multiple-choice test, all the correct answers are somewhere before you. On an essay exam, however, the only thing in front of you is a question and a blank sheet of paper. This blank sheet of paper can be intimidating to many students. Your job is to recall appropriate ideas for a response and pull them together under the central theme designated in the question. The following suggestions can help you respond effectively.

Translate the Question.   Frequently the "question" is not a question at all. It may be a statement that you must first turn into a question. Read and reread this statement that is called a *question*. Be sure you understand it and then reword it into a question. Even if you begin with a question, translate it into your own words. Simplify the question into straight terms that you can understand. Break the question into its parts.

Convert the translated parts of the questions into the approach that you will need to use to answer the question. Will you define, describe, explain, or compare? State what you will do to answer. In a sense, this is a behavioral statement. The following example demonstrates the process.

Statement to Support: **It is both appropriate and ironic to refer to Catherine as one of the great rulers of Russia.**

Question: Why is it both appropriate and ironic to refer to Catherine as one of the great rulers of Russia?

Translation: The question has two parts:

1. What did Catherine do that was really great?
2. What did she do that was the opposite of what you would expect (irony) of a great Russian ruler?

Response Approach: List what Catherine did that was great and list what she did that was the opposite of what you would expect of a great Russian ruler. Relate her actions to the question.

Answer the Question.   Your answer should be in response to the question that is asked and not a summary of everything you know about a particular subject. Write with purpose so that the reader can understand your views and relate your points to the subject. Padding your answer by repeating the same idea or including irrelevant information is obvious to graders and seldom appreciated.

Example: An inappropriate answer to the question "Why is it both appropriate and ironic to refer to Catherine as one of the great rulers of Russia?"

> Catherine was born in Germany and came to Russia as a young girl to marry Peter. It was an unhappy marriage that lasted for seventeen years. She...

(This response does not answer the question: it is a summary.)

Organize Your Response.   Do not write the first thing to pop into your head. Take a few minutes to brainstorm and jot down ideas. Number the ideas in the order that you wish to present them and use this plan as your outline for writing.

In your first sentence, establish the purpose and direction of your response. Then list specific details that support, explain, prove, and develop your point. Reemphasize the points in a concluding sentence and restate your purpose. Whenever possible, use numbers or subheadings to simplify your message for the reader. If time runs short, use an outline or a diagram to express your remaining ideas.

Example: To answer the previous question, think about the selection on Catherine and jot down the ideas that you would include in a response.

Use an Appropriate Style.   Your audience for this response is not your best friend or buckaroo but your learned professor who is going to give you a

I. <u>Appropriate</u>
1. Acquired land
2. Art, medicine, buildings
3. 34 years
4. Political skill & foreign
    diplomacy

II. <u>Ironic</u> (opposite)
1. Not Russian
2. Killed Peter
3. Serfs very poor
4. Revolt against her

grade. Be respectful. Do not use slang. Do not use phrases like "as you know" or "well." They may be appropriate in conversation, but they are not appropriate in formal writing.

Avoid empty words and thoughts. Words like *good, interesting,* and *nice* say very little. Be more direct and descriptive in your writing.

State your thesis, supply proof, and use transitional phrases to tie your ideas together. Words like *first, second,* and *finally* help to organize enumerations. Terms like *however* and *on the other hand* show a shift in thought. Remember, you are pulling ideas together, so use phrases and words to help the reader see relationships.

Study this response to the question for organization, transition, and style.

Catherine was a very good ruler of Russia. She tried to be Russian but she was from Germany. Catherine was a good politician and got Russia seaports on the Baltic, Caspian, and Black Sea. She had many boyfriends and there was gossip about her. She did very little for the Serfs because they remained very poor for a long time. She built nice buildings and got doctors to help people. She was not as awesome as she pretended to be.

(Note the total lack of organization, the weak language, inappropriate phrases, and the failure to use traditional words.)

Be Aware of Appearance.   Research has shown that, on the average, essays written in a clear, legible hand receive a grade level higher score than essays written somewhat illegibly.[6] Be particular about appearance and considerate of the reader. Proofread for correct grammar, punctuation, and spelling.

Predict and Practice.   Predict possible essay items by using the table of contents and subheadings of your text to form questions. Practice brainstorming to answer these questions. Review old exams for an insight both into the questions and the kinds of answers that received good marks. Outline answers to possible exam questions. Do as much thinking as possible to prepare yourself to take the test before you sit down to begin writing.

Notice Key Words in Essay Questions.   This is a list of key words of instruction that appear in essay questions, with hints for responding to each:

Compare: list the similarities between things
Contrast: note the differences between things
Criticize: state your opinion and stress the weaknesses
Define: state the meaning so that the term is understood, and use examples
Describe: state the characteristics so that the image is vivid
Diagram: make a drawing that demonstrates relationships
Discuss: define the issue and elaborate on the advantages and
         disadvantages
Evaluate: state positive and negative views and make a judgment
Explain: show cause and effect and give reasons
Illustrate: provide examples
Interpret: explain your own understanding of a topic which includes
         your opinions
Justify: give proof or reasons to support an opinion
List: record a series of numbered items
Outline: sketch out the main points with their significant supporting
         details
Prove: use facts as evidence in support of an opinion
Relate: connect items and show how one influences another
Review: overview with a summary
Summarize: retell the main points
Trace: move sequentially from one event to another

View Your Response Objectively for Evaluation Points.

Respond to get points. Some students feel that filling up the page deserves a passing grade. They do not understand how a whole page written on the subject of Catherine could receive no points.

[6]H. W. James, "The Effect of Handwriting upon Grading," *English Journal* 16 (1927): 180–185.

Although essay exams seem totally subjective, they cannot be. Students need to know that a professor who gives an essay exam grades answers according to an objective scoring system. The professor examines the paper for certain relevant points that should be made. The student's grade reflects the quantity, quality, and clarity of these relevant points.

Unfortunately, essay exams are shrouded in mystery. The hardest part of answering an item is to figure out what the professor wants. Ask yourself, "What do I need to say to get enough points to pass or to make an *A*?"

Do not add personal experiences or extraneous examples unless they are requested. You may be wasting your time by including information that will give you no points. Stick to the subject and the material. Demonstrate to the professor that you know the material by selectively using it in your response.

The professor scoring the response to the question about Catherine used the following checklist for evaluation.

Appropriate	*Ironic*
1. Acquired land	1. Not Russian
2. Art, medicine, buildings	2. Killed Peter
3. 34 years	3. Serfs very poor
4. Political skill and foreign diplomacy	4. Revolt against her

The professor determined that an *A* paper should contain all of the items. In order to pass, a student should give 5 of the 8 categories covered. Listing and explaining less than five would not produce enough points to pass. Naturally, the professor would expect clarity and elaboration in each category.

After the Test, Read an *A* Paper   Maybe the *A* paper will be yours. If so, share it with others. If not, ask to read an *A* paper so that you will have a model from which to learn. Ask your classmates or ask the professor. You can learn a lot from reading a good paper; you can see what you should and could have done.

When your professor returns a multiple-choice exam, you can reread items and analyze your mistakes to figure out what you did wrong. However, you cannot review essay exams so easily. You may get back a *C* paper with only a word or two of comment and never know what you should have done. Ideally, essay exams should be returned with an example of what would have been a perfect *A* response so that students can study and learn from a perfect model and not make the same mistakes on the next test, but this is seldom, if ever, done. Your best bet is to ask to see an *A* paper.

Study the following response to the previous question. The paper received an *A*.

To call Catherine one of the great rulers of Russia is both appropriate and ironic. It is appropriate because she expanded the borders of Russia. Through her cunning, Russia annexed part of Poland and expanded the frontier to the Black Sea, Caspian, and Baltic. Catherine professed to be enlightened and formed an art academy, a college of pharmacy, and imported foreign physicians. She built many architecturally significant buildings, including the Hermitage. For thirty-four years she amazed the Russian people with her political skill and diplomacy.

On the other hand, Catherine was not a great Russian, nor was she an enlightened leader of all the people. First, she was not Russian; she was German, but she had worked hard to "russify" herself during the early years of her unhappy marriage. Secondly and ironically, she murdered the legitimate ruler of Russia. When she seized power, she made sure the czar quickly died of "hemorrhoidal colic." Third, she did nothing to improve the lot of the poor serfs and after a bloody uprising in 1773, she became even more despotic. Yet Catherine was an engaging character who, through her cunning and intellect, has become known to the world in history books as "Catherine the Great."

(Note the organization, logical thinking, and use of transitions in this response.)

LOCUS OF CONTROL

Have you ever heard students say, "I do better when I don't study," or "No matter how much I study, I still get a *C*"? Rotter, a learning theory psychologist who believes that people develop attitudes about control of their lives, would interpret these comments as reflecting an external locus of control regarding test taking.[7] Such "externalizers" feel that fate, luck, or others control what happens to them. Since they feel they can do little to avoid what befalls them, they do not face matters directly and thus do not take responsibility for failure or credit for success.

People who have an internal locus of control, on the other hand, feel that they, rather than "fate," have control over what happens to them. Such students might evaluate test performance by saying, "I didn't study enough" or "I should have spent more time organizing my essay response." "Internalizers" feel their rewards are due to their own actions, and thus they take steps to be sure they receive those rewards. When it comes to test taking, be an "internalizer," take control, and accept the credit for your success.

SUMMARY

Test taking is a serious part of the business of being a college student. Preparation and practice can lead to improved scores on both standardized reading tests and content area exams. Both types of test require you to be mentally and physically alert, aware of procedures, and aware of environmental factors that affect your score. Items on standardized reading tests tend to follow a predictable pattern and include five major question types. Observations and suggestions for multiple-choice items apply to both standardized and content exams. Essay exam questions demand effort, energy, and organization.

[7] J. Rotter, "External Control and Internal Control," *Psychology Today,* 5(1) (1971): 37–42.

TEXTBOOK APPLICATION

- Can you transfer your reading skills?
- Can you plan your attack?
- Can you succeed?

TRANSFER YOUR SKILLS

This book contains many exercises designed to teach reading skills. Each skill discussion is followed by short excerpts from college textbooks for practicing these skills. Your success with this textbook is certainly a measure of your reading ability. However, the true measure of success in college reading comes, not from your grade at the end of the reading course, but from your grades in the college courses in which you apply the skills.

At the end of your college reading course, your challenge is to transfer these skills to the real world. Can you read and understand textbook material? Can you present the information necessary to make a passing grade in a psychology, sociology, or history course?

MEET THE CHALLENGE

In order to encourage your transfer of skills, this last section of *Bridging the Gap* contains a chapter from a popular sociology text. The chapter titled "Racial and Ethnic Minorities" begins with an array of examples to sensitize the reader and heighten curiosity. Then words like "race," "minority," and "ethnicity" are defined from the perspective of a sociologist. Ways in which society accepts or rejects minorities are explained with accompanying examples, and the chapter concludes with a history of six different ethnic groups. In its approach the chapter is a combination of sociology and history.

Your challenge is to work systematically through the material using the skills you have learned, to study the material, and to present that knowledge on a test. Two tests have been prepared to cover this material. One is a multiple-choice test and the other is an essay exam asking for a written response to two out of three questions.

ORGANIZE YOUR STUDY

Another purpose of including this sociology chapter in *Bridging the Gap* is to give you the opportunity to work with a long piece of textbook material while you still have the advantage of college reading instruction. Use the skills you have learned over the past months and organize your study around the three stages of reading. Use the following suggestions as guides.

Before Reading

Stage 1: Preview
Read the table of contents.
Glance through the chapter for an overview.
Selectively read subheadings.

Predict content and organization.
Establish a purpose consistent with expectations.
Set goals.
Activate your computer chip.

While Reading

Stage 2: Integrate Knowledge
Use the five thinking strategies as you read.

1. Predict 2. Picture 3. Relate 4. Monitor 5. Fix up

Process the material; separate the major ideas from the minor ideas.
As you finish a section, annotate it for later study.
Take notes using a system that works for you.

After Reading

Stage 3: Recall to Self-Test
Recite what you have read.
Refer to the table of contents for an overview.
Identify the major trends.
Recognize similarities and differences that link issues.
Predict exam questions and practice written responses.

1. For multiple-choice tests, study the specifics.
2. For an essay exam, predict questions and outline possible responses.

Take the initiative with this chapter and coordinate your own reading and studying. Study strategy suggestions and questions are inserted, but they do not constitute all that is needed for you to master this material.

RACIAL AND ETHNIC MINORITIES

Contents

Identifying Minorities
  Race
  Ethnicity
  Minority
Racial and Ethnic Relations
  Forms of Acceptance
  Forms of Rejection

Minority Groups in America
Native Americans
African-Americans
Hispanic-Americans
Asian-Americans
Jewish-Americans
White Ethnics

Introduction

The status of all minorities in the United States is generally better today than before. Coming closest to the American dream of success are Jews, Asians, and white ethnics, followed by blacks and Hispanics. Ironically, Native Americans, who originally owned this land, have experienced the least improvement in their lives. Of course, we still have a lot of prejudice and discrimination. But it is less than before, so that racial intermingling as shown here is now a common sight.

What are the major organizational sections of this chapter?
What is the purpose of each section?
How can you divide your reading and notetaking on this chapter?

From Alex Thio, *Sociology: A Brief Introduction*

A 46-year-old African-American woman describes how people react to her and her husband, who is white:

> In some churches, you're ignored. They won't sit beside you, especially at a church that is more white. At black churches, they raise eyebrows, but they don't do anything. We go to the malls, and people look at us, but it doesn't stop us from holding hands. Sometimes people see us, and they think, "Oh, nice. He can afford a housekeeper." When he puts his arm around my waist, they're in shock. "He's having an affair with his housekeeper" (Thompson 1989).

This is not the only way minorities encounter prejudice and discrimination. Nor does this social problem exist only in the United States. It can be found all over the world. Some 40 years ago about 6 million Jews were systematically murdered by the Nazis. More recently, many of the 700,000 Chinese in Vietnam, who made up the majority of the refugees who left the country between 1975 and 1979, were expelled—and forced to pay large sums before their expulsion. Many had to leave in small or leaky boats, and as many of them drowned at sea as reached land. At least one-third of the "boat people" were robbed, assaulted, raped, or killed by crews of other vessels from various Southeast Asian countries, which, like Vietnam, have a long history of discriminating against their own Chinese minorities (Sowell 1983). In Western Europe today, Pakistanis, Turks, Algerians, and other non-European minorities are often subjected to random insults and hostile stares, which tend to escalate into "a gang attack, an anonymous bullet, or a bomb thrown from a passing car" (Nielsen 1984). In Eastern Europe, minorities suffer the same fate; they include the Slovaks in Czechoslovakia, ethnic Albanians in Yugoslavia, ethnic Hungarians in Romania, and ethnic Turks in Bulgaria (Nelan 1990). In Japan, the Koreans, Burakumin (sometimes called *Eta,* meaning much filth), and Konketsuji (American-Japanese mixed bloods) are also targets of considerable prejudice and discrimination (Burkhardt 1983). In white-dominated South Africa, blacks, coloreds, and Asians continue to be legally segregated and discriminated against. These are only a few of the countless cases of mistreatment suffered by minorities in various countries.

In this chapter we examine the criteria for identifying minorities and the nature of prejudice and discrimination against them. Then we analyze the alternative ways in which a society may accept or reject a minority group and the possible responses by members of the minority. Finally, we find out how various racial and ethnic groups have fared in the United States.

What is the purpose of this introductory material?
Will these details be on the test?

IDENTIFYING MINORITIES

Americans are accustomed to thinking of a minority as a category of people who are physically different and who make up a small percentage of the population. Neither physical traits nor numbers alone determine whether people constitute a minority group. To get a clearer idea of what a minority is, we need first to see what races and ethnic groups are.

Should you annotate and then take notes on this material?
Before reading what sociologists believe, how would you define race, ethnicity, and minorities?
Should you list an example to illustrate each definition?

Race

As a biological concept, race refers to a large category of people who share certain inherited physical characteristics. These characteristics may include particular skin color, head shape, hair type, nasal shape, lip form, or blood type. One common classification of human races recognizes three groups: Caucasoid, Mongoloid, and Negroid. Caucasoids have light skin, Mongoloids yellowish skin, and Negroids dark skin—and there are other physical differences among the three groups.

One problem with the biological classification of races is that there are no "pure" races. People in these groups have been interbreeding for centuries. In the United States, for example, about 70 percent of blacks have some white ancestry and approximately 20 percent of whites have at least one black ancestor (Sowell 1983). Biologists have also determined that all current populations originate from one common genetic pool—one single group of humans that evolved about 30,000 years ago, most likely in Africa. As humans migrated all over the planet, different populations developed different physical characteristics in their adaptations to particular physical environments. Thus the Eskimos' relatively thick layer of fat under the skin of their eyes, faces, and other parts of the body provides good insulation against the icy cold of Arctic regions. The Africans' dark skin offers protection from the burning sun of tropical regions. Yet there has not developed a significant genetic difference among the "races." As genetic research has indicated, about 95 percent of the DNA molecules (which make up the gene) are the same for all humans, and only the remaining 5 percent are responsible for all the differences in appearance (Vora 1981). Even these outward differences are meaningless, because the differences among the members of the same "race" are greater than the average differences between two racial groups. Some American blacks, for example, have lighter skins than many whites, and some whites are darker than many blacks.

Since there are no clear-cut biological distinctions—in physical characteristics or genetic makeup—between racial groups, sociologists prefer to define race as a social rather than biological phenomenon. Defined sociologically, a race is a group of people who are *perceived* by a given society as biologically different from others. People are assigned to one race or another, not necessarily on the basis of logic or fact but by public opinion, which, in turn, is molded by society's dominant group. Consider, for example, an American boy whose father has 100 percent white ancestry and whose mother is the daughter of a white man and black woman. This youngster is considered "black" in our society, although he is actually more white than black because of his 75 percent white and 25 percent black ancestry. In many Latin American countries, however, this same child would be considered "white." In fact, according to Brazil's popular perception of a black as "a person of African descent who has no white ancestry at all," about three-fourths of all American blacks would *not* be considered blacks. They would be considered white because they have some white ancestry (Sowell 1983).

What is a race?
To what extent do we all share the same genetic pool?

Ethnicity

Jews have often been called a race. But they have the same racial origins as Arabs—both being Semites—and through the centuries Jews and non-Jews have interbred extensively. As a result, Jews are often physically indistinguishable from non-Jews. Besides, a person can become a Jew by choice—by conversion to Judaism. Jews do not constitute a race. Instead, they are a religious group, or more broadly, an ethnic group.

Whereas race is based on popularly perceived physical traits, ethnicity is based on cultural characteristics. An **ethnic group** is a collection of people who share a distinctive cultural heritage and a consciousness of their common bond. Members of an ethnic group may share a language, accent, religion, history, philosophy, national origin, or life-style. They always share a feeling that they are a distinct people. In the United States members of an ethnic group typically have the same national origin. As a result, they are named after the countries from which they or their ancestors came. Thus they are Polish-Americans, Italian-Americans, Irish-Americans, and so on.

For the most part, ethnicity is culturally learned. People learn the life-styles, cooking, language, values, and other characteristics of their ethnic group. Often Americans, in effect, choose ethnicity: they choose whether to continue to consider themselves as members of an ethnic group. Yet members of an ethnic group are usually born into it. The traits of the group are passed from one generation to another, and ethnicity is not always a matter of choice. A person may be classified by others as a member of some ethnic group, for example, on the basis of appearance or accent. In fact, racial and ethnic groups sometimes overlap, as in the case of Afro- or Asian-Americans. Like race, then, ethnicity can be an ascribed status.

How does ethnicity differ from race?
Whom do you know who has dropped their ethnicity?
Who has maintained their ethnicity?

Minority

A **minority** is a racial or ethnic group that is subjected to prejudice and discrimination. The essence of a minority, then, is its experience of prejudice and discrimination. **Prejudice** is a negative attitude toward members of a minority. It includes ideas and beliefs, feelings, and predispositions to act in a certain way. For example, whites prejudiced against blacks might fear meeting a black man on the street at night. They might resent blacks who are successful. They might plan to sell their houses if a black family moves into the neighborhood.

Whereas prejudice is an attitude, **discrimination** is an act. More specifically, it is unequal treatment of people because they are members of a group. When a landlord will not rent an apartment to a family because they are African-American or Hispanic, that is discrimination.

What is a minority?
What is prejudice?
What is discrimination?
Are you a member of a minority?

Questions for Discussion and Review

1. Why do sociologists define race as a social rather than a physical phenomenon?
2. What is ethnicity, and why do sociologists prefer to use this concept to explain the diverse behavior of minorities?
3. When does a racial or ethnic group become a minority group?

RACIAL AND ETHNIC RELATIONS

Prejudice and discrimination are an integral part of the relations between the dominant group and minorities. But the amount of prejudice and discrimination obviously varies from one society to another. Hence the racial and ethnic relations may appear in different forms, ranging from peaceful coexistence to violent conflict. In the following sections we analyze the various ways in which a society's dominant group accepts or rejects its minorities, and we also look at minorities' various responses to the dominant group's negative action.

What is the focus of this section?
What is the pattern of organization under each subheading?
What will you need to know after reading this section?
How are the boldface words connected?

Forms of Acceptance

If a society treats its racial and ethnic groups in a positive way, it will grant them rights of citizenship. Still, its acceptance of these groups is not necessarily total and unconditional. The dominant group, for example, may expect other groups to give up their distinct identities and accept the dominant subculture. Acceptance of a racial or ethnic group may take three forms: assimilation, amalgamation, and cultural pluralism.

Assimilation   Frequently, a minority group accepts the culture of the dominant group, fading into the larger society. This process, called **assimilation,** has at least two aspects. The first is **behavioral assimilation,** which means that the minority group adopts the dominant culture—its language, values, norms, and so on—giving up its own distinctive characteristics. Behavioral assimilation, however, does not guarantee **structural assimilation**—in which the minority group ceases to be a minority *and* is accepted on equal terms with the rest of society. German-Americans, for example, have achieved structural assimilation, but African-Americans have not. Taken as a whole, assimilation can be expressed as A + B + C = A, where minorities (B and C) lose their subcultural traits and become indistinguishable from the dominant group (A) (Newman 1973).

When the dominant group is ethnocentric, believing that its subculture is superior to others', then minority groups face considerable pressure to achieve behavioral assimilation. How easily they make this transition depends on both their attitude toward their own subculture and the degree of similarity between themselves and the dominant group. Minority groups that take pride in their own subculture are likely to resist behavioral assimilation. This may explain why Jews and Asians in the United States display a lot of ethnic solidarity. Groups that are very different from the dominant group may find that even behavioral assimilation does not lead to structural assimilation.

What is behavioral assimilation? Name a personal example.
What is structural assimilation? Name a personal example.
What factors encourage and prevent behavioral and structural assimilation?

Amalgamation   A society that believes that groups should go through the process of behavioral assimilation in order to be accepted as equals obviously has little respect for the distinctive traits of these groups. In contrast, a society that seeks amalgamation as an ideal has some appreciation for the equal worth of various subcultures. **Amalgamation** produces a "melting pot," in which many subcultures are blended together to produce a new culture, one that differs from any of its components. Like assimilation, amalgamation requires groups to give up their distinct racial and ethnic identities. But unlike assimilation, amalgamation demands respect for the original subcultures. Various groups are expected to contribute their own subcultures to the development of a new culture, without pushing any one subculture at the expense of another. Usually, this blending of diverse subcultures results from intermarriage. It can be described as $A + B + C = D$, where A, B, and C represent different groups jointly producing a new culture (D) unlike any of its original components (Newman 1973).

More than 70 years ago a British-Jewish dramatist portrayed the United States as an amalgamation of subcultures. "There she lies," he wrote, "the great melting pot—listen! . . . Ah, what a stirring and seething—Celt and Latin, Slav and Teuton, Greek and Syrian, Black and Yellow—Jew and Gentile" (Zangwill 1909). Indeed, to some extent America is a melting pot. In popular music and slang, for example, you can find elements of many subcultures.

What is amalgamation?
How does amalgamation differ from assimilation?

Cultural Pluralism Switzerland provides an example of yet a third way in which ethnic groups may live together. In Switzerland, three major groups—Germans, French, and Italians—retain their own languages while living together in peace. They are neither assimilated nor amalgamated. Instead, these diverse groups retain their distinctive subcultures while coexisting peacefully. This situation is called **cultural pluralism.** It is the opposite of assimilation and requires yet greater mutual respect for other groups' traditions and customs than does amalgamation. And unlike either assimilation or amalgamation, cultural pluralism encourages each group to take pride in its distinctiveness, to be conscious of its heritage, and to retain its identity. Such pluralism can be shown as $A + B + C = A + B + C$, where various groups continue to keep their subcultures while living together in the same society (Newman 1973).

To some extent, the United States has long been marked by cultural pluralism. This can be seen in the Chinatowns, Little Italies, and Polish neighborhoods of many American cities. But these ethnic enclaves owe their existence more to discrimination than to the respectful encouragement of diversity that characterizes true pluralism.

For many groups in America, cultural pluralism has become a goal. This became evident during the 1960s and 1970s, when blacks and white ethnics alike denounced assimilation and proclaimed pride in their own identities. But pluralism is not easy to maintain. It requires that society conquer prejudice and respect various groups equally. If it fails to do so, pluralism is likely to give way to either assimilation or outright rejection of minority groups.

What is cultural pluralism?
What are the dangers of cultural pluralism?

Forms of Rejection

When a dominant group rejects racial and ethnic groups, they are restricted to the status of minorities. They are discriminated against to some degree. The three major forms of rejection, in order of severity, are segregation, expulsion, and extermination.

Segregation   **Segregation** means more than spatial and social separation of the dominant and minority groups. It means that minority groups, because they are believed inferior, are compelled to live separately, and in inferior conditions. The neighborhoods, schools, and other public facilities for the dominant group are both separate from and superior to those of the minorities.

The compulsion that underlies segregation is not necessarily official, or acknowledged. In the United States, for example, segregation is officially outlawed, yet it persists. In other words, **de jure segregation**—segregation sanctioned by law—is gone, but **de facto segregation**—segregation resulting from tradition and custom—remains. This is particularly the case for African-Americans in housing. Like the United States, most nations no longer practice *de jure* segregation.

What is *de jure* segregation?
What is *de facto* segregation?

Expulsion   Societies have also used more drastic means of rejecting minorities, such as expulsion. In some cases, the dominant group has expelled a minority from certain areas. In other cases, it has pushed the minority out of the country entirely. During the nineteenth century, for example, Czarist Russia drove out millions of Jews, and the American government forced the Cherokees to travel from their homes in Georgia and the Carolinas to reservations in Oklahoma. About 4,000 of the Cherokees died on this "Trail of Tears." During the 1970s Uganda expelled more than 40,000 Asians—many of them Ugandan citizens—and Vietnam forced 700,000 Chinese to leave the country (Schaefer 1988).

© 1993 HarperCollins College Publishers

What are examples of rejection by expulsion?
Can you add examples of others not mentioned?

Extermination   Finally, the most drastic action against minorities
is to kill them. Wholesale killing of a racial or ethnic group, called
genocide, has been attempted in various countries. During the
nineteenth century, Dutch settlers in South Africa exterminated the
Hottentots. Native Americans in the United States were slaughtered by
white settlers. On the island of Tasmania, near Australia, British
settlers killed the entire native population, whom they hunted like
wild animals. Between 1933 and 1945, the Nazis systematically
murdered 6 million Jews. In the early 1970s, thousands of Ibos and
Hutus were massacred in the African states of Nigeria and Burundi.
Also in the early 1970s, machine guns and gifts of poisoned food and
germ-infected clothing were used against Indians in Brazil—20 tribes
were exterminated (Bodard 1972).

What is genocide?
What are examples of genocide?

Questions for Discussion and Review

1. In what different ways can the majority group accept members of a
   minority group?
2. What can happen when a dominant group decides to reject a racial or
   ethnic minority?

MINORITY GROUPS IN AMERICA

The United States is a nation of immigrants. The earliest immigrants
were the American Indians, who arrived from Asia more than 20,000
years ago. Long after the Indians had settled down as native
Americans, other immigrants began to pour in from Europe and later
from Africa, Asia, and Latin America. They came as explorers,
adventurers, slaves or refugees, most of them hoping to fulfill a dream
of success and happiness. The British were the earliest of these
immigrants and, on the whole, the most successful in fulfilling that
dream. They became the dominant group. Eventually they founded a
government dedicated to the democratic ideal of equality.

What is the focus of this section?
What major groups are discussed?

What seems to be the pattern of organization for the discussion of each group?

How detailed should your notes be?

How much will you need to know for the test?

What do you already know about the Native Americans?

How have the Native Americans fared in their own country?

Native Americans

Native Americans have long been called Indians—one result of Columbus's mistaken belief that he had landed in India. The explorer's descendants passed down many other distorted descriptions of the Native Americans. They were described as savages, although it was whites who slaughtered hundreds of thousands of them. They were portrayed as scalp hunters, although it was the white government that offered large sums to whites for the scalps of Indians. They were stereotyped as lazy, although it was whites who forced them to give up their traditional occupations. These false conceptions of Native Americans were reinforced by the contrasting pictures whites painted of themselves. The white settlers were known as pioneers rather than invaders and marauders; their taking of the Native Americans' land was called homesteading, not robbery.

When Columbus "discovered" America, there were more than 300 Native American tribes, with a total population exceeding a million. Of those he encountered around the Caribbean, Columbus wrote: "Of anything they have, if it be asked for, they never say no, but do rather invite the person to accept it, and show as much lovingness as though they would give their hearts" (Hraba 1979). In North America, too, the earliest white settlers were often aided by friendly Native Americans.

Moving the Native Americans   As the white settlers increased in numbers and moved westward, however, Native Americans resisted them. But the native population was decimated by outright killing, by destruction of their food sources, and by diseases brought by whites, such as smallpox and influenza. With their greater numbers and superior military technology, the whites prevailed. Sometimes they took land by treaty rather than by outright force—and then they often violated the treaty.

During the last half of the nineteenth century, the U.S. government tried a new policy. It made the tribes its wards and drove them into reservations. The land they were given was mostly useless for farming, and it made up only 2.9 percent of the United States. Even on the reservations, Native Americans were not free to live their own lives. The federal government was intent on assimilating them, replacing tribal culture with the white settlers' way of life. Indian men were forced to become small farmers, though they had for centuries been hunting and herding while letting women do the farming. Some of the tribal rituals and languages were banned. Children were sent away to boarding schools and encouraged to leave the reservation to seek jobs in cities. In 1887 those Indians who lived away from the tribe and "adopted the habits of civilized life" were granted citizenship. The government also disrupted the tradition of tribal ownership by granting land to the heads of families (Franklin 1981).

By 1890 the Native American population had been reduced to less than a quarter of a million. Changes in the government's policy toward them came slowly. In 1924 Congress conferred citizenship on all Native Americans. In 1934 the federal government reversed course and supported tribal culture by granting self-government rights to tribes, restoring communal ownership, and giving financial aid. In 1940 the Native American population, which had been reduced to 0.3 million, began to grow.

By 1980 there were 1.4 million Native Americans. Slightly more than half live on 261 reservations, mostly in the Southwest. The rest live in urban areas. After more than two centuries of colonial subjugation, Native Americans today find themselves at the bottom of the ladder—the poorest minority in the United States.

"Red Power"   Since the early 1960s Native Americans have begun
to assert their "red power." In 1963 they started a vigorous campaign
to have their fishing rights recognized in northwest Washington; these
were eventually granted by the Supreme Court in 1968. In late 1960
they publicized their grievances by occupying Alcatraz, the abandoned
island prison in San Francisco Bay, for 19 months. In 1972 they
marched into Washington to dramatize the "trail of broken treaties"
and presented the government with a series of demands for
improving their lives. In 1973 they took over Wounded Knee, South
Dakota for 72 days, during which they were engaged in a shooting
war with government troops. These dramatic actions were mostly
symbolic, designed to foster Indian identity and unity. In the 1980s,
however, they have been seeking more substantive goals. Thus, an
increasing number of Indian tribes have been filing lawsuits to win
back lands taken from their ancestors. They have also been fighting
through federal courts to protect their water and mineral resources as
well as hunting and fishing rights. Moreover, they are demanding
more government assistance with health, educational, and social
programs (Zuern 1983; Jarvenpa 1985).

   All this has sparked a national movement to recapture traditions, to
make Native Americans feel proud of their cultural heritage. Virtually
every tribe places a heavy emphasis on teaching the younger
generation its native language, crafts, tribal history, and religious
ceremonies. There used to be a lack of unity among the 300 tribes,
but today intertribal visiting and marriage are a common occurrence.
Moreover, in the last 15 years, more than 500 Indian men and women
have become lawyers—and more have successfully established
themselves in the business and professional worlds. Of course, the
majority of Native Americans still have a long way to go. Without a
viable economic base to draw on, they still find themselves
"powerless in the face of rising unemployment, deteriorating health
care, and a falling standard of living."

How did government policies devastate Native Americans?
How has "red power" been asserted?
How have Native Americans been accepted and rejected by society?

African-Americans

There are more than 28 million African-Americans, constituting about
12 percent of the U.S. population. They are the largest minority in the
nation. In fact, there are more African-Americans in the United States
than in any single African nation except Nigeria.

   Their ancestors first came from Africa to North America as
indentured servants in 1619. Soon after that they were brought here as

slaves. For the two-month voyage across the ocean they were chained and packed like sardines, often lying immobile for weeks in their own sweat and excrement. It was not unusual for half the slaves to die from disease, starvation, and suicide before reaching their destination.

From 1619 to 1820 about half a million of the slaves were taken to U.S. shores. Most lived in the southern states and worked on cotton, tobacco, or sugar-cane plantations. "Slave codes" that restricted their movement and conduct were enshrined in laws.

By the time the Civil War broke out in 1861, the number of enslaved African-Americans had reached 5 million. The end of the Civil War in 1865 brought the end of slavery and other new opportunities for southern African-Americans. For the first time they could go to public schools and state universities with whites. The greatest black advance came in politics, but little was done to improve the economic position of African-Americans.

Then, in 1877, federal troops were withdrawn from the South. White supremacy reigned, and whatever gains African-Americans had made during Reconstruction were wiped out. Many so-called **Jim Crow** laws were enacted, segregating blacks from whites in all kinds of public and private facilities—from rest rooms to schools. These laws were supplemented by terror.

As southern farms were mechanized and as the demand for workers in northern industrial centers rose during World Wars I and II, many southern African-Americans migrated North. When the wars ended and the demand for workers decreased, however, they were often the first to be fired. Even in the North, where there were no Jim Crow laws, they faced discrimination and segregation.

The federal government itself sanctioned segregation. In 1896 the Supreme Court declared segregation legal. In 1913 President Wilson ordered the restaurants and cafeterias in federal buildings segregated. Even the armed forces were segregated until President Truman ordered them desegregated in 1948.

Desegregation   A turning point in American race relations came in 1954. In that year the Supreme Court ordered that public schools be desegregated. The decision gave momentum to the long-standing movement against racial discrimination. In the late 1950s and 1960s the civil rights movement launched marches, sit-ins, and boycotts. The price was high: many civil rights workers were beaten and jailed, and some were killed. But eventually Congress passed the landmark Civil Rights Act in 1964, prohibiting segregation and discrimination in virtually all areas of social life, such as restaurants, hotels, schools, housing, and employment (Schaefer 1988).

Prejudice against African-Americans still exists. They still fall far behind whites in economics and housing, though they have shown

impressive gains in education and politics. This is not true for all African-Americans, however. A black middle class is emerging, now constituting about 40 percent of the African-American population, as compared with only 5 percent in 1940. While this group is getting richer, the larger number of African-Americans—the poor underclass—are getting poorer. This is, in William Wilson's (1980, 1987) view, due to the increasing number of well-educated African-Americans getting high-paying jobs. As these successful, well-off African-Americans move to better neighborhoods, they leave behind many ghettos full of poor people. These poor people have become poorer because they lack education.

The same economy, however, benefits the well-educated African-Americans. Thus Wilson argues that the significance of race as an obstacle to upward mobility is declining. While race is no longer as important in determining who gets ahead, however, it still remains significant today.

At any rate, taking into account the long history of black oppression in America, Sowell (1981) concludes: "The race as a whole has moved from a position of utter destitution—in money, knowledge, and rights—to a place alongside other groups emerging in the great struggles of life. None has had to come from so far back to join their fellow Americans."

What were Jim Crow laws and what were the effects?
How have African-Americans been accepted and rejected by society?

Hispanic-Americans

In 1848 the United States either won or bought what would become Texas, California, Nevada, Utah, Arizona, New Mexico, and Colorado from Mexico. Thus many Mexicans found themselves living in U.S. territories as American citizens. The vast majority of today's Mexican-Americans, however, are the result of immigration from Mexico since the turn of the century. The early immigrants came largely to work in the farmlands of California and to build the railroads of the Southwest. Then numerous Mexicans began to pour into the United States, driven by Mexico's population pressures and economic problems and attracted by American industry's need for low-paid, unskilled labor.

The United States also added Puerto Rico to its territory in 1898, by defeating the Spaniards in the Spanish-American War. In 1917 Congress conferred citizenship on all Puerto Ricans, but they may not vote in presidential elections and have no representation in Congress. Over the years, especially since the early 1950s, many Puerto Ricans have migrated to the U.S. mainland, lured by job opportunities and cheap plane service between New York City and San Juan. In the last two decades, though, more have returned to Puerto Rico than have come here.

Thus a new minority group emerged in the United States—Hispanic-Americans. The category actually includes several groups today. Besides the Mexican-Americans and Puerto Ricans, there are immigrants from Cuba, who began to flock to the Miami area since their country became communist in 1959. There are also the "other Hispanics"—immigrants from other Central and South American countries, who have come here as political refugees and job seekers. By 1990 the members of all these groups totaled about 25 million, constituting 10 percent of the U.S. population. This made them our second largest minority. Because of their high birthrates and the continuing influx of immigrants, Hispanic-Americans could outnumber African-Americans in the next decade (Kenna 1983; Davis, Haub, and Willette 1983; Salholz 1990).

The Spanish language is the unifying factor among Hispanic-Americans. Another source of common identity is religion: at least 85 percent of them are Roman Catholics. There is an increasing friction, though, between Mexican-Americans and the newly arrived immigrants from Mexico. Many Mexican-Americans blame the "undocumented workers" for lower salaries, loss of jobs, overcrowding of schools and health clinics, and deterioration of neighborhoods. According to a recent Los Angeles poll, 40 percent of the Mexican-

American respondents said there were "too many" Mexican immigrants in California. According to another survey, 66 percent accused illegal immigrants of taking jobs from American citizens and 54 percent believed that cheap immigrant labor had led to lower wages in general.

Differences in Hispanic Groups   There are, however, significant differences within the Hispanic community. Mexican-Americans are by far the largest group, accounting for 61 percent of the Hispanics. They are heavily concentrated in the Southwest and West. Puerto Ricans make up 15 percent and live mostly in the Northeast, especially in New York City. As a group, they are the poorest among the Hispanics, which may explain why many have gone back to Puerto Rico. Those born in the United States, however, are more successful economically than their parents from Puerto Rico. The Cubans, who constitute 7 percent of the Hispanic population, are the most affluent. They therefore show the greatest tendency toward integration with Anglos. The remaining Hispanics are a diverse group, ranging from uneducated, unskilled laborers to highly trained professionals (Fitzpatrick and Parker 1981; Nelson and Tienda 1985).

As a whole, Hispanics are younger than the general population. The median age is 23 for Hispanics, compared with 30 for other Americans. The youthfulness of the Hispanic population is due to relatively high fertility and heavy immigration of young adults. This is particularly the case with Mexican-Americans, who have the most children and are the youngest of all Hispanic groups. At the other extreme are Cubans, who even have fewer children and are older than *non*-Hispanic Americans, with a median age of 41.

Hispanics in general also lag behind both whites and blacks in educational attainment. But some Hispanic groups are more educated than others. Cubans are the best educated, primarily because most of the early refugees fleeing communist Cuba were middle-class and professional people. Mexican-Americans and Puerto Ricans are less educated because they consist of many recent immigrants with much less schooling. The young, American-born Hispanics usually have more education. Lack of proficiency in English has retarded the recent Hispanic immigrants' educational progress. As many as 25 percent of Hispanics in public schools speak little or no English, which has resulted in their having higher dropout rates than non-Hispanic students. Since 1968, however, many schools began to teach academic subjects such as math and science in Spanish while teaching English as a foreign language. They believe that the children can learn English much faster by picking up skills in both languages.

Although Hispanics' economic status has improved in recent decades, they remain primarily clustered in lower-paying jobs. They

© 1993 HarperCollins College Publishers

earn about 70 percent of the amount made by Anglos. They also have a higher rate of unemployment than the general population.

In short, Hispanics as a group are still trailing behind the general population in social and economic well-being. However, the higher educational achievement of young Hispanics provides hope that more Hispanics—not just Cubans—will be joining the higher paid white-collar work force in the future. As already shown by recent research, if Hispanics speak English fluently and have at least graduated from high school, their occupational achievement is close to that of non-Hispanics with similar English fluency and education (Stolzenberg 1990). Hispanics are also already a growing force in American politics. They now have 10 congressmen, two state governors (in New Mexico and Florida), and mayors in Denver, Miami, and San Antonio. Most importantly, the states with the largest concentration of Hispanics—California, Texas, New York, and Florida—are highly significant in both state and national elections.

What commonalities unite Hispanics?
What are the different Hispanic groups?
How do the different Hispanic groups differ in their economic status in America?

Asian-Americans

During the 1970s there was a large influx of refugees from Southeast Asia, and today there are over 20 different Asian nationalities. The Chinese and Japanese are the largest and best-known groups of Asian-Americans. The Chinese first came during the gold rush on the

West Coast in 1849, pulled by better economic conditions in America and pushed by economic problems and local rebellions in China. Soon huge numbers of Chinese were imported to work for low wages, digging mines and building railroads. After these projects were completed, jobs became scarce and white workers feared competition from the Chinese. As a result, special taxes were imposed on the Chinese, and they were prohibited from attending school, seeking employment, owning property, and bearing witness in court. In 1882 the Chinese Exclusion Act restricted Chinese immigration to the United States, and it stopped all Chinese immigration from 1904 to 1943. Many returned to their homeland (Kitano 1981).

Immigrants from Japan met with similar hostility. They began to come to the West Coast somewhat later than the Chinese, also in search of better economic opportunities. At first they were welcomed as a source of cheap labor. But soon they began to operate small shops, and anti-Japanese activity grew. In 1906 San Francisco forbade Asian children to attend white schools. In response, the Japanese government negotiated an agreement whereby the Japanese agreed to stop emigration to the United States and President Theodore Roosevelt agreed to end harassment of the Japanese who were already here. But when the Japanese began to buy their own farms, they met with new opposition. In 1913 California prohibited foreign-born Japanese from owning or leasing lands; other Western states followed suit. In 1922 the U.S. Supreme Court ruled that foreign-born Japanese could not become American citizens.

World War II   Worse came during World War II. All the Japanese, aliens and citizens, were rounded up from the West Coast and confined in concentration camps set up in isolated areas. They were forced to sell their homes and properties; the average family lost $10,000. The action was condoned even by the Supreme Court as a legitimate way of ensuring that the Japanese-Americans would not help Japan defeat the United States. Racism, however, was the real source of such treatment. After all, there was no evidence of any espionage or sabotage by a Japanese-American. Besides, German-Americans were not sent to concentration camps, although Germany was at war with the United States and there *were* instances of subversion by German-Americans. In 1976, though, President Ford proclaimed that the wartime detention of Japanese-Americans had been a mistake, calling it "a sad day in American history." In 1983 a congressional commission recommended that each surviving evacuee be paid $20,000. In 1987, when the survivors sued the government for billions of dollars in compensation, the solicitor general acknowledged that the detention was "frankly racist" and "deplorable."

And in 1988 the Senate voted overwhelmingly to give $20,000 and an apology to each of the surviving internees (Molotsky 1988).

Reverence for Learning   Despite this history of discrimination, Chinese- and Japanese-Americans, along with Jewish Americans, are educationally and professionally the most successful minorities in the United States today. They have higher percentages of high school and college graduates than whites. While Asians are only 1.5 percent of the U.S. population, they make up 8 percent of the student body at Harvard and 21 percent of the student body at the University of California at Berkeley. Among academics, scientists, and engineers, a higher proportion of Asians than whites have Ph.D.'s. Asian professors also publish more than their white colleagues. Moreover, Asian-Americans as a whole have a higher percentage of white-collar jobs and a higher median family income than whites. The success of Asian-Americans has been attributed to a traditional reverence for learning, parental pressure to succeed, and the support of close-knit families (Kasindorf 1982; McGrath 1983; Williams 1984b; Schwartz 1987).

Officials at Berkeley, Stanford, Harvard, MIT, and other elite universities have also been charged with discriminating against Asian-Americans. At those universities, admission of Asian-Americans has stabilized or gone down, even though the number of qualified Asian applicants has risen substantially. Today the proportion of admissions among Asian applicants is one-third lower than that among whites, despite comparable or higher academic qualifications. The university officials are apparently fearful of being "swamped" by Asian-American students, often pointing out that there are already numerous Asian-Americans on their campuses.

Now that they are being increasingly assimilated into the white culture, however, Asian-Americans have begun to assume a more confrontational stance on the issue of racism. They have complained to the U.S. Justice Department and to the press about discrimination at the universities. They have also sued companies for job discrimination. On the other hand, some corporations have begun to wise up, trying to correct past wrongs. Aware that the Asian nations are becoming ever more powerful in the global economy, they realize that they can get the competitive edge by making use of Asian-Americans' cultural backgrounds and language skills (Schwartz 1987). Perhaps elite-university officials will follow suit by actively recruiting Asian-American students. These students generally excel in math and science—the very skills that the United States urgently needs today to retain its technological preeminence against the increasing challenge from Japan.

What laws were passed against Asian-Americans?
How do Asian-Americans fare in the educational system?

Jewish-Americans

The first Jews came here from Brazil in 1654—their ancestors had been expelled from Spain and Portugal. Then other Jews arrived directly from Europe. Their numbers were very small, however, until the 1880s, when large numbers of Jewish immigrants began to arrive, first from Germany, then from Russia and other eastern European countries. Here they were safe from the pogroms (massacres) they had faced in Europe, but they did confront prejudice and discrimination.

During the 1870s, many American colleges refused to admit Jews. At the turn of the century, Jews often encountered discrimination when they applied for white-collar jobs. During the 1920s and 1930s, they were accused of being part of an international conspiracy to take over U.S. business and government, and **anti-Semitism**—prejudice or discrimination against Jews—became more widespread and overt. The president of Harvard University called for quotas against Jews. Large real estate companies in New Jersey, New York, Georgia, and Florida refused to sell property to Jews.

The Jewish population in the United States rose as European Jews fled the Nazis' attempt to exterminate them. During and after World War II, anti-Jewish activities subsided, but they increased again during the 1960s—including 14 explosions, 9 fire bombings, 4 attempted bombings, and 47 bomb threats against Jewish property (Marden and Meyer 1978). From 1964 to the present, however, anti-Semitism has declined sharply.

Jewish Success   Despite the past discrimination against them, Jewish Americans as a group have been very successful. Their success may stem from the emphasis Jewish culture gives to education, from a self-image as God's chosen people, and from parental pressure to succeed. Not all Jews are successful, though. They still have a significant amount of poverty in their midst—over 15 percent of New York City's Jewish population are poor. This poverty is largely due to the recency of their arrival in America, as can be seen in the experiences of three types of Jews. Most of the poor Jews are Orthodox, the most recent immigrants in the United States. Conservative Jews, who are more successful, have been in this country longer. Reform Jews, the wealthiest of the group, have been here the longest (Schaefer 1988).

While Jews as a whole are prosperous, they are not conservative or inclined to vote Republican, as other prosperous Americans are. Instead, they tend more to be liberal—supporting welfare, civil rights, women's rights, civil liberties, and the like—and to vote Democratic. Perhaps this reflects their ability to identify with the dispossessed and oppressed, people like themselves who came here to escape hunger and persecution in Europe. Jews are so successfully assimilated into

American society that they seem in danger of losing their Jewish identity. There has been a substantial decline in affiliation with synagogues and in ritual observance. Today about half of all Jews are not affiliated with a synagogue, and only 20 percent attend synagogue regularly. Marriage with non-Jews has increased greatly, with well over half of all Jewish marriages outside New York involving a non-Jew. This has recently intensified the dispute among Jewish leaders over who is qualified to be a Jew. While Reform rabbis would accept as Jews children of intermarriages involving a Jewish father and non-Jewish mother, Orthodox and Conservative leaders would not (Zenner 1985; Berger 1986).

What is anti-Semitism?
How have Jews been assimilated into society?

White Ethnics

Jews were not the only European immigrants to face discrimination. From about 1830 to 1860, European immigration surged, and conflict grew between the immigrants—especially Catholic immigrants—and native-born Americans, the majority of whom were Protestants. The Irish immigrants, who tended to be both poor and Catholic, faced especially strong hostility. The notice "No Irish Need Apply" was commonplace in newspaper want ads.

Toward the end of the nineteenth century, there was a new wave of immigrants. These people came not from northern and western Europe, as most of the earlier immigrants had, but from southern and eastern Europe. They were Poles, Greeks, Italians. Many native-born Americans proclaimed these new immigrants to be inferior people and treated them as such. This belief was reflected in the National Origins Act of 1924. It enacted quotas that greatly restricted immigration from southern and eastern Europe, a policy that was not altered until 1965.

Today, Irish, Italians, Poles, Greeks, and others from eastern or southern Europe are called **white ethnics.** Even in the 1950s and 1960s, they faced jokes and stereotypes about "dumb Poles" or "criminal Italians."

Prejudice against white ethnics has been called "respectable bigotry." The stereotype overlaps with the image of uneducated blue-collar workers. In fact, a rising number of white ethnics are middle class, and about half have attended college, the same proportion as many Anglo-Saxon Americans (Alba 1981, 1985). Several surveys have further shown that white ethnics largely favor "liberal" policies such as welfare programs, anti-pollution laws, and guaranteed wages. They are also relatively free of racial prejudice, perhaps because they can easily identify with African-Americans since, like African-Americans, many have held low-paying manual jobs and have been subjected to discrimination (Greeley and McCready 1974). Most significantly, white ethnics by and large can no longer speak their immigrant parents' language, do not live in ethnic neighborhoods any more, and routinely marry into the dominant group. In short, they have become such an integral part of mainstream American society that it is difficult to tell them apart (Steinberg 1981). Traces of prejudice toward some white ethnics still exist, though. Most Americans, for example, continue to associate Italian-Americans with organized crime, although people of Italian background make up less than 1 percent of the 500,000 individuals involved in such activities (Giordano 1987).

In conclusion, the status of all the minorities is generally better today than before. Getting closest to the American dream of success are Jews, Asians, and white ethnics, followed by blacks and Hispanics. Ironically, the original owners of this land—Native Americans—have experienced the least improvement in their lives. Of course, we still have a lot of prejudice and discrimination. But it is less than before, especially less than in South Africa, where racism is still an official policy. It is also less serious than in India and other countries, where a single incident of ethnic conflict often takes hundreds or thousands of lives. However, Americans tend to focus on their own current racial problem, without comparing it with how things were in the past or with similar problems in other societies. Interestingly, the lack of historical and cross-cultural concern may limit our understanding of race relations, but it can intensify our impatience with our own racial inequality. This is good for American society, because it compels us—especially the minorities among us—to keep pushing for racial equality. On the other hand, the historical and cross-societal analysis in this chapter, which shows some improvement in our race relations, is also useful. It counsels against despair, encouraging us to be hopeful that racial equality can be achieved.

What are the white ethnic groups?
What tend to be the economic status of white ethnics?

Questions for Discussion and Review

1. What different policies has the government adopted toward Native Americans, and why have they often been resisted?
2. Why are large numbers of black Americans still not fully equal?

3. Who are the different groups of Hispanic-Americans, and what factors unify all of them?
4. Why have Asian-Americans gained more educational and professional success than other minority groups?
5. How have the experiences of Jewish-Americans differed from those of other white ethnic groups?
6. Does the "American Dilemma" still exist, or have American intergroup relations improved?

Study Strategies

1. Recall the focus of each section of this chapter.
2. Make a study sheet including words like "race," "assimilation," and "anti-Semitic." Define them and give examples.
3. Create scenarios with fictional characters to illustrate a list of words like "cultural pluralism" and "expulsion" in preparation for application questions.
4. Connect your new knowledge by discussing recent articles that deal with some of the same issues in this chapter.
5. Brainstorm possible essay questions that connect the different sections of the chapter. Practice by writing answers to your questions.
6. Plan your attack by answering the following questions:
   How will the test look?
   What material will be covered?
   How will you study?
   When will you study?
   What grade are you honestly working to achieve?
   Study for success!

GLOSSARY

analogy: a comparison showing connections with and similarities to previous experiences

annotating: a method of using symbols and notations to highlight textbook material for future study

attention: uninterrupted mental focus

bar graph: an arrangement of horizontal or vertical bars in which the length of each represents an amount or number

bias: an opinion or position on a subject recognized through facts slanted towards an author's personal beliefs

cause and effect: a pattern of organization in which one item is shown as having produced another

chronological order: a pattern of organization in which items are listed in time order or sequence

cognitive psychology: a body of knowledge that describes how the mind works or is believed to work

comparison-contrast: a pattern of organization in which similarities and differences are presented

concentration: the focusing of full attention on a task

conclusion: interpretation based on evidence and suggested meaning

connotation: the feeling associated with the definition of a word

context clues: hints within the sentence which help unlock the meaning of an unknown word

Cornell method: a system of note taking that involves writing sentence summaries on the right side of the page with key words and topics indicated to the left

creative thinking: generating many possible solutions to a problem

critical thinking: deliberating in a purposeful, organized manner to assess the value of information or argument

deductive reasoning: thinking which starts with a previously learned conclusion and applies it to a new situation

definition: a pattern of organization devoted to defining an idea and further explaining it with examples

denotation: the dictionary definition of a word

description: a pattern of organization listing characteristics of a person, place, or thing, as in a simple listing

details: information that supports, describes, and explains the main idea

diagram: drawing of an object showing labeled parts

external distractors: temptations of the physical world that divert the attention from a task

fact: a statement that can be proven true or false

figurative language: words used to create images that take on a new meaning

fixations: stops the eyes make while reading

flowchart: a diagram showing how ideas are related with boxes and arrows indicating levels of importance and movement

humorous: comical or amusing

idiom: figurative expression that does not make literal sense but communicates a generally accepted meaning

imagery: mental pictures created by figurative language

implied meaning: suggested rather than directly stated meaning

inductive reasoning: thinking based on the collection of data and the formulation of a conclusion based on it

inference: subtle suggestions expressed without direct statement

internal distractions: concerns that come repeatedly to mind and disturb concentration

irony: a twist or surprise ending that is the opposite of what is expected and elicits a bittersweet, cruel chuckle

knowledge network: a cluster of knowledge about a subject; a schema

lateral thinking: a way of creatively thinking around a problem or a redefining of the problem to seek new solutions

learning styles: preference for a particular manner of presenting material to be learned

line graph: a frequency distribution in which the horizontal scale measures time and the vertical scale measures amount

main idea: a statement of the particular focus of the topic in a passage

map: graphic designation or distribution

mapping: a method of graphically displaying material to show relationships and importance for later study

metacognition: knowledge of how to read as well as the ability to regulate and direct the process

metaphor: a direct comparison of two unlike things (without using the words *like* or *as*)

mnemonics: a technique using images, numbers, rhymes, or letters to improve memory

notetaking: a method of writing down short phrases and summaries to record textbook material for future study

opinion: a statement of personal views or judgment

outlining: a method of using indentations, Roman numerals, numbers, and letters to organize textbook material for future study

pattern of organization: the structure or framework for presenting the details in a passage

personification: attributing human characteristics to nonhuman things

pie graph: a circle divided into wedge-shaped slices to show portions totaling 100 percent

point of view: a position or opinion on a subject

previewing: a method of predicting what the material is about in order to assess knowledge and need

prior knowledge: previous learning about a subject

propaganda: a systematic and deliberate attempt to persuade others to a particular doctrine or point of view

purpose: the author's underlying reason or intent for writing

rate: reading pace described in number of words per minute

recall: reviewing what was included and learned after reading material

regression: rereading material because of a lack of understanding

sarcasm: a tone that is witty, usually saying the opposite of what is true, but with the purpose of cutting or ridicule

scanning: searching to locate single bits of information in reading material

schema: a skeleton or network of knowledge about a subject

simile: a comparison of two things using the words *like* or *as*

simple listing: a pattern of organization that lists items in a series

skimming: a technique for selectively reading for the gist or main idea

study system: a plan for working through stages to read and learn textbook material

subvocalization: use of a little voice in the head, your inner voice, that reads aloud for you, enabling you to hear the words

summary: concise statement of the main idea and significant supporting details

table: listing of facts and figures in columns for quick reference

tone: the author's attitude toward the subject

topic: a word or phrase that labels the subject of a paragraph

vertical thinking: a straightforward and logical way of thinking that searches for a solution to the stated problem

CREDITS

Photo Acknowledgments

Cover—Eric Schweikardt/The Image Bank   1—Joel Gordon Photography   15—Nina Leen/*LIFE* Magazine, Time Warner Inc.   25—Brent Jones   37—UPI/Bettmann   41—Tom Turner/Design Conceptions   59—Lawrence Migdale   70—Detail of Painting, *The Herd Quitter,* by Charles M. Russell, 1897, Montona Historical Society, Gift of Col. Wallis Huidekoper. 80—Cynthia Haas/Woodfin Camp & Associates   99—Kolvoord/The Image Works 107—Courtesy, American Cancer Society   108—Photo by Lewis Hine/Library of Congress 112—Derek Hudson/Sygma   129—Dr. Harry F. Harlow/Harlow Primate Laboratory, University of Wisconsin   151—Frans Lanting/Minden Pictures   165—Felicia Martine/Photo Edit 185—John Watney/Photo Researchers   192—Sophia Smith Collection, Smith College, Northampton, Ma.   213—Joel Gordon Photography   240—Jean-Claude LeJeune 258—The Bettmann Archive   269—Elizabeth Crews/The Image Works   280—David Wells/The Image Works   296—Gary Brookins/Richmond Times   297—Dick Wright/ Reprinted by permission of United Feature Syndicate, Inc.   298—James L. Shaffer/Photo Edit 306—J.Griffin/The Image Works   313—AP/Wide World   320—James M. Poulson, (c)1992 by the Daily Sitka Sentinel, Sitka, Alaska   342—John Griffin/The Image Works 351—Reuters/UPI/Bettmann   356—Drawing by Dedini (c)1990 The New Yorker Magazine, Inc.   361—Photo Edit   374—Mario Ruiz/*TIME Magazine*   389—Susan Lapides/Design Conceptions   418—M.Wojnarowicz/The Image Works   430—Felicia Martinez/Photo Edit 434—Gatewood/The Image Works   437—AP/Wide World

Literary Acknowledgments

"A Chinese Reporter on Cape Cod," by Guan Keguang from Freedom of Choice Is Not an Option in China" from *The Cape Cod Times,* March 14, 1987. Copyright © 1987 by Guan Keguang. Reprinted by permission of the author. **232–4.**   From *Access & Excellence: The Open-Door College* by John E. Roueche et al., pages 145–8. Copyright © 1987 by The Community College Press. Reprinted by permission. **304–305.**   Rodolfo Acuna, "Legacy of Hate: The Myth of a Peaceful Belligerent" from *Myth and the American Experience,* Volume One, Third Edition, edited by Nicholas Cords and Patrick Gerater. New York, NY: HarperCollins Publishers, 1991, pages 285 and 301. **285.**   Figure, "Age Began Reading" from *The Gallup Pool Monthly,* No. 305, February 1991, page 52. Reprinted by permission of the American Institute of Public Opinion. **366.** From *America and Its People* by James Kirby Martin et al., pages 15–16, 440, 785–6, 902–903, 951, 953–6, and 989. Copyright © 1989 James Kirby Martin, Randy Roberts, Steven Mintz, Linda O. McMurry, and James H. Jones. Published by HarperCollins Publishers, Inc. **104, 252, 284–5, 289, 314–17.**   From *American Government: Incomplete Conquest* by Theodore J. Lowi. From *America Past and Present,* 2nd Edition, by Divine et al. © 1987 by Scott, Foresman and Company, HarperCollinsCollege Publishers. **248, 255, 286, 288.**   Maya Angelou, *I Know Why the Caged Bird Sings.* New York: Random House, Inc., 1969. **247.**   From *Anthropology,* Fifth Edition by Kottack, pages 24, 40–41, 172–3, 204, 327, and 348–9. Copyright © 1991 by McGraw-Hill, Inc.

INDEX